CHINESE
MILITARY
THEORY

CHINESE MILITARY THEORY

ANCIENT AND MODERN

Chen-Ya Tien

MOSAIC PRESS
Oakville - New York - London

CANADIAN CATALOGUING IN PUBLICATION DATA

Tien, Chen-Ya
    Chinese military theory

Includes bibliographical references and index
ISBN 0-88962-423-2 (bound)   ISBN 0-88962-422-4 (pbk.)

1.   Military art and science - China History.
I.   Title.

U43,C5T54 1991   355'.00951 C91-095605-7

Published by MOSAIC PRESS, P.O. Box 1032, Oakville, Ontario, L6J 5E9, Canada. Offices and warehouse at 1252 Speers Road, Units 1&2, Oakville, Ontario, L6L 5N9, Canada.

Mosaic Press acknowledges the assistance of the Canadian Council and the Ontario Arts Council in support of its publishing programme.

Copyright © Chen-ya Tien, 1992
Design by Marion Black
Typeset by Jackie Ernst
Printed and bound in Canada.

ISBN 0-88962-423-2 CLOTH   ISBN 0-88962-422-4 PAPER

MOSAIC PRESS:
In Canada:
    MOSAIC PRESS, 1252 Speers Road, Units 1&2, Oakville, Ontario, L6L 5N9, P.O. Box 1032, Oakville, Ontario, L6J 5E9, Canada.

In the United States:
    Distributed to the trade in the United States by: National Book Network, Inc., 4720-A Boston Way, Landham, MD 20706, USA.

CONTENTS

PREFACE

While doing research at Columbia University in 1975, the subject of this book first emerged in my mind when by chance I read a brief item in the newsletter of The American Learned Society. It reported that no research had been done on modern Chinese military thinking. This subject was related to the research I was doing at the time on the mass militia system and Chinese modernization, so I thought that perhaps I could write a book about it in the future. However, it was not until 1984 when the Mass Militia System was published by Mossaic Press in Canada that I had time to think about it again.

In the very beginning, I had several ideas about how to write this book. I could take a strict military point of view by limiting my discussions to military systems, strategies, tactics, and the use of the armed forces; or I could take a historical, socio-political and economic approach to extend my analysis to the development of modern Chinese military theories. I chose the later because I believe that the rise of a military theory is closely related to socio-economic conditions. In making this decision, I not only extended my discussion back to ancient Chinese military thought but I also referred to contemporary trends of development of Chinese strategies since the 1970s.

The book is not only a work for those who are interested in Chinese military theories, both ancient and modern, but to some extent, it is also for those who are interested in the socio-political and economic history of modern China.

With the assistance of a grant from the Social Sciences and Humanities Research Council of Canada, I was able to use the libraries of the University of Toronto, Harvard and Standford Universities, and National Chengchi University in Taipei. Under the sponsorship of the Beijing Institute of International Strategic Studies (BIISS), I made a research trip to China. With my host's arrangement, I held seminars with many prominent scholars and benefited from their comments and advice. General Gao Tiqian, Vice President of the Military Science Council of the People's Liberation Army, helped me the most.

From the first draft to final publication, Prof. Howard Aster and Prof. Peter Potichnyj of McMaster University, Prof. Mervin Y.T. Chen of Acadia University, Prof. Don Jackson of Algoma University College, and Mr. Steven Allen, a senior editor at CCH Canadian Limited, have either gone through part or all of the manuscripts and given their comments and suggestions. Prof. Aster and Mr. Allen especially spent a lot of time editing and proofreading. With their help, this book has arrived at its present form.

During my work on this book, my wife, Wennie, and our two children, Alexia and Homer not only sacrificed their happy hours of family life with me but came to my help, above all my wife. She spent many weekends and evenings typing my manuscripts. It would have been impossible for me to complete this work without their help and support. If this book represents a contribution to understanding modern Chinese military thought, all of aforementioned people and many others unmentioned here should share the credit. However, if anything is unsatisfactory, the author is solely responsible.

Chen-Ya Tien
Toronto, February 1991

CHAPTER 1

Introduction

Since the mid-1970s, the international political alignment has gradually departed from the track of bipolar power politics and tended to develop a new system of multiple poles. According to different sources, the emerging new centres of the global political power may include the European Community, the Soviet Union, the United States of America, Japan, and China. In terms of economic and military power, China is probably far behind the two superpowers. It may not even be as strong as the other two power centres for the foreseeable future. However, taking its large population, rich resources, and huge territory into account, no reasonable person would deny that without serious internal socio-political disruption, China could soon be the third superpower and would have a strong influence on the global politics and world peace.

Peaceful negotiation has become a relatively popular approach in dealing with inter-state problems. However, it is still commonly accepted that international relations is to a large degree dominated by power. No international problem referring to important national interest can be solved without a proper national power to back up its negotiations. National power consists of economic productivity, technology, national morale, geopolitical conditions, and military force, etc. Nevertheless, military force is always a symbol of national power. A country with a big military force needs a powerful military thought to guide its armed forces in organization, training, and choosing strategy and tactics. Without proper military thought, a military force with advanced weaponry and equipment is not guaranteed to win a war. On the contrary, should there be proper thought to guide the use of armed force, its performance in war could be improved greatly; it could even overwhelm an enemy armed with better equipment but with less advanced military thought and/or strategy. Therefore, it is proper to say that though the emergence of a military thought is to a considerable degree a reflection of the development of military technology, it is however the soul of the armed forces. It can help the armed forces to complete its mission. This is the primary reason for this book to concentrate on studying modern Chinese military thought.

Since the 1950s, students of Chinese military affairs in the Western world have primarily focused their attention on the People's Liberation Army (PLA), the theories of the people's warfare, or the military principles, doctrines, and defence policies of Communist China. Few writers in this field have ever extended their study from the contemporary Chinese military system to the historical development of modern Chinese military thought. A historical study of the development of modern Chinese military thought may not be closely related to policy making, but it is still important in understand- ing contemporary China and its military systems, because every modern system has its roots in history. This is a reason for this study to extend itself to part of ancient Chinese military philosophy to explore its continuation and influence on the development of modern Chinese military thought.

1. Power Politics and Military Force

Before Woodrow Wilson proposed to create the League of Nations in 1920 after the First World War, there was no international system able to regulate effectively the anarchic situation between nation-states. The only law that could rule their relations was power. Whoever has power, represents justice. Consequently, international politics, like all politics, is a struggle for power. Since the founding of international organizations, inter-state rela- tions have gradually improved. Many serious international conflicts have been solved with peaceful discussion or negotiations. However, the substance of traditional inter-state relations has not changed. Hans Morgenthau wrote that "whatever the ultimate aim of international politics, power is always the immediate aim. . .Whenever they strive to realize their goal by means of international politics, they do so by striving for power."[1] This concept is still alive in the minds of current political leaders. For example, George Bush, the president of the United States, stated publicly that he would protect American interests through a policy of peace abiding by force.[2]

Power is an ability to control others. When the use of power between the states refers to the actual exercise of physical violence, it starts to rely on military force. Therefore, in international politics, the use of armed force as a threat or a potentiality is the most important material factor making for political power of a nation.

A. National Interest and National Power

"Power is a means to other ends and not an end itself."[3] As a means of realizing national ends, military force may play an important role in international and national politics to protect national interest.

In discussing national interest, Morton Kaplan distinguished passion or sentiment from interest. The former may not actually relate to national interests and its objective may be more ephemeral than the latter, but it may also play an important role in the process of decision-making, in which the national interests and the means used to protect those interests are decided.[4] The passion and sentiment in many cases are expressed as national pride and are rightly or wrongly seen as part of national interests.

To serve as a means of national interests, the roles of national military force can be classified into three categories in accordance with the policy of the country. According to Arnold Wolfers, the goals of foreign policy can be divided into three headings, that is, national self-extension, national self-preservation, and self-abnegation. The self-abnegation primarily refers to self-control or self-sacrificing, it requires less support from the national military force except suppressing possible internal dissidents.

When a country pursues a policy of self-extension, it tends to demand a change of the status quo. The aim may be more power as an end in itself, or domination over other peoples, or territorial expansion, but it may also represent a quest for the return of lost territory, or the redress of some grievances such as unjust discrimination or control.[5] No matter what the basic motivation is, as long as a country is determined to pursue a policy of self-extension, it will inevitably meet the military resistance of other countries. Therefore, it needs a strong armed force to either wage war against its enemy or threaten to use force in order to bring its adversary to its knees or to the negotiation table.

B. Global Politics and National Security

Not every state in the world wishes to pursue a policy of self-extension, nor can every country afford to do so. There are more countries in the world that want to maintain the status quo than change it dramatically. This is called by Wolfers a policy of national self-preservation. However, under the name of national security, it may only request national independence and the territorial integrity of the nation; it may also include many other vital interests, from safety and influence zones to investments abroad, etc.

To fulfil the policy of self-preservation does not means to defend one's territory when it is actually under attack. The request for national secruity goes beyond mere maintenance and defence, it may in many cases "become so ambitious as to transform itself into a goal of unlimited self-extension. "[6] In examining the military confrontations of the superpowers since the end of the Second World War, one would see that a country pursuing national security could not stop at less than world domination.

Regardless of whether self-preservation is held to reasonable limitations, or aggressive self-extension is pursued, proper military preparation is always necessary. There is no country that could remain peaceful for long without a minimum armed force to maintain its security. This applies to both global politics and geopolitics. While the superpowers and other world powers are competing for more influence in the world, most middle and small powers are occupied with geopolitical problems with neighbouring states. Examples can be found in the Middle East and Africa. Though the superpowers want to negotiate for global disarmament, the military industry and weapon trades in the world market are extremely active. Regional wars have insured a thriving trade in military weapons.

C. The Political Role of the Military in the Developing Countries

While there are more than one hundred sixty countries in the world now, only two dozen or so can be considered developed countries, economically and politically. All of the rest are recognized as being developing or underdeveloped ones. In most cases they remain in a preindustrial or early industrial stage characterized by low productivity and authoritarian rule.

The national security problems of these countries are not due to the threat of foreign countries; on the contrary, they are due primarily to internal instability. Because of the lack of democratic traditions in solving their socio-political problems, the political struggles in the developing countries often become violent. The armed forces often intervene and replace the civilian government. Even if they do not replace the government with a military regime, they may still exercise a strong influence on the government. This is the most common phenomenon in the Third World today. The Philippines, South Korea and Pakistan are some notable examples. The military in those countries always play a dominant role in maintaining political stability.

Military force may also help the country in socio-economic development with or without a military regime. Generally speaking, military regimes in the developing countries have not had an impressive record in economic development except in Korea, where the military regime has continually suppressed the demand for political democracy and directed its efforts to economic development. It is now one of the few successful models of industrialization in the developing countries.

In addition, with its advanced equipment and efficient organization, the military can undertake socio-economic construction projects in order to prompt national modernization. However, this is rather an illusion in most developing countries because the armed forces in these countries are in many cases power brokers and are therefore a privileged class. They are not willing to serve as a labour force or army of producers. However, under a proper political machanism and ideological education, military force could become a vital force of production; it could use part of its manpower and equipment for economic projects. The reclamation of wasteland by troops in traditional China and the economic activities of the military in modern China are both convincing examples. This point will be further discussed in the following chapters.

Without directly engaging in economic activities, the military force in the modernizing countries can still assist in economic development. It could lend its advanced equipment to train the conscripts through regular military procedures and let them join economic development after discharge from the army, or help local government and business train the civilians through special arrangements, which will be able to raise the standard of the technol-ogy and promote the economic development of the country.

2. Modern Technology and Modern Military Thought

If war is deeply rooted in human nature, the use of weapons in war would be a special talent of man. The development of technology has its undeniable effect on the military, its organization, strategy and tactics. In other words, the development of military technology will inevitably affect the development of military thought.

A. Socio-Economic System and Military Force

Generally, in early human history, technology was very simple. The tools used in everyday living were also used as weapons in war. When manufacturing technology improved, weapons were gradually separted from working tools. Weapons were adapted to the special requirement of war. From studying world history, a modern Chinese military thinker, General Jiang Baili, found that when both the means of living and requirements of war are correlated with each other, a nation would be strong; otherwise it would be weak and might even perish. According to his findings, the unification of the means of livelihood and the needs of war could be achieved in two ways: one is the tools, the other the socio-economic system. The horse of the Mongos and the ship of the Europeans are the examples of the former; the system of "including all of the male peasants in the reserve" in ancient China and the mobilization system in modern Europe are of the latter. What Jiang tried to indicate is that there is a vital relationship between the national economy and the power of national defence.[7]

Similar to Jiang's finding, Paul Kennedy has drawn a far-reaching conclusion from his study of world history in the last 500 years in his recent book, *The Rise and Fall of the Great Powers*. He shows how the interaction of military and economic forces governs the progress of nations. Based on tremendous historical data, he suggested that there is a very clear connection in the long run between a great power's economic rise and fall and its growth and decline as an important military power, because economic resources are necessary to support a largescale military establishment. To him, as far as international politics is concerned, wealth and power are always relative.[8] This is very similar to the theories found in ancient Chinese military philosophies, which will be discussed in the second chapter of this book.

Kennedy did not try to propose any general theory about what kind of society and socio-political organizations are the most efficient in extracting resources in time of war, but he emphasized the effect of economic and technological change, and the interaction between strategy and economics on the relative position of the big power in the international system. However, he did point out that the market economy and the plurality of European power centres from the 16th to the 19th centuries may have promoted economic and technological development by competition. By stating so, he was unmistakably led to a conclusion that the centralization of a despotic oriental-style regime would be in a relatively disadvantageous position to stimulate technological change unless it was sponsored by the government itself.[9] The Chinese socio-political system after the Ming Dynasty is seen by Kennedy as a typical example.

B. The Impact of Modern Technology on the Balance of Power

When General Jiang mentioned the relationship between the means of living and the requirement of war, it already implied that the contemporary technology of a society has its effect on military force. Paul Kennedy goes further to show that the invention of the steam engine in the late 18th century not only started the modern industrial revolution in Europe but more importantly it totally shifted the world's balance of power for two hundred years in favour of the Western countries. The new technology derived from the industrial field was applied to the military and naval warfare a few decades later. Railways, telegraphs, quickfiring guns, steam propulsion, and armored warships took over the field one after another and became the decisive indicator of military strength. They greatly increased the firepower and mobility of the European military forces and helped them expand outside of Europe.

While the Europeans benefited from these new technologies, countries in Asia such as India and China were stuck in their old tradition. They not only knew nothing about the new technology but also abandoned some of their once very precious and advanced technologies. For example, the Ming emperors banned the Chinese shipbuilding industry and let their powerful ocean going fleet rot away in the middle of 15th century. Consequently, when the Europeans forced their way into China, the Chinese were unable to stop them. The Sino-British Opium War was fought under these circumstances in the

1840s. Since then China started her one hundred years of nightmare and struggled for survival by trying desperately to modernize her military force.

C. The Effect of Modern Technology on Military Strategy and Tactics

It is common knowledge today that the change of weaponry will immediately affect the organization of the armed force and its strategy and tactics. However, that was not the case when the new technology began to be applied to the military in the early 19th century. According to Kennedy, the European military commanders started to revise their ideas of strategy and tactics many decades after the army and navy were armed with the new weapons derived from the industrial revolution.[10] In China, however, the change in strategy took almost a century.

The Chinese experience of military modernization shows that the military leaders in the 19th century had pushed hard to get the new technology but did not think about the necessity of organizational and strategic changes until 40 years later. They started to build up Chinese military industry and began to copy the Western rifles and guns in the early 1860s, but they only began to adopt the Western military system and training manuals at the beginning of the 20th century when they were repeatedly defeated by Japan and the Western powers. Part of this long delay may be attributed to the shortage of financial resources and industrial bases to supply enough new weapons for the national military forces. Most of the country's armed force, except those of Li Hongzhang and Zuo Zongtang, were still equiped with traditional weapons. Many military leaders, therefore, may not have felt the urgent need for organizational changes in the middle of 19th century.

The most important reason, however, is probably due to the obsolete system of recruiting military officers. There was no military academy to offer standard military courses for the candidates. Like the civil servants, the military officers were selected through an imperial examination system, which primarily tested the archery and horsemanship skills of the candidates. Consequently, the military officers recruited from this system did not have any knowledge of the Western weapons and, above all, military systems. They were also not sensitive to organizational changes.

In addition, the Confucian bureaucrats with a strong Chinese ethnocentrism tended to reject any foreign ideas and systems. National humiliation of defeat in war reinforced the opposition to the adoption of Western systems. Even as late as the end of 19th century, some bureaucrats still asked the government to restore Chinese traditional weapons to fight the Western powers. Under these circumstances, the delay of drastic change of military systems was inevitable. It was not until the 1920s, when Chinese society was changed substantially by the revolution and civil wars that military leaders developed an awareness of the need for radical change.

The emergence of Mao Zedong's military thought did not mean that Chinese military modernization had succeeded, nor was it designed to take advantage of modern weapons. Instead, this military thought was developed to offset the tremendous power of the new weapons used by his enemies. It has been recognized as one of the few powerful military strategies of this century.[11] However, circumstances in the 1980s are totally different from those in the 1930s when Mao was fighting from a position of weakness. Today, the Chinese have a relatively modernized military industry, their armed forces are equiped with nuclear weapons and missiles second only to the two superpowers, the U.S.A. and U.S.S.R. While pushing for a further modernization of their military forces, they have been seriously reevaluating their once powerful people's warfare to make the necessary change in order to adapt to the new technology and weaponry they have.

3. Contemporary Chinese Military Modernization and Its Impact on People's Warfare

Since 1949, under the Communist regime there have been two major drives for military modernization. While the current one was started in the late 1970s and is not yet completed, the first one was initiated in the early 1950s after the end of the Korean War, but was virtually abandoned later for political reasons. Both of them have had their impact on the revered military doctrine of people's warfare.

A. Post-Korean War Military Modernization and Its Effects

Chinese involvement in the Korean War gave their armed forces the first opportunity to test themselves against the largest military powers of the world in conventional warfare. They earned the respect of the world but suffered heavy casualties. Since then the Chinese realized the important role of modern weapons in war and thus pushed for military modernization after the end of the war. While the whole leadership group was behind the modernization drive, the over-enthusiastic veterans of the Korean War and young officers offended the political leaders by rejecting the supremacy of Party leadership and political work system in the armed forces. This conflict eventually brought down Marshal Peng Dehuai, the major leader of the modernization drive, and his followers; it also caused a serious convulsion in the military force and the whole country. It, of course, delayed the modernization effort, at least partly, for more than a decade.

International factors also served to dismantle the drive. The deterioration of Sino-Soviet relations in 1958 and the withdrawal of Soviet military and economic aid played a significant role in delaying Chinese modernization. The Chinese were therefore forced to rely on themselves. Under the so-called "walking on two legs" policy, they kept their modernization effort independent of foreign assistance.[12] However, Chinese industrial capacity was not able to support the requirements of a modernized military force at that time. Nevertheless, the increasing tension between China and the United States, the

Suez Canal Crisis of 1956 and the landing of U.S. forces in Lebanon in 1958, for example, may have convinced the Chinese leaders that a Sino-American military confrontation was inevitable, and thus China must prepare herself for a war with whatever she could afford. Should China be forced to enter a war against the United States without military support from the Soviet Union, what the Chinese could do was to fight a people's war on their own land. This conclusion helped the Chinese leaders to further revolutionize their People's Liberation Army (hereafter PLA) and extensively expand the mass militia system by including almost all able-bodied men and women in the militia divisions in order to fight possible aggressors in the highly militarized Chinese countryside. They advocated a theory that the imperialists cannot destroy China with their nuclear weapons alone; they would have to send their armed forces to occupy China. When they stepped on Chinese soil, they would be immediately surrounded by the hostile mass militia and the PLA. They would be trapped in the occean of people's warfare and would be wiped out eventually.

At the height of the war preparation movement, Marshal Lin Bao, however, extensively politicized the PLA and expanded its political roles in the power struggles of the Cultural Revolution in sacrificing its military training. This is one of the most significant consequences of the Cultural Revolution, and the Chinese had to pay for this mistake later in the Sino-Soviet military conflict in Zhenbao Island (Damansky) in 1969 and the Sino-Vietnam border war in 1979. These hard lessons led the Chinese back to their military modernization plan again in the late 1970s after Deng Xiaoping resumed power. Under Deng's program military modernization is only a part of the official Four-Modernization drive, and is listed behind industry, agriculture, science and technology. The Chinese government wants to built military modernization on the basis of successful economic and technological development.

B. Current Military Modernization and the Strategic Debate

After almost two decades of political turbulence, the Chinese leaders began to realize the serious damage to Chinese socio-economic and military development caused by intra-party power struggle. Before his death, Premier Zhou Enlai had already decided to drive for national modernization, but it was effectively put on the government agenda only when the Gang of Four was purged from the party in 1976 after Mao's death.

When the current military modernization program was started in the late 1970s, the domestic and external circumstances were quite different from the 1950s. In 1978, when Deng resumed power, though China still felt the serious military pressure from the Soviet Union along her border, her diplomatic breakthrough with the U.S.A. made the Chinese leaders feel safer than they did in the 1950s. Under Deng's open door policy, China was given a limited opportunity to obtain Western new technology and weapons. This gave the modernization drive a better chance of success.

When military modernization was on the agenda again in 1978, the Chinese already had intermediate ballistic missiles, the hydrogen bomb, and satellites in space; their ICBM system was close to its scheduled test date. So the Chinese leaders knew much better about the destructive power of modern weapons and were in a better position to drive for military modernization.

Furthermore, though there was a strong demand to limit the overindulgence of the PLA in political activity as they did during the Cultural Revolution, there was no leader who publicly denied the supremacy of party leadership in the armed forces. On the contrary, the leaders still coupled revolutionization with regularization and modernization as the three goals of military modernization. They paid at least some lip service to political work in the armed forces, which to a considerable degree deflated strong dissent from the political commissars in the armed forces. As a senior political commissar, Deng Xiaoping may have also helped to crush any possible opposition. However, this does not mean that there were no dissenting voices within the PLA on the military modernization. As a matter of fact, debate over the applicability of Mao's people's warfare in modern war has not been completely silenced. While some senior military leaders continually claimed that should a war happen tomorrow, China would still be on the weak side and thus the PLA should be prepared to fight a people's war with the assistance of the mass militia and guerrilla forces, etc. The modernization-orientated leaders, however, did not deny the usefulness of people's warfare, but suggested that it be adapted to the new circumstances and realistic conditions. Meanwhile, the reformers keep a firm stand in improving weapon systems, reorganizing the armed forces, and emphasizing military training.

Thanks to a relatively peaceful political environment, the Chinese have been able to make impressive progress in both economic and military modernization. While they have been able to maintain an annual seven percent rate of economic growth, they have reduced their military expenditures from 17.5 percent of the total national budget in 1979 to 8.2 percent in 1987.[13] Nevertheless, they have also surprised the world by showing their achievement in ICBMs and other missiles, and new tanks and guns displayed in National Day parades. They have reduced the size of their armed forces by one million men within two years, established a retirement system for officers, introduced a better conscription system, improved their military school systems, and eventually restored the traditional military rank system. All of these are essential to a modern military force. Backed by these achievements, Zhao Ziyang, the then General Secretary of the Central Committee and the First Vice-Chairman of the Military Commission of the CCP, was able to say publicly in an important meeting that "in referring to the strategic problem of the armed force, it should be concentrated on the military modernization and trainning but not the old people's warfare."[14]

On another occasion, Zhao even went further to say that China should start to make an accurate estimate about the possible type of future war, the perspective of national defence, and the direction of potential development of the military.[15] The same source also revealed that the Chinese government has been reviewing their current national defence planning. They are trying to formulate an intermediate goal of military reform and national defence planning before working out their blue-print of military strategy for the next century.[16]

From these reports, there is no doubt that the Chinese are heading for a drastic change of their military thought in general and military strategy in particular. They are thinking not in terms of a decade from now, but 20 years or more in the future. No one knows exactly how the Chinese are going to change their current strategic doctrines and how drastic the change will be. However, we can examine the possible direction of change in accordance with some vital factors.

4. The Factors Affecting the Change of Chinese Military Thought

When a country decides on its strategy of national defence, the political and military leaders have to consider the objective conditions that they may have to face. They could go further to delineate the potential problems that may occur in future when national and international political developments reach a particular stage. Given these considerations, the leaders should decide their short-term, intermediate term, and long-term strategies of national defence. There may be numerous factors that can affect the choice of the policy makers, but the most important ones could be limited to the following six.

A. The Perspective of War and International Situation

The primary goal of national defense and strategy is to deal with potential wars and win them. Therefore, the defence planning and strategy of a country has to be based on a sound judgment of the perspective of the future wars. Is there any potential war threatening to the country? If the answer is yes, who could the enemy be? Would it be a general war or a regional one? Would there be any danger of being drawn into a nuclear war? Furthermore, if war is inevitable, when could it happen? In five years? In a decade? or in an indefinite future? The decision-makers must assimilate all the available information to make a correct judgment and then formulate their plans and strategies of national defense accordingly.

After the close of the Korean War, the cold war between the Western capitalist countries and the Communist bloc intensified. A general war was often seen as possible in connection with regional conflict. With their monopoly of the nuclear weapons, the U.S. leaders adopted a rather aggressive strategy. A strategy of "massive retaliation" would permit the U.S. to start any size of war including nuclear war in responding to local military conflicts. The disparity in nuclear weapons between the U.S. and the Soviet Union began to change in the late 1950s. The loss of her absolute superior position and concern about mutual destruction in a nuclear war forced the U.S.A. to retreat from her doctrine of massive retaliation and adopt a strategy of flexible or controlled response in the 1960s. When Nixon came to power in 1969, the national instability caused by the prolonged Vietnam War persuaded him to pursue de'tente with the Soviet Union and undertake a personal journey to China in order to defuse the longstanding hostility between China and the U.S.

Before Nixon's visit, the Chinese government had often declared that a general war between the imperialist and socialist countries would be inevitable, and the victory would go to the socialist countries. Based on this assumption, the Chinese were to prepare themselves for a general nuclear war. They even announced that should the war be inevitable, they would prefer to fight it sooner rather than later. When the Soviet Union disputed their strategy and withdrew its support for Chinese military and economic development, instead of giving up their decision, the chinese started to prepare themselves for a people's war. As mentioned earlier, they greatly expanded their militia force by mobilizing all able-bodied men and women throughout the whole country to join the militia. This strategy was pursued without significant change until the late 1970s after Deng assumed power. However, the change became clear only in the mid-1980s when Deng was quoted as saying: "We have changed our past point of view that the danger of war was getting close. Now we expect to have a relatively long period of peace without war, at least in the rest of this century. This is possibly not a mirage."[17] Since then China has stepped up her military modernization projects for peace time. Among other things, they discharged about one million of their four million armed forces in 1986.

Zhao Ziyang was also quoted as having said in an important military meeting that, based on current Chinese diplomatic relations with foreign countries and the general conditions of the international community, large-scale wars are unlikely. However, he asked the Chinese leaders to be alert to the possibility of regional wars. With these assumptions in mind, the Chinese leaders have started to think about the reorganization of their armed forces, defence arrangements for the border areas, and many other reforms of national defence. [18]

Since assuming power in 1985, Mikhail Gorbachev has continually stepped up his effort to clear historical issues between China and the Soviet Union in order to improve their relations. This has, of course, further confirmed the Chinese views of the international situation and, therefore, put their peace-time military building and new strategy on a more solid basis.

B. The Effect of Material and Technology

The vital effect of technology on national power and the armed forces has been discussed above. What we should further point out here is that while the Chinese armed forces may be superior or at least equal to the regional powers in Asia and thus be able to adopt a forward defence strategy or offensive defence in a regional military conflict, they would be still inferior to those of the superpowers. Therefore, in the event of military conflict with either of the superpowers, China would find it difficult to take advantage of a forward defence strategy. Instead, it may have to think about retrograde defence or positional defence along the border areas. With their modern equipment, the PLA will have to rely heavily on the supply of high technology products from China's industrial centres. Therefore, it is incredible to think that the PLA would give up the industrial centres and retreat to the countryside and/or the mountainous areas to practise their revered people's warfare before engaging the enemy in the border areas and the strategic economic centres.

However, it would also be wrong to think that in a defensive war against the superpowers on the Chinese mainland, the PLA would completely discard the old doctrines of people's warfare. It would still be useful should the PLA be forced to retreat from the initial campaigns in the border areas. To adapt to the new circumstances, the Chinese are considering a three-stage defence strategy, that is positional warfare, mobile warfare, and guerrilla warfare. Under this strategy, the intruders would have to face the fierce resistance of the PLA in the strongly fortified border areas first. If this defensive line is breached, a mobile warfare with the maneuvering forces such as armored army columns, air-borne forces, and other forces would be followed when the enemy goes inland. If both of these strategies failed to stop the enemy, guerrilla warfare would be the last strategy used to fight the enemy, which would of course be different from the traditional guerrilla war. It would be carried out with relatively modern weapons. [19]

C. National History and Culture

Military strategy is, to a considerable degree, affected by the national character which, among other things, includes primarily the history and culture of a country. History is the record of experience; culture is the customary beliefs, social systems and material traits of a country transmitted from generation to generation. These make up the heritage of a country.

As one of the oldest civilized countries, with more than four thousand years of history, China has had one of the richest national military legacies in the world. The development of modern military technology, the exposure to foreign military theories, and the repeated defeats in wars against the Western powers, have broken the monopoly of the ancient military theories but they are still highly respected and continually influence the thinking of Chinese military leaders. Therefore, when analyzing modern Chinese military thought, it is necessary to trace its roots back to traditional Chinese military philosophy. As to the development of future Chinese military strategies, instead of inventing a dramatically different new one overnight, it is expected to revise the old strategies step by step. Therefore, a comprehensive study of modern Chinese military thought including that of Jiang Jieshi and Mao Zedong would be helpful in forecasting possible changes against the contemporary socio-political reality of China.

D. Foreign Military Theories

Before the Opium War, Chinese military leaders were not familiar with Western military theories. Even after being defeated by the foreign powers, the Chinese did not readily change their military thought. Instead, these defeats just marked the beginning of a long and painful process that eventually brought Western theories to the Chinese leaders. Even when the Chinese accepted foreign military theories through alliances, military aid, weapon trades, and cultural and economic contacts, they were only superficially copied without being properly adapted to the Chinese reality of the time. Therefore, when the Chinese armed forces were confronted with the foreign aggressors, they were often easily defeated until they learned how to adapt the foreign military theories to Chinese socio-economic reality. Accordingly, modern Chinese military thought is neither a simple continuation of traditional Chinese military heritage nor a total copy of the imported idea. It is a new theory based on both Chinese and foreign thoughts. Since the open door policy was adopted in the 1970s, the Chinese have greatly increased their contact with the Western military by mutual visits and weapon and technology importation. Consequently, Western military theory will have an effect on the Chinese in the years to come.

E. Contemporary Political Ideology

Ideology is a systematic body of concepts about human life or culture.[20] Franz Schurmann defined it as a systematic set of ideas with action consequences.[21] Although Schurmann's use of this term is primarily aimed at its functions in serving the purpose of an organization, the concept of ideology can also be applied to personal actions. It can guide one's behaviour and way of thinking .

Traditional Chinese military theories are primarily based on ancient Chinese political ideology such as Confucianism, Doism, Legalism, and Moism. However, when modern military thought started to develop, the influence of traditional Chinese political ideology gradually decreased, and foreign political ideology increased its influence. This trend paralleled the process of Chinese military modernization. Zeng Guofan, the supreme commander of the Qing Army in suppressing the Taiping Army and a prominent military strategist in his time, had developed his military thought primarily based on his philosophy of *Lixue*--a Confucian school of idealism developed in the Song and Ming dynasties.[22] When the Guomindang fought the Communists in Jiangxi province in the 1930s, Jiang Jieshi still trained his Nationalist Army using part of Zeng's theories. Since the beginning of the Sino-Japanese War, with increasing military aid from and political contact with the Western countries, the influence of Western military thought along with their political ideologies has overshadowed that of traditional Chinese military thought on Jiang and other Guomindang leaders. By the same token, Marxism and Leninism have had a tremendous influence on the development of the military thought of Mao and other communist leaders.

The People's Liberation Army was directly led by the Communist party, which often identified itself with the interest of the socio-economically disadvantaged people, and, thus, relied on their support and cooperation to win the war. Therefore, Mao developed his people's warfare based on the support of the armed masses. Following the current political reforms and open-door policy, the traditional Marxism-Leninism has been gradually revised and merged with some new elements accepted from the Western world. This change of political ideology will sooner or later leave its imprint on Chinese strategy and military thought in the future.

F. Personality

The development of personality is a subject which has generated intense discussion among psychologists and anthropologists for a long time. There is a general consensus that individual personality is primarily shaped by the environment in which one is brought up. In other words, the development of personality is basically affected by the family and society through formal and informal education.[23] Therefore, the national history, culture, and the socio-political conditions, as discussed above, may all affect one's personality. However, some students believe that the effect of environmental factors on the shape of an individual personality only reveals part of the story. Part of the personality may be inherited.[24]. No conclusion has been reached in this controversy.

No matter whatever factors may contribute to the development of one's personality, the particular character of a leader often shows in his military thought. Jiang Jieshi, for example, with the strong heroism of a professional soldier often asked his generals to fight to the death at their positions, while Mao Zedong acted like Zhuge Liang, a prominent strategist in the period of the Three Kingdoms, who never demanded such personal sacrifice of his subordinates; on the contrary, he often preferred to play 'hide-and-seek' with his enemy, ready to pounce on and destroy them when the chance arose.

When these characteristics are reflected in military thought, Jiang tended to emphasize the virtue of bravery and fearlessness. He often wrote that it is possible to pit one against ten or pit ten against one hundred, should a soldier be ready to fight to the death.

Although Mao did not ignore the same virtue, as a strategist and game player, he obviously preferred to rely more on strategy than physical power. His idea was to pit one against ten in strategy but pit ten against one in tactics.

While these factors are vital to the development of military thought, they may not affect a person's thought equally. While some influence factor may have a significant imprint on one's thought, others maybe completely absent from it depending on the objective situation one faces. Accordingly, these factors will serve as a general guideline only in the later chapters based on the available materials.

5. Approach and Oranization
A. Approach

The development of modern Chinese military thought as discussed above is closely related to two basic elements: the development of modern Chinese socio-political history in general and the process of Chinese military modernization in particular. Therefore, this study will adopt a historical approach to analyze the phenomenon of Chinese military modernization at different stages in the development of modern China. It will examine the relevant socio-economic and political activities of the period in question in order to explore the relations between the historical cause and effect of various social changes.

To trace the cause of a particular socio-political change, it is essential to inquire into the existing system to expose the elements that may induce the change in question. Based on this assumption, the socio-political system, economic condition, and the military system immediately before the Opium War of 1840 will be examined in order to present a general background for further discussion of societal change.

While the traditional Chinese socio-political system before 1840 may have provided the basis for imminent social change and the drive for modernization, the Opium War and subsequent events were the immediate catalysts of Chinese modernization, and above all, military modernization. How did the Chinese respond to the Opium War? What were the reactions of the Chinese intellectuals? The ideas of the socio-political elites will be the major focus of the analysis at this stage in order to interpret the beginning of Chinese military modernization.

"Ideas grow out of history." Modern military thought is a product of history. Military leaders who played a certain role in this period of time may have more or less contributed to the final result of modern thought. Prior to analyzing any personal military ideas, his socio-political and educational background, and personal character will be briefly examined in order to probe the factors that have affected the development of his thought.

The military conflict of various socio-political forces after the collapse of the traditional system dominated political change for a long time and almost totally destroyed the country. However, after a long arduous struggle, China was saved from destruction, and unified under one government except for Taiwan. From the technological point of view, military modernization of China was far from completion in the 1940s. Among other factors, the emergence of modern Chinese military thought was the key to winning the war of national liberation and unifying herself from civil war. A comprehensive analysis of Jiang and Mao's military thought and the unique circumstances that promoted their development will give us an idea about how the Chinese leaders developed their theories; how they passed the serious test in the extremely arduous wars; and thus, to further show us how the Chinese masses were mobilized to participate in the unprecedented national liberation movement, which to some extent may have had a similar effect of the traditional social mobility, extensive social interdependence, mass participation, and national identity recognized as the characteristics of modern society and attributes of modernization.

B. The Organization

The book is divided into eight chapters: besides the introduction and epilogue, the other six chapters will be devoted to analyzing the following topics:

The second chapter will be a general survey of Chinese traditional military philosophy. It will not only summarize the schools and the content of ancient Chinese military theories, but also analyze the socio-economic background which helped produce them, and to maintain their attraction without drastic change for several thousands of years.

The third chapter will deal primarily with the Opium War and the transition of Chinese military system. It will discuss the traditional Chinese military system prior to the war, the impact of the war and the Chinese response, above all, the reactions of the intellectuals and bureaucrats. Ideas of military modernization and government policies such as the *Yangwu* movement and *Ziqiang* movement; the rise of regional military forces like Xiangjun, Huaijun and their effect on the Chinese military modernization in the coming years will be analyzed in detail.

Personal military ideas from Lin Zexu, Wei Yuan, Feng Guifen, Zeng Guofan, Li Hongzhang, Zuo Zongtang to Yuan Shihkai will be discussed individually.

The fourth chapter is basically a continuation of the transitional period after the Revolution of 1911. Ideas of curbing military power and pressing for demobilization of the armed forces, the rise of armed forces of political parties and their political work system, and the particular socio-political background will be discussed in detail. Personal thought singled out for analysis includes Li Yuanhong, Huang Xing, Cai E, Dr. Sun Yatsen, and Jiang Baili.

The fifth and sixth chapters will be completely devoted to military theories of Jiang Jieshi and Mao Zedong. They are the best representatives of modern Chinese military theories.

The seventh chapter will present a short analysis of the military reformation of Deng Xiaoping and the development of Chinese national defence strategy since the late 1970s.

6. The Material

The information used in this study comes primarily from four sources:

A. Personal Collections of the Author

Part of the research on ancient Chinese military philosophy, the works of Mao Zedong and Jiang Jieshi, and current military developments in China and Taiwan made use of the journals and newspaper articles in the personal collections of the author.

B. Libraries in North America

Much of the material used in this book comes from the East Asia Institutes at the University of Toronto, in Canada, and from Harvard University and Stanford University, in the United States.

C. Collections in Taiwan

Through both official invitations and personal requests, the author was also able to use resources in the East Asia Institute of National Chengchi University, and in the College of Military Political Workers of the Guomindang Armed Forces.

D. Resources from China

Under the sponsorship of the Beijing Institute for International Strategic Studies, the author spent three weeks in China meeting with many prominent scholars specializing in military history. Especially useful were seminars with the people of the Military Academy of the PLA, in Beijing. These meetings helped the author in clarifying several key issues and collecting information.

These research trips to the United States, Taiwan and China were made possible by the financial assistance of the Social Sciences and Humanities Research Council of Canada.

Footnotes

1. Hans J. Morgenthau, "Power and Ideology in International Politics," *International Politics and Foreign Policy*, ed. by Hans Margenthau (New York: the Free Press, 1968), pp. 170-77.

2. See "The World Lighthouse of Hope," a comment carried on the *Xing Dao Daily*, (in Chinese, issued in North America) Jan. 20, 1989.

3. Arnold Wolfers, "The Pole of Power and the Pole of Indifference," *International Politics and Foreign Policy*, ed. by Hans Morgenthau (New York: the Free Press, 1968), pp. 146-51.

4. Morton Kaplan, "The National Interest and Other Interests," *International Politics and Foreign Policy, op. cit.*, pp. 164-69.

5. Wolfers, "The Pole of Power and the Pole of Indifference," *op. cit.*, p. 147.

6. *Ibid*.

7. See Ch. 4, Section 5 of this book, The Military Thought of Jiang Baili.

8. Paul Kennedy, *The Rise and Fall of the Great Powers: Economic Change and Military Conflict from 1500 to 2000* (London: Unwin Human, 1988), p. XXii

9. *Ibid.*, pp.22-30.

10. *Ibid.*, p. 144.

11. Joseph C. Wylie, *Military Strategy: A General Theory of Power Control* (N.J.: Rutgers Univ., 1966), p. 38.

12. Chen-ya Tien, *The Mass Militia System and Chinese Modernization* (Toronto: Mosaic Press, 1982), pp. 45-46.

13. Louise Branson, "Chinese Military Peddles Wine, Toys to Boost Its Budget," a report on *The Toronto Star*, Oct. 23, 1988.

14. *The Xing Dao Daily*, March 26, 1988.

15. A report on *The Xing Dao Daily*, May 13, 1988.

16. *Ibid*.

17. "The Reforms and Open-Door Policy of the Chinese PLA," on *The International Daily*, May 30, 1986.

18. "Zhao Ziyang Worries about Regional War and Urges the Military Leaders to Keep Alert in a Military Meeting," *The Xing Dao Daily*, May 13, 1988.

19. "The Significant Changes of the Chinese Military Thought," *The International Daily*, Oct. 16, 1983.

20. Webster's New Collegiate Dictionary.

21. Franz Schurmann, *Ideology and Organization in Communist China* (Berkeley & Los Angeles: Univ. of Calif., 1968), pp. 23-4.

22. Zhang Yutian, *Modern Chinese Military History* (Liaoning: People's Press, 1983), pp. 232-35.

23. Hang Thaddaus, *A Study of the Chinese Nation* (Taiwan: Shangwu, 1966), p. 13.
24. *Ibid.*, p. 14.

CHAPTER 2

Survey of Ancient Chinese Military Theories

1. The Origin and Characteristics of Ancient Chinese Military Philosophy

The first book on the art of war in China can be traced to the legends of *Hetu* and *Luoshu*, which are said to be battle formations created by some unknown tribal leaders in Shaanxi Province, by the Yellow River, about 6000 to 7000 years ago. *Fuxi*, another tribal chieftain in Henan Province, was inspired by these works and subsequently created the well known *Bagua*, or the Eight Diagrams, a thousand years later, which is said to be a more advanced battle formation.[1] These works, however, are not real books, because a written language had not yet appeared in China. According to various ancient historical records, it seems that *Huangdi*, or the Yellow Emperor, founder of the Chinese nation, had written numerous books on military affairs. However, Chinese books on the art of war only began to proliferate in the later Zhou dynasty. Since then, more than a thousand works have been published.

According to Lu Dajie, the author of *An Introduction to Books on the Art of War of All Ages* (of China), there are one thousand three hundred forty military works, which include over six thousand eight hundred and thirty one volumes. However, the majority of these works have been lost. Only two hundred eighty-eight books, including two thousand one hundred and sixty volumes, are left. Furthermore, a considerable number of these remaining works are either preserved as the sole copy or are possessed by private collectors and are thus rendered inaccessible to the public. Consequently, only one hundred and seventy eight works can be purchased on the market.[2]

Lu made his estimate of the number of surviving works based on information contained in Emperor Qian Long's unprecedented encyclopedia *Si Ku Quan Shu* published in 18th century, which was a massive compilation of existing scholarly works in all fields. Since that time, China has experienced many wars, and it is quite conceivable that some of these military works were damaged or lost again. Therefore, the actual number of books in existence today may be much smaller than the figure given by Lu, although we cannot give a more reliable figure.

From the remaining works, some unique features of Chinese military philosophy can be noted by the researcher in this field. First of all, Chinese military theories were primarily developed in the later Zhou dynasty or *Chunqiu* (Spring and Autumn 770-476 B.C.) and *Zhanquo* (the Warring States 475-221 B.C.) period. Since then, the development of Chinese military philosophy tended to interpret the old works, or to solve some technical and trivial problems. Some works were even devoted to discussing superstitious rituals such as prayers, divination, and astrology. The subsequent publications are primarily supplementary ones; there are few works that have significant theoretical contributions. Therefore, studies of Chinese traditional military philosophy have overwhelmingly emphasized the works produced before the Qin dynasty or the pre-Qin period (*Xianqin*) and have paid very little attention to those of later years. This omission does not cause any significant bias to the study of traditional Chinese military philosophy. Indeed, as Lu Dajie says:

> The greatest military strategists in ancient China are Sunzi and Wu Qi. Ideas developed by those prior to Sun and Wu were inherited by them, while those after Sun and Wu were inspired by them. Although there have been tremendous changes in the development of the art of war in the past millenia in China, these changes have never deviated from the paths initiated by Sun and Wu. It is, therefore, safe to say that all of the writing on the art of war after Sun and Wu are indeed those of Sun and Wu.[3]

To many students of this field, this statement may be oversimplified, but it is quite correct to say that traditional Chinese military philosophy basically developed its unique shape in the later Zhou dynasty by Sunzi and Wuzi (Wu Qi); there have been no significant changes since then. The reasons for this phenomenon will be discussed later, but for the time being, it is enough for us to realize that the technological condition, the socio-eonomic and political systems have had a strong effect on it.

Secondly, the ancient Chinese military theories are limited neither to books on the Art of War, nor to works of military strategists; indeed, these theories are also found in the non-military works of philosophers and politicians. The books of Legalism, Confucianism, Daoism (Taoism), and others have contained some philosophies of war which in turn have strongly influenced the theories of military strategists. Generally, all books on the art of war embrace the basic elements of traditional Chinese political philosophy. Sunzi, for example, is often said to be influenced by Daoism, while Wuzi is said to be affected by Confucianism. Both works, however, show that the principle of humanity had primarily dominated the author's consideration of war. As a disciple of Confucianism, Wuzi advised rulers to observe moral principle and practice righteousness in governing their people.[4] "The Four Harmonies" must be achieved in one's own country before a ruler can go to war against other countries.

By emphasizing the importance of moral law in war, Sunzi consistently pursued a strategy of *"Quan"* in war which means keeping it complete without killing. "The best thing of all", he said, "is to take the enemy's country whole and intact; to shatter and destroy it is not so good. So, too, is it better to capture an army entire than to destroy it, to capture a regiment, a detachment or an entire company than to destroy it."[5]

As the principle of humanism is observed by strategists in discussing war, a comprehensive study of the ancient Chinese art of war is almost impossible without touching on the traditional Chinese political philosophies or value systems. Indeed, Zeng Guoyuan, the author of *The Philosophy of War Before Qin Dynasty (China)*, writes that the political philosophy of the pre-Qin period included the philosophy of war.[6] Therefore, to some degree, one inevitably refers to political philosophy when discussing Chinese military theories.

Thirdly, in using the ancient works on the art of war, one will have to deal with the problem of forged works , that is *Wei Tao* and *Wei Shu* in Chinese. Both refer to ancient books of dubious authenticity, but do not strictly mean the same thing. *Wei Shu* refers to ancient books that have been found to be forged, incorrectly dated or attributed to a wrong author; *Wei Tao*, without excluding the common definition, particularly emphasizes passing off modern works as ancient ones.[7]

Wei Shu and *Wei Tao* not only exist in the works on the art of war which may relate to the subject in question here. As Zeng Guoyuan wrote: "Books published before the Qin dynasty often confuse authentic elements with false ones. . .they are mostly found in the books of the *Zi* category, but books of *Jing* category are not totally free from forgeries."[8] To Lu Dajie, in regard to the authors, ancient books on the art of war are primarily *Wei Tao*. It is incredible that while Yellow Emperor and Xuannu are said to have written more than ten books each, Taigong (Jiang Shang), Huang Shigong, Zhuge Liang, and Li Weigong (Li Jing) are credited with anywhere from ten to thirty books each. It seems that the further we go back into history, the more prolific the writers seem to be. As a rule, this trend is unbelievable.[9]

The reasons for so many *Wei Shu* are that many ancient books were not written by the authors themselves; most of them were probably edited or compiled by their disciples or descendants in the later ages. Therefore, some additions and incorrect material may have been inserted. This kind of *Wei Shu*, according to Zeng Guoyuan, can be used without any difficulty. Should a book be entirely "counterfeit", its usefulness could be determined by the time that the book was written. If a book on the ancient philosophy of war was forged before the Qin dynasty by a person who lived in the same age, the counterfeit work has probably preserved some valuable information of that period. Therefore, it could be still used. As to the ancient books on the art of war, Zeng believes that most of them are of dubious origin, but with no other material available, one must use them cautiously, relying on one's own judgment of their value.[10]

With these problems and the limited goals set for this particular chapter in mind, it is necessary for us to set guidelines for our analysis in order to avoid being dragged into unnecessary controversies:

(1)   Although the existing ancient books on the art of war amount to only about 20 percent of the number as calculated by Lu, it would be still too ambitious for this researcher to go through all of them. Actually, it is not only impossible but also unnecessary, because according to Lu Dajie's explanation, the figure he actually gave included many books which either deal only partially with the philosophy of war or are interpretations of other books. No major points on the ancient concepts of war would be missed if one were to examine exclusively the major works available in this field. Accordingly, the books on classic military theories which will be used in this analysis are, for the most part, limited to those included in *The Great Collection of Chinese Books on the Arts of War*, edited by Li Yuri. This is a 15-volume collection including more than 30 major works.

(2)   With regard to the philosophy of war, information will primarily be based on the major works on the art of war. Non-military works will be only used on particular occasions in order to account for the philosophical and ideological origins of the philosophy of war. It is not the intention of this study to delve deeply into Confucianism, Daoism, and Legalism except where absolutely necessary.

(3)   More emphasis will be put on the theories contained in those works written before the Qin dynasty than on those of the later period, because the framework of Chinese military theories was developed during the former period. The value of the works produced after Qin, from a theoretical point of view, is insignificant. However, a brief comparison will be made before the close of this chapter.

2. The Socio-political Background and Its Effect on the Military Philosophy of the Pre-Qin Period

China's history dates back much further than the *Qin* dynasty. The legends containing the precepts of the art of war, as mentioned before, can be traced back to Yellow Emperor and *Fuxi* (6000 or 7000 B.C.). However, these legends are less than authentic and, thus, cannot be used for serious analytical purposes. Like most students of ancient Chinese military philosophy, the author has adopted a particular definition to limit the term '*Xianqin*' (prior to Qin or pre-Qin) to the period of Chunqiu and Zhanguo, because most important works were credited to people of this time. [11]

Chunqiu and Zhanguo was the golden age of ancient Chinese civilization. The greatest works of military philosophy and other philosophies of ancient China were products of this period. Sinologists would agree that this period was an unique and unprecedented age in terms of cultural development. It really deserves the honourable title of 'the age of a hundred flowers blossoming and a hundred schools of thought contending'. Confucianism, Daoism, Legalism, Moism, and many other philosophies which dominated Chinese socio-political development for more than two thousand five hundred years, are examples of the monumental products of that culturally active age. Why were the Chinese able to develop these great philosophies, and above all military theories, in this period? And why did no similar monumental works emerge in later periods? The answer can be found from the socio-political background of that age.

A. The Socio-Political Background of the Later Zhou Period

With the overthrow of the Shang dynasty and the subsequent emergence of the Zhou dynasty in 1118 B.C., China was able to enjoy an unprecedented long, peaceful and prosperous period before the invasion of the *Quanrong*, an ancient barbarian tribe in northwest China in 771 B.C. Allied with the reigning King Yu's father-in-law, the invaders captured the capital and put the King to death.

After the new King Ping ascended the throne, he was forced to move his capital city from the three hundred year old city of Hao, near the modern city of Xian in Shaanxi Province, eastward to Luoyang in Henan Province. Since Luoyang is located to the east of Hao, the Zhou dynasty after 771 B C is now referred to as East Zhou. From 771 B.C. to its complete dethronement in 249 B.C., East Zhou never regained the stablility and prosperity of the preceding age. A turbulent age of war prevailed.

With the decline of the central authority, local feudal lords started to extend their power by military conquest. In the 8th century B.C., when East Zhou was first established, there were still about 200 states in China, but after the conquest of feudal lords, all states with a few exceptions were merged into seven large states, further fighting continued for two and half more centuries until the final surrender of Qi State to Qin State in 221 B.C. [12]

During the almost five hundred years of fighting, the central authority was gradually weakened, and subsequently, the whole country fell into a state of anarchy. The disintegration of the political system and the weakening of the ruling class provided an opportunity for commoners to come to power. Social morality no longer existed, and people lived under extremely miserable conditions. Social and political changes were so pronounced in character that they significantly affected Chinese military philosophy.

After the national government was weakened and later disappeared, while the local feudal lords were occupied with power struggles against each other, government control over ideological matters was lost, academic activities were completely liberated from government censorship. Instead, private schools started to operate. It seems that freedom of speech and travel were enjoyed by the people in this period. People could not only say whatever they wanted, but they could also move freely from one state to another to sell their ideas to any ambitious local leaders who would listen. Under these circumstances, whoever had the skill and ideas to help the warlords could expect rapid advancement in the military hiearchy. This situation provided the impetus for "a hundred schools of thought contending together".[13] Various philosophies and theories on the art of war were developed by the newly formed social class *Shi*, which consisted of the educated commoners and the descendants of the nobles.

B. Contemporary Political Thought and its Effect on Military Theories

The miserable life of the people was entirely due to the decline of central authority and the fighting between feudal lords. The Confucianists believed that if the old political order, the Zhou system, was restored, the chaos would cease.[14] Confucius denounced the fighting between states and the coups d'état among feudal lords.

Although Confucianists failed to restore the Zhou authority and stop the fighting, their unflagging support of the orthodox political ideologies such as the policy of *Ren*, the deeds of model rulers, and the importance of virtue in a prosperous society, helped keep these ideas in the forefront of the minds of contemporary military strategists, and thus, influenced their theories on war.

About one hundred years after the death of Confucius, Moism became a very popular school of thought. It is said that *Mo Di*, the founder of Moism, had learned from the Confucians but later became dissatisfied with Confucianism and turned his back on it. In the earlier stage of the Zhanguo period, Moism became a major rival of Confucianism.[15] Moists shared with Confucians the view of good government; they wanted to restore the old political system in order to improve the lives of the people. The Moists were opposed to any offensive war, but supported defensive ones.[16] *Mo Di* once even personally led his disciples to help the Song State against the invasion of

Chu.[17] The anti-offensive war (*Feigong*) attitude is closely related to the Moist philosophy of universal love, which extended the concept of loving one's relatives and friends to loving everybody.

The first step towards achieving universal love is to stop hating each other. "Hatred is the biggest source of war." The Moist's philosophy of *Feigong* is primarily based on a utilitarian point of view, because the loss and suffering brought about by war outweighs any possible advantage that could be gained through it.[18] However, defensive wars are not denounced. The evil is in aggression or offensive war only; if people give up aggression, peace would be achievable.

In comparison with Confucianism and Moism, Daoism has a negative attitude towards both political systems and war. The philosophy of Daoist[19] is often seen as a mystery. It sees the origin of the universe is based on *Dao*, which is the supreme principle upon which everything comes into being. To the Daoist, *Dao* is the mother of everything, but is also nothingness. In turn, it means that everything comes from nothingness. It is a natural law.

To other schools of ancient philosophy, *Dao* was seen as the general principle of human beings, a moral law, but not a natural law.[20] When it is applied to the arts of war, Sunzi and Wuzi used it as a moral law.[21]

Daoists were against all wars, but the interesting thing is that their inactive attitude is often credited by students of military affairs as having a significant effect on the theories of ancient Chinese military strategists. Because the Daoists believe that inactiveness can control activeness (or active energy), the weaker can defeat the stronger. Similarly, the soft can overcome the hard. Water is "soft" in nature and can adapt to any ground. However, it can break dams and destroy anything that stands in its way.[22] Sunzi, for example, compared the shape of water with the form of an army. "Now an army may be likened to water, for just as flowing water avoids the heights and hastens to the lowlands, so an army avoids strength and strikes weakness. And as water shapes its flow in accordance with the ground, so an army manages its victory in accordance with the situation of the enemy."[23]

Different from all other schools, Legalists were the most prominent and active of the social forces that wholeheartedly embraced the social changes in the Xianqin period. They were even eager to initiate further change.

The founder of Legalism is Guan Zhong of the Qi State. As the first minister, Guan carried out a series of policies that strengthened the country's military force and economic systems. His policies can be summarized in two words: "order and strength". To achieve order, he emphasized the rule of law; for strength, he set up a militia system. It was called *Ji Junling Yu Neizheng*, a name emphasizing the coupling of the military force to local political systems.[24] This system not only brought other states under the hegemony of the Qi State and created a relatively peaceful situation in the interstate community for more than forty years, but it also affected the Chinese military system and philosophy of war.

Legalism was later accepted in various degrees by almost all of the feudal states. When the armed force was greatly expanded under the militia system, military strategies, tactics, and the command of the army were so complicated that generalship became a highly professional post. Therefore, military strategists with their special knowledge of military affairs were promptly appointed to key positions by the federal lords. Sunzi, Wuzi, and many others got their names and books known this way. This may be why the most prominent books on the art of war were produced in this period.

The change of military system made war extremely costly. The casualties were so large that they seriously affected the attitude of Chinese philosophers toward war. Confucianists, Moists, and Daoists all took negative attitudes towards war to different degrees. Mencius, a Confucianist in the Zhanguo period, for example, denounced war and vehemently condemned the prominent warriors of the time. He said: "those who are skillful in fighting should suffer the highest punishment. The death penalty is not even enough for those who have slaughtered men till the land and city are filled with bodies".[25] These negative attitudes toward war had a tremendous effect on the ancient strategists. Most of them took a rather prudent attitude towards war and thus tended to be more defensive than offensive, at least in the initial stages of war.

Legalism was fully carried out in the Qin State under the leadership of Shang yang. Its policies could be simplified into two categories: the military merit system and the rule of law. The peasantry of the Qin State were totally organized into militia units; they were taught to till their land in peacetime and to fight together with their units in war. Based upon the military merit system, the highest honours and rewards went to those who killed the most enemies. The second policy ensured the supremacy of law; even the crown prince had to answer for any violations of it. The result of these policies was the establishment of the hegemonic status of the Qin State over the other six states. China was eventually unified under Qin in 221 B.C. after five and a half centuries of fighting.

The Legalists were divided into three factions with different emphasis in policy: one emphasized the authority of the rulers; the other stressed schemes, maneuvers, and/or stratagem played by the rulers; and the third concentrated on law. They were later unified by Han Fei.[26] Under the unified theory, the ruler of the country has the absolute authority not only to make laws, but also to decide whether the law is violated and what punishment should be meted out to a particular person. The emphasis on stratagem and maneuver gives the ruler the right to use whatever means he may choose to manipulate his subjects. In practice, the ruler would become a tyrant; the law would be a straitjacket for the masses, and the death penalty may fall on anybody for minor offenses.

Due to the emphasis on military force, the Legalists in the Zhanguo period were concurrently military strategists, and vice versa. Li Li and Shang Yang were said to have commanded armies and written books on the art of war, but they were also Legalistic politicians. Wuzi was a military strategist and a Legalist politician. Therefore, students of philosophy of war in Taiwan, for example, Zeng Guoyuan, link ancient military strategists with the Legalists.[27] The emphasis on strict military discipline, the insistence on absolute power of the commander, and the justification of the use of deception by military leaders on the enemy as well as on their own soldiers can be interpreted as the adoption of Legalist philosophy by the strategists.

C. Interstate Relations and Military Theories

Unification under a single central authority has long been a dominant concept accepted by the Chinese as the basis of a peaceful political life. Indeed, history shows that upon the collapse of the central government, many ambitious local leaders fought to unify the country and to succeed the throne left by the previous emperor; very few of them attempted to set up their own separate political regime. It was thus difficult for the Chinese warring feudal lords to establish stable interstate relations with each other. The only exception to this rule in Chinese history occurred in the Chunqiu period, when the fighting feudal lords successfully worked out an interstate relationship and applied modern diplomatic principles based on equal status.

As mentioned above, in the 7th century B.C., when central authority declined, the political disintegration in China gave the less civilized tribes of the north (and later of the South as well) the opportunity to invade China. The situation had sometimes degenerated to a point where the barbarians had directly threatened the existence of several states. For their own security, the princes of the states were forced to put aside their own differences temporarily and to form a united front against the barbarians. Huangong of Qi, with the help of his first minister Guan Zhong, had achieved a hegemonic status over the other princes and called for their cooperation under the slogan of "Respect to the central authority and repulsion of the barbarians." He was said to have gone to war twenty-eight times during his forty-three years of reign. To strengthen his leadership among these states, Huangong invited the rulers of the Chinese states together twenty-six times to hold interstate summit meetings. Agreements were signed. Among other things, all princes pledged non-aggression amongst themselves. Huangong was asked to serve as arbitrator should dispute arise among them.[28] Though there were some violations, peaceful interstate relations generally prevailed.

The prince of Jin succeeded Huangong to assume the leadership through a series of wars upon the latter's death. During the long fighting for the interstate leadership, Jinggong, the prince of Jin, cleverly played states against each other, looked for suitable allies and isolated his enemies; he was thus able to eventually defeat them one by one.[29]

Without subjecting any states, a non-aggression conference of all important states was initiated by a small state of Song in 546 B.C. A multilateral agreement was finally reached after much backroom politicking, and all signatories pledged non-aggression against their neighbours. This agreement paved the way for a peace that lasted more than forty years.[30]

These diplomatic activities in the Chunqiu period were unique in Chinese history. However, the effect of diplomatic maneuvers on the military theories of ancient strategists was significant. Sunzi, for example, insisted that the supreme goal of war is to attack the enemy's strategy; next best is to disrupt his alliances.[31] Similarly, Wuzi also considered the diplomatic relations of the enemy as a major factor in deciding whether one should go to war against it.[32]

3. The Concept of National Defence and Grand Strategy in the Pre-Qin Era

As mentioned earlier in this chapter, many books on the art of war attributed to the Chunqiu and Zhanguo period are steeped in controversy about their authors and dates of origin. However, most students of military philosophy in China have agreed in principle that Liutao, Sunzi, Wuzi, Simafa, and Weiliaozi were actually produced in either the Chunqiu or Zhanguo period.[33] Therefore, our discussion hereafter will primarily be limited to the uncontroversial books.

In ancient China, there was no strict division between military leaders and civil officers. The nobles who were civil officers in peacetime were also trained and subject to call for military service in wartime. The Chinese have proudly claimed this system as *Wen Wu He Yi*, that is to unify literary education with martial skill training together. Professional military leaders emerged only in the later period of Chunqiu and Zhanguo.[34] Consequently, most writers on art of war in ancient China were not only military strategists but also high-ranking civil officials. In many cases, their books only marginally related to military affairs. From a modern point of view, however, the non-military subjects included in these books can be referred to as basic concepts of national defence and grand strategy, which are far beyond the traditional concept of military strategy. The first two chapters of *Liutao*, for example, discussed socio-economic and political subjects, which have been classified by Xu Peigen as subjects of revolutionary strategies and/or political strategies.[35] Wuzi started his discussion with a chapter of "Tuguo", which primarily refers to the principles of governing. As to Weiliaozi, he devoted more pages than other authors to the relationship between military operations and the socio-economic system. He even paid attention to market management, which can be helpful in collecting information and controlling economic activities. He wrote: "should one ignore the market management, he would be unlikely to win a war even if he has well organized armed forces."[36] Sunzi primarily concentrated on military subjects in his book, but he did not ignore the importance of political strategies. The concept of national defence and grand strategies discussed in these ancient books can be simplified as follows:

A. Attitude toward War

Few ancient Chinese strategists bothered to give a definition of war in their books, but they were conscious of clarifying the causes and purposes of war. By discussing these subjects, most of them clearly demonstrated their attitude towards war.

Based on the motives behind war, ancient Chinese strategists divided war into just and unjust ones. While just war was acceptable to the Chinese, unjust war should be avoided.

As a revolutionary, Taigong believed that a revolutionary war should only be started when there is significant evidence to show that Heaven has demonstrated its displeasure of an oppressive ruler by causing natural disasters. In other words, a rebellion was only justified when the government was extremely oppressive.[37] Wuzi enumerated five motives of a ruler for going to war: fame, advantage, animosity, internal disorder, and famine. Based on these motivations, he further classified wars into righteous, aggressive, enraged, wanton, and insurgent ones. Wars to suppress violence and quell disorder are righteous.[38] All others, therefore, are unrighteous.[39]

Like Wuzi, Weiliaozi is often seen as a Legalist, but his concept of war stemmed from the basic principles of Confucianism. "War should not be used to attack a state of innocence and to kill people who are faultless .... It should be used to punish those guilty of committing violence, cruelty, and tyranny, and to stop unrighteous actions."[40] "A punitive expedition initiated by a king against those causing violence and disorder must be based upon the principle of benevolence and righteousness."[41] Therefore, Weiliaozi was also opposed to unjust wars.

To Sunzi, the only purpose of war is to compete for "advantage" (Li in Chinese). It seems that beyond Li, there is nothing else. However, his prudent attitude toward war led readers to believe that there is a distinction between just and unjust in his mind. He said, for example, "a sovereign should not go to war because he is enraged, nor should a general fight because he is resentful."[42] Therefore, "if you are not in danger, do not fight."[43] It means that he supported defensive and non-aggressive wars only.

From the conception of war and its purposes, it is obvious that the majority of ancient Chinese strategists saw war as a means to achieve righteousness and stop unrighteousness. A typical statement can be quoted from Simafa, which has been recognized by the Chinese student as a model of ancient military regulations governing matters of national defence in the early Zhou dynasty:

In ancient times, the King governed his country with righteousness based on the principles of benevolence. This is the normal way of ruling. However, should the rule of benevolence fail to achieve its goals, it should be replaced by force. Indeed, it is justifiable to kill those who have threatened the peace and safety of other people; it is thus also permissible to attack a state in order to save and/or liberate its people from a cruel tyrant. To stop a war by war is acceptable.[44]

In ancient China a righteous war was of three types: the first and primary form of war was a punitive expedition carried out by the central authority against a local feudal ruler for offences. This is the most justifiable and acceptable form of war under the traditional political system. The second form was revolutionary war or rebellion, which was justifiable only when the king or emperor seriously deviated from the publicly accepted deeds of a ruler and subsequently inflicted extreme hardship on the people. This kind of war is supported by traditional Chinese political philosophy. The Confucians in China have often quoted from Mencius to justify a revolution and the execution of a tyrant king: "He who outrages the benevolence proper to his nature is called a robber; he who outrages righteousness is called a ruffian. The robber and ruffian we call a mere fellow. I have heard of the cutting off of the fellow Zhou, but I have not heard of putting a sovereign to death."[45] The third form was a war started by the feudal ruler of a state against the ruler of another state. This extraordinary phenomenon only happened when central authority was extremely weak. Even so, they were more or less affected by the traditional political ideology. By the same token, the ancient military strategists could not help but relate their theories to the principle of righteousness. In addition, due to the antiwar attitude of the Chinese philosophers of various schools, the military strategists of this period also held a prudent attitude toward war. Sunzi, as mentioned above, warned the ruler that "if you are not in danger, do not fight." Wuzi told Marquis Wen that "there was the lord of Yu Hu who relied solely on his armed forces and the valour of his troops, and thereby lost his power."[46] He also said "it is easy to win a war but difficult to retain the result of the victory."[47] Therefore, a ruler should not go to war only for personal pleasure. Weiliaozi had a similar philosophy that war should not be waged to satisfy the personal whims of the ruler.[48] He agreed to defensive war only. "Should violence arise, for protecting national interests, we should strike only after the adversary has started the war. All in all, while we should not start the war first, but be always ready to defend ourself".[49] The ideological justification for this attitude is found in Simafa, which reads: "Even a large country would be subjugated if it becomes too belligerent; although the 'Under-the- Heaven' is secure, it can be endangered, should the ruler take a reckless action of war against others."[50]

This philosophy has strongly influenced the attitude of the Chinese towards war. The Chinese have consistently maintained this attitude with very few exceptions up to now.

B. Eliminating the Cause of War

Under the traditional concept of 'Under-the-Heaven', China was different from a modern nation-state. The ruler of China was called the son of Heaven, and was expected to be the symbol of virtue and harmony. As long as he implemented the policy of benevolence, behaved gracefully and set an example for his subjects, Heaven would bless him with peace and prosperity; he thus would get his mandate From Heaven. All of the people on the land under Heaven were his subjects and obligated to pay their loyalty to him as well. This principle not only applied to the Chinese people but to various degrees also applied to the barbarians around the Chinese borders.

To fulfill his role of maintaining peace and order, the king was responsible for eliminating any actual and potential violence that might interrupt the peaceful life of the kingdom. The worst type of disorder is, of course, war. The national strategy for quelling violence and preventing potential wars was two-pronged, and can be described as "wealth and strength." The former refers to the management of the national economy; the latter refers to military preparation.

As Taigong said in the Liutao, if one is poor (or not rich enough), there is no way for one to fulfil the virtue of benevolence. Therefore, the ruler must commit himself to increasing the wealth of the country.[51] In fact, strength presupposes an affluent society. According to Taigong, a ruler has to manage his three treasures properly: agriculture, industry, and commerce. When people are permitted to run their own businesses, the country would have enough food and goods and the ruler would be blessed with a stable and secure reign.[52]

Simafa advised the ruler to govern in accordance with the law of nature and to commit himself to economic development. By doing so he would be able to command the respect of the princes of the states and attract foreign countries to ally themselves with him. If so, the jails of the country would be emptied and no wars would occur.[53]

Sunzi and Wuzi, as military strategists, paid less attention to socio-economic policies in their discussions, except to the extent that they might affect the outcome of war. Sunzi, for example, mentioned that the ruler should cultivate "moral law" (*Xiu Dao*) and preserve "a proper system or organization" (*Bao Fa*) in order to formulate victorious policies.[54] By doing so, people will most likely be in complete accord with their ruler, so that they will follow him regardless of any danger to their lives.[55] Wuzi believed that when a ruler plans war against another state, he should surely first teach his people and display affection towards them. If the people know that their ruler loves them and grieves at their deaths, they would face crises together with him and would consider it glorious to advance and die for him ,and shameful to save their own lives by retreating.[56] What Sunzi and Wuzi were really concerned about was victory in war. Harmony and order may thus be relevant to their discussions, but not economic development.

Weiliaozi emphasized the winning of war by Dao or moral influence; winning by Dao is called the victory of the ruler, which is a victory accomplished without even showing one's weapons. How can a ruler do this? "A ruler should be concerned about all those who have settled in his state; he should cultivate all the wastelands. When the land is fully cultivated, the state would be wealthy and his people would be well fed. Then, when his population increased and was properly governed, the state would be secure. When a state is both wealthy and secure, its authority will be enough to govern the entire 'Under-the-Heaven'."[57]

The ancient strategists seemed to believe that as long as a ruler can rule his country by virtue and by the policy of benevolence, he would not only be able to keep the country in peace and order, but also likely attract the tributes of foreign countries to China. By achieving this, the threat of war or disorder will be eliminated. However, this does not mean that the ruler should give up all armaments. Confucius, for example, emphasized both the necessity of food and armament for good government. He even warned that a ruler's failure to teach his subjects military skills is tantamount to abandoning them.[58] Weiliaozi saw that the preparation for war is as important as fighting itself.[59]

To the ancient philosophers, as long as a country can achieve "wealth and strength", it would be able to please those who are near and to attract those who are far off. This philosophy was later adopted by the Legalists who emphasized the importance of strength in interstate relations. They believed that when a country is strong, foreign countries will pay tribute to it; when it is weak, however, it probably has to pay tribute to other countries. Consequently, the Legalists focused on "farming and fighting" as the mainstay of their policies in many states during the Zhanguo period.

C. The Use of Alliance

Instead of totally relying on the elimination of war, the ancient strategists often made alliances with other states in order to prevent or win wars.

As mentioned before, during the Chunqiu and Zhanguo period, the warring princes had developed interstate relations similar to modern diplomatic relations between nation-states in order to stop wars. Later, when wars became unavoidable, alliances were used as an important means to strengthen one's forces and weaken the enemy.

As Sunzi said: "To disrupt the enemy's alliance is the second best method of winning a war; it is second only to attacking the enemy's strategy. This is to subdue the enemy without going to war." [61] When Wuzi discussed the factors that may affect a ruler's decision to go to war, he said that "when the neighbouring states do not come to aid the enemy, one may fight without recourse to divination. On the contrary, when there is aid from all sides and the enemy is assisted by powerful states, you must without doubt avoid him."[61] Weiliaozi did not trust alliances. To him, while a country pays tribute and concedes its land for aid from an ally, that ally may be still unreliable, because no soldier would fight for other countries as enthusiastically as he would for his own country.[62]

The concept of looking for an alliance in the Chunqiu and Zhanguo periods was a unique phenomenon among the princes of the states. It did not apply to the central authority itself. Under the traditional Chinese system, if there was any reason for the emperor to go to war against any local prince or barbarians, he just simply announced the criminal offence and summoned the princes or local governments to join him to punish the offender.[63] The local princes were obligated to answer the call and join him. Therefore, there was no alliance between the emperor and princes.

The most significant example of applying alliances to the struggles for power among competing states in China after the Chunqiu and Zhanguo era was the Three Kingdoms. Diplomatic manipulations between the states of Wei, Shu, and Wu were prominent examples of the process of making alliances and disrupting those of their enemies. In conjunction with the use of secret agents, the foundation of alliances and disrupting the enemy's alliance have become a vital part of strategy in China. Under the doctrine of people's warfare, secret activity led by the underground party organization of the Communist Party had had a tremendous effect on the outcome of the Civil War between the CCP and the Guomindang in 1949. The famous United Front was a masterpiece of strategy used by Mao in allying with various social elements against his enemy. All of these strategies can be traced to traditional military thought.

D. Preparation for War

Before a country decides to go to war, certain steps have to be taken in order to ensure victory.

(a) *Estimating the enemy's forces and the planning of war*: As Sunzi said, war is a matter of vital importance to the state; it is the province of life or death and the road to survival or ruin. Therefore, before starting a war, the ruler and his ministers have to correctly estimate the enemy's forces from both strategic and tactical aspects in order to decide whether and how the country can win the war.

At the strategic level, the sovereign and his advisers should take the following into account: the adversary's socio-political and economic situation; international relations; the war resources, morale and fighting power of its armed forces, its dispositions, and the terrain in the expected war zones.

Tactical matters primarily refer to the use of armed forces in a given condition to fulfil the strategic goals. The disposition of the enemy's armed forces, its morale, supply conditions, and the terrain, weather and other occasional factors in the battlefield likely to affect the result of operations should be correctly estimated in time by the military commanders at the front.

In estimating the strength of an adversary's forces, some ancient strategists, such as Sunzi and Taigong, discussed both strategy and tactics in detail; others made only brief discussions without strictly distinguishing strategic subjects from tactical ones.

In this section we will deal primarily with strategic subjects and leave tactical matters to the next section.

According to Sunzi, war is governed by five constant factors which should be taken into account in one's deliberations. They are the moral law, weather, terrain, the commander, and regulation and organization. When seeking to determine the military conditions, they are further used as the basis of a comparison with seven elements: which ruler possesses the moral law; which general is more able; which army obtains the advantages of nature and the terrain; on which side are regulations and instructions better carried out; which troops are stronger; which side has better trained officers and men; and in which army are both reward and punishment given out in a more enlightened manner.[64] Calculating carefully with these factors and elements, one would be able to forcast which side will be victorious and which side will be defeated.

In estimating the enemy's situation, Wuzi gave an arbitrary review of the military condition of the warring states based on their national character and political situations. He did not try to distinguish strategic considerations from tactical matters. For example, in estimating the enemy's situation, he first listed eight conditions in which one may fight him without recourse to divination. All of them refer to special advantageous opportunities in the field, in which one may attack the enemy immediately, for example: "in times of strong wind and great cold when his men (enemy) are awakened early ; move and break ice to ford the rivers and do not shrink from hardship. Second, in the scorching heat of mid-summer when they rise late and are pressed for time. . .and eight, when the enemy's array is not yet drawn up, when he has not completed his encampment, or when he is marching in hilly country. . ."[65] All of these items are tactical in nature. However, following these, he listed six situations in which one should absolutely avoid attacking the enemy; they are referred to as strategic matters. For example,

> First where his country is extensive and his people many and prosperous. Second, where the superiors love their inferiors and their benevolence grows and spreads. Third, where rewards are reliable and punishment is carefully considered and where these are administered appropriately. Fourth,

where those who display merit are given suitable positions, where responsibilities are given to the wise and employment to the able. Fifth, where the army is large and well equipped. Sixth, when there is aid from all sides and the enemy is assisted by powerful states. Generally when unequal to your enemy in these matters, you must without doubt avoid him. "[66]

These six situations are similar to the five fundamental factors quoted above from Sunzi, which should be carefully calculated by the court before starting the war. No single factor can be simply determined on the battlefront after the war is started.

In preparing for war, Weiliaozi emphasized the improvement of national socio-economic and political conditions. The fortification of economic and population centres, reclamation of wasteland, and attraction of immigrants in order to add to the national wealth and security are all important strategies. In pursuing these strategies, according to Weiliaozi, the ruler may extend his authority over the whole land Under-the-Heaven without using his armed forces.[67]

He did not discuss how to estimate the enemy and how to decide whether one should go to war except to say that "when one sees the possible chance of winning, one should fight, otherwise avoid it".[68] However, he suggested a five-step plan for war: first, decide the basic strategy in the council meeting; appoint the commander; plan attacks and defensive strategies; and, last, initiate attacks. He emphasized the strategy of destroying the enemy's morale in order to force him to retreat without fighting.[69]

Taigong's discussion of strategic matters was spread over the entire first half of his Liutao. He analyzed political strategies including domestic policies, personnel policies, the use of stratagems, and the principles of military operations. Some of these are undoubtedly related to the estimate of the enemy's strength.

Taigong paid a great deal of attention to strengthening the revolutionary forces and weakening the enemy power prior to starting armed rebellion. Based on this consideration, he advised King Wen to cultivate his own virtues, pay respect to the able and virtuous persons, and carry out benevolent policies in his country in order to win support from the masses. Meanwhile, he designed various stratagems including bribery, sexual baits, and spies to cause corruption, disorder, and rebellion in the enemy's camps to impair their political and military unities. He carefully observed changes in the enemy's public policies, his personal virtue and behaviour, his trusted ministers and personal attendant, and those who are close to the ruler and those who become estranged. When he found the adversary had met with serious natural and man-made calamities, he advised King Wen to initiate his rebellion.[70]

He estimated the situation of the Shang regime and advised King Wen that "the ruler of Shang has been surrounded by treacherous and evil officials and has overindulged himself in a sexually promiscuous life with his beloved concubine, and thus left his responsibility unfulfilled. Furthermore, farms are full of weeds rather than grain; his court has many more evil and crafty persons than loyal and virtuous servants; officials have been ruthlessly torturing the people, violating laws without any consciousness. This is the time of national collapse."[71]

With this analysis, Taigong told King Wen that if he held high his revolutionary flag and started armed rebellion, wherever his army went, everyone would accept his leadership and obey his authority.[72]

At the tactical level, Taigong was quite like Sunzi and Wuzi. He emphasized the principles of direct observation at the front and the application of deception in accordance with terrain, weather and other situations.[73] These will be discussed futher in later sections.

In discussing the preparation for war, Simafa, like Weiliaozi, paid special attention to establishing proper regulations, appointing proper personnel, campaigning for public support of the war, and collecting war materials, etc.[74] If all of these have been done, then the ruler should further consider five factors: nature, materials, morale, terrain, and weapons.[75] Using these factors as the criteria, he should be able to predict whether his country would be able to win the war. This is strictly a strategic subject to be considered in the court before war. When it turned to discuss the principles of tactical activity in the battlefield in later chapters, it dogmatically listed particular actions in responding to given situations. For example, "No army group should be requested to combat continuously for more than three days, no company for more than half a day, and no soldier for more than two hours."[76]

(b) *The Appointment of Commanders and Independent Exercise of Commanding*: The appointment of commanders and the independence of commanding are always vital subjects in the ancient art of war. The desirable qualities and virtues of a general are seen as the important factors that may affect the outcome of war. When a general was appointed to lead the army to war in ancient times, the ceremony was a major event. It must be presided by the sovereign himself and symbolically confer the commander with absolute power to act independently in the field without any intervention from the ruler.

According to Sunzi, a competent commander must stand for the virtues of wisdom, sincerity, benevolence, courage, and strictness. As long as he possesses these qualities and is appointed to lead the army, the sovereign should have faith in his judgments and not try to run the army by himself. A ruler may bring misfortune upon his army if he is ignorant of military affairs but tries to share the power of command.[77] Therefore, Sunzi suggested that there are occasions when the commands of the sovereign need not be obeyed.[78]

Wuzi believed that the commander of an army must have the combined acumen of the civil and martial leaders. He must concentrate on five matters: administration, preparation, determination, prudence, and economy. He must, of course, have majestic virtue, humanity, and courage sufficent to lead his people. If a country has this kind of general in charge, it will be strong. If it loses him, it will suffer.[79]

Weiliaozi likened the commander to the heart of a man, while his subordinates were like the arms and legs.[80] When a commander acts in war, he should be governed totally by his own judgment subject to neither meteorological phenomena nor the conditions of terrain. He may also ignore the orders of the sovereign and the presence of the enemy. He should be as brave as tigers or wolves and act as quickly as storms and lightning. He should not be easily enraged and corrupted.[81] These virtues are the basis for conferring absolute power on the commanders. Weiliaozi particularly emphasized the strictness of discipline. There is no mercy for offenders. Death is the only punishment for them. As he said: "I heard about the good commanders of ancient times, those who dared to kill half of their soldiers for offences were able to conquer the "Under-the-Heaven"; those who dared to kill one third of them were able to impose their will on the princes of states; and those who dared to kill one tenth of their men were able to ensure that their orders would be obeyed."[82] This strictness of discipline had a tremendous effect on the Chinese forces. However, Weiliaozi did not only preach killing. He also asked the commanders to lead by virtuous examples. When an army is in a difficult situation, for example, its commander must personally take part in it and share the hardship with his soldiers. As he wrote:

There should be no umbrella to protect himself from scorching sun, no extra coat for himself during the bitter cold winter. When there is a difficult road ahead, he should get off his carriage and horse to walk together with his soldiers. He should not drink except when there is enough water for his soldiers; no food for himself except when food is ready for his soldiers; no camp for himself until the army is encamped. No matter how difficult the situation may be, he must share it with his army together. As long as he can do so, the army will be able to keep its morale in any lengthy engagement.[83]

In referring to independent commanding, Taigong went further to say: "Military affairs are not subject to the order of the sovereign. Every order must come from the commander." To guarantee the independent exercise of a commander's power, Taigong particularly emphasized the ceremony of appointment. The sovereign had to publicly make a solemn statement that confers absolute power on the commander.[84]

(c) Rear Service Problems and Supply from the Enemy

Every military leader knows that shortages of supply would seriously weaken the fighting power of an army. If the shortages are acute, they may even endanger the survival of the army. The ancient Chinese strategists were sensitive to this problem. Sunzi discussed this issue in detail. When he estimated the expense of a hundred thousand men army in the field, he wrote:

In the operations of war, where there are in the field a thousand swift chariots, as many heavy chariots, and a hundred thousand mail-clad soldiers, with provisions enough to carry them a thousand Li, the expenditure at home and at the front, including entertainment for guests, small items such as glue and paint, and sums spent on chariots and armour, will reach the total of a thouand ounces of silver per day. Such is the cost of raising an army of 100,000 men.[85]

According to Sunzi, when an army engages in actual fighting, weapons are likely to get dull and damaged; the daily cost of maintaining the army and its activities will increase proportionately. Should the campaign be prolonged, the resources of the state would be exhausted and leave the outcome of war in doubt.

To solve this problem, besides encouraging haste in war, he suggested that "those adept in waging war do not require a second levy of conscripts nor more than one provisioning."[86] Instead, he suggested the idea of supplying from the enemy. "They carry equipment from the homeland," Sunzi said, "but rely on the enemy for provisions. Thus the army is plentifully provided with food."[87] When an army feeds "on the enemy, one bushel of the enemy's provisions is equal to twenty of his own; one hundred weight of enemy fodder to twenty hundred weight of his own."[88]

In fact, Sunzi even suggested that one can take the enemy's equipment and soldiers to supply one's own army. When chariots are captured from the enemy in war, for example, he would replace the enemy's flags and banners and mix them with his own. Captives should be treated well. This is called "winning a battle and becoming stronger."[89]

It seems that Wuzi did not agree with this principle because he did not allow his soldiers to take booty from captured cities. "Where the army encamps, you must not cut down trees, destroy dwellings, take away crops, slaughter the domestic animals, or burn the granaries."[90]

Nevertheless, Sunzi's idea of "taking from the enemy to supply one's own army" has been completely accepted by Chinese strategists.

4. The Main Principles of Strategy and Tactics in the Pre-Qin Period

The equivalent terms for strategy and tactics in Chinese are *Zhanlue* and *Zhanshu*, which are not found in the ancient Chinese works on the art of war. The terminology used in these books similar to the meaning of Zhanlue and Zhanshu probably are *Taolue* and *Zhen*. While the former can be translated as strategy, the latter can be only translated as formation and disposition, which to a large extent is similar to tactics. Like many Chinese authors on other subjects, the ancient military strategists did not provide definitions for these conceptual terms.

From the works of modern Western strategists, one would not likely confuse the concept of tactics with that of strategy. Karl V. Clausewitz, for example, made it clear that the two terms refer to the subjects of different levels. Strategy refers to the whole and higher level, while tactic, the particular and lower. He defined tactics as the theory of the use of military forces in combat, and strategy as the theory of the use of combat for the object of war.[91] While the role of tactics is to decide how to fight a battle or what form should be used in a battle, the role of strategy is to fix when, where, and with what forces a battle is to be fought.[92]

To facilitate discussion in subsequent chapters, we will summarize the major principles of strategy and tactics in the ancient Chinese books on the art of war in the remainder of this chapter.

A. The Principle of Deceit

Is war a science or an art? Clausewitz is perhaps the first man in modern history to have seriously dealt with this question. He believed that war is a subject of science as far as planning is concerned, but a subject of art where judgment is concerned. All rules or principles regarding war are scientific, but their application in battle is a matter of art.[93]

There is no similar discussion in the ancient Chinese works on war, but the works of Sunzi and Wuzi and many others show that the Chinese strategists had combined scientific method and the application of art in war 2500 years earlier than Clausewitz. Sunzi, for example, began his book with a chapter on planning or calculation (Shiji); he listed five fundamental factors which can be used to estimate the objective circumstances of the enemy and oneself. The result of the calculations can help one to forecast the probability of victory or defeat.[94] Similar information can be found in Wuzi and other books. Estimates of the enemy's situation are recognized as the first priority before deciding to go to war.[95]

The application of scientific method in war is primarily related to accurate information. The authors of the art of war in ancient China paid particular attention to the collection of information. As Sunzi said: "Know the enemy and know yourself; in a hundred battles you will never be in peril. When you are ignorant of the enemy, but know yourself, your chances of winning or losing are equal. If ignorant both of your enemy and of yourself, you are certain in every battle to be in peril."[96] The procedure of "knowing" is actually a collection and analysis of information in war.

Accurate information and correct estimates of the condition of the enemy and oneself may present one with an indispensable chance of winning. However, it does not automatically guarantee a victory. One must prevent the enemy from "knowing" one's real situation and feed him with wrong information in order to mislead him into making decisions and thus cause his defeat. The ancient Chinese strategists called this the application of deceit. Since then it has become a golden rule of military operations in China. This is a matter of art. In applying this principle to war, Sunzi was undoubtedly the first and said it best.

When you are able, feign incapacity; when active, feign inactivity. When near, make it appear that you are far away; when far away, that you are near. Offer the enemy bait to lure him; feign disorder and strike him. . .Anger his general and confuse him. Pretend inferiority and encourage his arrogance. Keep him under strain and wear him down. When he is united, divide him. Attack where he is unprepared; sally out when he does not expect you.[97]

Taigong expounded a similar idea of *Yinmou* and *Yongjian* in his Liutao. Both of these words refer to the stratagem of using spies. He called the use of stratagem "*Wenfa*"; by which he meant, agents are assigned to work in hostile countries. They are not only expected to collect information, but are allowed to do everything with every possible method to cause problems for the enemy. Money and women are the most important resources used to corrupt the enemy, and to buy double agents.[98]

Deception remains an important strategy once military operations are underway. As Taigong told King Wen: "show the enemy chaos when you are actually in good order; show him hunger though you are well fed; show him dullness and weakness though you are acute and strong;. . .if you intend to strike at the west, you should strike at the east first."[99] This is almost the same advice as that of Sunzi.

Though this principle has long been accepted by the military world, it is, however, often criticized in China. The Confucians think that the unlimited use of deceit and stratagem in war is immoral. Therefore, some of them tend to praise Wuzi for emphasizing the traditional principle of benevolence and righteousness in war.[100] However, one would be naive to believe that Wuzi never used deceit in war. The following quotation tells how Wuzi thought about the use of deceit:

If the enemy's general is stupid and places his confidence in others, you can deceive him, and lure him into traps. If he is covetous and careless of his reputation, you can bribe him. If he changes his mind easily and lacks stratagems, you can tire him out and wear him down. If the superiors are rich and

arrogant and the inferiors poor and resentful, you can divide
and separate them. [101]

Weiliaozi also believed that using stratagem is a necessary part of war.
"When one has force, pretend not; when one does not, make it look like that
one does; one should always try to supply the enemy with false information
in order to reinforce their wrong decisions." [102]

The doctrine of deceit as an art applying to military operation is not
limited to this. It also refers to the principle of *Qi* and *Zheng,* and *Xu* and
Shi.

B. The Principle of *Qi* and *Zheng, Xu* and *Shi*

If one accepts the principle of deceit as a basic doctrine in Sunzi's *Art
of War,* one would likely believe that the principle of *Qi* and *Zheng,* and *Xu*
and *Shi,* is the essential practice of deception. Any significant analysis of
Sunzi must deal with the principle of *Qi* and *Zheng, Xu* and *Shi.* [103]

Qi is the short name of *Qibing,* which can be translated as extraordinary force; *Zheng* or *Zhengbing* is the opposite of *Qibing,* which can be
translated as normal force.

Xu means void, while *Shi* means solid. They are used to indicate the
strength of the military disposition. "Void" represents the weak area; "solid"
the strong position. *Qi* and *Zheng,* and *Xu* and *Shi,* are two pairs of opposite
military disposition with complementary functions. For example, one may
use the normal force to engage the enemy, but use the extraordinary force to
win the battle. [104] While the normal force is deployed to confront the enemy at
the front, the extraordinary force is assigned to attack his flanks or rear. [105]
Coordinating these two forces properly in operation would likely result in
victory. No matter how big a military force may be, there will always be
strong positions and weak ones. If one knows how to use one's solid strength
to hit the enemy's void position, the result can be likened to a grindstone
against eggs. [106]

There is no comment that can better indicate the importance of the
principle of *Qi* and *Zheng, Xu* and *Shi,* and their complementary functions
than Tang Taizong's monologue delivered to Lee Weigong:

> To me there is no book on the art of war better than Sunzi, in
> which nothing is more important than the principle of *Xu* and
> *Shi.* . .Teach the generals how to apply *Qi* and *Zheng* to
> operations first, and then the disposition of *Xu* and *Shi.* When
> they do not know how to use *Qi* as *Zheng* or *Zheng* as Qi, you
> cannot expect them to know that *Xu* can be made like *Shi,* and
> *Shi* as *Xu.* The use of *Qi* or *Zheng,* can basically be decided by
> oneself, but the situation of *Xu* and *Shi* is based on the array of
> the enemy. The alternative use of *Qi* and *Zheng* in operations

is to match the enemy's disposition of *Xu* and *Shi*. If the enemy's position is solid, we should use the normal force; if void, extraordinary force. Should a general not know the use of *Qi* and *Zheng*, even if he knows how to take advantage of the weakness and strength in the enemy's position, he is unlikely to apply it properly.[107]

Although some commentators have suspected the authenticity of this monologue and questioned the consistency of the discussion on the application of *Qi* and *Zheng*, the basic concept of, and the mutual relationship between, *Qi*, *Zheng*, *Xu*, and *Shi* is still acceptable.[108]

It is true to say that no other books on the art of war have dealt so comprehensively with these principles as Sunzi did. Wuzi, Weiliaozi and Taigong only occasionally mentioned these terms in their books; they did not give any systematic treatise.

The purpose of using *Qi*, *Zheng*, *Xu*, and *Shi* is to concentrate a superior force at a chosen point to defeat the enemy by making a surprise attack.

C. Numerical Superiority

Common sense dictates that the first principle in any operation is to concentrate one's forces on one front and to overwhelm the enemy by absolute superior power. When Sunzi dealt with the subject of offensive strategy, he said: "when ten to the enemy's one, surround him; when five times his strength, attack him; if double his strength, divide him."[109]

From this quotation, we realize that Sunzi preferred absolute numerical superiority. When one's force falls short of that standard, one would have to use the principle of *Qi* and *Zheng*, *Xu* and *Shi* to manipulate the situation. Even when one's force is still double that of the enemy, one should not attack the enemy without diverting part of his force away from the front in order to weaken him further and to create an absolute superiority for one's own force. Consequently, when one's force is only equal to that of the enemy, Sunzi expected the outcome to be indecisive. If one's force is numerically smaller than the enemy, he would suggest withdrawal and escape in order to avoid being captured by the enemy.[110]

Although strategists such as Wuzi, Weiliaozi, and Taigong did not emphasize the importance of numerical superiority as Sunzi did, they also proposed to overpower the enemy by a superior force. Taigong, for example, expounded the principle of "one". Among other things, "one" means that one's force should always be concentrated on one point or one front. By doing so, a commander can expect to crush the enemy with the maximum power he has.[111] A similar principle can be found in Weiliaozi. He said that an army could win a battle with its force concentrated properly, but could lose it with its troops dispersed and separated.[112]

Wuzi said almost mothing about the advantage of numerical superiority. On the contrary, he often emphasized the principle of subduing a numerically superior enemy with a small and elite force; he particularly insisted that if an army can choose its attack properly, it can rout an enemy ten times its size. [113]

As a matter of fact, while one cannot always expect to have an absolute superior force, one cannot simply withdraw when the enemy is stronger than one's own force. Even Sunzi did not really want a numerically smaller army to always refrain from engaging the enemy. What he wanted to do was to change this disadvantageous situation by using the principle of *Qi* and *Zheng*, or of *Xu* and *Shi*. As Sunzi said: "that the army is certain to sustain the enemy's attack without suffering defeat is due to operations of the extraordinary and normal forces." The possible combinations are limitless; no one can anticipate all of them. [114]

If one knows how to use the principle of *Qi* and *Zheng*, one is likely to keep the initiative in the field. To be the master of one's enemy, one has to choose one's own time and place to do battle; one must be able to keep the enemy ignorant of one's own disposition while finding out the enemy's exact position. By doing so, when one wishes to give battle, his enemy, even though protected by high walls and deep moats, cannot help but engage him, because he may attack positions that his enemy must succour. When one wishes to avoid battle, he may defend himself simply by drawing a line on the ground; the enemy will be unable to attack him, because he will have diverted his enemy going where he wishes. [115]

If one can do what Sunzi suggested, one would be able to concentrate one's force, while the enemy has to be divided. Consequently, one can use one's entire strength to attack a fraction of the enemy. At that point, one will be numerically superior to one's enemy. [116]

D. Terrain and Tactics

In different degrees, people's activities are always affected by the physical features of the land. Depending on one's purpose, the effect of terrain on man's actions may be either negative or positive. If a general can keep the initiative, he will be able to reap the advantages of the potential energy of the terrain. This is why Sunzi said that terrain could be a great assistance in battle. [117]

Among the ancient strategists, no one had committed so much of his work to discussing the significance of terrain on operations as Sunzi did. Of the 13 chapters of his *Art of War*, four chapters are devoted to discussing the impact of various terrains on operation. He classified the important types of terrain and listed their disadvantages in operations. He also described what an army should do if confronted with certain type of terrain in operation. [118] He did not discuss how an army can take the advantage of a particular terrain in battle against his enemy. Nevertheless, it would be unfair to say that Sunzi denied the possibility of using terrain in operation. On the contrary, he insisted that in operation, one's force should always arrive at the field and control the physical factors in order to keep one's initiative. He said: "generally, the one who occupies the field of battle first and awaits his enemy is at ease; he who comes later to the battlefield and rushes into battle is weary".[119] "While one is well rested, the enemy is exhausted. This is control of the physical factors."[120] While Sunzi emphasized the importance of numerical superiority, he felt that numbers alone are not decisive.[121] With the principles of *Qi* and *Zheng*, and *Xu* and *Shi* in mind, Sunzi would not ignore the possible advantage gained by using terrain effectively in war.

Although Sunzi was the man who presented the most systematic treatment of terrain and various tactics related to terrain, it was Wuzi who paid the most attention to the advantage of land. He emphasized the importance of the potential energy of terrain to strengthen a numerically inferior force. He often wrote that the number of soldiers under one's command is not always the determinant factor in war. A good disciplined force with better training and the advantage of terrain can defeat an enemy ten times its size. Once, in answering Marquis Wu's question about the imminent attack of a numerically superior enemy, he replied:

> If the ground is easy, avoid him; if a defile, encounter him. For it is said that when one attacks ten, no place is better than a defile; for ten to attack a hundred, nothing is better than a precipitous place; when one thousand attacks ten thousand, nothing is better than a mountain pass. Now, if you have a small force and suddenly attack the enemy in a narrow road with gongs sounding and drums rolling, his host, however large, will be alarmed. And therefore, it is said that one employing large numbers seeks easy ground, one employing small numbers constricted ground.[122]

Based on this realization, Wuzi listed terrain as one of the four factors which a general must be familiar with before deploying his troops. "Where roads are constricted and dangerous, where there are famous mountains and great bottlenecks and where if ten men defend, a thousand cannot pass, this is potential in respect to terrain."[123]

Taigong had been asked many times by King Wu about various tactics under different circumstances. There are some points that are similar to those of Sunzi and Wuzi, but Taigong delved even further into the issue and paid more attention to operations in difficult terrain, especially in offensive operations.

As a revolutionary and faced with the powerful army of the Shang dynasty, Taigong realized that to successfully defeat the enemy with a small force and to replace the Shang regime would be impossible unless he could create a new tactic that would confuse the enemy. To achieve this goal, Taigong designed a powerful new chariot pulled by four horses and many other new weapon systems. For those new weapons, Taigong also developed a set of tactics.[124] Taigong was the only ancient strategist who discussed coordinated actions of different kinds of armed forces in various terrains; he discussed the use of the chariot and calvary units, and the use of infantry in different situations.[125]

In his long discussion with King Wu on military tactics, he covered almost all operations in various terrains, such as operations in mountainous areas, rivers and lake areas, and in forests. It is conceivable that, as a revolutionary, Taigong tended to be an offensive strategist. Nevertheless, when he analyzed the potential energies of terrain, he was able to take a rather balanced point of view. He did not ignore the advantage of terrain in defence, above all, when discussing the principle of attacking a numerically superior enemy with a small army. He emphasized the use of special terrains such as valleys and precipitous cliffs to stop the approach of an enemy's cavalry and chariots.[126]

In discussing operations in mountainous areas, Taigong suggested a special tactic called "dark clouds formation (*Wuyunzhen*)", by which an army is disposed properly to guard virtually all accessible directions.[127]

According to General Xu, the author of *Taigong Liutao Jinzhu and Jinyi*, the dark clouds formation can be likened to the flying crows and flowing clouds that disperse, gather, and move constantly. A reserve force is held back in order to respond to the unexpected needs of an operation.[128] It seems that the distinction between an attacking force and a reserve force was first introduced in ancient China by Taigong.

On the use of terrain in operations, Simafa suggested having heights to one's rear and right, and precipitous and dangerous terrain to cover one's flanks.[129]

E. Defeating the Enemy by Detroying His Morale

Besides numerical superiority and the potential energy of terrain, one can use special occasions to launch an unexpected attack to defeat the enemy easily. Sunzi called this principle the control of morale, mental, physical, and circumstancial factors.[130]

Sunzi often emphasized that a commander should always exploit the situation of the enemy and seek advantages from it that may lead to victory. Using force in fighting can be likened to rolling logs and stones. While logs and stones are "on stable ground, they are static; on unstable ground, they move. If square, they stop; if round, they roll. Thus, the potential of troops skillfully commanded in battle may be compared to that of round boulders which roll down from mountain heights.[131]

Different from the potential energy of land and numerical superiority, the "situation" mentioned above is primarily related to the mental and physical conditions of the human body, which may be affected by weather, food supply, or working conditions. As Sunzi said: "When one's army is close to the field of battle, they wait an enemy coming from afar; at rest, an exhausted enemy; with well fed troops, hungry ones."[132] Should one seize this particular moment to engage the enemy, one would be able to win the battle as easily as setting a ball in motion on a stiff slope. The force applied is minute but the result is enormous.[133]

An even better opportunity for an army to rout its enemy may emerge when its rival is in disarray, confused and in low morale, due to bad commanding or internal discord. Sunzi warned that the intervention of an ignorant sovereign may confuse the army and engender doubts in the minds of the officers. If an army is in such a state, it would likely be easily defeated by its rivals in battle.[134] This is probably why Sunzi said, "An army can be robbed of its spirit and its commander deprived of his courage". If an army has been deprived of its morale, its general will also lose his heart.[135]

Wuzi's discussion of this issue consists more of concrete cases than general theories. He lists eight occasions in which one may attack the enemy without hesitation. As a matter of fact, these occasions are often moments when an army is physically tired and in low morale due to inclement weather, shortages of proper supplies and bad relations between officers and soldiers.[136]

In addition, there are some occasions when an enemy is also in a relatively disadvantageous position and can be easily thrown in disarray and destroyed without much of a fight, for example, when an enemy is approaching but has not yet properly formed his line; or when he has encamped and has not deployed sentries. When an army chances upon these opportunities, it should attack promptly, and it will likely win the battle.[137]

As a revolutionary, Taigong's favourite strategy was to pit one against ten, or to defeat a numerically large force with a small elite one. To achieve this goal, he explored various tactics. He analyzed the proper time to strike. For example, he listed fourteen occasions in which an enemy can be easily destroyed.[138] When the enemy is terrified, exhausted, encamped, or when there is a storm and, thus, sentry duty is difficult, one should immediately take the advantage to attack him. He is likely to defeat such an enemy ten times larger than one's own force.[139]

Simafa has a similar description of how to choose the occasion to attack in order to defeat an enemy easily. It suggests that the proper moment of attack is when the enemy is indecisive or in a rush; and that when the enemy is already in a panic, to add to his terror with a surprise attack.[140]

F. Information Collection and Employment of Secret Agents

The outcome of a campaign to a large degree depends on the commander's correct judgment, which in turn is based on the availability of accurate information about the enemy's disposition. Sunzi made it clear that "know the enemy and know yourself; in a hundred battles you will never be in peril".[141] He also emphasized the necessity of concealing oneself from the enemy in order to maintain freedom of action in battle. As he said: "If I am able to determine the enemy's dispositions while at the same time, I conceal my own, then I can concentrate and he must divide. . .There, [at the points of my choosing], I will be numerically superior."[142] There is no doubt that by the proper use of information about the enemy army, one can choose the time and location for a battle, and subsequently, the chances of winning are increased. However, if there is no information, the commander knows neither the battleground nor the day of battle, and his troops will be unable to aid each other.

To know the enemy and to know oneself requires a complex process of information collection on two levels: strategic and tactical. At the strategic level, relevant information would include a nation's socio-political, economical, and military situation as mentioned earlier in this chapter. Information at this level can be acquired either from official documents for the public, or from documents collected by special agents or spies. Tactical information is basically collected in the field by the armed forces themselves.

In his *Art of War*, Sunzi devoted a whole chapter to exploring this subject. According to Sunzi, if one is ignorant of the enemy's situation in a decisive battle, one is completely devoid of humanity. If an enlightened sovereign and a wise general can conquer the enemy whenever they move, it is because they have "foreknowledge", which "cannot be elicited from spirits, nor from gods, nor by analogy with past events, nor from calculations. It must be obtained from men who know the enemy situation."[143] The "men", in Sunzi's word, are secret agents.

Sunzi regarded secret agents as the precious treasure of a sovereign. There is no one in an army who can be closer to the commander than the secret agent. To Sunzi, a commander, who is not wise, humane and just, cannot use secret agents. He may be the most sensitive ancient strategist in the use of secret operations. He not only sent his own agents to the enemy's camps but also realized the importance of recruiting native and inside agents from the enemy's country or camps. He even sensed the possibility of developing double agents by employing the enemy's agent. He talked about living agents who are supposed to return with information, but also expendable ones who are deliberately given wrong information and expected to be killed by the enemy when they were defeated for using his information. To Sunzi, "there is no place where espionage is not used."[144]

The collection of tactical information takes place in the field by the army itself with direct observations. Sunzi summarized the usual phenomena and their meanings in the field based upon a soldier's experience. "When the enemy is nearby, but lying low, he is relying on a favourable position. When he challenges to do battle from afar, he wishes to lure you to advance, for he is on easy ground, where he is in an advantageous position. "[145] "When the trees are seen to move, the enemy is advancing;" "birds rising in flight is a sign that the enemy is lying in ambush; when the wild animals are startled and flee, he is trying to take you unaware." "Dust spurting upward in high straight columns indicates the approach of chariots. When it hangs low and is widespread, infantry is approaching."[146]

Secret operations were listed by Wuzi as the third of the four potentialities in using an army. "Be skillful in employing spies and agents" was his maxim. With coordinated actions of light troops maneuvering to divide the enemy forces, Wuzi expects to use spies and agents to cause mutual resentment between the enemy's sovereign and his ministers, and let the superiors and subordinates blame each other. It would eventually cause losses for the enemy. Wuzi called the employment of secret operation as the potential in respect to the situation.[147]

Weiliaozi did not discuss the use of secret operations as Sunzi did, but he suggested close self-protection systems in his army in order to stop the possible penetration of enemy spies and the leakage of information. The first method he adopted is a joint liability system, by which officers and soldiers of the same unit are all responsible and punished for violating military regulations by any of their collegues, if they fail to uncover or stop it in time.[148] The second method he suggested is communication control between different army units. When the army is encamped, no travel between different camps is allowed except on presentation of the official security pass. Punishment by death is given to all violators, at least in the war zone.[149] By carrying out these devices, Weiliaozi believed that his army would be able to conceal their actions.[150]

Taigong placed as much importance on secret operations and information collecting as Sunzi did. He listed twelve methods of clandestine operations which can be summarized as: corrupting the sovereign of the enemy and his ministers with women and gifts; bribing his high officials and cultivating agents inside the country; and befriending his social elites and other leaders.[151] Information collected from these channels was primarily limited to strategic matters.

In collecting tactical information, Taigong listed the signs that can distinguish a strong enemy from a weak one. When a commander sees these signs, he will be able to make a sound judgment as to whether he should launch an attack against the enemy or avoid a confrontation with him.[152]

Simafa used four Chinese characters to indicate the information collection methods: *Jianyuan and Guanmei*. They may be translated as: using secret agents to detect the situation of an enemy far away, but observing the nearby enemies directly.[153]

G. Psychological and Political Warfare

In previous sections, we have mentioned several times the effect of morale on the outcome of war. For example, Wuzi listed morale as one of the four potentialities that a general must know before employing his troops. Weiliaozi thought that the reason why a general is able to win battles is that the people under his command are willing to fight. When they have high morale, they fight well, and when they have low morale, they are apt to retreat.[154] Both Wuzi and Weiliaozi had emphasized the importance of destroying the enemy's morale, while maintaining that of their own armies. It is something like psychological and political warfare in the modern age.

The strategies for carrying out psychological and political warfare can be applied at different levels:

First, the sovereign and the supreme commander are asked to cultivate their moral influence in order to promote harmonious relations between the leaders and their people. "When the sovereign treats his people with benevolence, justice, and righteousness", as Zhang Yu commented, "and responds with confidence in them, the army will be united in mind and will all be happy to serve their leaders."[155]

Moral influence was discussed by almost all strategists in ancient China. According to Wuzi, the four harmonies are the most important doctrines for a sovereign to fulfil before going to war. When the country, the army, the battle formation, and the operation itself are all ruled by harmony, the country would be in a position to engage in war and likely win it. Otherwise, it should not go to war.[156] Wuzi particularly emphasized political education with ritual and righteousness in order to cultivate honour among the soldiers. As he said: "it is necessary to instruct the people by using ritual, and to encourage them with righteousness so as to inculcate the sense of honour. If a man's sense of honour is great, he will be able to campaign; if not, he will be able to defend."[157]

This may be the earliest theory of political education and political work for the armed forces.

Weiliaozi listed victory by moral influence as the first choice in employing troops. To him, this is political warfare. He said: "continually improve one's own political, economic, and military strength and to reinforce one's knowledge of the enemy in order to weaken and destroy its morale. Although its physical force is kept intact, it would not be able to fight any longer. This is called victory through moral influence."[158]

Though Weiliaozi did not use the term psychological and political warfare, it is conceivable that if one can defeat one's enemy without destroying it physically, psychological and political warfare is unavoidable.

Taigong probably was the first strategist in China and even in the world who discussed political and psychological warfare systematically.

Instead of using the modern terminology of political and psychological warfare, Taigong chose the word *Wenfa* to express a similar concept. *Wenfa* in Chinese means to "attack with non-military methods", or "striking without using arms". *Wenfa* in a broad sense can be applied to one's enemy and one's own people as well. When it is applied to one's own people, it is primarily aimed at promoting the morale of one's army.

When it is applied to the enemy, Taigong mentioned three different methods to deal with various people.

When it is applied to the enemy's sovereign and his close advisers, Taigong's basic strategy is to sow discord between them. It is called in Chinese *Liqin*. Taigong mentioned twelve methods, which can be summarized as using bribery, sexual bait, and secret agents to corrupt them, drive wedges between the ruler and his trusted advisers, and even buy collaborators among them.[159]

The same strategy is also applicable to the enemy's armed forces. However, a particular strategy was designed to blind the enemy with feigned weakness in order to increase its egotism and overconfidence. When the enemy becomes arrogant, it tends to underestimate its adversary and, thus, is likely to be lured into a trap and to be smashed easily. Taigong called this strategy "attacking a powerful enemy by making it feel even stronger" or *Gongqiang Yiqiang* in Chinese.[160]

To apply political warfare to the masses of the hostile country, Taigong's strategy is to separate the masses from their rulers and leaders by giving whatever one can afford to them and thus attract them to one's side. Taigong called this method as *Sanzhong Yizhong*.[161]

When political and psychological warfare apply to one's own army, it is primarily designed to keep the soldiers' morale high through the battle in order to win the war. Taigong's primary strategy to achieve this is to ask his commander to share joys and sorrows with his soldiers. As he wrote:

> A commander who does not wear furs in winter, does not use fans in summer, umbrella in rain and exposes himself together with his soldiers in the cold, warmth, and rain, would be called a wise general; otherwise he would not be able to understand the real situation of his troops. When an army is in action, if a commander gets off his horse and walks together with his people through the difficult narrow pass and terrain, he would be called a courageous and energetic general; otherwise, he would not be able to realize the hardships that his men may have suffered. When his troops have encamped, he will encamp; while their meal is not ready, he will not eat;. . .Then, he would be called a commander of controlled desires. Should a general share the cold and warmth, hunger and satiation, and ease and hardship together with the masses of his armies, they would fight to the death with him in order to win the battle.[162]

With similar but simpler wording, Weiliaozi suggested this same strategy for maintaining the morale of one's own troops in battle,[163] which can be seen as part of modern military political works. Sunzi dealt with this subject in a more affectionate way. He likened the officer and soldier relationship to one between a father and son. He said: "Because such a general regards his men as infants, they will march with him into the deepest valleys. He treats them as his own beloved sons and they will die with him."[164]

The concept of "father-son army" has now become an important doctrine in China. It is a basic tenet of the Chinese military organization, and many modern Chinese leaders have restated this doctrine on different occasions.

Political and psychological warfare has become an important part of modern military strategy exercised by both civilians and military political workers. The military political system in both the PLA and the Nationalist Army, for example, was introduced by Jiang Jieshi from the Soviet Union in the 1920s, but its functions can be mostly traced back to ancient Chinese military thought.

5. The Development of Chinese Military Theories in the Post-Qin Era

Since the very beginning of this chapter, it has been made clear that Chinese military theories were fully established before the unification of the Qin dynasty. Since then it has become stagnant. Though there have been large numbers of publications added to this subject, the basic content has not changed substantially. Based on this observation, this study has decided to review the selected works of ancient Chinese military theory from the pre-Qin age rather than extend its discussion to the works of all ages. However, it may be beneficial to provide a brief review of the works of the post-Qin era because otherwise a large gap would exist between ancient and modern China.

From the available information, most books on war since Qin were produced in a few periods in different dynasties. According to Mr. Lu's figures, almost 60 percent of the total 805 known military works were produced in three dynasties, which are all belonged to the post-Qin era. With 268 works, Ming was the most prolific dynasty, while Song and Qing were second and third with 104 and 101 on record, respectively.[165] All three of these dynasties had been faced with strong external enemies and were repeatedly defeated by them. It is, therefore, true to say that military theory, among other things, is a product of social necessity. Crisis forces people to struggle for survival and leads to new ideas.

However, these efforts only increased the quantity of works, and did not lead to any theoretical breakthroughs. This failure can be partly blamed on the stagnation of Chinese society, which in turn was caused by the cultural and political monism after Qin, and above all, after the Han Dynasty.

Before and during the Chunqiu period, only the aristocrats were subject to military service. Military training was not separated from civilian education. Soldiers, therefore, had both an extensive civilian and military training. During the Zhanguo era, however, due to the decline of the aristocracy and the imminent threat of war, the peasantry replaced the aristocracy as the backbone of Chinese military forces. The quality of the average soldier may have declined somewhat, but Chinese society at that time was blossoming both culturally and militarily. After the unification by Qin and Han, Chinese society lost its dynamic nature under the strict monism of the empire. Military training was separated from civilian education; soldiers were no longer versed in letters; and the ordinary peasants became indifferent to national affairs and thus were reluctant to serve in the armed forces. This change made the Chinese lose their martial spirit. Prof. Lei Bai-lun described this phenomenon as "a culture without soldiers."[166] The quality of Chinese armed forces since then declined even further. This may be one of the reasons that there were few prominent works on war produced in the long period after Qin and Han.

In addition, many of the military works of this period were produced by civilian scholars rather than military leaders. Without military experience, these Confucian scholars either heavily borrowed ideas from the ancient military works such as Sunzi and Taigong, or wrote about trivial subjects in great detail. The following few points are enough to indicate the development of military theories in this period.

A. Formation:

Formation is an arrangement of troops in operation; it is also called "disposition", which can be applied to both offensive and defensive operations. Principles of strategy and tactics are primarily affected by weapon systems and equipment. Modern weapon systems are totally different from the traditional spears, knives, bows and arrows. Therefore, the ancient military formations cannot be applied to modern military operations without substantial change.

Generally speaking, the ancient Chinese strategists before the Qin dynasty discussed only the very basic priniciples of formation. Sunzi, for example, discussed the principle of tactical dispositions (Xing) in great detail, but mentioned formation (Zhen) a couple of times without any discussion.[167] Wuzi also did not discuss this subject in detail. Weiliaozi and Taigong devoted only a few words to this subject, just referring to the principles of making formation. For example, Weiliaozi said: "In general, all formations should face the enemy. However, there are formations that may have the soldiers to face both inwards and outwards in defending dispositions, and formations that require the soldiers to stand or sit. The standing formation is for attack, while the sitting formation defence."[168]

The discussion of formations after Qin has in many cases become a central theme. Some authors even specialized in a particular formation.

He Liangchen, one of the few military authors in the Ming dynasty with military experience, gave a thorough description of the unhealthy development of formations. His conclusion is that the more complicated a formation is, the less practical it would be. If anyone actually used it in battle, he would inevitably be defeated. [169] Emperor Shenzong of the Song dynasty once pointed out the impracticality of some formations designed by the so-called experts:

> Nowadays, military theoreticians often borrow the pictures of formation from Li Quan's *Yingfujing* to bewilder each other. It is useless. Based on the theories, it seems that when two hostile armies meet on the battlefield, they have to send envoys to choose a mutually agreed date and ground of fight, then go to cut off the bushs and grasses, level to the ground, and fill up the holes to make a wide and even plain as a playground in order to adapt to the ideal shape of formation. I am sure that it does not work at all. [170]

It is true that the study of formations in the post Qin era has gone too far and thus has totally departed from reality. If their studies had been limited to a tactical level, they would not have received so much criticism. The problem is that some so-called experts often tried to design formations for several hundred thousand soldiers. For example, the *Fie Zhen* designed by Xu Dong was planned for an army of one hundred thousand people. With this in mind, the true value of Emperor Shenzong's criticism is seen in perspective.

B. The Emphasis on Technical Development

Most works on war before the Qin dynasty presented their principles without going into the finer points of the subject. This phenomenon had begun to change even before the end of the Zhanguo period. For example, Liutao and the recently unearthed Sunbin's *Art of War* both showed this tendency. Mao Yingbai, the author of *An Introduction to the Arts of War of Sunzi and Sunbin,* wrote that since Sunzi already produced an incomparable amount of theories which were then regarded as essentially complete, people after Sunzi could not add any more on it. Consequently, they chose to write technical subjects in detail. [171] This tendency becomes very significant in the works after the Han and Tang dynasties. For example, in *The Collection of Li Weigong's Art of War,* Li Jing discussed many technical subjects, which were later plagiarized by Li Quan in his *Taibaiyinjing.* [172] These works described in detail the techniques of building walls, bunkers, tunnels, moats, crossbow launchers and other defense instrument, as well as the design of equipment for river crossings, fire attacks, and banquet arrangements, etc. In *Huqianjing*, Xu Dong of the Yuan dynasty discussed the use of flags and banners, drums, and camp medical problems, etc. [173]

In the Baizhanjing, Wang Minghe of the Ming dynasty devoted many pages to training. He not only drew pictures of formations and camps but provided quite a few pictures to demonstrate the different kinds of postures of getting on and off the horses.[174]

This development had its positive effects as well. Soldiers and young officers, who do not have battle experience, could use these materials as training manuals to help themselves handle the training subjects and day-to-day military affairs.

C. Weapon Designs

Many military works of the Ming and Qing dynasties discussed the design of weapons. Some of them include drawings of weapons in their books which not only instructed people on how to use these weapons, but also taught them the techniques of manufacture. Wang Minghe, for example, devoted his book to discussing the musket and gun, the ingredients of gunpowder, and its process of manufacture.[175] An anonymous author, who used a writing name of Huilu Jiumin, wrote a book of *Bingpi Baijing Fang*. He described various weapons, defensive equipment, and formations in detail. He not only did what Wang Minghe had done in describing the method of manufacturing new weapons such as muskets, artillery, and gunpowder, but he also drew pictures of spears, knives and bows. He even gave the exact measurement for walls and watch towers.[174]

The discussion of weapon systems in the military publications of the Ming and Qing dynasties has its particular historical bases. Since the middle of the Ming dynasty, communication between China and Europe greatly increased. Western weapons were imported to China in this period. According to He Liangchen, the author of Zhanji, muskets were imported from the south barbarians, which probably means from Europe by sea through Indo-China to China. He compared the capacities of the Western musket with those of Japan and the traditional rockets of China.[177]

Although firearms were occasionally used in the Chinese army during the Ming dynasty, and the authors of military publications discussed the capacity of the new weapons in detail in their books on war, no strategist, however, had analyzed the impact of these weapons on strategies and tactics. As a matter of fact, discussions of traditional formations had reached an impractical stage, which continued to dominate the minds of Chinese strategists for several centuries, until the late 19th century, after the repeated defeat of China in wars against the intrusions of the Western powers. Indeed, the Chinese military leaders such as Zeng Guofan and Li Hongzhang started to realize that the military training of Goldon's Ever-Victorious Army was different from the Chinese, and started to partly change Chinese military organization and tactics when muskets and rifles were used in the Chinese army. Even so, they still closely followed the traditional formation concept. Zeng Guofan, in a letter to one of his generals, wrote of his high regard for the formations in *Woqijing* designed by Li Quan. Nevertheless, Zeng was flexible; he did not personally control the actions of his commanders. For example, he told a commander that "to a company, Yuanyang (Mandarin duck) and Sancai formations should be important; to a battalion, any formation must keep the principle of maintaining one normal force, two extraordinary forces, one reserve unit, and an ambush unit." Apart from this, he let his commanders choose their own formations.[178]

In fact, the Chinese never completely understood the impact of modern weapons on military strategy and tactics during that period, and thus, did not reorganize their armed forces based upon a totally new concept of strategy and tactics. A complete adoption of the Western military organization and its training methods only began in the last decade of the 19th century under Yuan Shikai's leadership. However, the changes of strategy and tactics were even slower. It did not go beyond the stage of "coping" until the civil wars and the Sino-Japanese War of the 1930-40's, which mobilized the Chinese physically and intellectually as well. Some Chinese leaders started to develop their own strategies and tactics in order to adapt to the objective situation using whatever means available.

D. *Yin Yang* and Superstition

It is quite understandable that early political rulers relied a great deal on superstition to govern. But this does not apply to ancient Chinese military strategists. None of the pre-Qin works mentioned in the previous sections had seriously referred to superstitions. Sunzi and Wuzi did not mention *Yin Yang* and other superstitions in their works, while Weiliaozi totally denied the usefulness of *Yin Yang*. Indeed, in answering the questions of King Lianghui, Weiliaozi even said: "What Huangdi did is to punish the unrighteousness by armed forces and to rule the country by virtue. He did not rely on the theory of astrology, *Yin Yang*, and divination to make his decisions."[179]

Taigong probably was the only ancient strategist who applied some superstitious theories to military affairs. He is probably the first man who tried to establish a theory of predicting the results of battle by reading the meteorological phenomenon of the field.[180] General Xu Peigen explained Taigong's theory with modern meteorological theories such as wind direction, the flow of dust, and smoke, but it may not be the basis of Taigong's own opinion and, thus, is not very convincing.[181]

The intensive discussion of the effect of *Yin Yang*, *Wuxing*, astrology, divination, and meteorology on the conduct of battle emerged in the works written after the Qin and Han dynasties. The thought of Daoists and those of *Yin Yang* were first shown in the *Yinfujing*, which was written by Li Quan of the Tang dynasty in the name of *Huangdi*. Instead of military affairs, the thirty articles talk about heaven, earth, the universe, nature, reason, opportunity (or chance), and *Yin Yang*. They are full of metaphysical terms.[182] This is often seen by strategists as evidence that ancient Chinese military philosophy was affected by Daoism. This phenomenon appears in many other works of this period. The extreme examples are likely found in Xu Dong's *Huqianjing*, which was comprised of 120 volumes and 450 pages in total. He spent almost half of his book dealing with astrology, divinations, funeral orations, and other superstitions. Seven volunmes are devoted entirely to the subject of astrology and divination, and other volumes also refer to these subjects. [183]

The theory of *Yin Yang*, *Wuxing* and divination can be traced back to those at the very beginning of Chinese history, such as Huangdi, Fuxi, and many others. However, it became a major school of philosophy during the Chunqiu and Zhanguo periods. It eventually became a popular philosophy and permeated all aspects of society. Indeed, when Emperor Wu of the Han dynasty decided to exclude all schools of philosophy except Confucianism from the empire's official ideology, the thought of *Yin Yang* and *Wuxing* still existed among the people, even within the ranks of royalty.

To many Chinese scholars, the ancient Chinese military strategists such as Sunzi were strongly affected by Daoist, and *Yin Yang* and *Wuxing* theories. Though it may be difficult to prove the falsity of this belief, it is probably correct, however, to say that Sunzi and others who developed their theories before the Qin dynasty were less affected by Daoism and *Yin Yang* and *Wuxing* than those after the Hang and Tang dynasties. The reason is apparent. Military theories represent only part of the national culture and have their roots in it. Therefore, the development of military theory cannot be free from the effect of the mainstream of national culture.

E. Postscript

The four points which have been singled out for analysis are the primary characteristics of development of Chinese military theory after the Qin dynasty, but they are not the only ones. There are many good works that have not been mentioned yet. There are basically three reasons for their omission: First, some works may be good but do not have significant meaning in terms of military theory. Huang Shigong's *Sushu*, for example, was simply written to teach political leaders how to behave themselves as members of the sovereign's entourage, and how to govern the country. There is nothing that refers to military affairs. As to Huang Shigong's *Sanlue*, although it has long been treated as a book on the art of war, it only briefly deals with this subject. Indeed, as General Wei Rulin, the auther of *Huang Shigong Sanlue Jinzhu Jinyi* said that in fact the book deals primarily with the principles of governing and pacifying the country. [184] Besides, the authenticity of the book and its legendary author, Huang Shigong, are questionable; the work was probably fabricated by people of a much later age. [185]

Another reason why many books were omitted from our discussion is that they contain few original ideas and are basically interpretations of ancient works. *The Dialogue between Tang Taizong and Li Weigong* is a typical example. The content is primarily a discussion of Sunzi's book; it concentrates on the subject of *Qi, Zheng, Xu,* and *Shi* as mentioned in the previous sections of the chapter. In addition, some authors either closely followed Sunzi's model,[186] or only tried to edit a war history.[187]

Finally, we have omitted some books because certain subjects, generalship for example, which had occupied an extremely important status in almost all ancient works on war, are no longer so significant.[188] The disproportional emphasis on this subject by ancient strategists was due to the lack of institutionalized training of officers in ancient China that had caused military commanders tremendous problems in choosing their officers. However, the institutionalized modern recruiting system and training program have greatly redressed this problem. No person in the modern age can be appointed to a high command without proper training and the necessary experience. This fact has not only improved the quality of the officer group, but also relieved part of the higher commanders' hardship in the recruiting procedure. Therefore, it is a less significant subject now than it used to be in ancient China.

Footnotes

1.   Xu, Peigen, *History of Chinese National Defense Thought* (Taipei: Zhongyang Wenwu, 1983), pp. 197-211. (Hereafter referred to as *Defense Thought.*)
      General Xu seems to be the first person to treat the *Hetu, Luoshu,* and the *Bagua* as battle formations. Before him, most Chinese scholars had discussed these diagrams as astrology and divination. This fresh theory is logically sound and thus acceptable.
2.   Lu, Dajie, *An Introduction to Books on Art of War of All Ages* (of China)(Hong Kong: Zhongshan, 1969), pp. 26-30.
3.   *Ibid.*, pp. 32-33.
4.   Wuqi is said once learned from Zengzi and dressed as Confucian scholars. See *Siku Quanshu Tiyao* (a digest of Siku Quanshu), V.53, Z.15, section: Military Strategist, p. 3. Also Wuzi, *The Arts of War*, Ch. 1, *Tuguo* (the governing of a country), in *Wuzi and Weiliaozi on the Arts of War*, annotated by Peng Daxiong (Taipei: Dahua).
5.   Sunzi (Sun Tzu), *The Art of War*, trans. with a introduction by Sammuel B. Griffith (London: Oxford Univ., 1971), Ch. 3, Attack by Strategem, sec. 1.
6.   Zeng, Guoyuan, *The Philosophy of War Before Qin Dynasty* (Taipei Shangwu, 1972), p. 1. Pre-Qin (*Xianqin*) is used to indicate the ancient Chinese history before Qin dynasty, but many times, it particularly emphasizes the Later Zhuo dynasty, that is the period of Chunqiu and Zhanguo.
7.   See the explanation in a *Chinese-English Dictionary* (Beijing:Shangwu, 1978).
8.   Zeng, *The Philosophy of War, op. cit.*, p. 3.
9.   Lu, *Books on Arts of War, op. cit.*, p. 3.
10.   Zeng, *The Philosophy of War, op. cit.*, p. 4.
11.   The definition of *Xianqin* is a common term used by Chinese students of history, literature as well as philosophy. It is used particularly by Zeng, Guoyuan, in his *The Philosophy of War, op. cit.*, p. 8.
12.   There are different theories of dividing the period of Chunqiu from that of Zhanguo. Some students use 481 B.C., the last year covered by the book of Chunqiu, as the year of division line, while others use 453 B.C., the year of partition of Jin by its three big houses--Han, Zhao, and Wei. This study prefers to use 473 B.C. as the division line. It is the year when the Yueh State conquered the Wu State, which has been used by Lei, Bailun, the author of *Chinese Culture and the Chinese Soldier* (Taipei: Wannianqing, 1971), and also used by the *Chinese-English Dictionary* (Beijing: Shangwu, 1981).

13. Wang, Tongling, *Chinese History* (Taipei: Qiming, 1932), pp. 319-322.

14. To Zeng Guoyuan, Confucianism was not only a conservatism but also a thought that was totally out of the tone of the age. Legalism was the major stream of thought in the later period of Chunqiu and Zhanguo. See Zeng, *The Philosophy of War*, p. 15.

15. Feng, Youlan, *Chinese History of Philosophy* (Beijing: Shangwu), Vol.1, p. 107.

16. The Moist's "Anti-Offensive War" in Chinese is Feigong. Some students translated it as "Non-Militarism". However, non-militarism by definition means not only anti-offensive but other military matters. The Moist did not oppose defensive war, so *Feigong* can only be seen as anti-offensive war, or anti-aggression.

17. Feng, *Chinese History of Philosophy*, p. 112.

18. *Ibid.*, pp. 127-28. Quoted from *Mozi*, Vol. 5, pp. 2-5.

19. For a long time, the translation of Chinese Daojia has been Daoist; while Daojiao, the religion, has been interpreted as Taoism. To avoid confusion, students of Daojia have adhered to the old way. In this study, I use Daoism to represent the philosophy of Daojia; Daoist to represent Daojia.

20. See Feng, *Chinese History of Philosophy*, op. cit., p. 218.

21. Li, Yuri, *A General Comment on Sunzi's Art of War* (Hong Kong: Xin Feng), pp. 38-40. To me, the Dao used in the books of art of war emphasized the moral law which is the standard used to comment on the policies of a country.

22. *Ibid.*, pp. 38-47.

23 Sunzi (Sun Tzu), *The Art of War, op. cit.*, Ch. VI, sec. 27 and 28.

24. The system is as follows: 5 households make up a *Gui*; 5 men, each from a household, form a *Wu* headed by the leader of *Gui*; 10 *Gui* make up a *Li* and the 50 militiamen of the *Li* form a *Xiaorung* headed by the head of *Li*; 4 *Li* make up a *Lian*, and the 200 militiamen form a *Zu* led by the head of *Lian*; 10 *Lian*, a *Xiang*, and 2000 militiamen form a *Lu* and headed the leader of *Xiang*; 5 *Xiang* a *Shi*, and 10000 militiamen, an army headed by an army marshal. There were 15 agricultural *Xiangs* in the Qi State, and, thus the total military force was put together with 3 armies. See Xu, Peigen, *Defense Thought, op. cit.* ,p. 328.

25. *The Works of Mencius*, Book IV, Le Low, Part 1, Ch. 14, sec. 2&3. See *The Four Books*, trans. in English by James Legge (Taipei: Culture, 1981).

26. Shen Dao and Guan Zhong were attributed to the first faction; Shen Buhai represented the second faction; and, Shang Yang was the third faction. Han Fei was the man who integrated all of those three factions

and put the different theories together into a unitary system of legalism--*Hanfeizi*. See Feng, Youlan, *Chinese History of Philosophy, op. cit.*, pp. 389-94.

27. Zeng, Guoyuan, *The Philosophy of War*, op. cit., pp. 13-14.
28. Dun J. Li, *The Ageless Chinese: A History* (New York: Charles Scribner's Sons, 1971), pp. 50-52.
29. Xu, *Defense Thought, op. cit.*, pp. 335-6.
30. Li, *The Ageless Chinese, op. cit.*, p. 53.
31. Sunzi, *The Art of War, op. cit.*, Ch. 3, Sec. 4,5.
32. Wuqi, *Wuzi on the Art of War, op. cit.*, Ch. 2.
33. See *Siku Quanshu Tiyao*, Vol. 53, Z1&5, pp. 1-6; also Zeng Guoyuan, *The Philosophy of War, op. cit.*, pp. 29-39.
34. *Ibid.*, p. 2. Generalship was said to be first used in Zuo Zhuan (up to 464 B.C.).
35. Xu, Peigen, *Taigong Liutao Jinzhu Jinyi*: A Modern Interpretation and translation on the Six War Doctrines of Taigong (Taipei: Shangwu, 1976), pp. 14-18. (Hereafter referred to as *Taigong Liutao.*)
36. Weiliaozi, *The Art of War*. Ch. 8. See Peng, Daxiong, *Wuzi and Weiliaozi on the Art of War* (Taipei: Dahua), p. 124.
37. Taigong *Liutao, op. cit.*, Ch. I, sec. 12, p. 80.
38. *Wuzi, op. cit.*, Ch. II, sec. 5: 1, 2.
39. Zeng, *The Philosophy of War, op. cit.*, p. 43.
40. *Weiliaozi, op. cit.*, Ch. 8, p. 120.
41. *Ibid.*, Ch. 23, p. 200.
42. Sunzi, *op. cit.*, Ch. 12: 18.
43. *Ibid.*, Ch. 17.
44. *Simafa*, Ch. 1. See Liu Zhongping, *Simaifa Jinzhu Jinyi*: A Modern Interpretation and Translation of Simafa (Taipei: Shangwu, 1975), p. 1.
45. Mencius, op. cit., Book 1, Part 2, Ch. 8, sec. 3. See *The Four Books*.
46. *Wuzi, op. cit.* Ch. 1, p. 5.
47. *Ibid.*, p. 10.
48. *Weiliaozi, op. cit.*, Ch. 2, p. 79.
49. *Ibid.*, p. 104.
50. *Simafa, op. cit.*, Ch. 1, p. 1.
51. *Taigong Liutao, op. cit.*, Ch. 1, sec. 7. p. 64.
52. *Ibid.*, Ch. 1, sec. 6, pp. 59-60.
53. *Simafa, op. cit.*, Ch. 1. p. 2.
54. *Sunzi, op. cit.*, Ch. 4, sec. 16.
55. *Ibid.*, Ch. 1, sec. 4.
56. *Wuzi, op. cit.*, Ch. 1. p. 6.
57. *Weiliaozi, op. cit.*, Ch. 2. p. 78.
58. *Confucian Analects*, Book 13, Ch. 30, p. 312.

59. *Weiliaozi, op. cit.*, Ch. 1, p. 76.
60. *Sunzi, op.cit.*, Ch. 3, sec. 5.
61. *Wuzi, op. cit.*, Ch. 2, Appendix 1, pp. 156-7.
62. *Weiliaozi, op. cit.*, Ch. 2, pp. 86-7.
63. *Simafa, op. cit.*, Ch. 1, p. 2.
64. *Sunzi, op. cit.*, Ch. 1, sec. 3-14.
65. *Wuzi, op. cit.*, Ch. 2, sec. 1-2.
66. *Ibid.*
67. *Weiliaozi, op. cit.*, Ch. 2, pp. 77-88.
68. *Ibid.*, p. 79.
69. *Ibid.*, Ch. 4, p. 91.
70. *Taigong Liutao, op. cit.*, Ch. 2, sec. 12, p. 80.
71. *Ibid.*, p. 81.
72. *Ibid.*
73. *Ibid.*, p. 99.
74. *Simafa, op. cit.*, Ch. 3, p. 57.
75. *Ibid.*
76. *Ibid.*, p. 95.
77. *Sunzi, op. cit.*, Ch. 3. p. 81.
78. *Ibid.*, p. 113.
79. *Wuzi, op. cit.*, Ch. 4, sec. 1, p. 162.
80. *Weiliaozi, op. cit.*, Ch. 4, p. 101.
81. *Ibid.*, p. 128.
82. *Ibid.*, pp. 209-210.
83. *Ibid.*, p. 97.
84. *Taigong Liutao, op. cit.*, Ch. 3, sec. 21, p. 117.
85. *Sunzi, op. cit.*, Ch. 2, sec. 1.
86. *Ibid.*, Sec. 9.
87. *Ibid.*, sec. 10.
88. *Ibid.*, sec. 15.
89. *Ibid.*, sec. 18, 19, 20.
90. *Ibid.*, Appendix: Wuzi, Ch. 5, sec. 10.
91. Karl Van Clansewitz, *On War* (New York:Barnes & Noble, 1966), Vol. 1, p. 86.
92. *Ibid.*, pp. 89-94.
93. *Ibid.*, p. 120.
94. *Sunzi, op. cit.*, Ch. 1.
95. *Ibid.*, Appendix: *Wuzi*, Chapt. 2, Estimating the Enemy, sec. 1, p. 154.
96. *Ibid.*, Ch. 3, p. 84.
97. *Ibid.*, Ch. 1, pp. 66-69.
98. *Taigong Liutao, op. cit.*, Ch. 2, sec. 14, pp. 90-92.
99. *Ibid.*, Ch. 2, sec.16, p. 99.

100. A typical comment may be found in the *Siku Quanshu Tiyao*, Vol. 52, Z:1,5, p. 3.
101. *Sunzi, op. cit.,*, Appendix: Wuzi, Ch. 4, sec. 2. p. 163.
102. *Weiliaozi, op. cit.*, Ch. 12, p. 150.
103. One can find a similar statement from "The Dialogue between Emperor Taizong and Duke Wei of Tang dynasty," Li Yuri, ed., *Collection on Art of War*, Vol. 1, p. 117.
104. *Sunzi, op. cit.*, Ch. 5, p. 91.
105. *Ibid.*, see Li, Chuan's comment.
106. *Ibid.*
107. *The Dialogue between Emperor Taizong and Duke Wei of Tang Dynasty*, op. cit., pp. 117-18.
108. See *Siku Quanshu Tiyao*, Vol. 53, Z: 1, 5, p. 6.
109. *Sunzi, op. cit.*, Ch. 3, p. 79.
110. *Ibid.*, p. 80.
111. *Taigong Liutao, op. cit.*, Ch. 2, sec. 16, p. 99.
112. *Weiliaozi, op. cit.*, Ch. 5, p. 100.
113. *Sunzi, op. cit.*, Appendix: *Wuzi*, Ch. 2, sec. 3, p. 157.
114. *Ibid.*, Ch. 5, pp. 91-92.
115. *Ibid.*, Ch. 6, p. 97.
116. *Ibid.*, p. 98.
117. *Ibid.*, Ch. 10, pp. 127-8.
118. *Ibid*, Ch. 9-11.
119. *Ibid.*, Ch. 6, p. 97.
120. *Ibid.*, Ch. 7, p. 109.
121. *Ibid.*, Ch. 9, p. 122.
122. *Ibid.*, Appendix: *Wuzi*, Ch. 5, p. 164.
123. *Ibid.*, Ch. 4. The four potentialities are: morale, terrain, situation, and strength.
124. *Taigong Liutao*. In the first part of this book, the author analyzed the historical socio-political background of Taigong and the strategies which Taigong designed to cope with the Shang Army: The new chariot, weapons, etc; see pp. 14-26. Also see Ch. 4, sec. 31, the treatise of weapons, pp. 147-150.
125. *Ibid.*, sec. 32-33, pp. 151-54; also see sec. 43: operation in forests; sec. 45: operation in nights, p. 182.
126. *Ibid.*, Ch. 3, sec. 27, p. 133.
127. *Ibid.*, Ch. 5, sec. 47, p. 187, operation in mountaineous areas.
128. *Ibid.*, p. 188.
129. *Simafa, op. cit.*, Ch. 5, p. 124.
130. *Sunzi, op. cit.*, Ch. 7. pp. 108-09.
131. *Ibid.*, Ch. 5, p. 95.
132. *Ibid.*, Ch 7, p. 109.

133. *Ibid.*, p. 95. See Zhang Yu's comment.
134. *Ibid.*, pp. 81-82.
135. *Ibid.*, p. 108.
136. *Ibid*, Appendix: *Wuzi*, Ch. 2, sec. 2, 3, , p. 157.
137. *Ibid.*, p. 158.
138. *Taigong Liutao, op. cit.*, Ch. 6, sec.52, p. 200.
139. *Ibid.*, Ch. 3, sec. 27, p. 132.
140. *Simafa, op. cit.*, Ch. 5, p. 124.
141. *Sunzi, op. cit.* Ch. 3, p. 84.
142. *Ibid.*, Ch. 6, p. 98.
143. *Ibid.*, Ch. 13, p. 145.
144. *Ibid.*, p. 147.
145. *Ibid.*, Ch. 9, p. 118.
146. *Ibid.*, pp. 118-119.
147. *Ibid.*, Appendix: *Wuzi*: Ch. 4, p. 162.
148. *Weiliaozi, op. cit.*, Ch. 14, p. 156.
149. *Ibid.*, Ch. 15, p. 160.
150. *Ibid.*, Ch. 2, p. 76..
151. *Taigong Liutao, op. cit.*, Ch. 2, sec. 14, pp. 90-91.
152. *Ibid.*, Ch. 3, sec. 29, p. 138, the signs of victory and defeat; Ch. 4, sec. 42, the signs of retreat of the enemy; and Ch. 6, sec. 52, p. 200, the opportunity of winning the battle in the field.
153. *Simafa, op. cit.*, Ch. 3, p. 58..
154. *Weiliaozi, op. cit.*, Ch. 4, p. 91.
155. *Sunzi, op. cit.*, Ch. 1, p. 64.
156. *Ibid.*, Appendix: *Wuzi*, Ch. 1, p. 151.
157. *Ibid.*, p. 152.
158. *Weiliaozi, op. cit.*, Ch. 4, p. 90.
159. *Taigong Liutao, op. cit.*, Ch. 2, sec. 14, *Wenfa*, pp. 90-92. Also see sec. 17, Sanyi, pp. 102-03.
160. *Ibid.*, pp. 102-03.
161. *Ibid.*
162 *Ibid.*, Ch. 2, sec. 23, pp. 122-23.
163. *Weiliaozi, op. cit.*, Ch. 4, p. 97.
164. *Sunzi, op. cit.*, Ch. 10, p. 128.
165. Lu, Dajie, *Books of Arts of War, op. cit.*, p. 16.
166. Lei, *Chinese Culture and Chinese Soldiers, op. cit.*, pp. 3-25.
167. *Sunzi., op. cit.*, Ch. 7, p. 109. Also, Ch. 9, p. 120.
168. *Weiliaozi, op. cit.*, Ch. 23, p. 202.
169. He, Liangchen, "Zhenji", Ch. 3, pp. 87-88, in Li's *Collections on Art of War, op. cit.*, Vol 7.
170. Tao, Luzi, "A Note of the Use of Formation (Yongnzhen Zhalu)," Li, *Collection on Art of War, op. cit.*, Vol. 3, p. 90.

171. Mao, Yingbai, *An Introduction to the Arts of War of Sunzi and Sunbin* (Hong Kong: Yinghua, 1979), p. 20.

172. Wang, Zhongyi, The preface to "The Collection of Weigong's Art of War," Li, *Collection on Art of War, op. cit.*, Vol. 3, p. 107.

173. Xu, Dong, "Huqianjing," Li, *Collection on Art of War, op. cit.*, Vol. 5.

174. Wang, Minghe, "Bingfa Baizhanjing," Li, *Collection on Art of War, op. cit.*, Vol. 7.

175. Ibid.

176. Huilu Jiumin, "Bingpi Baijing Fang," Li, *Collection on Art of War, op. cit.*, Vol. 11, pp. 147-206, 291-363.

177. He, "Zhenji," *op. cit.*, pp. 67-68.

178. Tao, "A Note of the Use of Formation," *op. cit.*, Vol. 3, pp. 93-97, the author quoted from Zeng Guofan.

179. *Weiliaozi, op. cit.*, Ch. 1, p. 73.

180. *Taigong Liutao, op. cit.*, Ch. 3, sec. 29, p. 139.

181. *Ibid.*, see General Xu's translation and comment, p. 141.

182. "Yinfujing," Li, *Collection on Art of War, op. cit.*, Vol. 4.

183. Xu, *Huqianjing, op. cit.*, Vol. 10 to 20 deal primarily with these subjects; only Vol. 10 partly refers to medicine, health and treatment etc. which are useful indeed.

184. Wei, Rulin, *Huangshigong Sanlue Jinzhu Jinyi* (Taipei: Shangwu, 1975), p. 39, see Footnote.

185. Many scholars believe that these books are written by people far later than Han dynasty. *Ibid.*, pp. 12-13.

186. "*Toubi Futan*," written by Sihu Yishi, is an example. The author, who was probably a Confucian scholar of the Ming dynasty, wrote his book in the same patten as Sunzi did. It included 13 chapters. See Li, *Collection on Art of War, op. cit.*, Vol. 7.

187. Historical approach seems to be a popular method in this period. Wei Xi, for example, edited two books such as *Bingji* (A Mark of Military) and *Bingmu and Bingfa* (Military Strategem and Art of War); he quoted a lot of historical facts from Zuo Zhuan and modeled it. See Li, *Collection on Art of War, op. cit.*, Vols. 8-9.

188. In Zhuge Liang's "Xinshu," there are 46 articles in total, out of which 11 articles are discussions of generalship, but only seven refer to the principles of operations. See Li, *Collection of on Art of War, op. cit.*, Vol. 4.

CHAPTER 3

The Opium War and the Transition
of the Chinese Military System

1. The Chinese Military System Prior to the War

From the developmental point of view, students of modernization agree that change is a permanent phenomenon, which exists in all societies at all times. As a matter of fact, the concept of change is not a modern one; it has at least a twenty-five-hundred year old history in Western culture. In China, the concept of change was accepted as a law of the universe as early as the Zhou dynasty. However, many sinologists believe that Chinese history, after the Qin dynasty, became a static one; no substantial changes occurred until the modern age. Lei Bailun, for example, wrote in his article "A Culture without Soldiers" that Chinese history before Qin was dynamic with constant socio-political changes, but since then, it has become static. There have only been cycles of order, chaos, and turbulence, but no real changes. Thus, under the fixed social conditions, similar political histories are repeatedly and cyclically displayed again and again. It can even be said that Chinese political history since the Han dynasty is only a repetition of Han. In referring to the military, the characteristic of Chinese culture since Han, to Lei, is that there have been no real soldiers. By this, he means that there are no citizens and no political life. To simplify this, he described the phenomenon as a culture without soldiers.[1]

The unification of China under a single central authority may have caused the loss of its political dynamics. However, change is a law of nature.

A failure of government to direct effective and peaceful social change will inevitably precipitate revolution in the long run. The cyclical repetition of Chinese political history is in fact cyclical revolutions to promptly bring about social change. Power causes corruption and absolute power causes absolute corruption. The longer a government stays in power, the more corrupt it becomes. The central authority of imperial China, like all other monarchical systems, was unable free itself from this political maxim. The loss of dynamics in China under the absolute monarchical system not only signified the failure of the system in bringing about the necessary social changes, but also demonstrated its impotence in maintaining an efficient military system. It is, therefore, correct to say that the Chinese military system in imperial China was often a victim of political corruption. Many times, the military force was virtually indistinguishable from gangs of marauding armed men, as mentioned by Lei. However, it may not be proper to judge this phenomenon from a cultural point of view and to attribute the failure of China in dealing with external military invasions to the "culture without soldiers" phenomenon as described by Lei. If cultural elements at one time or another caused the decline of the Chinese military system, the phenomenon would not be unique to China. Indeed, no country, before the modern age, had developed a democratic system that vested citizenship and political rights in its people. Prof. Wang Ermin, a modern military historian, has criticized Lei's conclusion as an emotional statement influenced by the feelings of sorrow he had because of China's inability to defend herself in modern times.[2]

To this writer, however, the failure of the Chinese military system in the modern era is part of the total bankruptcy of the Chinese political system under the Qing regime. To blame the armed force for China's defeat in wars without referring to the dramatic effect of the deterioration of the Chinese socio-economic and political situation as a whole is unsatisfactory. Therefore, a brief review of the socio-economic and political situation of China prior to the Opium War will be helpful in presenting a clear picture of the conditions of the Chinese military system of that time, and thus, pave the way for analyzing the various suggestions for reform that appeared later.

A. Socio-Economic Problems

In the early 19th century, many European countries had completed their economic, political, and even religious revolutions. Armed with the beliefs of nationalism, Christianity and capitalism, and backed with modern military forces which were equipped with the latest weapons, the Europeans started to expand outside of Europe, while China, under the Manhchu regime, had just begun her downward cycle from a relatively glorious and prosperous age.

As an agricultural country, China has always had land shortages. If a government could solve the land problem, it would likely enjoy a peaceful and prosperous reign without serious trouble. In the early stages of Chinese history, the government was able to grant land to each adult. Later, however, as the population grew too large, the government was unable to guarantee that each peasant would have his own land. Serious land shortages and economic hardships would inevitably lead to peasant rebellion and eventually bring down the government. The Qing dynasty in the early 19th century had just reached this point.

According to Hu Sheng, the amount of useable land in China in 1820 was about 808 million Mu, which was about 40 million Mu less than that available in 1393 (Ming dynasty).[3] However, the population had grown to several times that of 1393. In 1835, prior to the Opium War, the Chinese population was 400 million, which was 300 per cent more than the population in the 17th century, and 200 per cent more than that in the 1740s, when Emperor Qianlong just started his long reign.[4]

It was said that in 1835 the average amount of land per person was only 2 Mu, but the actual situation was even worse, because land was highly concentrated. According to Mu Anshi, 50 to 60 per cent of the tillable land in the early years of Emperor Qianlong's reign, was owned by rich landlords.[5] In addition, the royal family and the so-called 8 Banner imperial clansmen also owned a lot of land. Consequently, the peasants, who made up more than 90 per cent of the total population, only owned about 40 per cent of the land. When they worked on rented land, they had to pay 50 per cent of their crops to the landlord. This would not leave very much for themselves to feed their families.[6]

Under these circumstances, the Chinese peasantry was overwhelmed with economic hardships. The whole society was like an active volcano waiting to explode; peasant rebellion was imminent. It only needed a spark to light it. When the Opium War occurred, the rebellions followed within a few years.

B. Political Corruption

The Qing dynasty began in 1644, but it only totally pacified the rebels and brought China under a single central authority in 1683 when Taiwan was incorporated into China as a prefacture. After that, under Emperors Kangxi, Yongzheng, and Qianlong, the dynasty experienced a hundred years of glory and prosperity with military conquests and territorial expansion. However, political corruption also began to appear. It became so serious in the later part of Emperor Qianlong's reign that the country was faced with socio-economic bankruptcy in the early 19th Century. When the Opium War occurred 40 years later, the Empire was never be able to recover from the defeat. Political corruption which made the peasants suffer so badly subsequently brought the country to the edge of collapse. Two examples will illustrate the extent of this corruption.

First, Emperor Qianlong was like his grandfather Emperor Kangxi and often travelled around the country. During his reign, he travelled the south to Jiangsu and Zhejiang provinces six times; east to Shandong Province five times; northeast to Shengjing in Manchuria three times; west to Wutai Mountain six times; and to Henan Province once. His summer vacations in Rehe, annual hunting trips in Mulan during the eighth month, tours to the nearby Tianjin, and visits to the east Royal Mausoleum were so frequent that no records were kept any more. The emperor's entourage in travels always consisted of the Emperor-mother, the queen, and thousands of attendants and armed escorts. His travel schedule usually lasted several months. Furthermore, his annual summer vacation in Rehe lasted at least two months. To please the Emperor, the local officials always tried to do their best to provide for his expenses. All of these extra expenses were eventually impossed on the local peasantry, and thus added to their hardship.[7]

According to Wang Tongling, the author of *A General History of China*, many officials tried to persuade the Emperor to stop his extravagant trips because of the financial hardships they imposed on the local people, but the Emperor would become very angry and would indiscriminately punish them. Consequently, no one dared to speak out any longer.[8]

When the Emperor took long trips out of the Capital City, he left most of his political duties to his trusted minister He Shen, who was an infamously greedy man and, thus promptly added to the corruption of the government. Under He's leadership, bribes were seen as a normal way among the officials; ethics were no longer respected; official titles and government positons could be bought. Whoever was able to flatter and fawn his way into He's good graces, could do whatever he liked, including making a fortune overnight through taking bribes.

Second, flood prevention in China has always been an important responsibility that any government must fulfill. The Qing regime was no different from other dynasties. During the reign of Qianlong, however, the commissionership of flood prevention became an attractive prize for the He Shen followers and those officials who were looking for fortunes through government positions.[9]

Under these circumstances, no matter how much money the government spent in flood prevention works, no good was done except to increase the personal fortunes of the responsible officials. Consequently, floods often occurred, swallowing both lives and property. According to Wang Tongling's record, during the reign of Qianlong, the Yellow River flooded its banks 20 times in Henan and Jiangsu provinces within 45 years, almost once every two years. After the death of the Emperor, there were 17 floods within 22 years, caused by other rivers. On these occasions, governments spent multi-million taels of silver in repairing the broken banks, which gave the officials further opportunity to make money.[10] The peasants in the flooded areas became double victims. While their lands and houses were washed away and their relatives were lost, they were always asked to do the repairs.

C. Military Problems

In ancient China, the ideal military system had long been the so-called *Bingnong Heyi* or *Yubing Yunong* system, which combines the military system with the peasants. Every peasant or a selected group of peasants was obligated to serve in the armed forces for a period during his lifetime.[11] However, no dynasty in Chinese history was able to use this system for long. Generally speaking, it only worked briefly in the beginning of several dynasties but was then left unattended after peace reigned and was eventually abandoned. The Banner Army system of the Qing dynasty was close to the Chinese idea of the *Bingnong Heyi* system, and its fate was also similar to its predecessors. Although the system was kept alive after the conquest of China, its martial spirit was lost after one generation, because it was no longer an organization of warriors but a group of parasites feeding off the rulling class. They were extremely corrupt and could not fight.

The Banner Armies in Qing dynasty were divided into three groups: the Manchu Eight Banners, the Mongolian Eight Banners, and the Han Eight Banners. The Manchu Eight Banners were a political-military organization built on the basis of tribes and were the forces used by the Manchus to conquer China. Different coloured flags were used to identify the eight army groups. All of the soldiers and commanders were Manchus. They were deployed to defend the Capital and other strategic areas after the Manchus assumed power. Posts in this Banner Army were hereditary and thus were handed down from father to son. Consequently, a newborn baby might be registered as a soldier and would be paid as such, even if he later never received military training and learned nothing about martial arts.[12]

Mongolia was unified by the Manchus prior to their conquest of China. Like the Manchu Eight Banners, the Mongolians were organized into Eight Banners based on their tribes. They were the most trusted allies of the Manchus, and were used extensively in the conquest of China. Therefore, their Banner Armies were held in high esteem. The Mongolian Banners were primarily calvary and were able to maintain their strong fighting power without significant decline until the late 19th century, when they were badly defeated in a campaign against the Nian Army in the 1860s.[13]

The Han Eight Banner was organized by Chinese, who collaborated with Manchus prior to their invasion of China. The Han Banners, similar to the Manchu eight Banners, consisted of soldiers who were related to each other. Consequently, while they were not organized on a tribal basis, clan colours flew in most of the individual units. This set the Han Banners apart from the Green Banners and the Green Battalions, which were organized from the remains of the Ming armies and still kept their old systems of organization.[14]

After the unification of China, the primary source of Green Banner recruits were Chinese volunteers. Unlike the eight banners, Green Banner was not hereditary. The soldiers had to be discharged when they were old.[15]

It is said that the Banner Army, which included 24 banners together, had 280,000 soldiers in total when they conquered China.[16] They were the field armies. The Green Banner Army, however, consisted not only of the field armies, but also police forces which were assigned to protect communication lines and ensure local civil obedience. There were about half of a million people in the Green Banner forces in the early years.[17]

The commanders of the Manchu Banners were all Manchus, while the high commanders of the other armies were also Manchus. The Chinese could only be commanders of low rank in the Han Banners and the Green Banners.

Like the Manchu Banners, the Green Banner Army became corrupt after the country was at peace for a while, and lost its military skill and discipline. Furthermore, because the soldiers' salaries were low, it was often difficult to fill the vancancies with enough volunteers. The officers often had to hire people from the street temporarily in order to meet the occasional inspections of the higher commanders, so that they might be able to keep the salaries of the vacant members for themselves. It was said that even the positions of officers in the Green Banners were for sale. This not only lowered the quality of the commanders, but encouraged illegal activities such as bribe-taking and misappropriation of soldiers' wages by the officers. It was said that sometimes the army was 50 per cent understrength.[18]

Such a military force cannot be expected to defend the country effectively when war occurs. Unfortunately, this was exactly the situation of the Chinese military forces in the middle of 19th century. Besides, their obsolete weaponry and equipment did not help them to counteract the weaknesses in morale and command. By the middle of 19th century, the Western countries had started to use modern weapons. Rifles, machine guns, mortars, and land mines, for example, were consistently used in the American Civil War in the 1860s; torpedoes and submarine mines were also used in sea wars,[19] but the Chinese army still relied on spears, pikes, bows and arrows, and knives as their major weapons in the Opium War. Ten years after the First Opium War, Zeng Guofan's Xiangjun was still armed with muskets and Chinese traditional cannons (Taiqiang) in fighting against the Taiping Army in the 1850s. Rifles were introduced to China by the so-called Ever-Victorious Army led by F.T. Ward and C.G. Gordon in the 1860s when they helped the Imperial army to fight against the Taiping rebels but they were not available to the Chinese army yet. Li Hongzhang's Huaijun probably was the first Chinese armed force to use these new weapons in the early 1860s. However, the rifle did not become a standard weapon in the Chinese army until the 1880s.[20]

While the condition of the army was so dismal, what about the condition of the Chinese navy? The Chinese called their navy a water force. While the western countries had already used steam engines and modern guns to develop the powerful gunboat, the Chinese still used the small, frail, wooden rowboats and junks, armed with a few old guns. The personal weapons of the water forces were no different from those of the Banner Army: knives, arrows, and spears were still used on the ships. Many seashore defence installations were not kept in operational condition. According to a report from Yu Qian, the Viceroy of Liang-Jiang (Jiangsu-Zhejiang), the situation of the water force in Zhejiang prior to the Opium War was very bad. It was said that in an exercise, only one officer knew how to operate the coast gun; they even did not know how much firepowder a gun should take.[21] Common sense tells us that if soldiers do not learn to use their weapons, no matter how advanced they may be, they are useless. When a Western Christain priest and also a opium trader saw the situation, he wrote later that "the whole Chinese fleet of a thousand large and small boats together would not be able to cope with a single warship."[22] Although he might have exaggerated the power of the gunboat, he was not too far from the truth.

Furthermore, the practice of bribery also severely weakened the water forces. It was reported that the Tianjin coastal batteries were built in spring and collapsed in autumn of the same year. The soldiers, after taking bribes from the contractors, only used half the regular amount of firepowder in their test shots in order to guarantee passing of the official inspection. However, when the guns were fired later with the proper amount of firepowder, many batteries collapsed immediately.[23]

2. The Impact of the Opium War and the Chinese Response
A. The Opium Trade and the Opium War

As early as 16th century, Westerners had already started to bring opium to the Far Eastern countries. The first traders were the Portuguese, who were followed later by the Spanish, the Dutch, and eventually, the British. The Western opium traders, at that time, were often no different from pirates and gangs, so they often had military confrontations with Chinese armed forces. In most cases, the Chinese forces were able to drive them out of the Chinese seacoast until the 19th century when the British government sent its modern military forces to support its traders and to force a way for them to China.

Realizing the damage of opium to personal health and the national economy, the Qing government started to ban opium trade in 1729, but it was only a symbolic action and was not seriously enforced until the volume of opium trade became much bigger later. It was about 200 boxes annually when the first ban order was issued, but it increased to 1000 boxes annually within 40 years. Opium was used as madicine in the beginning, but after the British conquered India and organized its East Indian Company to handle opium production and trade, the uses of opium totally changed. In 1838, prior to war, the total imports of opium to China reached 34,776 boxes annually.[24] That is about 35 times the 1767 figure.

In 17th century, the British spent a lot of silver in importing teas from China. However, since the dramatic increase of opium trade, they not only balanced their trade with China, they also enjoyed a substantial surplus. According to Mu Anshi's figures, from 1817 to 1833, the British traders shipped out 51,961,000 dollars of silver from Canton within 17 years. In addition, the East Indian Company transported 4,441,000 dollars of silver out of Canton from 1830 to 1832. The loss of silver alarmed the Chinese government. It caused serious inflation in China. The exchange rate of silver to the legal copper was one tael per thousand coppers in 1810, but it became one to 1,362.8 in 1833. This hit the peasants badly and caused serious economic problems in China.[25]

To stop further loss of silver and to save the health of the Chinese people, the Qing government, after a period of debate, decided to ban the opium trade. Regulations became tougher year after year. In 1838, Chinese society reached a conclusion that the ban of opium trade in China was not only necessary but also possible. Therefore, the government appointed Lin Zexu as the special commissioner to Canton to handle this work. When he arrived at Canton in 1839, he immediately started to enforce the opium trade ban. Meanwhile, the British government, after tasting the huge profits from the opium trade, was reluctant to abandon it; under the pressure of the opium traders and also spurred by the arrogant attitude of the Chinese Emperor in refusing to accept its envoys, Britain decided to forcibly open the doors to the Chinese market.

Western scholars, in writing the history of the Opium Wars, often classified the Chinese officials as either hardline advocates (of the opium ban) or conciliators based on their attitude toward the opium trade. Lin Zexu was classified as a hardline advocate, while Qi Shan, Lin's successor, as a conciliator.[26] To the Chinese historians, however, Lin not only was a hardline supporter of the ban, but also an honest and able official, a great patriot, and a reasonable person. So when he was appointed as the viceroy of Hu-Guang, he not only performed his duty of banning the opium trade, but also made military preparations in his jurisdiction. Consequently, when the War eventually occurred, he was able to repulse the British forces in several areas and won an initial victory.

The Chinese historians have not been very kind to Qi Shan. Their attitude did not arise because he was a conciliator, but because he was an extremely corrupt, incompetent, and ignorant person. The criticism against him is not limited only to his performance in negotiating the truce agreement and the draft treaty of Chuanbi in 1841, in which he agreed to pay compensation, concede Hong Kong and give many other concessions to the British, but also based on his performance as a commander-in-chief in defending Canton after replacing Lin. He could have continued Lin's policy in strengthening military defence installations while taking a conciliatory position in trade affairs, but he did not do so. It was said that he totally abandoned Lin's policy and adopted a passive attitude in order to achieve peace by negotiation. What was even worse is that he misplaced his trust to a collaborator, who eventually betrayed him. Consequently, he was completely trapped by the British negotiators and lost the war and his own position.[27]

Although Lin Zexu had prepared for war when he was banning opium smuggling, the corrupted officials in other areas were not alarmed and, thus, did not strengthen their defence installations. When the British expeditionary forces had difficulty in breaking Lin's defence, they withdrew and went north. When they failed to take the coast of Fujian Province, they sailed further north to Zhejiang, where they took the unprepared local officials by surprise and were able to occupy Zhoushan Island off the coast of Zhenhai. When the British forces entered the Yangtze valley and sailed further north to Daguko, the Emperor and his government lost their nerve and decided to negotiate for peace. With the signing of the Nanjing treaty in 1842, more concessions were made at the expense of the Chinese. However, that was not the last Chinese experience of defeat, more foreign intrusions and national humiliations were to come. China was to a considerable degreee subordinated to foreign control and was even subjected to the threat of partition by the world powers. Two things which had a certain influence on modern Chinese military thought are worth mentioning here. One is Lin Zexu's military thought, and the other the militia movement in the Sanyuanli operation.

(a) *Lin Zexu's Military Thought*: His support for the banning of opium was seen by some Western scholars as xenophobic, but in fact it was not. It was part of his national defence thought. During the debate over whether opium should be banned from China, he pointed out to the Emperor that permitting the smoking of opium would cause tremendous damage to the country. "If we still hesitate to take any determined action to ban it, within ten years there would be no soldiers that can be deployed to defend the country from foreign invasion; nor would there be any money left to maintain our army. Could we remain unfrightened when we think about that?"[28]

In resisting the British naval attacks, Lin also showed that he clearly understood the objective circumstance he was facing and, thus, was able to deal with it properly. Generally, his military thought, which was primarily developed during the Opium War, can be analyzed from two aspects. First of all, he believed that weaponry plays an important, if not determinant, role in the result of war and realized that the British forces had solid ships and efficient guns, which were superior to those of the Chinese. Therefore, he publicly stated that China should learn the new technologies from her enemy and try to make warships and guns by herself.[29] Before China could make these weapons herself, she should buy them from the foreigners, even from the British.[30] It was said that he had bought a British ship which had been used against China a few months earlier.

Secondly, he recognized the power of the people in wars against foreign aggressors and was willing to rely on it to resist the British invasions. He once told the opium smugglers and the warmongers that if the British did not stop their opium exports, he would call for the masses to join the fighting; they would be "more than enough to annihilate the enemy". He also publicly stated that in case the British navy dared to penetrate to the inland rivers, the local masses could kill them with impunity.[31] When the British forces occupied Dinghai City, Zhoushan Island, he advised the Emperor that "instead of fighting the enemy on the sea without being sure of victory, it would be better to induce them inland where they would be helpless and, thus, be easily subdued."[32] This is to some extent a strategy of retrograde defence.

In the same report, Lin indicated his concept of guerrilla warfare. He advised the Emperor that the government should assign soldiers in plain clothes and local peasants with military training to go back to the occupied areas. As soon as the plain-clothes soldiers outnumbered the enemy, they could launch raids against them. By doing so, they could expect to annihilate the Brtish forces easily.[33] Lin's concept of relying on numerical superiority to drown the enemy in a human sea is very much like Mao's people's warfare theory. Although the Emperor did not use his advice, the Chinese people in Zhejiang Province adopted Lin's strategy voluntarily upon sighting the landings of British naval forces in their areas. Some enemy soldiers were killed and captured by the peasants in this way.[34]

(b) *The Sanyuanli Militia and People's War*: When Qi Shan replaced Lin Zexu as the Viceroy of Hu-Guang in Canton, the British forces also left Daguko and returned to Canton with an impression that Qi Shan was going to satisfy their demand. As soon as they realized that Qi Shan was unable to satisfy their wishes but was not prepared to fight either, they took the opportunity to strike immediately. The Chinese defence lines were easily breached. During their advance to Canton, the British forces were so ruthless in looting, destroying, molesting women and killing people, that the Chinese were greatly enraged. When a peasant woman was raped by a British soldier, with the help of other peasants, her husband started to raid the British forces. Before long, the majority of the peasants in Sanyuanli area were mobilized; more than 15,000 peasants armed with pikes, knives, and even hoes joined by the local militia and a battalion of the water forces and were ready to fight the enemy. From May 29 to 31, 1841, the peasant army surrounded a British battalion which had been attacking them. The British forces were only rescued by the local officials (Head of Prefecture) and a timely storm, with moderate casualties and losses. This boosted the spirit of the local people and became a legend in the militia movement of modern Chinese history. Its effect was not limited solely to the prompt withdrawal of the British forces from the Canton area, but it also saved as a useful model for people's warfare and clearly demonstrated to the world that peasants could play an important role in a national war against imperialists. This battle, therefore, is worthy of further analysis.

Generally speaking, the peasants are a relatively conservative group of people. Their working enviroment limits them to a very small perspective of the world. They care little about things beyond their village. This is why Marx and Lenin did not emphasize the importance of the peasantry in their revolutionary schemes. Nevertheless, the peasants are willing to fight to their death if there is a common cause strong enough to mobilize them. In the Sanyuanli case, the reason for the peasant mobilization was the ill treatment received from the British forces. This angered them and subsequently mobilized them.[35]

However, had the behaviour of the British been the only motivation for mobilization, the size of the peasant army would have been much smaller, or it would have most likely been limited to one or a few villages at a time; but the Sanyuanli case was beyond that level. While 15,000 peasants could be mobilized and armed within a couple of days,[36] at least two conditions existed. First, there must have been a common cause beyond the village level that could mobilize such a large number of peasants over such a large geographical area; secondly, there must have been some one to provide leadership of the peasants.

The Common Cause: The common cause that helped mobilize the large number of peasants to join the militia was nationalism. The British attack against China was seen as an act of aggression. The collapse of the Qing army without fighting badly hurt the pride of the Chinese. When Qi Shan signed a truce with Captain Charles Elliot on May 27, 1841, the entire nation took it as a national humiliation . Those who lived in the suburban area of Canton had themselves seen the development of the entire incident and personally felt the humiliation immediately after the truce was signed. Their anger was explosive.[37] Consequently, when a peasant woman was raped they were immediately mobilized.

Leadership: As a social class, the peasantry is unlikely to take any significant collective action unless someone can provide the necessary leadership to organize them. Modern Western sinologists have often mentioned the cooperation between peasantry, Confucian scholars, and military leaders in making revolutions. Based on this assumption, they have further rationalized the cooperation between the peasantry and the Communist Party.

According to C.P. Fitzgerald, while the modern Chinese peasantry still played the old role of followers and supporters as their ancestors did, the Communist Party replaced Confucian scholars to provide the leadership of the revolution.[38]

From a different point of view, Lei Bailun, a Chinese historian, has reached a somewhat similar conclusion. To Lei, Chinese history can be seen as a drama in which the leading role was played in turn by the Confucian scholars (Shi) and the crooks (military person). In peacetime, the Confucian scholars always assumed the leadership and put the crooks under control. However, when the political order fell apart and the country was in chaos, the scholars became helpless and had to give way to the crooks. Nevertheless, when the crooks took over the leadership, they still needed the Confucian scholars to help them. While they had the muscle, the scholars had the brains. By cooperation, they were likely to establish a new order. Of course, the peasants always played the same role as usual.[39]

Applying these theories to the Sanyuanli case, it is apparent that when the peasants were angry and enthusiastic to fight, they were put in operational form by the local scholars and military leaders.

In the Sanyuanli area, there was a community evening school presided over by local gentry, Mr. He Yucheng, a *Juren* degree holder, and a teacher, Mr. Huang Biao. Besides offering evening classes to the local peasants, these Confucians also organized the peasants into self-defence corps to pacify the local order, which served as a core of the peasant army in the Sanyuanli resistance.[40]

In addition, a battalion commander of the water force was involved in this incident. According to the commander's diary, he called a meeting to mobilize the peasant support for strengthening local defense May 29, 1841, which was attended by representatives from every district (Xiang). General principles of organizing local forces and operations were reached without defining any particular course of action. However, an incident happened in Donghuali on the same day and, thus, sparked the initial military action of the whole campaign. Based on his own record, it can be seen that he had played an important leading role in this operation.[41]

Sanyuanli was not the only site of resistance during the course of the Opium War, but it was the only place where an organized effort occurred; all other movements consisted of isolated resistance. These peasant militia resistances, however, had a psychological effect on the British forces, which reached its culmination in the Sanyuanli battle. It forced the British forces to withdraw from Canton within a few days and brought the truce into effect.

There is no direct evidence to prove that the Sanyuanli militia movement was part of Lin Zexu's military preparation when he was the Viceroy of Hu-Guang. It is reasonable, however, to think so, because when Lin was in Canton, he repeatedly called for the masses to rise against the British if they dared to penetrate the inland river valleys, as mentioned before.

Militia movements have been used by various regimes in different periods of time since then, but, for the most part, they were organized to maintain order in local areas until the Sino-Japanese War in the 1940s, when the Chinese Communists organized guerrilla warfare in the Japanese occupied areas.

Favourable Terrain: A militia force in most cases does not have advanced weapons and equipment, nor does it have the necessary military training to fight a conventional war against a well-equiped enemy. The chances for a militia force to win a battle in a regular war are slim. It has to be assisted either by favourable terrain or from the regular forces or both. The operation of the Sanyuanli militia force had been assisted by the water force battalion as well as favourable terrain.

The fighting primarily took place in the Niulangang mountain area, which has a stretch of marshland in front. The militia knew everything about the surrounding terrain and had the advantage of choosing the battle ground; they deployed their forces before the enemy entered the field. As Sunzi said: "he who occupies the field of battle first and awaits his enemy is at ease; he who comes later to the scene and rushes into the fight is weary."[42] When the British forces rushed to the field, the militia was already waiting for them. A timely storm dampened the gunpowder of the British troops, so they could not fire. Then, with hand-to-hand fighting, the militia's spears and pikes easily overpowered the enemy's bayonets. The British were saved from annihilation only when the Chinese officials intervened.

The Sanyuanli operation has been deliberately singled out as a sucessful model of people's militia in modern China. While it may be too arbitrary to claim that the mass militia movement in contemporary China is directly related to the Sanyuanli system, it would be equally wrong to say that Mao's ideas on people's warfare were totally unrelated to the Sanyuanli movement.

B. The Response of the Intellectual Circles

Intellectuals are the most politically sensitive elements of a society and are likely to react to any socio-political changes. Their reactions usually reflect public opinion and are the guiding force of political reforms.

In the wake of the Chinese defeat in the Opium War, the reaction of Chinese intellectuals focused primarily on military-related subjects which were believed to be the fatal factor that directly caused the national disaster.

Among the numerous discussions, those of Wei Yuan and Feng Guifen have often been mentioned by modern historians as the typical reactions of the intellectuals, which significantly affected government policies later.

Wei Yuan was a friend of Lin Zexu and belonged to the same group of intellectuals. From communicating with Lin, Wei Yuan was well informed about the military disparity between China and the British, and about the world situation. His opinion, to a large degree, was close to Lin Zexu and had a widespread influence.

Wei Yuan's major work is *The Atlas of Countries Beyond the Oceans*; it was first published in 1842 when the Treaty of Nanjing was signed. His thought relevant to military affairs consisted primarily of a series of articles titled "The Overall Planning of Coastal Defenses" (Chou Hai Pian) and can be summarized as follows:

(a) *Learning from the Enemy*: Like Lin Zexu and most other intellectuals, Wei realized that the weapons of the Western countries were superior to those of the Chinese. To defend China, it was absolutely necessary to have ships and guns. Instead of importing weapons from other countries, he thought that China should learn how to manufacture them. However, Wei went further; he insisted that the superiority of the Western countries was not limited to their solid ships and effective guns, but also included high wages and benefits of the soldiers and their strict training and rigid discipline. Because the soldier's pay was high, it was possible to attract the best recruits; with rigorous training and strict discipline, the soldiers can be always under the control of the commanders. "Should an armed force have solid ships and effective guns without effective control, it would be like having no guns and ships; if there is no reasonable renumeration system, it would be impossible to recruit the best soldiers." He continued, "therefore, prior to recruiting soldiers and starting to train them, it is necessary to reform the salary system. It is even better to have a small military force with higher salaries."[43]

(b) *Retrograde Defence and Luring the Enemy in Deep*: Wei Yuan strongly argued against the public opinion that "defending inland rivers is not as good as defending seaports; defending the seaports, in turn, is not as good as defending oceans."[44] Instead, he believed that on the huge ocean, it is relatively easy for the enemy's ship to move and, thus, it is unlikely for the Chinese to destroy them; meanwhile, the Chinese seacoast is too long to be defended properly. If the Chinese try to protect their entire coastline from attack, they would be exhausted while the enemy would be at ease; the Chinese would be divided, while the enemy would be concentrated. Consequently, he suggested that defending the seaports is better than defending the oceans, and defending the waterways is better than defending the seaports.[45]

What Wei Yuan tried to explain is actually a strategy of retrograde defence. By using this strategy, he intended to induce the enemy into a carefully arranged battlefield in the inland rivers, or lure them to a chosen area, where the enemy would be trapped by the Chinese defending installations and could be destroyed completely. He particularly used the Sanyuanli operation as an example to support his argument.

(c) *To Control One Barbarian by Another*: In discussing offensive operations, Wei Yuan suggested the old strategy of checking one barbarian by another. He thought that if China were able to ally herself with Russia,

France, and the U.S.A., she might pursue the Russians to attack East India from land, while have the French and the Americans to engage the British on the ocean. With this strategy, the British could be defeated easily without sending a single Chinese soldier to the front.

Wei Yuan's strategy was based on an assumption that Russia, France, and the U.S.A. were enemies of the British and, thus, it was possible for China to manipulate them to fight against the British, as China occasionally did in fighting off the ancient barbarians on the Chinese borders. However, the real situation was not as simple as Wei Yuan thought. This is why Feng Guifen criticized him that "it is likely a way to put oneself down, should one indulge in playing stratagems without strengthening oneself."[46] Nevertheless, if Wei Yuan's discussion was limited to proper diplomatic activities and military alliances with other countries, it could still be useful in getting assistance from the international community.

(d) *Open Doors to Foreign Trade*: Wei probably was the first man of his time to have recognized the advantage and necessity of opening Chinese doors to foreign trade and communication. When he discussed this problem, he did not follow the traditional view of using "trade" as a method of pacifying the barbarians, but as a mutually beneficial method of conducting economic activity. Prof. Feng Youlan pointed out this particular concept as a progressive perspective on international relations.[47]

It seems that the Chinese have long been familiar with using trade as a strategy to achieve their diplomatic purpose in controlling neighbouring countries. However, they never used trade as a strategy to improve their economic situation as Wei suggested.

In the 19th century, if the Qing government had realized the advantage of trade strategy it might have avoided some confrontations with the West. It might at least have been able to trade for new Western technology and weapons in order to strengthen her economic and military forces. Unfortunately, the Qing government did not take Wei's suggestion in time. So when it wanted to purchase weapons, it just paid cash without referring to import and export trades.

Wei's work was well known and widely read in the 1840's when the Chinese were anxious to find different ways to save the country in the wake of defeat in the Opium War. His concept of learning from the West and building arsenals to make ships and guns was accepted and carried out by the government later. It is known as the *Yangwu* Movement, which will be discussed further in later sections.

C. Feng Guifen and His Influence

Feng was younger than Wei. His work first became known in the 1860's, after Wei had already died. His thought is, to a large degree, similar to Wei's, but he went further in some respects. He showed a broader perspective of the Western world, and suggested the necessary socio-political reforms in China. Therefore, his influence on Chinese society was even more substantial.

(a) *Learning from the West and Self-Strengthening*: Similar to Wei, Feng completely agreed that the Western ships were solid and guns effective, and, therefore, China should adopt the Western weapons. In learning from the West, he emphasized two points that made his thought more influential than Wei Yuan's on Chinese society: first of all, Feng realized that when China wanted to learn from the West, she should not only buy the Western weapons, but also learn how to make them by herself; not only copy from the West, but create or invent new models; and eventually, she should be able to manufacture, repair, and use the Western arms herself. China must do her best to master these technologies, and turn them into a Chinese technology. Until China could do so, she would not be able to defend herself and free herself from foreign threats. This is called self-strengthening.[48]

Secondly, he believed that if China wanted to master Western technology, she must reform her education system and offer equal degrees and status to those who are willing to learn Western technologies with certain achievement. Feng's suggestion was not limited to learning the Western technologies, but included Western basic sciences such as mathematics, chemistry, physics, and even astronomy. By learning these sciences, China could not only quickly improve her military industry, but she could build up the necessary foundation for long-term development of the Chinese socio-economic system.

In addition, Feng suggested that the Chinese government should set up foreign language schools or translation centres in Canton and Shanghai to teach the young people foreign languages so that they could translate foreign books. That would greatly facilitate the flow of knowledge from the Western world.[49]

(b) *On the Armed Forces*: In discussing the effect of weaponry on the fighting power of the armed force, Feng briefly made two points. First, the defeat of the Chinese army by the British forces was not completely due to the inferiority of the Chinese ships and guns; the training and fighting formations of the enemy were also better than those of the Chinese army. Second, China should not rely on imported weaponry to support her armed forces. She must promptly develop her independent arsenals; otherwise, she would not be able to start an offensive war beyond her borders in order to pursue the defeated enemy and destroy them in their home base once and for all.[50] This was an extremely ambitious opinion at that time as far as the Chinese situation was concerned. However, Feng's idea has been proven valid in many cases in history. While the military forces were strong enough to suppress internal rebellions, they often became impotent in fighting their foreign suppliers of weapons.[51] If it is difficult to rely on foreign weapons to defend oneself, it is virtually impossible to rely on foreign supplies to build a military force capable of attacking a potential enemy beyond one's own border.

As to the military organization, Feng strongly advocated a small but elite military force. He pointed out that there were about one million soldiers in China, of which about two hundred thousand were assigned to protect flood works. They could neither maintain local order nor defend the country from attack. Therefore, they should be discharged completely. Feng also pointed out that many army units were undermanned. According to Feng's figure, some battalions were 40 to 50 percent undermanned and 20 percent of their personnel were non-fighting or aged and weak soldiers. Consequently, less than 50 percent of the soldiers could be used in war.[52]

Based on this analysis, Feng made a bold suggestion that two-thirds of the armed forces should be discharged, while the wages and provisions of the remaining active servicemen should be tripled. Feng decided that no racial preference would be considered; both the Manchus and the Han people were to be treated equally as long as they could meet the military requirements.[53]

(c) *The Tiyong Philosophy and its Effect on Chinese Modernization*: To Feng, there is no need for China to learn from the Western countries about socio-economic reforms, because China may do better than the foreign countries as long as it can insist upon the ethics and principles of Confucianism coupled with the advanced Western technology. It would be enough to make a prosperous and strong society.[54] This approach was later further developed into the theory of *Tiyong*, which insists upon the traditional Chinese value system as the essential substance of the society with Western technology as a means. This theory dominated the political development of China for several decades after the middle of 19th century.

Tiyong theory was later criticized by the revolutionaries and blamed for the failure of the *Yangwu* movement. However, if one examines the contemporary modernization movement in the developing countries, *Tiyong* theory has in different degrees been followed and has also been accepted by students of this field as a healthy phenomenon. National culture and tradition are increasingly respected in the process of modernization in most developing countries. As far as modern China is concerned, while the Guomindang never agreed to accept an overall Westernization in its long years of revolution, the Communists, after the turbulent revolutionary years, have shown that they are more or less willing to accept the once unmercifully denounced traditional Chinese culture. While they are campaigning for the Four Modernizations now, they have emphatically held high the flag of Four Insistences, which serves as the *Ti* in its campaign to introduce advanced Western technology in order to regenerate its economy by a new *Yangwu* movement.

However, when this philosophy was applied to military modernization, the insistence on the Chinese traditional system (Ti) has created endless problems and made the advanced foreign means useless in defending the country against external enemies. Therefore, it is vital for one to distinguish those traditions which may help or at least not hinder the process of modernization and those which are obviously out of date and may impede the process of modernization.

D. Social Instability and the Self-Strengthening Movement

Less than 10 years after the signing of Nanjing Treaty, the social order of China deteriorated rapidly. Popular movements highlighted by the Taiping and Nian rebellions almost toppled the already shaken Imperial system. Within two years, the quickly growing peasant rebel army, Taiping, easily swept into Southern and Central China from a small village in Guangxi Province. After taking Nanjing in March of 1853, they were able to send an expeditionary force marching to the North to threaten the Imperial government's capital city. The Chinese army, which had not yet recovered from the defeat of the Opium War, could not stop the expansion of the Taiping Army into the Yangtze area. The Emperor was forced to call for the Hunan provincial militia forces led by Zeng Guofan to fight the Taiping rebels. The rebellion was only crushed after Nanjing was retaken in 1864. Nevertheless, the country's resources were further exhausted and the government fell deeper into trouble.

While the Imperial army was engaged in fighting the Taiping and Nian rebels, the Second Opium War began in 1856; the Qing regime was trapped in an extremely difficult situation. The result of the two-front operation was two more unequal treaties with more concessions of rights and interests to the Western countries.[55] The increasing national humiliation and social instability brought the country to an unprecedented difficult situation. The Chinese intellectuals demanded reforms in order to save the country from total defeat by the Western powers.

As the country was clamouring for reforms, people were ready to listen to any suggestions. Therefore, Wei Yuan and Feng Guifen's works found their audience. Feng's work was completed and first presented to Zeng Guofan in 1860 when Zeng was still commanding his Xiangjun and engaging the Taiping Army.

Although Feng's work was not published until after his death, the high praise from Zeng Guofan greatly increased its popularity and, thus, was circulated among the bureaucrats and the intellectuals. The idea of Ziqiang or Self-strengthening was quickly accepted by the society. However, the Imperial government only paid attention to his suggestions on technical matters such as building military industries and opening foreign language schools. It did not pay any attention to the suggestion of educational reform, nor did it ever consider changing its military system and political system in order to adapt to the new situation. If the Qing government had adopted his suggestion of changing the educational system and the traditional civil servant system, it would have laid a much better foundation for Chinese economic modernization in general and military modernization in particular in the late 19th century. Unfortunately, this suggestion was not put into practice until the end of the century.

The *Ziqiang* movement is better known as *Yangwu* Movement. It started in 1860 when the Beijing Treaty was signed but resulted in total failure in 1895, when China was badly defeated in the Sino-Japanese War and was forced to sign the Treaty of Shimonoseki, in which the Chinese suffered the most serious loss of territory and other rights to date.

Publications on the *Yangwu* movement both in China and abroad have become numerous in recent years. No matter what attitudes the researcher may have, it is generally agreed that the primary motivation of the movement was to improve the Chinese military status. In other words, the initial goal of the movement was to procure the Western technology in order to make solid ships and effective guns. Though the movement was later extended to non-military industries and other businesses, it was still dominated by the original military goals.

From 1860 to 1895, under the effort of the *Yangwu* politicians, the Chinese military force had reached a relatively modern level in terms of guns and ships. Compared to the Japanese forces, the Chinese navy and land forces were numerically greater. Nevertheless, the Chinese forces were defeated, and in some cases, even totally destroyed without much heavy fighting. There were many discussions on the failure of the *Yangwu* movement in general and the military build-up in particular. Hu Sheng, the president of Chinese Academy of Social Science, believed that the failure of the *Yangwu* movement was primarily due to the backward production relations of the Chinese feudal society, which provided no solid foundation for developing any industry, above all modern military industry. Sun Yutang, a Chinese historian, convinced his readers that the failure of modern Chinese military industry in the Qing dynasty was because it was imported from foreign countries without growing out of the solid foundation of the Chinese socio-economic system.[56] When one examines the Chinese armed forces of this period, one would further find that while the Chinese troops were equipped with foreign weapons and trained by the foreign instructors according to Western military principles, they did not really understand what they were doing and why they were doing it. In other words, mentally and psychologically, the Chinese soldiers in some cases were not prepared to face a modern war. Instead of taking their military training seriously, the soldiers and officers were like comedians acting out a farce.

A British navy officer gave the following comment after he reviewed the military training performance of the Chinese armed forces:

> From what we saw in their performance, the soldiers acted as
> if they were only playing the role of soldiers, and were not real
> ones. It made us believe that they did not in fact even slightly
> know the real purpose of the funny roles they were playing. .
> .I am afraid that in case they are confronted by the enemy, they
> may forget all of their training much sooner than they learned
> it.[57]

To support his comment, he give two examples to indicate how
mentally unprepared and undisciplined the Chinese forces were. First, after
target shooting, the above-mentioned soldiers washed their rifles in a stream
which was of course not very clean.

Second, once a commander wanted to show his foreign guest how
successful the performance of his Chinese soldiers would be in emergent
military situations. One quiet night, with his guest present, the officer rang
his emergency alarm to call his soldiers into action. He tried every possible
method to call them out, but no one reacted. They stayed in their living
quarters laughing and thinking that the officer was playing a similar joke on
them as he did before. They wanted to turn the tables around on the officer.[58]

The situation of the navy was not any better. China hired Captain
Luxmore, a British navy officer, as the commander of its largest warship
Yangwu, in 1870. The highest Chinese commander on the ship was a Tidu
(similar to the rank of a general), who was described by Captain Luxmore as
follows:

> I could not see what the Tidu did on the boat, because he was
> rarely seen on the ship. When he did come, he usually locked
> himself in the cabin at the center of the ship and rarely came out.
> In his cabin, there was the image of a Goddess (Ma Zu), who
> was believed to be able to ensure the safe navigation of the boat
> on sea. The old man stayed in the cabin without doing anything
> except worshipping and meditating. . .It is not clear how this
> old general could assume this position, because he knew
> neither the steam engine nor English which was the only
> working language on the ship. [59]

The focus of the country during the *Yangwu* movement was on military
modernization, but up to 1880, the results were just like this. To the author
of *The Navigation of Lupwing*, the problem with the Chinese military force
was lack of discipline, organization, leadership, and morale. He wrote:

> Everyone knows that it is useless and even harmful if an army
> has only manpower but no discipline and organization. Fur-
> thermore, even the best fleet and army can be defeated if they
> do not have a competent commander with the necessary knowl-

edge and skills. Considering the huge size of the Chinese armed forces, it is sad to say that the commanding officers are seriously lacking in leadership skills.[60]

His final comment on the Chinese armed forces was that: "judging by European standards, the Chinese army was better in form than substance. Organization, if such a word could be used to describe the Chinese system, was a joke. The Chinese armed forces were simply an unorganized mass of armed people with no discipline at all."[61]

These quotations help us to realize that the failure of the *Yangwu* movement and, above all, the military modernization at this stage was due to more than the backwardness of Chinese production relations or the capacity of military industry. It was primarily due to the misunderstanding of the essence of modernization. The majority of the Chinese including the high bureaucrats and soldiers were not ready to change their attitude in order to meet the needs of modernization. There is no doubt that the extreme corruption of Chinese governmment and the military forces as mentioned before were additional impediments to the success of military modernization. How to properly adapt the Chinese military organization to the imported new weapons and military strategy and tactics was only vaguely understood by a few enlightened leaders but was totally unknown to the majority of military persons. This caused failures of the Chinese initial effort of military modernization. In addition, as mentioned earlier, the Chinese leaders did not realize that basic reform of the educational system should be undertaken, which would not only promote a change of social attitudes but most impor-tantly lay a solid foundation for modernization.

3. The Rise of Regional Military Forces and Chinese Military Modernization

After the defeat of China in the Second Opium War and the increasing threat of the peasant rebellions, the Qing government was forced to initiate reforms. While the *Ziqiang* movement was a result of social reactions to the defeat in the Second Opium War, regional armed forces, Xiangjun and Huaijun, were the major products in suppressing the internal peasant rebel-lions. Because the important supporters of the *Ziqiang* movement were basically the intellectuals and the leaders of the Xiangjun and Huaijun and because the major policies of the *Ziqiang* movement were primarily concen-trated on military modernization, the immediate result of the social movement greatly assisted the growth of modern Chinese regional militarism, which has had far-reaching effects on the socio-political development of China.

A. Zeng Guofan and the Xiangjun

Zeng Kuofan was a Confucian bureaucrat who had close connections with the intellectual community and, thus, supported its self-strengthening movement ideas. When the Taiping rebellion expanded to central China, he was in mourning for his mother and stayed at home in Xiangxiang in Hunan Province. He shared the fear of the mass rebellions of Taiping and Nian with the local people, and, thus, had a strong desire to support the government in fighting the rebels. Therefore, when Emperor Xianfeng ordered him to help organize local militia forces in Hunan, he immediately committed himself to this job in 1853. Due to his realization of the weaknesses of the current military system under the Eight Banner Army and the Green Battalions, he began to develop his own military thought in organizing the militia forces and later the Xiangjun, which caused the rise of the regional military forces, and subsequently, warlord politics in modern China.

(a) *Zeng's Reform of Chinese Military Organization*: The Chinese military establishment in the mid-19th century was often criticized for at least three weaknesses. Firstly, the lack of training prevented the Chinese army from fighting effectively. Secondly, the low salary of the soldiers failed to give them any incentive to do their duty properly. Thirdly, in war the army unit was often composed of soldiers from different units and led by temporarily appointed commanders, in whom the soldiers had no confidence and subsequently, there was no 'team spirit' in the army. With these problems in mind, Zeng decided to build a new military system that could avoid them.

When he accepted the order to organize the militia in Hunan Province, he asked the local officials at the county level to organize the masses into militia units and give them some initial military training. Then he selected the best elements of the local militia and gave them further intensive training in Changsa, the capital city of Hunan.[62] He personally supervised the training and later commanded these elite militia forces in war. After the first successful test that the militia underwent against the Taiping Army in Hunan, the Emperor ordered him to fight outside the province. His militia forces soon replaced the Green Battalions to lead the campaigns against the rebels.

Encouraged by his initial success and in order to meet the increasing needs of the war, he decided to further expand his forces. He wrote a military regulation in describing the military organization, the renumeration system, and the military training program. The militia force was transformed into a powerful armed force, which was later known as Xiangjun.

In organization, Zeng Guofan adopted a totally different system. He personally recruited his immediate subordinate commanders, and in turn, offered them the authority to choose their own subordinates. The same procedure was applied to every level down to the squad, where the squad leader was permitted to recruit his own soldiers. Soldiers were required to obey only orders from their immediate commander. Organized in this way, the army automatically developed a close relationship between the commanders and their subordinates, much like a father-son relationship, and subsequently developed a strong team spirit.

While the old problem which afflicted the Green Battalions was solved, a new one gradually took its place and caused serious military and political problems in the coming years. Under the Green Battalion and the Banner systems, the military forces were under the direct control of the central government. They belonged to the country, not to any individual person. The emperor, through the ministry of war, had the sole authority to appoint commanders and through them to command every unit. However, after the Hunan militia was established, the central authority no longer retained the right of command; the soldiers would only obey the person who recruited them and subsequently worked with them. The consequence was that the army became a private force. Under this system when a commander was removed, his entire supporting staff and sometimes even the entire unit had to be dissolved so that a new commander could recruit them again in order to develop the same close relationship with those people.[63]

As a regional force, the Xiangjun was not treated as a regular army unit in China until many years had passed. During this long period, it was not financed by the central government but by the regional authorities, and for this reason, the Xiangjun was paid more than the regualr army. This discrepancy in wages forced the central authority to accelerate its effort to improve the salaries of the regular armed forces.

(b) *Confucian Rationalism and the Political Education in the Xiangjun:* When Zeng Guofan started to build up his militia and later the Xiangjun, he wanted to correct the bad habits of the existing military force and guarantee a high moral quality for his army. He was a student of rationalism, which was a new Confucian school developed in the Song and Ming dynasties and required an individual to look inwards and monitor his own mental activities in order to avoid any slight deviation from his right conscience.[64] Zeng particularly emphasized self-cultivation of his conscience in order to achieve moral perfection. To improve the moral quality of his force, Zeng applied the rationalitic theories to his new army in the recruiting process and training programs in accordance with Confucian ethical codes.

As a devout Confucian scholar, Zeng was also extremely unhappy about the Taiping rebels, who were self-proclaimed Christians. In his official statement of declaration of war against the Taiping, he denounced the Taiping army for trying to destroy Confucian ethics. Zeng, therefore, called on all who were courageous and righteous to fight for the cause of national civilization.

To imbue the Xiangjun with Confucian ideas, he chose his officers from the ranks of Confucian scholars. Relying on those scholars as the inner core of his army, he started to set up a new moral foundation for the armed forces of China. In addition, he recruited his soldiers from the peasantry in the mountainous areas of Hunan Province. He purposely excluded the urban hoodlums from his army, because he thought that the simple nature of the farmers would be compatible with the requirements of a well disciplined army.

In training his force, Zeng emphasized the principles of "loyalty, righteousness, courage and uprightness". Loyalty and righteousness are the basic Confucian ethics, the core of Chinese civilization. Loyalty requires every citizen to pay allegiance to his legitimate sovereign and government, and to his superiors. Righteousness demands that person behave in accordance with divine and moral laws and be free from any guilt and sin. Courage and uprightness are the chief traits of all soldiers.

This was probably the first time in Chinese history that a military force consciously used the values of traditional Chinese culture as a weapon against its enemy. Zeng's military success, therefore, can be partly attributed to the ideological training of his army.

As mentioned above, the officer group of the Xiangjun were all Confucian scholars and, thus, the best political instructors in the army. Furthermore, there were full-time instructors attached to Zeng's headquarters staff. These officers were also responsible for overseeing these ideological matters.[65]

(c) *The Strategies of the Taiping and Nians and Their Effect on Zeng's Military Thought*: As a Confucian scholar, Zeng did not have any military experience prior to being ordered by the Emperor to train the Hunan militia in 1853. Therefore, his military thought was primarily developed in the process of suppressing the Taiping and Nian armies.

The Mobile Warfare of the Rebels: In the initial stage of a rebellion, when the rebel is still weak, it usually does not take positional warfare. Instead, it prefers to use guerrilla and mobile warfare to play hide-and-seek games with its enemy in order to exhaust them. It will pounce on and destroy them when the chance arises.

When the Taiping and Nian began their rebellion, they followed the same rule and avoided engaging the Qing army in positional warfare. From 1850 to 1852, the Taiping army was able to fight their way to Hunan Province with this strategy. They captured a lot of cities without serious fighting until arriving in Changsa, the capital city of Hunan in central China. They surrounded the city for more than two months and fought fiercely but failed to take it. Then they turned to the east down the Yangtze River to take Nanjing after Wuchang. This action took the Qing army by surprise and, thus, they easily captured the city. After taking over Nanjing, however, the Taiping decided to set up their capital there. Instead of using their major force to fight to the north, they were kept to defend the capital city and the adjacent areas. Though they still dominated the battlefield of central China for years to come and continued their mobile warfare in this area, but they lost their strategic initiative forever and fell into a passive positional warfare.

However, the Nian army used mobile warfare up to their final extinction. Their loss was due to the lack of a secure base, not the lack of initiative. In a letter to his younger brother, Zeng Ranpu, a field commander of the Xiangjun, Zeng Guofan described how the Nian army used mobile warfare in fighting the Imperial army:

> ...While they are able to fight but never engage themselves in operation imprudently. They rather wait for us to move and then hit us on moving. This is exactly the strategies taken by the Taiping army in their initial stage of rebellion. Fourthly, they act like a storm. Sometimes they march a thousand Li within several days without stopping, other times they simply swing in circle around a small one.[66]

In the same letter, he even quoted the Nian's own words to indicate the power of the mobile tactics. He wrote: "In the Nians, there is a well known secret of tactics. They said: 'should we swing in circle for a while, the pursuing Imperial army would be exhausted.' The loss of Prince Zeng (a Mongolian) was exactly caused by the Nians with this strategy."[67]

While Zeng took the rebels' strategic advantages seriously, he did not ignore their disadvantages in designing his own strategies. For example, he wrote to his brother that:

> The Nians have three weakness in operation. Firstly, they don't have any firearms, and, thus, are not able to take fortified positions. Therefore, as long as the Imperial army can hold the walled cities and the peasantry militia can hold their stockaded villages, the Nians cannot get advantage from us and even cannot loot food. Secondly, they don't encamp but stay in the farm houses at night. They are, therefore, vulnerable to night raids. Thirdly, they always take their baggages and stores, dependents, and cars and animals with them in a campaign. If the Imperial army can raid their baggage and stores, they are likely to suffer a heavy loss.[68]

Based on his analysis of the advantages and weakness of his enemies, he developed his own strategies and tactics.

Zeng's Military Principles

(a) *Concentration of Force*: When Zeng began his campaign against the Taiping and Nian later, he often experienced a shorage of competent commanders able to act indepedently in the battlefield while he had to face an enemy numerically several times larger than his own forces. Consequently, he often advised his commanders to concentrate on one front and not use their force in a separate front. As he wrote to his brother: "To divide the force is an extremely difficult matter. If there is no competent commander to lead the separate force they may suffer."[69]

(b) *Keeping Solicitude in Operation*:   As a serious Confucian scholar with the realization of the disparity between his forces and the rebels, he was so cautious in operation that he often advised his commanders to keep a solicitous attitude in battle in order to avoid any feeling of arrogance. He often quoted from both Laozi and Confucius to justify his theory. "When two opposing armies meet each other, the victory goes to those who have a feeling of grief or sadness." "Confucius was always solicitous when he was faced with any incident." "To keep a solicitous attitude, one is likely to be free from being arrogant." To Zeng, arrogance is the source of defeat. One must always maintain a feeling of grief in using military forces. He once wrote: "war is an extremely sinister matter. One should always take it seriously with feelings of sadness and grief as if one were attending one's parent's funeral, or one should maintain a solemn and respectful mind as if one were attending religious sacrificial rites."[70]

(c) *The Master of Field Belonging to the Defenders*:   Zeng had such a cautious attitude towards war that he often took defensive positions and opposed offence, even when his force was engaging in an offensive operation. He went so far as to say that "the defender is always the master of the field and the attacker, the guest. . .In fighting, the one who shoots first is the guest, the one who shoots later, the master; in a hand to hand struggle with spears, the one who strikes first is the guest, the one who strikes after repulsing the attack, the master."[71]

Zeng's theory of 'master and guest' is rather controversial. If one is always afraid of striking first, one cannot get the advantage of initiative, which is extremely important in operations. His cautious attitude even permits his force to wait in the front of the enemy positions until they come out and rush to his force. It is conceivable that Zeng designed this strategy in order to deal with the mobile warfare of his enemy.

(d) *Keeping a Big Maneuver Force*:   Although Zeng preferred adopting defensive strategies, he often asked his commanders to keep a maneuver force that could be used for attacks. Based on this idea, he insisted on dividing his forces into two units. One is called the "dumb force" (*Dai Bing*), the other, the active one (*Huo Bing*). While the former is deployed to engage the enemy in positional operations in either defence or offence, the latter is used for strikes, which is known in modern military terminology as the maneuver force or reserves. He repeatedly advised his front commanders to keep at least half of his force as maneuver force. To Zeng, it would be better to keep a bigger active force rather a large dumb one. Half and half would be ideal for him.[72] However, one may sense a contradiction between the theory of 'master and guest' and that of 'the active and dumb forces'. It seems that if one emphasizes the positive role of the active force, one is likely to follow more offensive than defensive strategies.

The reserve force in China's military history may have long existed in fact, but it was not considered a significant subject by the ancient strategists, as mentioned in last chapter except the concept of Qibing. Therefore, Zeng's emphasis on keeping a maneuver force in the front becomes an outstanding point. However, his big reserve theory may also lead readers to ask how big a reserve force should be? Half and half may be a little too big.

(e) *The Emphasis on Human Factors over Weapons*:   While Zeng was a prominent supporter of the self- strengthening movement and was one of the few pioneers who started modern Chinese military industries in the mid-19th century to copy the new Western weapons, he insisted on the supremacy of the human factor over weapons in war. On some occasions, he even let his readers believe that he looked down upon Western military technology and was opposed to arming his forces with modern Western weapons. He once wrote to a friend:

> The most reliable factor in attack and defence, in my opinion, is man not weapons. I had instructed my bother repeatedly that he should not overrely on foreign guns. . .The superiority of the foreign military forces lies primarily in the strictness of their discipline and the quality of their organization. They win battles not by totally relying on their firearms. . .Therefore, it is clear that there is no absolute way to win a battle by relying on weapons only.[73]

This quotation not only tells us that Zeng did not overestimate the effectiveness of the foreign guns as many others did, but it also indicates that Zeng emphasized the role of the human factor in war over that of weapons. Therefore, Zeng was actually a predecessor of the modern Chinese strategists who oppose the theories of weapon determinism.

Generally speaking, Zeng Guofan did not make any unusual contribu-tion as a great strategist. However, he had a gift to attract talent to work for his cause, and this trait helped him win the war against the Taiping. Li Hongzhang and Zuo Zongtang were the most prominent members of his staff. They also affected the development of modern Chinese military thought.

B Li Hongzhang and Chinese Military Modernization

Like Zeng Guofan, Li Hongzhang was also a Confucian scholar-bu-reaucrat and held the highest degree of the imperial civil servant examination (*Jin Shi*). Prior to joining Zeng's staff, he had been training local militia and fighting the Nian and Taiping armies for several years in his home province. His talent was highly praised by Zeng long before he joined Zeng's staff. Zeng, therefore, sent him to organize a new force in his home province, Anhui. This force was later known as Huaijun, which primarily followed the system of Xiangjun except for the supremacy of Confucian scholars in the officer group.[74] The officers of the Huaijun were recruited from various sources and were not as idealistic as the Xiangjun officers, who were driven by a highly sacrificial spirit to defend Chinese civilization and, above all, the Confucian ethical code. Instead, the motivation behind the Huaijun officers was self-interest and careerism. For this reason, the discipline of the Huaijun was not as good as the Xiangjun. It is said that the soldiers often robbed without hesitation during operations. Sometimes, they even fought against the local militias if they dared to stand in their way of robbing.[75]

When the Taiping army attacked Shanghai in 1862, Zeng sent Li Hongzhang to lead an attachment to reinforce Shanghai. After he repulsed the attack and restored part of Jiangsu Province from Taiping occupation, he was appointed as Xunfu, the supreme military leader of the province. He then succeeded Zeng step by step, from the acting Viceroy of Liangjiang, the Commander-in-Chief in the campaign against the Nian army, the Viceroy of Liangjiang, and eventually the Viceroy of Zhili and concurrently the Minister of Beiyang after Zeng's death in 1870.

During the campaign against Taiping, as a regional commander, he did not show any particular strategy and tactics different from those of Zeng. Even when he replaced Zeng as the Commander-in-Chief in suppressing the Nian campaign, he still followed Zeng's strategies without dramatic change. For example, when Zeng insisted on containing the rolling Nian army with fortified positional defence in the strategic areas and communication lines,[76] Li suggested a strategy of strengthening the defence and clearing the field to isolate the Nian from looting food. As he wrote:

> If we want to find an effective strategy to defeat the Nian army, there is no other way except instructing the local people in Hebei, Anhui and Henan provinces to strengthen the defence and clear the field. . .Otherwise, the rebels would be able to continually loot food and expand their forces. If the provinces concerned do not train their forces and hold the important strategic areas in order to stop the rebels from continually swinging freely. . .We would not be able to siege and extermi-nate them.[77]

After this strategy succeeded, he started to organize striking forces to attack the Nians and eventually won the campaign.

In assessing his contribution to military modernization, Li Hongzhang's great achievement was introducing modern Western weapons to China, building modern military industries, establishing a modern navy, and other relevant military systems.

(a) *Systematically Introducing Western Weaponry*: Although the Chinese had learned the effectiveness of Western weaponry since the Opium War in 1840, there was no single Chinese army unit that was armed with them. As mentioned before, when Li arrived at Shanghai in 1862, he personally witnessed the power of the Western firearms in the foreign mercenary army led by F. Wards and repeatedly wrote to Zeng Guofan and his collegues in Xiangjun showing his admiration of them. Although Zeng maintained a skeptical point of view on the effectiveness of the Western weapons, it did not affect Li's favourable attitude. He began to arm his force with these new weapons and hired instructors from the Western military officers in Shanghai to train his force with Western training manuals. This not only helped him to successfully repulse the Taiping rebels in Shanghai and restore Jiangsu Province from Taiping occupation, it also helped him to win the campaign against the Nian later. When he was required to lead the campaign against the Nian in 1865, his Huaijun was entirely armed with Western rifles and artillery. As he reported to the Emperor in 1865:

> Because the Western firearms are much more powerful than those of the Chinese, therefore, since 1863, I have instructed all of my forces to employ foreign instructors in order to teach them to use rifles and artillery. After continually hard work, they have mastered the secrets of operations of these weapons.[78]

According to his reports, a battalion of 500 soldiers was armed with 400 rifles and artillery. It needed several tons of ammunition to support a battle. When it was on the move, it had to have dozens of big ships or wagons to transport its ammunition, and baggages and stores.[79] There is no doubt that it was a highly modernized army unique in the Chinese armed forces in the 1860s. Due to his positive attitude toward Western new weapons, it strongly affected other military leaders and accelerated the process of Chinese military modernization. Furthermore, to meet the urgent need for new weapons, the Chinese were no longer satisfied with purchasing weapons from the Western- ers; they wished to make their own weapons. This ambition helped China to establish modern military industries. Li Hongzhang was one of the most important leaders in pushing for its success.

(b) *The Establishment of Military Industry:* Under the self-strength- ening movement, there was a popular theory in China that "the way of governing a country is to rely on self-strengthening. To achieve this goal under the current circumstances, it has to build up an effective armed force.

The top priority of military building, however, is to get weapons."[80] Based on this theory, almost all leaders of China were anxious to build military industries in their jurisdictions. Li Hongzhong was probably the most prominent one, who started to build arsenals in Shanghai and Suzhou in 1862. Though they were small in the beginning, due to the urgent needs of his army, they were promptly expanded in order to supply the ammunition for his force within a short period of time.

In 1863, he was able to accept soldiers assigned by the Imperial government in Beijing to learn the new technology of manufacturing Western weapons in his arsenals.[81]

In 1865, he purchased a factory in Shanghai and boasted that it was a "machine of machine manufacturing", which can make various kinds of machines. According to his report to the Emperor, the Chinese would be able to copy and develop whatever machines they wished without worrying about foreign interruptions. However, he particularly mentioned in his report that for the time being, it would primarily be used to make weapons. After integrating it into his existing arsenals in Shanghai, he called it the General Bureau of Jiangnan Manufactory, which became the biggest military industry of China in the 1860s.[82] About the same time, he moved the Suzhou arsenal to Nanjing and renamed it the Bureau of Jinling Manufactory. It was also greatly expanded. Two years later, a factory similar to the Jiangnan Manufactory was set up in Tianjin near Beijing. It also came under his control in 1870 when he was appointed the Viceroy of Zhili.[83] Since then, many arsenals of different size were built up in provincial capitals. Some of them not only produced weapons and ammunition, but also warships and steamships. The Fuzhou Bureau of Shipyard, for example, built by Zuo Zongtang, the Viceroy of Minzhe, in 1866, was the biggest shipyard in modern China for many years.[84]

As mentioned earlier in this chapter, military industry was one of the major pillars of the *Yangwu* movement in the 1860s. While the *Yangwu* movement was completely discredited in the wake of China's defeat in the Sino-Japanese War of 1894 and the Allied Expeditions of 1901, the military industry was not abandoned with it. On the contrary, it became the foundation of Chinese industrial modernization by transforming part of its capacities to produce goods such as steamships or machines for other industries.

(c) *Strengthening the Maritime Defense and the Establishment of the Navy:* Since he was sent to reinforce Shanghai by Zeng Guofan in 1862, the development of his career thereafter showed two consistent trends. First of all, most of the time he worked in the maritime area or close to it. Secondly, he had more opportunity than other leaders of China to deal with Westerners, governmental representatives and civilians. These facts not only earned him a reputation as a *Yangwu* expert, but also an advocate of maritime defence at the expense of other parts of the country.

His national defence strategy and the theories behind it are revealed in his memorial to the throne on the issue of Maritime Defence and his comment on the memorial of the *Zongli Yamen* to the throne on the national strategies in 1874.

Li's basic theory of national defence is that "the ocean people respect power not reason. While China is weak but wished to convince them with reason, it would not work. Therefore, it should strengthen its military force."[85] According to Li, the enemy of China in the 19th century was different from her traditional adversaries, who were from the northwest. While China has national borders to separate it from its neighbours in the northwest area, there are ten thousand Li of ocean to the East and Southeast; any ocean people can arrive by ship. If China cannot protect her coastline from foreign invasion, she would be immediately in danger. This is an unprece-dented circumstance that China never experienced before. Therefore, the government must take some action to deal with this new situation. It should not bind itself with traditional thinking.[86]

Li wanted the Emperor and his advisers to change their traditional thinking of border defence in the Northwest area, that is Xinjiang, in order to concentrate the nation's limited financial resourses to strengthen the maritime defence in the East.

To convince the Emperor, he argued that even when Xinjiang was at peace the country still had to spend 3 million taels of silver to run the local administration and support the garrison force annually. If the government wanted to remove the Moslem rebels from the area with armed force, it had to devote more resources to support the military action, which the country could not afford without seriously cutting off other important projects. Furthermore, while China was weak, the countries bordering Xinjiang, such as Russia, Turkey, and British India, became stronger day after day. They were all waiting for opportunities to grap this land. If China started war in Xinjiang, it might hand them an excuse to get into it, which would make the situation even worse. Consequently, he advised the Emperor to stop the armies from crossing the Yumen pass to the West and even ask them to turn back if they already went over the pass. He suggested that the army should defend the Yumen pass for the time being.[87]

Although the Emperor did not take his advice at this point and Xinjiang was restored by Zuo Zongtang after about ten years' fighting without inter-vention from the Russians and British. However, his maritime defence strategy was accepted by the government.

In designing his maritime defence system, Li believed that China is a continental country, and it does not have a naval power strong enough to match the foreign navies. Therefore, it should primarily rely on its army to defend the coastline and harbour areas assisted by some naval ships in order to block the enemy navy from landing. Based on this concept, he suggested a two-fold strategy. First, harbour and strategic areas should be protected by stationary troops with strongly fortified position, gunboats, and torpedo installations. Second, a strong maneuverable army group and ocean-going fleet should be set up and ready to take attack against any landing enemies in time.[88]

To meet the needs of the first strategy, Li suggested that Garrison Battalions be organized in the strategic harbour and coast areas. Meanwhile, he proposed the establishment of three fleets known as the Beiyang (North Ocean), Nanyang (South Ocean), and Dongyang (East Ocean) fleets.[89]

In the following 20 years, the Imperial government basically carried out Li's maritime defence strategies. On the eve of the Sino-Japanese War of 1894, Li Hongzhang reviewed the Beiyang and Nanyang fleets and found that they were in satisfactory condition. However, only four months later, when they met the Japanese navy at sea, they were almost completely destroyed within a few weeks.

Many different reasons have been given for China's defeat in the war. However, from a military point of view, the basic reason may be that Li and his maritime defence strategy paid too much attention to weapons and missed the essence or spirit of the Western military system. As Mr. Song Yuren, the author of *A Study of Current Affairs*, commented prior to the war on Li's policy that "they (the Yangwu experts) only copied the Western weapons but did not learn their fundamental principles or method in arranging maritime defence. Consequently, they have exhausted almost all of the country's resources but failed to achieve their goals--to be prosperous and strong."[90]

(d) *The Beginning of a Modern Military Education System--the Establishment of a Military Academy:* If Song Yuren's comment on learning the Western military system is correct, Li Hongzhang did not totally ignore the essence of Western military systems. He actually advised the Emperor to change the traditional examination system in recruiting military officers. Instead of testing archery and horsemanship, he quoted other leaders' proposals and suggested new subjects such as firearms, Western arts of war, *yangwu*, etc.[91]

In 1872, China began to send students to Western countries to learn technologies of manufacturing and operating warships and firearms. In the memorial to the throne on the appointment of the returned military officers, Li further analyzed the difference between China and the Western countries in selecting military officers. He suggested adopting the Western method in order to improve the Chinese system. As he wrote:

> Although the arts of using military force in both of China and
> the Western countries are similar, the methods of selecting
> military officers are quite different. While China chooses its

officers from those who have passed the test of operations in the field, the Western countries, however, cultivate their officers in military schools.[92]

Based on this understanding Li Hongzhang started to set up military schools in Tianjin of Zhili under his supervision. As mentioned earlier, Zuo Zongtang established a Bureau of Shipyard in Fuzhou in 1866, under which a school was set up to train engineers. This would be the first of these kinds of schools in China. Li Hongzhang established his Naval Academy in 1881. A year later, he set up a Naval School of Machinary and offered new courses such as astronomy, geography, physics, mathematics, and survey and mapping. In 1885, he set up an Army Academy. To encourage students to enrol in these schools, he even asked the Emperor to grant them the privilege of taking the civil servant examination at the provincial level in 1887.[93] Since then China began to train her officers in modern military schools. However, it is still too early to think that the graduates of these schools would be able to have a revolutionary effect on the Chinese military modernization in the coming decade, because the conservative forces in the military establishment were still standing in their way and were not ready to give up their positions in the armed forces.

The *Yangwu* movement and Li Hongzhang's personal political career were badly damaged by the defeat in the Sino-Japanese War of 1894 and the Allied Expedition of 1900, but Li's effect on the Chinese military modernization cannot be totally discredited. His over-emphasis on weapon modernization without matching it with the necessary reforms of the whole military system should be partly blamed on Chinese society in general for its lack of understanding the essence of modernization and the conservative bureaucrats in particular for their strong opposition to reforms.

C. Zuo Zongtang's Military Thought

Zuo Zongtang was a Hunanese and a holder of the *Juren* (the second highest degree). He had served for eight years as a military adviser to the *Xunfu* of his home province before joining Zeng Guofan in 1860. With his experience and good reputation, Zuo was immediately put in charge of an army unit, which was known as Chujun, and was sent to fight the Taiping in Jiangxi Province. After winning a series of campaigns, he was assigned to head the military force and, later, appointed as the *Xunfu* of Zhejiang Province in 1862. He was further promoted in 1864 to the viceroy of Min-Zhe (Fujian and Zhejiang provinces).

After the victorious conclusion of the campaign against the Taiping Army in 1864, he initiated a coastal defence project and a military industry plan. Nevertheless, before completing this task, he was given the viceroyship of Shaangan (Shaanxi and Gansu provinces) in 1865, and assigned to suppress the Moslem rebellion there. Zuo not only crushed the rebels and restored the local order, but captured Xinjiang in 1877 and integrated it into China as a province later.

His military career in Northwest China made his military thought different from Li Hongzhang. He not only pushed for a powerful maritime defense project but also strongly argued against Li and others who suggested giving up Xinjiang in order to strengthen the maritime defence. Zuo insisted on a more balanced policy of national defence and advocated an aggressive strategy in dealing with the Russian and British intrusions in Xinjiang. His stubborn attitude and careful preparation won the support of the Emperor and won back the strategic area of Yili in Xinjiang from the occupation of the Russians without drawing the country into a war with Russia.

(a) *Maritime Defense and the Establishment of Modern Shipbuilding Industry:* In 1866 before he moved from the Viceroyalty of Minzhe to the Viceroyalty of Shaangan, he sent a memorial to the throne about his shipbuilding project. Though he emphasized the economic and financial objects of his project, it was in fact a military industrial plan. He told the Emperor that "if we want to avoid the disadvantage but reap the advantage of the ocean, the only way is to reenforce our waterforce; but to build a waterforce, we have to build up a shipyard in order to manufacture steamships."[94]

When he realized that the Japanese might have steamboats within a few years, he started to worry about it. If China does not catch up as soon as possible, one day when she has to compete with Japan on the ocean, "while they have the means, the Chinese would have nothing. It would be like crossing a river while others are rowing in a boat, we are making a raft; it would also be like racing on a donkey against people who are riding horses."[95]

With the help of two French officers, d'Aiguebelle and Giquel, Fuzhou Shipyard was built under the direction of Shen Baozhen, a trustee of Zuo. By 1874, in addition to the docks, yards and workshops used for shipbuilding, it also operated an arms and ammunition factory, metalworks producing laminated iron, a translation department, and a school in which French, English, mathematics, drawing and navigation were taught. Two thousand Chinese and fifty foreigners were employed there.[96] It became one of the four biggest arsenals in China. Due to the successful establishment of the Fuzhou arsenal, the Chinese naval force particularly in the Fujian coastal area was reenforced with its production. However, Zuo's strategic perspective of national defence was not limited to this achievement, nor he was totally occupied by the maritime defence. His involvement in suppressing the Moslem rebellion in Xinjiang area gave him a fresh outlook about the potential dangers to Chinese national defence and, thus, he promptly shifted his attention to the priority of inland defence.

(b) *Moslem Rebellion and Its Effect on Zuo's Military Thought:*
Many Chinese emperors in different dynasties had campaigned in the Xinjiang
area. Some were successful after paying a heavy price, while others failed
miserably. The operation itself was difficult to accomplish, even when the
empire was powerful and prosperous. A weak and corrupt regime, the Qing
Government, after being repeatedly defeated by the Western countries and
shaken by the Taiping and Nian rebellions, was not in the position to initiate
a military expedition there. This is why Li Hongzhang suggested bolting his
expedition. In early 1875, when the Campaign of Suppressing Moslem
Rebellions in Gansu and Shaanxi was victoriously concluded, and the Qing
government was ready to send its army to recover Xinjiang from the Russian
supported Moslem rebels, a debate on the priority of strengthening maritime
defence or recoving the Northwest territory among the government was still
going on. Li Hongzhang was the leading figure insisting that the country
should withdraw its army from the west of Yumen Pass and take a defensive
position behind it in order to save the financial resources for strengthening the
maritime defence installations.

When the Emperor asked for his advice on this issue, Zuo strongly
opposed Li's opinion and suggested that the Emperor should stand firm in his
decision of recovering Xinjiang. His argument was that the Western countries
were primarily interested in trade. As long as China permits them to trade,
they would not cause any serious problems. However, the Russians and even
some British in India were trying to grab Chinese territory in Xinjiang. In
addition, after the successful completion of the Fuzhou Shipbuilding Yard,
with the current budget it would be enough to maintain its productivity in
order to strengthen the maritime defence force. It needs no extra money to
expand the defence installations, nor is there any urgent need to stop and
withdraw the Expedition Force in Xinjiang in order to transfer its budget for
the use of maritime defence.[97] His most important point, however, is that if
China abandons the Campaign of Recovering Xinjiang, it would lose all of the
strategic points that are vital in national defence. He wrote:

> If we take a defensive position behind Yumen Pass and no
> longer try to recover Wuyuan, there would be no strategic
> point that can be used to defend the country. . .If so, not only
> the Longyou region would be endangered, even the north of
> Tianshan Mountain such as Kebuduo and Wuliyasutai etc.
> would also fall prey to the enemy. Consequently, I am afraid
> that while we may not be able to benefit from strengthening our
> maritime installations by moving the expenditures of the
> Expedition Force in the west, the border defence would be
> seriously damaged by it.[98]

The Emperor accepted his advice and appointed him as the special commissioner, the Commander-in-Chief, of the Expedition Force to recover Xinjiang in the same month.

(c) *The Supply Problems of the Expedition Force and Zuo's Solution:* During the Taiping and Nian rebellions, the campaigns were usually fought in southeast and central China, which were the most prosperous areas in China. Therefore, it was possible, if not easy, for a commander to acquire provisions at the local level. However, as far as northwest China was concerned, it was not only a war-torn area but also an extremely poverty-stricken region. Agriculture production could not even meet the minimum needs of the local people, let alone those of an army such as Zuo's, which totalled several hundred thousand men.[99]

An old popular Chinese maxim said: food and fodder should go before troops and horses. As Zuo knew that he could not expect to get supply for his army from the war-torn areas and, thus, he had to keep an almost ten thousand kilometres of supply line without modern highway and railroads in order to guarantee the flow of supplies. This reality had a tremendous effect on his military strategy during the expedition.

Zuo started to set up a supply system in 1866. First, he established five rear service centres in China proper from southeast to northwest around the country (they were Shanghai in Jiangsu, Tianjin in Hepei, Finzhou in Shanxi, Boning, and Shunqin in Sichuan), from where provisions, weapons and other equipment were purchased and transported to the war areas. Major army service stations close to or in the war zones such as Xian in Shaanxi, Tianshui in Gansu were set up to accept materials shipped out from the rear service centres and to supply the forces at the front by stretcher teams, carts, and camels crossing another thousand kelometers of desert area. Between the major army service stations and the rear service centres, there were one to several intermediate stations to transfer the materials. Hankou, for example, served as a rear grain distribution centre of the Shaangan front, from which supplies were shipped to Xian following different roads.[100] With such a supply system, Zuo was able to maintain the supply flow without any interruption.

Opening Wasteland with Stationed Troops: In addition to setting up supply lines from maritime areas, Zuo Zongtang even picked up an old strategy to help him solve military supply problems. He ordered his army to open wasteland in their garrison locations in order to produce grain for their own needs. This strategy had been used from the Han dynasty in the first and second centuries up to the late 18th century, when the Qing regime quartered its army in Xinjiang.

Opening wasteland in the border areas was primarily considered as a strategy of solving military supply problems, but it also had socio-economic and political significance. Instead of stationing troops to open wasteland, sometimes the government gave seeds, tools, animals and lands to the peasants, and let them farm. After the harvest, the government purchased their extra grain to supply the army. This is known as *Mintun* or civilian reclaiming land. It can help the local government to pacify the local peasants and restore social order. [101]

Stationing troops to open land in the war areas, like the case in Xinjiang during the expedition, is a special strategy which may affect the combat performance of the forces and thus may cause military losses in operation. Therefore, whenever it is possible, the higher commander never hesitates to transfer their reclaimed land to the local peasants without asking for compensation. [102]

In addition, Zuo ordered his forces to repair irrigation systems, build roads, and plant trees. It is said that during the whole campaign, his army reclaimed more than 19,000 *Mu* of land, planted 568,000 trees, built 96 bridges, constructed 800 *Li* of roads, and repaired 13 irrigation and river projects. [103] These works not only allowed his Expedition to achieve victory but also helped the country to restore socio-economic and political order in the postwar period. This strategy has had a significant impact on the modern military system.

Slow Moves but Quick Decision: To adapt to the difficulty of supply, Zuo was forced to choose a special strategy. It was called *Huan Jin Su Zhan* or "slow move but quick decision in fighting". [104] In other words, Zuo's strategy was to spend as much time as necessary in preparing his military action. He would deploy his troops only after supplies were stored properly. When everything was ready, he attacked quickly at his chosen area and smashed his adversary as soon as possible. Therefore, strategically it was a protracted war, but tactically a series of quick and sure blows striking at the enemy.

To guarantee his army getting proper supply and protection in movement, he moved his force forward step by step in accordance with the preparation of supplies. He wrote:

Before the first group starts to move from Suzhou to Yumen, enough food and fodder must be transported from Ganchuan and Liangzhou to Yumen. When the first group arrives in Yumen, they should pick up the necessary supplies with their own camels and carts and move further to Anxi. . .Other groups would move forward following the same procedure. All army groups would take a break in Anxi and then march to Hami carrying their own foods. The whole army would move forward like this, group after group and step by step in order to save the energy of the soldiers and animals, and to keep the army morale always fresh. This would likely enable us to avoid any serious accident. [105]

Before artillery was used extensively in war, the primary Chinese strategy of seizing a strongly fortified position was to besiege it and cut off enemy supplies for months and years in order to starve it, and thus force it to fight out of its forts. This protracted surround strategy was extensively used in the campaigns against the Taiping army by Zeng Guofan. For example, in seizing Nanjing, the Capital City of Taiping, Zeng Guochuan quartered about 50,000 soliders around the fortified city for more than two years before he could take it in 1864 when the Taiping army was forced to break the siege.

If a similar tactic had been used by Zuo in the Expedition campaign, it could have been a disaster in terms of supply. So, he adopted a tactic of quick decision in each battle.

A tactic of coordinated action by various army units in operation was a significant method to fulfil the quick decision in the whole expedition. Zuo often concentrated his artillery and cavalry to the major front taking coordinated actions with the infantry. Night action and surprise attack were typical tactics applied in the decisive battles.

Artillery was extensively used in modern war in China by the so-called Ever-Victorious Army against the Taiping Army. The Xiangjun adopted it later. However, none of the Chinese forces had used it so much in operation that it became a significant new tactics in China later. A typical tactic used by Zuo's army in seizing fortified positions was to move their cannons ahead under the cover of dark and take positions close enough to bombard the fort before dawn. A surprise attack with infantry followed the bombardment by the artillery of the enemy defence installation. The infantry in many cases was able to run into the destroyed forts without serious casualties. [106]

The coordinated action in operation and the extensive use of artillery in attack greatly reduced the time of battle and the whole campaign of the expedition. According to Lu Fungge, Zuo spent almost six years preparing for the expedition in Xinjiang, but it only took him one and half years to complete his operation in recovering the whole Xinjiang except Yili which was occupied by the Russians and was returned to China after long negotiations. [107]

As one of the prominent military leaders during the so-called Tongzhi Restoration, Zuo's contributions to Chinese military modernization can match those of Li Hongzhang. For example, he set up the shipbuilding yard and arsenal industries in Fuzhou and Lanzhou. His military strategy and tactics in the expeditions were more significant than those of other leaders of his time. According to Lu Fungge, his supply system and front army group organization are close to the latest systems used by the Germans in the Prussian-Austrian War of 1866. However, to Lu, Zuo did not copy the German system but initiated it by himself. [108]

In addition, his project of opening wasteland with the armed forces and civilians, and other projects in helping restore local socio-economic order are more than a military strategy in solving supply problems. They had a longterm effect on regional economic and political development.

4. Yuan Shikai and the New Chinese Military System

After the close of the campaign against the Nian rebellion in the mid-1860s, Li Hongzhang and his Huaijun dominated the Chinese military scene for about 30 years until it was badly defeated and almost completely destroyed in the Sino-Japanese War of 1894. In the wake of this defeat, both government and public opinion held that China should totally abandon her old military system and build a new one based on Western methods. Encouraged by public opinion, Yuan Shikai, like many other people, submitted a proposal for building a new army to the government.

Yuan Shikai was different from Zeng, Li, and Zuo; he did not hold any degree, and thus, was not a traditional Confucian scholar-bureaucrat. Nevertheless, he was not an uneducated person either. Due to the connections of his late grand uncle, he was offered a job in Huaijun in 1880 and was later assigned to Korea with the Chinese army. When his military leader was called back two years later, Yuan succeeded him and became the head of the Qing army in Korea. He earned his reputation as a able man there. Partly due to his relationship with Huaijun, he got the strong support of Li Hongzhang. After an interview with Rong Lu, a powerful member of the Military Council (*Junji Chu*), he was groomed to head the training of the new army in Xiaozhan near Tianjin in Hebei Province. In his first report to the Superintendent (*Duban*) of the newly established army, Yuan wrote: "Although the reason of our defeat could be partly attributed to the mistakes of commanding, it was primarily due to the weakness of our military system. If we do not make thorough changes and adopt the Western method of training our army, I am afraid that the previous experience of defeat may happen again in the future."[109]

In his proposal, Yuan suggested that if China decided to use the Western training method, it would also have to adopt the Western military organization, otherwise, it could not work properly in war time. According to his understanding, the division (Finjun) in the West was the largest army unit, which included 12,000 infantry soldiers and an extra artillery unit, a cavalry unit, and an engineering unit.

However, at the initial stage, he made allowance for the country's financial hardships, and thus, only organized a unit of 7,000 people, which included five infantry battalions, one artillery battalion, one cavalry battalion, and one engineering battalion. Each of the infantry and artillery battalions had 1000 soldiers, while the cavalry and engineering battalions only had 500. After this initial stage, the newly established army unit was expanded to five units within three years and was named *Wuwei jun*. Each unit had only about 10,000 people. Yuan was appointed to lead the Right Army (*Yujun*). Of these five armies, only Yuan's Right Army was carefully recruited and trained; the other units were either transferred from the old army units or recruited from various sources without proper training. Consequently, Yuan's army was the only real elite unit at that time.

When *Wuwei jun* was destroyed in the invasion of the Allied Force in 1900 following the Boxer Rebellion, Yuan's Right Army was saved, because it was deployed to defend Shandong Province and thus, was far away from the centre of the crisis.

Li Hongzhang's death and his control of the best army in China easily propelled Yuan to the most powerful position, the Viceroy of Zhili (Hebei) and the Minister of Beiyang. His army was then moved back to Xiaozhan. After the signing of the Peace Protocal of 1901, he started his New Army build-up work again. Yuan not only had the necessary power to do whatever he wished, but also got a better idea about the modern military system. Consequently, the new army system set up by Yuan in the first decade of the 20th century was relatively close to the current Western system. It has been seen as the basis of the modern Chinese military system.

In 1895, Yuan decided to follow the German model of military organization, and hired quite a few German instructors to help him train his forces. In 1901, however, he switched to the British system, and the reorganization of the army showed the following characteristics:

A. Standing Army and the Reserve Forces

A standing army is an army maintained on a permanent organizational basis in peacetime as well as in time of war. A reserve force means that men or units in the armed forces are not on active duty but subject to call up.

In ancient China, under the system of *Bingnong Heyi* or *Yubing Yunong*, the armed forces were combined with the peasants. Every peasant was automatically listed as a reserve unless he was on active duty, physically unfit, or too old. [110]

However, this system has long been abandoned in China. There was no reserve system during the Qing dynasty; all armed forces under the Banner system were standing army as mentioned in the earlier section. In accepting the modern Western military system, Yuan decided to establish both a standing army and a reserve force. Although the reserve force was not actually established at that time, the idea was still valuable in the development of modern Chinese military modernization.

(a) *The Standing Army:* Under Yuan's new army system, the highest combat organization of the standing army was an "Army" which included two divisions (*Zhen*). Each division had two infantry brigades (*Xie*), one calvary regiment, one artillery regiment, one engineering battalion, and one service battalion. Each brigade included two regiments (*Biao*); each regiment, three battalions (*Ying*); each battalion, four companies (*Lian*); each company, three platoons (*Pai*); and each platoon, three squads (*Pong*). The calvary regiment was similar to the infantry, the only difference being that each platoon included only two squads.

The artillery regiment consisted of three battalions; each battalion, three companies; each company, three platoons; each platoon, three squads.

The engineering battalion consisted of three companies; each company, three platoons; each platoon, three squads.

The service battalion consisted of four companies; each company, two platoons; each platoon, three squads.

In all units, each squad consisted of 14 soldiers which included four firstclass privates, eight secondclass privates, and one leader and one vice-leader. There were 12,512 soldiers in each division, which included 748 officers and clerks, 10,436 combat soldiers, and 1,328 non-combant workers.[111]

This system was later adopted by almost all provinces which decided to organize their own new army. It was occasionally changed slightly in individual areas in order to adapt to their particular situation. However, the system as a whole was kept intact for several decades until the 1930's, when China was preparing to confront the Japanese. However, even at that time, the changes were minimal.

(b) *The Reserve Force (Xubei jun):* Under Yuan's new army system, the soldiers of the Standing Army were supposed to be discharged after three years on active service. When they became civilians, they were supposed to be still paid in part and registered as members of the Reserve Force, and were subject to call for active duty in times of war. The government would appoint an officer to lead the reserve force in areas where there were a hundred or more members. Once a year, they would be called up to receive a month of military training. This was called firstclass reserve force or *Xubei jun*.

After three years in the Reserve Force, a soldier would then be registered in the Secondclass Reserve Force (*Houbei jun*); he would be paid 50 percent of the wages of members of the firstclass reserve force and he would be called to receive a month of training every other year. After finishing four years in the secondclass reserve force, he would be once again discharged and no longer be recalled for any training. However, he would be still subject to call up in time of war until he was 45 years old,when he would be permanently relieved from any military obligations.[112]

The modern European military system is based on conscription by which every qualified male citizen is obligated to serve in the armed forces for a certain number of years. After active service, soldiers are discharged and automatically put on the list of reserves. However, in China, there was no conscription law under the Qing Empire. Yuan's New Army was still based on the volunteer system. Soldiers were not necessarily discharged after three years in active service. Therefore, there was no basis for a reserve system at that time.

B. Officer Corps and Officer Education

Following the organizational change of the army, the officer hierarchy also changed. Before the 1901 reformation, the military officer hierarchy was not clearly defined. Under the New Army system, Yuan reclassified the officers into three classes; each class was further divided into three ranks. The total officer corps thus consisted of nine ranks. The top class was the equivalent of modern generals, and included the ranks of general, lieutenant general, and major general; the second class was the same as modern colonels, and included the ranks of colonel, lieutenant colonel, and major; the third class was the equivalent of the modern lieutenants, and included the ranks of captain, first lieutenant, and second lieutenant. [113]

From 1880, Zuo Zongtang, Li Hongzhang and many other leaders started to establish military schools in their jurisdictions. Because these schools were usually attached to particular military units, the cadets were usually assigned to the same units after finishing their training. However, due to the uncooperative attitude of the senior officers, who knew nothing about modern Western military training and weapons, the graduates were not given any commanding appointment, but relegated to inconsequential positions. In operation, it was still the old officers taking command. Therefore, the newly graduated officers were not able to change the Chinese armed forces in accordance with the Western system they learned in school. [114]

When Yuan assumed the Zhili viceroyship and began using Western training methods again, he set up a military academy in Baoding of Hebei Province, which included three tiers of training: lower, intermediate, and higher classes. Each level of education lasted for four years. The Baoding Military Academy was better organized and set a model for the modern Chinese military education system. It educated the first generation of modern Chinese military officers who dominated the Chinese military and political scene in the coming decades. [115]

C. The Staff Organization

In ancient China, the high commanders always had some kind of staff to give them advice. However, there was no regular organization or clearly defined functions in these staffs. When Yuan was appointed to train the New Army in Xiaozhan in 1895, he began to set up various staff systems with clearly defined functions. They were further developed in 1901 when he assumed the viceroyship of Zhili and the Ministership of Beiyang.

The staffs in the Headquarters of Military Training Centre (*Lian Bing Chu*) were known as the Office of Military Affairs (*Junwuchu*). It was divided into three sections: the Departments of Staff, Education, and Armament. The first branch was in charge of operations planning; the second, training; and the third, weapons, equipment and supplies. Two years later, the staff organizations were further changed and renamed the Military Command (*Jun Ling*), Military Education (*Jun Xue*), and Military Administration (*Jun Zheng*). Since then it was accepted as a standard system and was adopted by the central government and other regional military forces.

By modern stardards, Yuan's staff organization may not be well differentiated yet; however, it was probably the first such organization in Chinese military history.[116]

D. The Military Police Force

Since the signing of the Protocol of 1901 with the Allied Forces, China was not allowed to deploy military forces in Tianjin. To meet this requirement and maintain local order, Yuan transformed part of his armed forces into a police force so that they could remain in Tianjin without violating the protocal. It turned out to be a good idea. Many provinces followed Yuan's model and set up their own police forces. The program was later adopted by the central government, and a ministry of police was set up to head the national police force in 1905.

The military police, however, was established later than the civil police force. It was probably set up in 1908 based on the Experimental Regulation of Military Police Forces issued by the Ministry of the Army.[117] Although there is no evidence to show that this was also Yuan's idea, it is, however, likely related to his idea of civil police forces.

E. The Publication of Army Training Manuals

Although Yuan's primary contribution to Chinese military modernization was to introduce Western military systems to China, it is not, however, limited to this aspect. As the leader responsible for training the New Army, he presided over the writing of training manuals, rules and regulations. *A six-volume Record of Military Scheme of the Newly Established Army (Xinjian Lujun Binglue Lucun)* and a twelve-volume *Minute Description and Illustration of Training Manuals (Xunlian Caofa Xiangxi Tushuo)* were published separately in 1898 and 1899.

Both of those works consist of the general rules, prohibitions, precepts, and the rules for military drills. The latter further introduces the methods of searching and caption of march, offence and defence in different terrain, and the use of artillery, cavalry and military engineering units in operation.

Generally speaking, these books have absorbed the essence of the Western military training manuals in general and the German training method in particular. Of course, these publications also represent Yuan's personal military thought.[118]

In the *Minute Description and Illustration of Training Manuals*, Yuan showed two important guiding philosophies which inevitably affected the political attitude of his forces in the future. First of all, he emphasized the importance of political training. Soldiers were taught to be loyal and righteous to the Emperor. As he wrote in the Essentials of Training:

> Your ancestors. . .have received benefits from the country, none of it was not granted by the royal court. Even if you were not a soldier you should still try to repay the kindness of the Emperor. As a soldier you are paid with high salaries, how can you face your father and grandfather, if you do not pay your loyalty to the Emperor?[119]

Since loyalty and righteousness are paid to the royal court or Emperor and not to the country or nation, they could be easily transferred to Yuan personally under the regional military force, which requires the soldiers to accept orders only from their immediate commander, who recruited them. This tendency was strengthened by his belief that the traditional ethics of father and son, and master and attendant, should apply to the relationship between officers and their soldiers.[120]

The second guiding philosophy in his training manuals is utilitarianism. He encouraged his soldiers to work hard to earn promotions and higher salaries. As he wrote in the same context: "There are no barriers for you to be promoted to higher ranks and to get higher pay step by step; they can be reached easily." "Since ancient times, many generals and prime ministers have been privates." "If you are lucky in fighting and come back safely, you would be automatically promoted."[121]

From these quotations above, one is likely to find that the two guiding doctrines may not be always consistent with each other. While the soldiers are encouraged with utilitarianism to pursue personal interests, they may ignore the ethics of loyalism and righteousness and thus become warlords and bandits. This may be part of the reason for the long turbulence and wars among the warlords after the overthrow of the Qing Emperor.

Yuan was a controversial personality in modern Chinese history. He can be blamed for betraying the Republicans and trying to restore the monarchy in China, and for the warlord fighting that splintered the country after his death. Although Yuan did not have any great experience of war and thus did not leave any grand theory of strategies and tactics, it is clear that as a talented organizer, he had gone a big step further than Zeng, Li, and Zuo in modernizing the Chinese military organization and training methods.

5. Conclusion

The Chinese spent more than half a century to modernize their armed forces but did not go through the modernization of weapons and the organization until the first decade of the 20th century. While part of the delay could be blamed on the corrupt Qing political system and the conservative social forces, the overemphasis on weapon system and technological improvement among the military leaders without referring to organizational change and other socio-political coordinative reforms are primarily responsible for this delay. Yuan Shikai was the first man in modern China who carried out a systematic reform of the military system and its training manual. Though it was primarily copied from the Western countries, particularly the German system, it, however, opened a new era for the Chinese military system. The way for further change was now totally clear. No one wanted to restore the traditional system, nor did anyone try to stop further adoption of the Western system. The following stage of Chinese military modernization should logically begin to develop a set of strategy and tactics which might be better adapted to the Chinese reality if there were no interruptions.

Although the Chinese leaders were blamed for their overemphasis on technology and weapon modernization without paying enough attention to socio-political and organizational reforms, their costly investment in military industry cannot be totally ignored. If they had not done so, the industrialization of China might have been postponed for several decades, because there was no individual entrepreneur who could organize enough capital and talent to start modern industry and, above all, military industries at that time. For this reason, Dr. Sun Yatsen, the leader of the revolution and founder of the Republic of China, still advocated public investment and the leading role of government in key industries, which were either too expensive for any individual businessman to operate or too important to the public interest to be left to the private business sector. [122]

The state ownership and public investment in key industry was later inherited by the Guomintang regime after China was reunified in the 1930s. The government still controlled the development of arsenals. Since the 1950s, under the Communist regime, public ownership has been the only system for all enterprises. Although the open door policy has recently permitted individuals to operate small enterprises, there is no indication to show that the government is going to allow the private operation of military industry. As a matter of fact, in the past 40 years, no matter how many political crises China has had, or how seriously her economic development has been interrupted, the military industry has always been firmly controlled by the Party and government without suffering political impact. Their achievement in modern weapons and high technology could not have been so impressive if the government had not taken the leadership in this field. Perhaps this achievement should be partly attributed to the initial efforts of the *Yangwu* movement.

Footnotes

1. Lei, Bailun, *Chinese Culture and Chinese Soldier* (Taipei: Wanniangin, 1971), p. 126.

2. Wang, Ermin, *The Collection of Studies of Military History of Qing Dynasty* (Hong Kong: Luanyu Press, 1979), p. 3.

3. Hu Sheng, *From Opium War to May 4th Movement* (Beijing: People's Press, 1980), pp. 3-5. (Hereafter referred to as Opium War to May 4th.)

4. The figures are taken from Hu Sheng's *Opium War to May 4th*, p. 11, and Dun J. Li, *The Ageless Chinese: A History* (New York: Charles Scribner's Sons, 1971), p. 325.

5. Mu, Anshi, *The Opium War* (Shanghai: People's Press, 1982), p. 90.

6. *Ibid*.

7. Wang, Tongling, *Chinese History* (Taipei: Qiming, 1960), Vol. 2, Part 4, pp. 263-64.

8. *Ibid*.

9. *Ibid.*, p. 416.

10. *Ibid.*, pp. 416-17.

11. Chen-ya Tien, *The Mass Militia and Chinese Modernization* (Toronto: Mosaic, 1983), pp. 32-34. A brief discussion on this subject is available.

12. Wen, Gongzhi, *The Chinese Military History of the Last Thirty Years* (Taipei: Wenhai, 1971), pp. 3-8. (Hereafter referred to as *History of Last 30 Years*.)

13. Hu, Sheng, *Opium War to May 4th, op. cit.*, Vol. 1, p. 268.

14. Wen, Gongzhi, *History of the Last 30 Years, op. cit.*, pp. 4-9.

15. Wang, Tongling, *Chinese History, op. cit.*, Vol. 2, Part 4, p. 307.

16. Wen, Gongzhi, *History of the Last 30 Years, op. cit.*, p. 4.

17. *Ibid.*, p. 10.

18. *Ibid*.

19. J.F.C. Fuller, *War and Western Civilization 1832-1932* (London: Duckwork, 1932), p. 97.

20. Zhang, Yutian, et al, *Modern Chinese Military History* (Shengyang: Liaoning Renmin Press, 1983), it shows in 1850s when Xiangjun was organized, it was equipped with traditional weapons only. Since 1861, Zeng Guofan started to set up his first factory in Anqing to try to make new weapons. From 1865 to 1885, new military industries were built up over the country. It was said that 15 factories were in operation. Therefore, new weapons were available to the Chinese army in the 1880s. pp. 228-254.

21. Mu, Anshi, *The Opium War, op. cit.*, pp. 93-4.

22.   *Ibid.*
23.   *Ibid.*
24.   *Ibid.*, pp. 3-21. Each box is 100 to 120 Jin, or 133.3 to 159.96 pounds.
25.   *Ibid.*, pp. 35-36.
26.   Jean Chesneaux, et al., *China -- From Opium Wars to the 1911 Revolution* (New York: Pantheon, 1976), pp. 62-62.
27.   Mu, Anshi, *The Opium War, op. cit.*, pp. 196-224.
28.   Lin, Zexu, *Political Writing of Lin Wenzhong Gong*, Vol 2, Ch. 5, in The Works of Lin Wenzhong Gong (Taipei: Deszhi, 1963), p. 145.
29.   *Ibid.*, Ch. 4.
30.   When he was the Viceroy of Hu-Guang, he bought more than one third of the coast guns installed in Humei fort area. See Feng, Youlan, "The Opium War and Lin Zexu," *The Essays of Modern Chinese History of Thought* (Shanghai: People's Press, 1958), p.8. (Hereafter referred to as *Essays of Thought*.)
31.   Lin, Zexu, "A Public Announcement to the People about the Possible Invasion of the British Forces," quoted in "The Opium War and Lin Zexu," by Feng Youlan, in *Essays of Thought, op. cit.*, p. 7.
32.   Idem, *The Political Writing of Lin Wenzhong Gong*, Vol. 2, Chapt. 4, "A Secret Investigation Report about the Situation of the British Forces in the Occupied Dinghai City." Quoted in Feng Youlan's "The Opium War and Lin Zexu," *op. cit.*, p. 7.
33.   *Ibid.*, pp. 7-8.
34.   It was said that when Captain P. Anstruther, accompanied by his servant, was climbing a hill, a peasant with a hoe in hand followed them and hit the servant to death in a raid; when the captain ran into the nearby valley, the local peasants beat gongs and drums to call for the masses to help. The peasants surrounded the valley and eventually captured him. See Mu, Anshi, *The Opium War, op. cit.*, p. 191.
35.   *Ibid.*, pp. 234-238.
36.   On May 29, 1841, the local people held a meeting and decided to work together to protect themselves, but no date was set up. However, after a fight occured on the same day, there was almost a 20,000 strong peasant army available on May 30. See Ibid., pp.240-42.
37.   *Ibid.*, p. 239.
38.   C.P. Fitzgerald, *The Birth of Communist China* (New York: A Pelican Book, 1964), Ch. 1, pp. 16-42.
39.   Lei, Bailun, "A Culture Without Soldier," in *The Chinese Culture and Chinese Soldier, op. cit.*, pp. 138-142.
40.   Mu, Anshi, *The Opium War, op. cit.*, p. 243.
41.   *Ibid.*, p. 240.
42.   Sunzi (Sun Tzu), *Arts of War*, trans. with an introduction by Samuel B. Griffith (London: Oxford Univ., 1971), Ch. 6, p. 96.

43. Wei, Yuan, "The Overall Planning of the Coast Defense (3)," ed. by Shi, Jun, *Reference Materials of Modern Chinese History of Thought* (Beijing: Sanlian, 1957), Vol. 1, p. 46. (Hereafter referred to as *Reference of History of Thought*.)

44. Idem, "The Overall Planning of the Coast Defense (1), in Shi, Jun's *Reference of History of Thought, op. cit.*, Vol. 1, pp. 34-35.

45. *Ibid.*

46. Feng, Guifen, "A Discussion on Learning the Technology of Making Foreign Weapons," in Shi Jun's *Reference of History of Thought, op. cit.*, Vol 1, p. 141.

47. Feng, Youlan, "The Thought of Wei Yuan," in *The Essays of Modern Chinese History of Thought* (Shanghai: Renmin, 1958), p. 17.

48. Feng, Guifen, "A Discussion on Learning the Technology of Making Foreign Weapons," *op. cit.*, pp. 140-43.

49. Idem, "A Discussion on Adopting the Western Learning Subject," in Shi, Jun's *Reference of History of Thought, op. cit.*, Vol. 1, pp. 138-139.

50. Idem, "A Discussion on Learning the Technology of Making Foreign Weapons," *op. cit.*, p. 141.

51. These facts were confirmed by Jean Chesneaux in *China, op. cit.*, p. 165.

52. Feng, Guifen, "A Discussion on Reducing the Number of the Armed Forces," quoted from Feng Youlan's *Essays of Thought, op. cit.*, p. 33.

53. *Ibid.*, also see Feng's "A Discussion on Saving Expenditure," quoted from Feng Youlan's *Essays of Thought, op. cit.*, p. 33.

54. Idem, "A Discussion on Adopting the Western Learning Subjects," *op. cit.*, p. 139.

55. Tianjin Treaty of 1858, and Beijing Treaty of 1890.

56. Tian, Ping, "A Discussion on the Historical Functions of the Yangwu Movement," *The Essays of Modern Chinese History* (Beijing: Zhonghua, 1979), p. 1125.

57. *The Navigation of the Lapwing by Shoule*, translated by Zhang Yanshen, in *Yangwu Movement -- The Selected Materials of Modern Chinese History*, Vol. 8, pp. 382-83.

58. *Ibid.*, pp. 383-85.

59. *Ibid.*, p. 390.

60. *Ibid.*, p. 377.

61. *Ibid.*, p. 399.

62. Zhang, Yutian, *Modern Chinese Military History, op. cit.*, p. 221.

63. *Ibid.*, pp. 225-27.

64. Don J. Li, *The Ageless Chinese, op. cit.*, pp. 221-22.

65. Li, Dingfang, *Zeng Goufan and His Staffs* (Hong Kong: Yuandong, 1978), pp. 8-10.

66   A letter to brother Ran, on 22nd, Month of Twelve, Tongzhi 5 (1866), in *The System of Zeng Guofan's Words and Deeds*, ed. by Zhao Zenghui (Taipei: Lanxi, 1975), p. 296.

67.   *Ibid.*

68.   *Ibid.*

69.   *Ibid.*, p. 276.

70.   *Ibid.*, pp. 277-278

71.   *Ibid.*, p. 282, Diary.

72.   *Ibid.*, p. 283. See a letter to brother Ran.

73.   Wang, Ermin, *A Record of the Huaijun* (Hong Kong: Lianyu Press, 1979), p. 201.

74.   Li, Shoukong, *Biography of Li Hongzhang* (Taipei: Xuesheng, 1978), p. 48.

75.   *Ibid.*, pp. 48-49.

76.   A letter to brother Ran, in *The System of Zeng Guofan's words and Deeds*, op. cit., p. 296.

77.   Li, Hongzhang, "A Confidential Memorial to the Throne on Suppressing the Nian Army, 1865," *The Works of Li Wenzhong Gong (Li Hongzhang)*, 1980, Vol. 1, p. 290, in *Collections of Modern Chinese Historical Documentations*, ed. by Shen Yunlong (Taipei: Wenhai).

78.   *Ibid*, p. 289.

79.   *Ibid.*

80.   *Yiwu (Foreign Affairs) in the Tongzhi Reign*, Vol. 25, p. 1. Quoted from Hu Sheng, *Opium War to May 4th*, op. cit., Vol. 1, p. 329.

81.   Li, Hongzhang, "A Memorial to the Throne on the Soldiers from Beijing Garrison Force to Learn the Technologies of Weapon Manufacture, 1863," *Works of Li*, op. cit., Vol. 1, p. 247.

82.   Idem, "A Memorial to the Throne on Purchasing the Steel and Machine Factory, 1865," *Works of Li*, op. cit., Vol. 1, p. 322.

83.   Hu, *Opium War to May 4th*, op. cit., Vol. 1, p. 313.

84.   *Ibid.*

85.   Li, Hongzhang, "A Memorial to the Throne on the Issue of Maritime Defence," *Works of Li*, op. cit., Vol. 2, p. 828.

86.   *Ibid.*

87.   *Ibid.*, p. 832.

88.   *Ibid.*, p. 831.

89.   *Ibid.*

90.   Song, Yuren, *A Study of Current Affairs*. Quoted from Hu, *Opium War to May 4th*, op. cit., Vol. 1, p. 344.

91.   Li, Hongzhang, "A Comment on the Six Articles of the Important Matters of National Defence Submitted by *Zongli Yamen*," *Works of Li*, op. cit., p. 834.

92. Idem, "A Memorial to the Throne on the Appointment of the Returned Military Officers to Instructorships," *Works of Li, op. cit.*, Vol. 2, pp. 1126-27.

93. Idem, "A Memorial to the Throne on Granting the privilege of taking Civil Servant Exams at the Provincial Level (Xiangshi) to School Students, 1887," *Works of Li, op. cit.*, Vol. 3, p. 1783.

94. Zuo, Zongtang, "A Memorial to the Throne on His Proposal of Purchasing Machine and Hiring Foreign Engineers to Building Steamships, 1866," *The Works of Zuo Wenxiang Gong (Zuo Zongtang)* 1979, Vol. 2, p. 691, in *Collections of Modern Chinese Historical Documentations*, ed. by Shen Yunlong (Taipei: Wenhai).

95. *Ibid.*

96. Jean Chesneaux, *China, op. cit.*, p. 208.

97. Zuo, "A Memorial to the Throne on the Issue of Maritime Defence, Northwest Border Defence, and Situations of Campaign and Supply in the West of the Pass, 7th, Month of 7th, Year 7th of Tongzhi," *Works of Zuo, op. cit.*, Vol. 4, pp. 1842-45.

98. *Ibid.*, p. 1844.

99. Lu, Fungge, *A General History of the West Expedition of Zuo Wenxiang Gong* (Taipei: Wenhai, 1972). (Hereafter referred to as *West Expedition of Zuo.*) There were several figures about Zuo's force in this campaign. In Gansu and Shaanxi, there were about 120,000 soldiers. Once, in a major operation in Xinjiang, he used about 70,000 soldiers. It is quite possible that the entire size of the army used in the Shaan-Gan-Xin campaigns was more than 2000,000 strong.

100. *Ibid.*, pp. 109-114.

101. Zuo, "A Memorial to the Throne on Pacifying the Moslems and Helping Them to Open Wasteland in 1870," *Works of Zuo, op. cit.*, Vol. 3, pp. 1415-16.

102. Zuo's military reclaiming land project was an important strategy in his expedition. For example, when he sent "A Memorial to the Throne on the Army Advance Forward by Groups and the Preparation for Grain supplies," in 1874, he already firmly decided to use this strategy to solve part of the supply problems. See *Works of Zuo*, Vol. 4, pp. 1753-56.

He even instructed his front commander Zhang Langzhai in detail how to run the land reclaiming project with the armed force (See Vol. 7, pp. 3137-38). However, he realized the problems too. For example, in "A Secret Memorial to the Throne," in 1875, he explained to the Emperor that the traditional policy of quartering the soldiers in the peasantry and military reclaiming land are no longer reliable now. See Vol. 4, pp. 1847-48.

Also see "A Letter to Answer General Zhang Langzhai," *Works of Zuo*, Vol. 7, pp. 3175-76, and Zhang Jiayun, *Zuo Zongtang*, in *The Series of Strategists*, No. 4 (Taipei: Lianming Wenhua, 1981), pp. 115-16.

103. Zhang, Jiayun, *Zuo Zongtang, op. cit.*, pp. 115-116.

104. Zuo, "A Memorial to the Throne on the Campaign in Taking Dabancheng, Takesun, and Tulufan, and the Name of Casualty, Injured, Merits Recommending for Awards, on 25th, Month of 7th, the Third Year of Guangxu (1877)," *Works of Zuo, op. cit.*, Vol. 4, pp. 1997-2001.

105. Idem, "A Memorial to the Throne on a Proposal of Army Move and Supply Procedure, and on the Awards of the Staffs, on 10th, Month of 12th, the 12th Year of Tongzhi (1874), *Work of Zuo, op. cit.*, Vol. 4, p. 1757.

106. These tactics were repeatedly used in the campaigns to seize Wurumqi and Dihua. See Zuo, "A Memorial to the Throne on the Campaigns of Taking Gumudi, Wurumqi, Dihua, and Many other Fortified Cities, on 18th, Month of 7th, the 3rd Year of Guangxu," *Works of Zuo, op. cit.*, Vol. 4, pp. 1929-30. Also see "A Memorial to the Throne on the Campaigns of Taking Dabancheng, Takesun, and Tulufan, and the Name of Casualties, Injured, and Merits Recommending for Awards, on 25th, Month of 7th, the 3rd Year of Guangxu," *Works of Zuo, op. cit.*, Vol. 4, pp. 1997-2000.

107. Lu, Fungge, *West Expedition of Zuo, op. cit.*, p. 128.

108. *Ibid.*, pp. 108-128.

109. Wen, Gongzhi, *History of Last 30 Years, op. cit.*, p. 16.

110. Reference on *Yubing Yunong* and *Bingnong Heyi*, see *The Mass Militia System and Chinese Modernization*, by Chen-ya Tien, *op. cit.*, Ch. 3.

111. Wen, Gongzhi, *History of Last 30 Years, op. cit.*, pp. 40-41.

112. *Ibid.*

113. Yuan's classification named high class, middle class, and low class. Each class was further classified as 1st, 2nd and 3rd ranks; meanwhile these ranks were further matched to the traditional 9 category ranks from the 1st rank down to 7th rank (Cong Yi Pin to Zheng Qi Pin).

114. The Chinese defeat in the Sino-Japanese War was interpreted as a proper case, by Tian Buyi, see *A History of the Beiyang Warlord*, (Taipei: Chunqiu, 1967), p. 39.

115. Tao, Jiuyin, "A History of the Beiyang Warlord Governing Period," *Life, Study, and New Knowledge* (Shanghai), Vol.1, 1957, p. 16.

116. Tian, Buyi, *A History of the Beiyang Warlord, op. cit.*, pp. 99-101.

117. Wen, Gongzhi, *History of last 30 Years*, *op. cit.*, p. 44.
118. These publications and their basic contents were paraphrased from a letter of General Gao Tiqian, the Vice-President of Military Science Council of the Chinese People's Liberation Army, to the author of this book on Sept. 20, 1987.
119. *Ibid.*
120. *Ibid.*
121. *Ibid.*
122. Sun, Yatsen, *Sanmin Zhuyi* (Taipei:China Publishing), pp. 180-181.

CHAPTER 4

The Development of Military Thought in the Early Republican Period

1. Warlord Rule and the Setback of Military Modernization

Chinese military modernization suffered a temporary setback after the 1911 Revolution.

In the latter part of Empress Ci-xi's rein, Yuan Shikai had become so powerful that he had to face the suspicion and hostility of some members of the royal family and high Manchu officials. Although Yuan had voluntarily handed over part of his powers to the royal family, he was immediately removed from all positions upon the death of Empress CI-xi.

Emperor Guangxu and Empress Ci-xi both died within two days in the middle of November 1908. The nephew of Guangxu, a three year-old baby boy, Xuantong, succeeded to the throne; his father, Prince Zaifeng, became the regent and held decision-making powers. The regent was so angry about Yuan's betrayal of his brother, Emperor Guangxu, in the power struggle between Ci-xi and Guangxu in the so-called Hundred Days Reform of 1898 that he wanted to kill Yuan. He only spared Yuan's life under the pressure of some high-ranking officials. Yuan left Beijing for home, but he still kept in close contact with his former army officers. When he later reappeared on the Chinese military scene, the Manchu regime was promptly forced to give up its power to Yuan, and thus began the warlord period.

A. The Origins of the Modern Chinese Revolution

Since the defeat of China in the first Opium War, the Manchu regime had been plagued by peasant rebellions, which greatly increased in number in the last decade of the Dynasty. Xingzhonghui, the forerunner of the Guomindang founded in 1894 following the disastrous defeat of China in the Sino-Japanese War, carried out its first uprising in 1895. Among the numerous popular movements, Xingzhonghui was not the most powerful one in the beginning, but it became the most successful revolutionary organization later and eventually overthrew the Qing Dynasty.

The Xingzhonghui was primarily organized and led by the modernized Chinese intellectuals, and was initially organized outside China. This fact not only gave it the chance to mobilize support among the overseas Chinese and Westerners, but also provided protection from political persecution from the Qing Government, when it was still too weak to face the enemy.

Because the initial members were drawn from the intellectual circles, it was much easier for it to develop an exclusive political program appealing to the majority of the Chinese masses. Many other peasant rebellions without the necessary leadership from the intellectuals were often handicapped by their lack of long-term political appeal and proper organization. They were usually mobilized due to famines or economic hardship and thus were strongly motivated by economic gains. As soon as the economic situation improved, their support for the rebellion would promptly fade. Strong political programs that appeal to the society are only possible when the movements are led or joined by the intellectuals who are competent to provide political guidelines.

Furthermore, most leaders of the Xingzhonghui were not armed fighters themselves but good political organizers and agitators. This made it possible for them to organize uprisings and military actions without their personal involvement in fighting, which reduced the casualty rate of its important leaders and made it possible to continue its struggle even after repeated military defeats. Most leaders of the peasant rebellions, however, were armed fighters and were often directly involved in the military actions. The movement was often abruptly brought to an end with the death of its leader in a military campaign. The Xingzhonghui had suffered ten defeats prior to its final victory in October of 1911, but that did not destroy its revolutionary organization.[1]

Due to these organizational characteristics, the Xingzhonghui and its successor, Tongmonhui, had shown two more distinguishing features in their revolutionary campaigns against the Qing dynasty. First of all, they developed a close cooperation wtih the Chinese anti-Manchu secret societies in their early stage of military uprisings. Since the Manchus conquered China in the 17th century, many of the former Ming dynasty supporters had turned into secret societies hiding among the peasantry and working classes. In the late 19th century, although most of them already lost their political identities, they were still beyond the control of the Qing government, especially those which were located in Hong Kong and in the overseas Chinese communities. When Xingzhonghui started its anti-Manchu activities, it spared no effort seeking the support of these societies. It was said that the first military uprising led by the Xingzhonghui in 1895 consisted of three thousand men being recruited from the membership of the Sanhehui in Hong Kong. To prepare for the second uprising, the Xingzhonghui had even formed a unified organization (Xinghanhui) with the Sanhehui and Gelaohui. It was chaired by Dr. Sun Yatsen in 1899.[2] These secret societies may have been nationalistic, but they were primarily apolitical. Indeed, after the Qing dynasty was overthrown, they promptly disappeared from the political stage and no longer played any significant role in the post-revolutionary period.

Secondly, in the later stage of the revolution, Tongmonhui, the successor of Xingzhonghui, relied primarily on the support of the junior officers and soldiers of the Qing army to carry out its military campaigns. As mentioned in the last chapter, after Yuan Shikai was asked to train new armies in Xiaozhan, the government further ordered each province to organize one or two new army divisions or to reorganize their old military units based on the organizational guidelines of the new army. Though the new army units had greatly expanded, many old army units still existed on the eve of the 1911 revolution. This parallel military system complicated the situation and created tremendous conflict in the Qing military forces. However, it gave the revolutionaries a rare opportunity to recruit their force from the army itself. They recruited pro-revolutionary young officers and soldiers from both the new and old army units. This development greatly reinforced the revolutionary force for the last few uprisings.[3] Some military rebellions were actually led by them without strong support from the Tongmonhui. The last uprising, for example, carried out on October 10, 1911 in Wuchang, was completely led by these Qing officers. The revolutionary leaders took over the command much later.

While the secret societies promptly withdrew from political activity after 1911, the pro-revolution military forces were not big enough to resist Yuan's Beiyang Army. Furthermore, few of these pro-revolution officers were fervent revolutionaries. As soon as the Manchu Empire was gone, under the manipulation of Yuan Shihkai, many of them joined in the warlord fighting to further their own interests. This change left the Guomindang helpless in consolidating its power and unifying the country in the post-revolution years; it also contributed to the further dissolution of political order in China and prolonged the warlord period.

B. The Historical Background of the Warlord Period in China

In Chapter 2 of this book, Lei Bailun's work was quoted as saying that China was a country without real soldiers. He repeatedly compared Chinese soldiers with bandits. To Lei, there had been no real soldier in China since the collapse of the ancient militia system in the Han dynasty. Soldiers were often recruited from the ranks of ruffians, bandits, and hooligans, who only lent their loyalty to the generals who were able to control them. The military forces no longer belonged to the country but became a personal force. When the country was at peace and when the emperor could properly pay them, the soldiers were loyal to him. In case he failed to do so, or when the country was in a state of chaos, a few of the more ambitious generals sometimes tried to claim the throne in order to establish their own empire. Other generals became common bandits. This chaotic state would last until the country was unified again by one of the fighting generals.[4] This process may last for several decades. In such a situation, the whole society crumbles, disrupting normal economic and cultural activities. In many cases, disorder not only holds back social development, but destroys its previous achievements, and even causes regression. The Chinese situation in the 1920s was in fact a typical case of Lei's argument. The warlord fighting not only temporarily ruined the revolution and the country, but also damaged Chinese military modernization, which had been the first priority of the country for more than half a century.

During the Qing dynasty, as mentioned in the last chapter, the Banner military force was centrally controlled, when Zeng Guofan began to organize his Xiangjun. Instead of following this Manchu tradition of military centralism, he built a local army based on the principle of personal control. Li Hongzhang and Yuan Shikai also became adherents of this principle, when they started to train their own armies. Scholars have called such a force a regional military force, to distinguish it from a centrally controlled national armed force.

When Yuan was appointed to train the new army in Zhili, Zhang Zhidong, the Viceroy of Hu-Guang, had also began to train his new army in Hubei Province, which became known by three names: Ziqiangjun, Nanyangjun, and Anjun.[5] As the best units in Southern China, the Ziqiangjun shared the dominant status with the Beiyangjun in Northern China respectively. Pleased with this success in their military buildup, the Qing regime hurriedly decided to expand the new army to thirty-six Zhens (divisions) in total. To achieve this goal, the government formally requested in 1901 that the provincial authorities begin building their own military units using either the Beiyangjun or the Ziqiangjun as a model. Furthermore, in 1906, the government decreed that provincial military budgets were to be a minimum of 20 percent of the provincial revenues. Although the goal of thirty-six Zhens was not achieved, the military power of local authorities was further bolstered.[6] This increase in the military capacity of regional leaders lay the groundwork for the future warlord wars, and thereby supported Lei's theory of dynastic cycles.

C. The Warlord Fighting and the Setback of Chinese Military Modernization

After Wuchang was occupied by the revolutionaries on October 10, 1911, the Qing government immediately sent Feng Guozhang and Duan Qirui's armies to suppress the rebellion. Both Feng and Duan were Yuan Shikai's former subordinates and still kept close contact with him. On Yuan's advice, the two commanders purposely delayed moving against the rebels. Subsequently, the government was forced to ask Yuan to lead the campaign against the rebels.[7]

Yuan could have crushed the Wuchang revolution at that time if he wished to do so. But, in fact, Yuan resented his dismissal two years before, and no longer had any intention of supporting the Qing regime. Now, all he wanted was to bring down the empire and take over by himself. After several weeks of negotiating, Yuan was able to conclude a peace agreement with the revolutionaries at the expense of the Manchu throne. He was elected as the provisional president of the Republic of China in Feburary of 1912. In return, he promised to support the Republic.[8]

Yuan's acceptance of the presidency was only the first step in achieving his political ambition. He neither liked the Republic nor was satisfied with the ceremonial head position under a parliamentary system designed by the revolutionaries in Nanjing on March 11, 1912.[9] Yuan did not intend to accept any restrictions imposed on him by a cabinet or parliament. Therefore, the conflict between Yuan and the revolutionary government was fateful from the very begining.

In early 1913, the newly founded Guomindang, which integrated several political organizations into the revolutionary Tongmonhui, won a huge majority in the senate elections. Song Jiaoren, the most enthusiastic supporter of parliamentary system and the actual leader of the Party, would probably be elected as the prime minister. However, Song was assassinated in Shanghai when he was leaving for Beijing on March 20, 1913. After it became clear that Yuan had been behind the assassination plot, he was left with no alternative but to eliminate the revolutionary opposition by force. The Guomindang was forced to fight in July 1913. This is now known as the Second Revolution.[10]

After the Beiyangjun successfully crushed the pro-Guomindang armed forces, Yuan removed all of the pro-revolutionary leaders from all national and local governments, dissolved the parliament and outlawed the Guomindang, and thus cleared the way for him to establish his own dynasty. From 1914 to the end of 1915, Yuan used different methods to manipulate public opinion and to mobilize support for restoring the monarchy. Under the threat, the National Assemblies voted unanimously in supporting him to assume the throne of the Chinese Empire (*Zhonghua Diguo*) by the end of November 1915. He decided to take the throne on New Year's day, 1916.[11]

It is obvious that Yuan had misjudged the public opinion; he did not realize that the Chinese had been mobilized by the revolutionaries to abandon the monarchy. On December 25, 1915, Cai E, a Tongmonhui member and a prominent general, announced the independence of Yunnan Province and started to organize an expeditionary force against Yuan. This action is now known as the War of Defending the Republic (Huguo Zhanzeng). While Cai's army was not large enough to overthrow Yuan's regime, his brave actions were immediately supported by the leaders of many provinces, including some of Yuan's close followers and supporters. Consequently, Yuan was forced to abandon the monarchy system on March 22, 1916. This unexpected failure caused both his physical and mental collapse. He died within three months.[12]

As mentioned earlier, Yuan had made the Beiyang army a personal force and trained them to be loyal to him only. After his death, no one could command these forces as he did. Consequently, the secondary leaders such as Feng Guozhang and Duan Qirui started to develop their own groups. Feng headed a Zhili faction; Duan led an Anfu faction known as Anfu Club. While Feng and Duan did so, other minor military leaders at the local level within and without the Beiyang factions followed suit to expand their forces and establish military regimes in their own areas.

Many military leaders in the southwestern provinces, who either had been members of Tongmonhui or in one way or another had taken part in military uprisings during the 1911 revolution, also lost their revolutionary enthusiasm. They not only joined the warlords in search of personal gains, but even turned their guns against the revolutionary Party and its leaders. Men such as Cen Chunxuan, Tang Jiyao, Lu Rongting, Mo Rongxin, and Chen Jiongming betrayed Dr. Sun Yatsen, who was the commander-in-chief of the campaign for Defending the Provisional Constitution in 1918, and made a truce agreement with the Beiyangjun that left Dr. Sun helpless.[13] Chen Jiongming even started a military coup against Sun in Guangzhou. He bombed Sun's official residence and forced him to take refugee on a warship.[14]

From the death of Yuan Shikai in 1916 up to 1922, when Sun was forced to abandon his North Expedition, there had been endless fighting between the warlords. They divided the country into various independent regimes and carried out military autocratic rule. China was completely immersed in a chaotic and dark age, which continued to worsen until Jiang Jieshi led a Northern Expedition Force to defeat the warlords and nominally unified China in 1930.

There were more soldiers and weapons during this long period of war than there had been in the Qing Empire, but in terms of military modernization, no new military thought developed except the call to curb the powers of the warlords and demobilize the armed forces. Instead, most military leaders were occupied with fighting for political power and, subsequently, became very corrupt. They would not hesitate to kill people who failed them; meanwhile, they themselves were loyal to no one. Deceit and betrayals were commonplace in their ranks. Though the warlords were always fighting, no one cared about military training or studied tactics and strategies. There were no armed forces, only armed bandits. When the Guomindang took over these forces and sent them to fight the Communist guerrillas and Japanese armies without proper retraining, many of them were easily defeated.

2. The Voices of Military Reform in the Early Republican Period

During this warlord period, some leaders began to call for curbing the powers of the local military forces and initiating military reforms; there was also discussion of military preparation for the inevitable war against the Japanese. Later in the 1930's, when the Civil War between the Comnmunist and the Guomindang armies arose, Mao Zedong and Jiang Jieshi's military thought began to take shape. Both Mao and Jiang had dominated the modern Chinese military and political arena for half a century. Their military theories have been revered by their followers and have become the mainstay of modern Chinese military thought, which will be analyzed separately in the later chapters. What remains for us to discuss in this Chapter are the military ideas of Li Yuanhong, Cai E, Huang Xing, Dr. Sun Yatsen, and Jiang Baili, who have more or less contributed to the development of modern Chinese military thought.

A. Li Yuanhong's Suggestion of Curbing Military Power

Li Yuanhong was a brigade commander of the Qing army and was stationed in Wuchang of Hunan Province on the eve of the revolution of 1911.[15] He was pushed into the position of Governor General by some of his junior officers who had secretly joined the revolutionary organization, *Tongmonhui*, and started the uprising. Although he was not a revolutionary or a sympathizer of the revolutionary cause, he was a respected military commander in that area. So when the rebels badly needed a prestigious military leader, he was the only qualified candidate.

Because of his competent leadership in the initial period of the 1911 Revolution, he was later elected as the first Provisional Vice-President of the Republic of China (Dr. Sun Yatsen was the first Provisional President) and became a prominent political figure in the following decade. He was once again elected to the vice-presidency during Yuan Shikai's presidency and succeeded to the presidency twice in the post-Yuan era during the warlord rule.

His connection to Yuan in the post-revolution years had ruined his relations with the revolutionaries. However, his refusal to support Yuan's plot of restoring the monarchy saved at least part of his reputation as a major leader who had played an important role in the founding of the Republic.

(a) *The Separation of Military Authority from Civilian Affairs:* Although modern Chinese historians have linked him to the warlords, Li was different from other warlords in that he consistently advocated a policy of curbing the powers of the local military leaders, and insisted upon the separation of military authority from civilian affairs. He expounded this policy from the beginning of the Republic until he left the political arena in 1923. All his major points are fully explained in his famous long telegram to Yuan Shikai on April 10, 1912.[16] His major points were simplified by Yuan as the "ten harms" and "three nots"'.[17] The so-called "ten harms" referred to the damage done to society and the whole country by conferring both military and civilian authorities on a single leader, the Governor General (*Dudu*) or the supreme military commander (*Dujun*), while the "three nots" concerned the negative effects of putting all of these powers in the hands of the provincial military leaders.

The "ten harms" caused by military rule can be further simplified into four points. First, both military and civilian affairs require expertise. It is difficult to get a person who can be competent in both areas, and thus local administration would likely be spoiled.

Secondly, if the country is put under military rule, martial law would likely be enforced and the civilians would subsequently be endangered by the potential abuse of power by the military leaders.

Thirdly, power struggles between local military leaders would result in armed conflict that would bring further misery upon the people.

Last of all, the expansion of the military power of the local leaders would likely encourage their ambition to disobey the central government in an attempt to assert their independence; as a result, the country would be fragmented by separatist warlord rule as experienced in the Zhou and Tang dynasties.[18]

The "three nots", or the three negative effects of military regionalism on society, can be summarized as follows: first of all, military regionalism would cause extensive corruption in the armed forces and thus damage their martial virtues. Secondly, soldiers would begin to ignore discipline and laws, which would result in the downfall of the military organization. And finally, the soldiers would lose their sense of duty and responsibility. He even stated that the corrupt lifestyles of the soldiers already made them ignore their military training; they were ignorant of contemporary strategy and tactics. If there was a war, they would not be able to defend the country and protect the people.[19]

For these reasons, Li suggested that the *Dudu* or *Dujun* in the province should be limited in his powers, leaving the nonmilitary affairs to the civilian leaders. By doing so, the military leaders could concentrate on their military duties. Following his own suggestion, he immediately resigned all his civilian posts and asked the provincial legislature to elect a civilian governor for Hubei Province.[20]

(b) *Conscription System and Everyone a Soldier:* In addition, Li recommended a conscription system to replace the current volunteer system; he called it a system of "everyone a soldier".[21] The national government should assign military officers to provinces to train soldiers drafted from the local population. All soldiers should be discharged after finishing their training and returned to their home.

With all of these problems in military rule, he eventually proposed a policy of "abolishing the viceroyship and demobilizing the armed forces" (*Feidu Caijun*).[22] Although this was a very popular policy and was advocated by many prominent figures including Dr. Sun Yatsen,[23] it was ignored by the warlords because they would have been the only losers. Li resigned the presidency in 1923 and departed from the Chinese political stage permanently without achieving his policy. However, the effect of this proposal on reforms in the military system cannot be totally ignored, because this old issue took the centre stage again when the country was later unified in the 1930s.

B. Huang Xing and his Military Thought

Huang Xing was one of the prominent revolutionary leaders in modern Chinese history. He was born in Changsha County of Hunan Province in 1874 and organized his revolutionary organization Huaxinghui in 1903. He planned an armed uprising in his home town of Changsha in 1904, but he was exposed by the Qing authority and was forced to take refugee in Japan where he first met Dr. Sun Yatsen, and joined him together with his organization in 1905. He worked closely with Sun until his death.[24]

During the long period of revolutionary actions before 1911, Huang was often the acting leader of the Tongmonhui when Sun was expelled from Hong Kong, Japan and other Asian countries. Huang personally directed more armed uprisings than anybody else, and subsequently, was recognized as the best military leader of the Party in its early years. When the 1911 Revolution took place in Wuchang, he immediately rushed to the front from Hong Kong and assumed the position of Commander-in-Chief of the revolutionary force. He stayed at that job for 24 days in resisting the attacks of the Qing army, and bought the necessary time for the rebellion to mobilize support from other povinces in demanding the abdication of the monarch and the establishment of a republic.

After the Republic was established, he was appointed as the Minister of the Army and the Chief of Staff of the Armed Forces in 1912 by the provisional government. When Yuan Shikai succeeded Dr. Sun Yatsen as the Provisional President and moved the capital to Beijing, Huang was required by Yuan to remain in Nanjing to clear up unfinished business. He then resigned from office and refused to take part in politics again.

During his long career as a revolutionary, Huang was known as a revolutionary practitioner compared with Dr. Sun, who was regarded as a revolutionary theoretician. Huang did not leave many written works behind him. What we do know about his military thought comes from a few telegrams and speeches. However, as the supreme military leader of the revolutionary forces, Huang's influence on the development of Chinese military thought in the early Republican period is still significant. It is, therefore, worthwhile to briefly describe his thought with the limited information available.

(a) *Universal Military Education for all Students:* He was probably the first leader in modern Chinese history to have proposed a universal military education for all students. In 1916, when he spoke to members of the Parliament from the southern provinces, he attributed the unacceptable behavior of the armed forces to the absence of general military education. Referring to the huge numbers engaged in the European theatre during the First World War, he believed that only a militarization of Chinese education could allow a large armed force to be mobilized in time of war. He wrote:

China should emphasize the militarization of national education. If we add some military courses to the current curriculum of the students at every stage of our school system--from public school to university--we would have more people undergoing military training. In case there is a war, when a mobilization order is issued in the morning, we can have tens of million of soldiers in the army by evening. This is a military reform which I have had in mind for a long time, but have never spoken publicly about before.[25]

It is obvious that when Huang talked about a universal military education for all Chinese school children, he actually had a conscription system in mind. Although there are no more references on this subject, his idea is still clear; otherwise, it would be difficult to envision what he meant by a ten million man army which could be made ready within 12 hours by an order.

(b) *Curbing the Role of the Armed Forces in Civilian Affairs:* Like Li Yuanhong, who proposed a policy for abstracting the military leaders from concurrently taking civilian posts at provincial and local levels, Huang Xing had made similar suggestions when he was the Minister of Army and the Chief of Staff of the Armed Forces in the Provisional Government of the Guomindang in 1912.

As early as February 1912, only a little more than one month after the Republic was established, he began sending telegrams to the Vice President and governors of the provinces asking them to dismiss the district military government except in the war zones and let the civilian officials take over local administration.[26]

Huang Xing realized the danger of the military autocracies. So after the 1911 Revolution, the revolutionary leaders were anxious to curb the powers of the military leaders, who just wanted to take advantage of the chaos to expand their powers. Only those who were under the direct influence of those leaders such as Huang, Li, and Cai E were willing to give up their civilian powers.

(c) *Other Military Reforms:* Following the announcement of dissolving the district military administrations, Huang started to demobilize armies under his command.

As mentioned above, Huang was appointed to head the administration of Nanjing in April 1912 after Yuan moved the government to Beijing. The reason for his appointment was probably that Yuan wanted to use Huang's prestige to control the armed forces in Southern China, over which Yuan himself had little control.

From April 6 to the end of May 1912, Huang was able to reorganize the armies under his control. More than 20,000 soldiers were discharged and sent back to their homes; several brigade, division, and even army commanders were willing to dismantle their entire forces, while others agreed to discharge part of their forces. On May 13, Huang was able to report that his task was done, and subsequently, he submitted his resignation.[27]

Demobilization was a difficult and complicated task. After the 1911 Revolution, China was still in a state of chaos and was not unified in any sense. Any successful demobilization can only be accomplished with considerable financial support, something which China at the time could not afford. The discharged soldiers were only given travel expenses. No arrangements were made concerning living subsidies or future jobs. Consequently, many of the soldiers remained in the cities, thereby creating new social problems.[28] Some joined other army units, while others just became bandits. Huang ordered the local leaders to suppress the latter group.[29]

Huang's military reforms in Nanjing did not induce the Beiyang warlords to follow suit. Instead, they continually expanded their forces. Furthermore, some of Huang's own generals secretly disobeyed his orders and continued to bolster their own forces.[30] It is evident that Huang's initiatives did not cause widespread military reforms. By unilaterally disarming, he may even have contributed to his own defeat in the Second Revolutionary War against Yuan Shikai, after the assassination of Song Jiaoren. However, Huang's determined actions set a model for future reforms. Indeed, China's efforts at military modernization in the 1950s involved partial demobilization of the country's large army.

3. Cai E and the Militarization of China

Cai E was one of the most prominent military leaders in the early years of the Republic. He won the respect of the Chinese by his heroic action in defending the Republic in 1916.

Cai E was born in Shaoyang County of Hunan Province in 1882. He was a student of Liang Qichao, who was a prominent scholar and a constitutional monarchist at the beginning of the 20th century. With the help of Liang, he went to Japan and attended the Japanese Military Academy in 1903. After he returned to China, he worked as an instructor and superintendent of military academies in Guangxi and Yunnan provinces for many years. By doing so, he established his status in the Chinese army, particularly in South China. He was appointed a brigade commander of the Yunnan army in 1911. With the support of his young officers, he announced that he was joining the revolution a few days after the uprising of Wuchang on October 10, 1911. He was elected the Dudu of Yunnan Province by the officers.

Cai's pro-Republic stand cost him the governorship of Yunnan Province and he was recalled to Beijing in 1913 by Yuan Shikai, who was planning to restore the monarchy in China. Cai escaped from Beijing to Yunnan in late 1915 and declared war against Yuan for his betraying the Republic. Yuan was brought down in 1916. However, Cai died of cancer in Japan only a few months after the war was over. He left behind several works on the military.[31]

Cai's major military ideas can be summarized in the following points:

A. The Recovery of National Martial Spirit

In 1900 when he was only 19 years old, he wrote an essay on "National Militarism" (*Jun Guomin Pian*) carried by a newspaper in Japan. Cai focused his discussion on a single subject that the Chinese (Han) have lost their martial spirit and become an extremely weak and cowardly people. The only way for China to free herself from being conquered and partitioned by foreign powers was to restore her martial spirit.[32]

There are several reasons for the Chinese losing their national martial spirit; however, the decisive factor for Cai was their education system, which killed the initiative of Chinese children by teaching them to behave in accordance with the supreme principles of the Confucian school such as kindness, righteousness, wisdom, and the three cardinal guides and the five constant virtues. It totally ignored physical education, which is important to the development of children.[33]

Besides physical education, he emphasized the education of national spirit, national history, and heroic models and saints in order to arouse national pride.[34]

B. The Promotion of Military Virtue

As mentioned before, the corruption of the armed forces in the early Republican period was so serious that there was almost no difference between soldiers and bandits. Cai felt that if the undisciplined behaviour of the armed forces could not be changed, the rise of martial spirit would only intensify the warlord fighting and worsen the misery of the people. Based on this consideration, Cai compiled a pamphlet of *Quotations of Zeng (Guofan) and Hu (Linyi) Regarding the Administration of the Armed Forces* in 1911 for his officer corps in order to promote their moral standards and leadership.

To Cai, it seems that all of the military virtues have their roots in loyalty, righteousness, courage and uprightness. "Whoever has had these basic virtues will automatically have other virtues and talents of a military commander. On the contrary, if one does not have these basic virtues, he is hardly likely to have other talents and virtues."[35]

Accordingly, Cai simplified the Chinese traditional military virtues as wisdom, faith, benevolence, righteousness, courage, and strictness. They are now accepted as a common creed and included in many Chinese military regulations and handbooks. He also recommended that a commander should always keep one's good conscience, courage and uprightness. They are more important than other virtues.[36]

C. National Defence Plans and the Conscription System

If the essay on "National Militarism" is a diagnosis of the disease afflicting the Chinese, the writing of "military plan" would be Cai's prescription for that disease.

In his last major military writing, Cai laid down a national defence plan for China. From the purpose of army building to military education systems, he analyzed the relationships between national power, military power, the armed forces, military service system, weapon system, and military organization. Although most of the subjects he discussed were familiar to most Western military leaders, in China they were relatively new. Therefore, his systematic discussion had a tremendous effect on modern Chinese military systems, above all, the conscription system and the military education system.

According to Cai, every nation must have its own innate character to maintain its continuity and survival. He called it the national foundation (Guo Ben), which has its roots in the characteristics of national history and geographic conditions. Based on this foundation, a nation would decide its basic policy in order to cope with various situations and maintain its security. A national strategy would then emerges. Strategic conflict between nations causes war and, thus, a country needs to maintain an armed force, which is the basic instrument for carrying out national strategies and policies.[37] No country can long neglect its armed force without compromising its national interest and security.

As far as military build-up is concerned, most modern world powers prefer a conscription system at least in wartime. However, as late as the 1930s, China was still using a volunteer service system. Although Yuan Shikai had suggested a conscription system in his report to the Qing government in the 1890s, it was never put in practice.

The basic requirement of a military system is to supply an armed force with enough soldiers of the best quality. According to Cai, only universal military service can meet this target. "If a country wants to keep its armed forces in supreme condition with a limited budget," he wrote, "it should adopt a conscription system, because only this system can provide enough soldiers without compromising its qualities under a limited budget."[38] It permits a country to hold its standing army to a minimal size in peacetime but keep training as many reserves as possible. As long as the reserves are regularly called for retraining, they would be able to fight effectively in war.[39]

A conscription system cannot achieve its goals unless five conditions are met: firstly, the drafts should be able to report to the army in time; secondly, the military organization should be able to train them properly; thirdly, the discharged soldiers should be ensured a stable life after returning home; fourthly, they should be able to answer calls for duty immediately; and finally, as soon as they are gathered, they should be able to fight effectively. However, to Cai these preconditions can only be achieved by a well-organized government and armed force.[40]

D. Universal Military Training and Militarization

With his unique military experience as an instructor and superintendent, Cai made some convincing statements on military education. The main goals of military education are to achieve moral harmony and to unify the military forces. However, they are not achieved in school, but in combat units. According to Cai, under an effective conscription system, the armed forces are actually the military training schools for all citizens in peace time. As he said:

> Soldiers are the elite of the citizens of a country; a proper and successful training for the armed forces can affect social morale. Should each citizen be honest and vigorous, the country would be strong and powerful. . .To train a good soldier is actually to make a good citizen."[41]

Cai's concept of national militarism was, in fact, a big plan for militarizing Chinese citizens in order to change the historical weakness of the Han people as mentioned earlier.

To achieve the primary goals of military education--strengthening moral harmony and unification--Cai set up four key criteria: skill, cooperation, discipline, and patriotism.

A military education system must be able to train the soldiers to master the skills of using their weapons and learning to cooperate with each other. To achieve this goal, the training must follow a procedure of "from form to spirit", that is, from external uniform to the internal unity of every soldier. Therefore, soldiers have to wear uniforms, walk in step, and perform the same functions together.

A military education system must also be able to promote discipline in an armed force. According to Cai, discipline is the lifeblood of an armed force; it is based on a commonly shared confidence. The soldiers believe in their commanders and follow their orders without hesitation; they believe that their superiors and fellow soldiers will not desert them. It is this mutual confidence that can bring an army together and allow it to cooperate closely in operation, and to pursue final victory over the enemy together.[42]

Finally, a military education system must be able to instill the entire military force with a deep sense of patriotism, which is the basic motivation that causes soldiers to fight to death for their country. A military education system, according to Cai, has to teach the soldiers to honour their national flag, the national anthem, and to learn the national history and geography in order to promote their patriotism.[43] What Cai actually proposed was to develop a political identity among the armed forces. By doing so, Cai wished to unify all soldiers under the central government, thereby ending the chaotic warlord rule in China during the early Republican period.

E. Strategy and Tactics

As discussed in the previous chapter, Zeng Guofan often talked about the principle of Zhu (master) and Ke (guest) in strategy and tactics. He preferred to be the master of the field by taking a defensive position. To a large degree Cai agreed with Zeng's conservative strategy. As he wrote:

> . . .in discussing strategy, Zeng and Hu had insisted on the theory of Zhu and Ke. Zhu means defensive; Ke is offensive.
> . .This theory is similar to those of the Western strategists before the Franco-Prussian War. . .All of their [Zeng and Hu's] theories were tested in war and forged through experience. They are consistent with the theories of modern strategists in the world. When I think about their words, I cannot help but sincerely admire them."[44]

Cai, however, did not blind himself by Zeng's words; he realized that after the Franco-Prussian and Russian-Japanese wars, strategists of the world had been talking about the advantages of the offensive. No one wants to insist upon defensive strategies except when one's force is extremely weak, or because other particular situations overwhelmingly favour defensive strategies.[45]

133

However, by the same token, Cai did not unconditionally follow the current offensive theories of his time. He believed that "in chosing strategy and tactics, one should consider the realistic circumstance and not be bound by any theory. If one does not understand the basic principle behind the theory but blindly applies it, one will inevitably fall like the lame man who tries to run."[46]

After examining the Chinese military force in terms of training, weapons, supplies and communications compared with her enemies, Cai denied the advantages of offensive strategy and presented his own idea, which was considered by Chinese strategists as applicable to the Chinese situation. Cai wrote:

> If China is militarily confronted by another country in the near future, it would be better for it to adopt the Boer tactic rather than to risk everything on a single venture by taking any other strategies. China should primarily take a delaying resistance and retrograde defensive strategy to preserve its own forces while luring the enemy in deep. When the enemy is exhausted and does not have enough force to support itself, China can wipe it out with one strike. The experience of the Russians in defeating Napoleon's army could be learned by China in dealing with the foreign aggressors.[47]

Cai was one of the most prominent military leaders in China at that time. He was not only respected as a very knowledgeable man, but was also highly respected for his great personality. He never compromised the national interest for personal advantage; on the contrary, he had in time decided to withdraw from public life in order to promote national unification. His personal character made both his military and political ideas more attractive than many others at that time and, thus, strengthened his influence on the development of modern Chinese military thought. Indeed, the "Quotations of Zeng and Hu Regarding the Administration of the Armed Forces" was published with an introduction from Generalissimo Jiang Jieshi and distributed to the officers and cadets of the Huangpu Military Academy, when Jiang was the president of the school.[48]

4. Dr. Sun Yatsen and the Revolutionary Army
A. Sun and the Chinese Revolution

Dr. Sun Yatsen was born in 1866 in Xiangshan County of Guangdong Province, two years after the Qing army took over Nanjing and totally destroyed the Taiping Rebellion.

During his childhood, Sun was told countless stories of the Taiping Rebellion. His sympathy for the Taiping gave him a strong anti-Manchu feeling, which became much stronger when he grew up and watched the

Chinese socio-political situation deteriorate further. In 1879, he left China for Hawaii to pursue a Western education. In 1886, he was admitted to The Chinese Medical School of Hong Kong, and opened a clinic in Macau after finishing his school in 1892, but he was forced to close up within a few months by the competing European doctors. He subsequently moved to Guangzhou.[49]

According to his memoirs about the London incident, he joined the Xingzhonghui in 1892 and started his political agitations in Macau.[50]

After Xingzhonghui was established in Hawaii in 1894, Sun became the supreme leader and personally led the first armed uprising in Guangzhou in 1895. He then travelled to many countries around the world in order to gather support for his revolution among the overseas Chinese community.

As mentioned in the previous sections, after the first armed uprisings, Sun was expelled from many East Asian countries. Subsequently, he could not directly lead the revolutionary activities and armed uprisings. The revolutionary forces were greatly strengthened when Xingzhonghui and Huaxinghui combined to form Tongmonghui in 1905. Sun was then able to leave the day-to-day leadership to others, such as Huang Xing and Song Jiaoren, and spend more time on his theoretical work. Furthermore, Sun had travelled extensively in the West and had a good command of English, and was thus able to incorporate Western political theory in his own thinking. Consequently, he assumed the ideological leadership of the Tongmonhui.

During his life, he published more works than any other leader of his party. His most famous works include *San Min Zhu YI, The Theory of Dr. Sun Yatsen,* and *The Proposal of International Development of Chinese Industry.* Although these works were published in the early 1920s, more than one decade after the 1911 Revolution, the basic ideas had long been spoken of. *The San Min Zhu Yi,* which combined Western nationalism, democracy, and socialism together with Sun's own explanation of traditional Chinese socio-political ideas, served as a general guideline of the Revolution. It also later served to regulate the socio-political system of the Republic of China. The other two works were designed to build up a moral as well as material foundation for the young Republic, and his military thought was partially reflected in this foundation.

The Proposal of International Development of Chinese Industry was submitted to several Western Powers in 1921 in order to persuade their political leaders to invest their discharged military manpower, equipment, and industries in China to help China develop modern industry and transportation projects.[51] From a military point of view, China would be greatly strengthened if Sun's plans could be carried out.[52]

The Sun Wen Xue Shuo was written to persuade the Chinese to follow his ideas in constructing a modern China. In this book, Sun focused on one single principle: to know how to do something is much more difficult than actually carrying it out.[53] Based on this precept, he encouraged his Party members and the ordinary Chinese to carry out the work of the revolution in accordance with his revolutionary theories. If *The Proposal of International Development of Chinese Industry* was a blueprint for the material construction of the young Republic, then the *Sun Wen Xue Shuo* was aimed at strengthening the resolve of the Chinese to achieve the goals of the Revolution. Using his own experience as an example, Sun repeatedly told the Chinese, above all the Party members and the soldiers, to emphasize the spiritual factor in the revolutionary struggle.

Sun was elected as the first Provisional President of the Republic of China in 1912, but he resigned in favour of Yuan Shikai in exchange for his support of the Republic. However, Yuan's betrayal and attempt to reestablish the monarchy, and his subsequent death after the rebellion of his generals against him caused a long period of warlord rule and civil war.

While the Chinese revolution suffered one blow after another, the Communist revolution in Russia succeeded. This fact affected Sun's political attitude. With the help of advisers from the Soviet Union and the Communist International, he reorganized the Guomindang in accordance with the model of the Communist party. He also decided to build a revolutionary army or party military force based on the model of the Soviet Union.[54] He sent General Jiang Jieshi as his personal representative to the Soviet Union to study its military and political systems. Upon his return, Jiang was appointed President of the Huangpu Military Academy in order to use what he had learned to build a revolutionary army. It was at this school that the political commissar system was first introduced. This system has since become a regular and significant part of the Chinese armed forces of both the Guomindang and the Communists.[55]

As a revolutionary leader and, above all, an ideological leader, Sun's political writings are much richer and better organized than his military ones. However, his influence on the modern Chinese military system has been felt more profoundly than that of many other military leaders of his time. It is, therefore, worthwhile to examine his thought in more detail.

B. National Defence Planning and Economic Development

In a letter to Leo Zhongkai in 1921, Dr. Sun revealed his plan for writing a book about Chinese national defence. He intended to call the book *A Ten-Year Plan of National Defence*, and he made a 62-item list of all the topics he planned to discuss. There is no evidence that he ever wrote such a book; therefore, it is unlikely for us to uncover his systematic theory of national defence.[56] Nevertheless, some information on the listed topics can be indirectly obtained from his lectures and other writings. The 62 topics covered a broad area; they can be summarized in the following 10 subjects:

    (1)   the principles, directions and policies of national defence;
    (2)   national defence and foreign policy;

(3)   national defence and the national political system including constitution and central and local governments;

(4)   economy and national defence: a discussion which includes plans concerning military industry, agriculture, mining, commerce, transportation and communications, and education. It would also include the relationship between national defence and the development of national industries;

(5)   plans of military build-up and military systems, including those for the army, navy and air force;

(6)   military education and exchanges of military ideas with foreign countries;

(7)   national defence and demographics, including such ideas as resettling people from overpopulated areas to the border areas;

(8)   weapon systems - standardizing weapons;

(9)   operation planning and military drills;

(10)   comparison between the military education of spirit and material.

Information about half of these items can be obtained from his other writings and speeches. The relationship between national defence and national economy, for example, can be found in *The Proposal of International Development of Chinese Industry*. His ideas concerning military education and strategic and tactical principles can be found in his speeches to the armed forces.

One may say that Sun's industrial development plan was a national defence project tailored to fit Chinese needs. To him, the development of industry was a crucial matter which directly relates to China's future.[57]

Sun's proposed method mainly focused on the resolving of transportation problems - he dedicated four sections of his six section work to discussing these problems. By improving transportation, Chinese sovereignty at the border areas could be maintained by resettling people to these areas, and providing the necessary supplies to any troubled areas. Furthermore, by facilitating transportation to and from China, China could receive technology, resources and goods from the Western countries, thereby allowing her to maintain and perhaps accelerate her industrial development. Sun's plan also called for the development of an automobile industry and the development of mines.

Sun's discussion of transportation problems was limited to improving harbours, railways, inland river systems and highways.

First of all, Sun planned to construct three first class harbours along the Chinese coast, which were to be known as the Great Northern Harbour of Zhili Bay in Hebei, the Great Eastern Harbour at Hangzhou Bay in Zhejiang or at Shanghai, and the Great Southern Harbour at Guangzhou. Furthermore, severl dozen second and third class harbours were to be constructed either along the sea coast or along the major inland rivers.[58]

Sun also emphasized the importance of improving navigation on the Yangtze River and the Grand Canals in order to link the extensive rich inland with the Great Eastern Harbour. The building of the secondary and tertiary harbours along these inland rivers was his proposed method.

To link all these projected harbours with economic and strategic areas over the country, he designed seven major railroad systems.

The Northwest railroad system would start from the projected Great Northern Harbour and run through Mongolia to the western part of Xinjiang, and finally to the border of the Soviet Union. Branch lines were also planned to link border towns and strategic areas of Mongolia, Gansu, and Xinjiang provinces with the main line. A resettlement plan was organized by Sun to shift people from the crowded inland areas to these outlying areas for both military and economic reasons. The projected length of this line was about seven thousand kilometres.[59]

In addition, he planned to build two railroad lines that would connect the Great Eastern Harbour with the inland cities and the border areas. These were to be called the Central Railroad system and the Southeast Railroad System. The Central line was to run along the Yangtze River toward the Western city of Xian in Shaanxi, then to Chongqing in Sichuan, and then turn to the north to Mongolia and Xinjiang by linking with the Northwest Railroad System. The Southeast line was to run south to the Great Southern Harbor in Guangzhou. In the process, the Southeast line would also pass through the inland provinces of Jiangxi, Jiangsu, Anhui, Hubei, and Hunan. These two lines were projected to be about 16,600 and 9,000 kilometres, respectively.[60]

A fourth line was planned by Sun which would help the projected Great Southern Harbour become a first class port. Sun proposed that this fourth line run from the Southern harbour, through Hunan, Guizhou, Guangxi, Yunnan and finally to the Sino-Burmese and Sino-Vietnamese borders.[61]

In addition to the above four major railroad systems, Sun also suggested three more railroad systems. One was to be called the Highland Railroad system, and it would run through Tibet, Qinghai, part of Xinjiang, Sichuan, Yunnan, and Guizhou provinces. It would help the Chinese repulse any intrusions from India and Indo-China.[62] The second line was called the Northeast or the Manchuria Railroad System, and it was to connect Manchuria with the projected Great Northern Harbour and other areas of Hebei Province. This line served the purpose of strengthening the Chinese ability to withstand Soviet or Japanese intrusions into Manchuria.[63] The third one was to be called the Extended Northwest Railroad system. After the completion of this extension, the Northwest line would reach all of the important strategic border towns in Xinjiang and Mongolia, thereby helping China contain the Soviet Union within its own borders.[64]

Finally, Sun proposed to build a million kilometres of highway to further facilitate transportation.

Sun's other objectives of the proposal were to develop an automobile industry and mines. He particularly emphasized the importance of steel, coal, oil and copper, as well as the development of a machine-manufacturing capability.[65]

In this proposal, Sun emphasized the possible advantages for the world powers in helping China develop her industrial capabilities. What he did not mention, but what is intuitively obvious, is that the result of this project would be a stronger Chinese military capability and an end to foreign intrusions.

C. The Establishment of Revolutionary Forces

Although the Tongmonhui once opened a military school in Tokyo in 1902 to train revolutionaries,[66] and also helped Chinese students enrol in Japanese military academies, Sun and Guomindang did not build their own revolutionary force until 1924, when the Huangpu Military Academy was set up.

Sun did not properly define the concept of a "revolutionary force", but he did make an effort to distinguish a revolutionary force from other military forces based on their spirit, tactics, and the loyalty to the cause of revolution. From those discussions, one can sense the concept of revolutionary force.

In distinguishing revolutionary armed forces from other military forces, Sun said: "Each revolutionary soldier can fight against one hundred enemies, or at least fight against ten. When the term revolutionary is applied to army units, one thousand soldiers of a revolutionary army can defeat ten or even one hundred thousand enemies. To be able to defeat a numerically superior enemy, therefore, is the criterion of being a Revolutionary Army."[67]

To pit one against one is a normal rule of engagement. Only in special circumstances can one soldier be expected to fight against more than one. Therefore, Sun's criterion of revolutionary army is indeed unusual. To him, revolution is an extraordinary business, and it can only be carried out by an extraordinary revolutionary force. And the only way to create a revolutionary armed force is to learn from the revolutionary party members. It is essential to learn their spirit of struggle and their courage to fight against one hundred. Indeed, Sun said: "Should an armed force be able to struggle as the revolutionary party members did, it could then be called a Revolutionary Army."[68] From what he said above, one is likely to realize that a revolutionary army is an armed force which particularly emphasizes the factor of spirit. With this unusual spirit of struggle, a revolutionary force can defeat a numerically superior force.

Before the creation of the revolutionary army, Sun and the Guomindang had primarily relied on the support of regional armed forces in the southern provinces. He often thought about transforming them into a revolutionary force. As he said: "If we want to rely on the existing military force to complete our revolution, the most important task for the Party members to do is to transform these soldiers into Party members themselves, so that they would be willing to sacrifice themselves for the cause of San Min Zhu Yi."[69]

Sun was obviously unsuccessful in transforming the local armies into an ideal revolutionary one. Consequently, he set up the Huangpu Military Academy to create his own revolutionary force. Sun admired the Russian revolution, and planned to train his own force using the Russian model. Indeed, Sun once wrote to General Jiang Jieshi in 1924, that "our revolution would never succeed unless we learn from the Russians."[70] What should be learned? Sun said: "If we want to complete our revolution, we have to learn the method, organization, and the training of the Russians."[71] The eventual outcome was to reorganize the Guomindang and establish a revolutionary force.

D. Sun's Revolutionary Tactics.

If Dr. Sun had ever developed a military strategy for his revolutionary army, it would be based on the principle of defeating an enemy with a numerically inferior force. He repeated this principle in many of his speeches and writings. Once, he wrote to Jiang Jieshi about his ideal army: "If the army is organized and trained in accordance with my idea and is under my command, I would be able to lead them to beat an enemy ten or even one hundred times larger than it. This strategy has not been mentioned by any strategist in the existing books on war."[72]

Sun was not correct to claim this principle as his own. To beat an enemy with a numerically inferior army is not a new idea. The ancient Chinese strategists had discussed this principle. And while the ancient strategists had developed some theories for carrying out this strategy, Sun himself did not leave any convincing method of carrying out his strategy except by emphasizing revolutionary spirit and guerrilla tactics.

Using his bodyguards in the Guanyinshan incident of 1922 as an example, he said that thirty men equipped with pistols were able to hold their positons for more than ten hours against several thousand rebels until they exhausted their ammunition. Sun said, "Only the bodyguards who fought in the Guanyinshan incident are qualified to be the ideal model of a revolutionary soldier: one who can pit himself against one hundred."[73] According to Sun, this soldier can beat the odds only if he does not fear death and is willing to sacrifice himself for the revolution.

Besides this spiritual element, the only other way Sun described by which a revolutionary army can beat a numerically superior enemy is to use guerrilla or You-Yong tactics.

It seems that Sun obtained the idea of guerrilla tactics from the Boer War, in which the Boers fought against the British in South Africa with tactics of ambush. The Vietnamese also used similar tactics against the French, and this also probably influenced Sun. Therefore, Sun suggested that guerrilla tactics should be used in wars against foreign invaders and against the Beiyang warlords.[74]

Generally speaking, Sun's discussions of guerrilla warfare were primarily limited to technical matters. According to Sun, there are five kinds of skills in You-Yong tactics to be learned: target shooting, ambushing, bearing hardships, walking, and eating coarse food. In discussing target shooting, Sun mentioned a principle of obtaining supplies from the enemy in guerrilla warfare. Sun said: "The supply of ammunition may come from our rear or from the front. However, the guerrilla force cannot get its ammunition supply except from the enemy. Therefore, their supply is not from the rear but from the enemy in front."[75] As to "bearing hardships, walking, and eating coarse food", instead of being skills, they are rather the physical training which may help the guerrillas to overcome the handicap of inferior weapons and equipment. And finally, the term "ambush" can be treated from either a technical level or a tactical one. The former emphasizes personal safety by using natural conditions such as terrain and shelters to protect oneself from the enemy fire; the latter, however, refers to a tactic by which a surprise attack on the enemy is emphasized. Sun's discussion focused primarily on the former case.[76]

E. The Determinant Factor of War - People

Sun did not have any particular strategy or tactic which could help him pit one against ten or one hundred. The only strategy he mentioned repeatedly was the superior spirit of struggle for the cause of revolution. As mentioned in the previous sections, he emphasized the extraordinary nature of revolutionary war and thus believed that it needs an extraordinary spirit of struggle. Indeed, Sun said, "one should ask himself whether he has the revolutionary spirit or not; if he has it, the success of the revolution is ensured."[77]

What is spirit? His definition is very simple: "whatever is not material is spirit."[78] Spirit and material are complementary and cannot be separated. However, to Sun, spirit is the major element, material, the minor. While weapons belong to the category of material, they can only be used properly by people with spirit. Therefore, the determinant factor in war is primarily human spirit, which Sun considers nine times as important as material.[79] The following quotation illustrates the importance which Sun placed on the factor of spirit in war:

> If one has an abundance of ammunition but is in low spirits, he is likely to leave all his ammunition to his enemy when they meet in the battle. An army like this is simply a transportation team that is carrying war booty to the enemy. Therefore, when two hostile forces want to destroy the fighting power of each other, they can simply do it by destroying the other's fighting spirit.[80]

Most people would agree that spirit is an important factor which can affect the outcome of war; however, some may still feel that Sun overestimated the role of spirit in war.

Generally speaking, the objective situation gives revolutionary leaders little choice but to preach the supremacy of spirit. Indeed, a revolutionary force is usually badly equipped without reliable supplies. It would be self-defeating if a revolutionary leader were to insist that weapons are more important than human will in war. In most cases, modern Chinese have consistently fought with obsolete weapons against their enemies equipped with advanced weapons. Subsequently, they have to convince themselves of the supremacy of spirit. For example, Mao Zedong called the atomic bomb a paper tiger because it looks terrible but in fact is not.[81] The real reason behind his statement was that China did not yet possess a nuclear capability. He did not want the People's Liberation Army to be intimidated by the possibility of fighting the enemy who had the atomic bomb.

However, one must realize that the consistent emphasis on spirit as the determinant factor has now become a distinctive feature of Chinese military thought. It is shared to different degrees by all military leaders.

F. The Function of Political Propaganda in War

Sun's strategy of using a small force to defeat a much larger force requires an army with extremely high morale. Raising the fighting spirit of one's own force while destroying that of the enemy, therefore, becomes the key to victory for the revolutionary force. The best way, according to Sun, was through the use of propaganda. Indeed, Sun said: "After the reorganization of the Guomindang, we are going to emphasize propaganda, not military means."[82]

Propaganda may turn an enemy into a friend. The 1911 Revolution in Wuchang, for example, was successful mostly because the Qing army also revolted. And the revolt of the Qing army at that time was due to the effect of the propaganda of the revolutionaries. Sun said: "By propaganda, we made them understand our San Min Zhu Yi and made them willing to fight for the revolution. Therefore, the success of the revolution was due to the success of propaganda."[83]

Furthermore, according to Sun, without propaganda, even a revolutionary force may not be able to win a battle, because "if we do not give any propaganda to our soldiers, they would not know why they should fight for the revolution."[84] Consequently, Sun said that "the fastest method to carry out a revolution is to rely 90 percent on propaganda, and only 10 per cent on the armed forces."[85]

The emphasis on propaganda in war is not only an important part of Sun's revolutionary strategy but also the foundation of the political work system of the modern Chinese military system. It is conceivable that Mao's argument against the purely military point of view in the Red Army during the Jinggangshan period may be partly traced back to Sun's philosophy.[86]

G. Stopping War and Discharging the Armed Forces

In discussing the nature of war, Sun believed that war is basically a manifestation of an evil aspect of human nature. He also believed that the more developed man becomes, the less chance there will be for this evil nature to reveal itself in war. However, as a general rule for the modern world, whoever can fight will survive, and whoever cannot will live in peril. Therefore, "one cannot help but go to war in order to stop war."[87] This is part of traditional Chinese military philosophy, and still dominates the minds of modern Chinese military leaders.

Discharging the armed forces has been a major issue since the 1911 revolution. Sun's voice on this issue was not only louder but more convincing than all others because he proposed a framework in which the demobilized soldiers could be employed by industry. Sun said, "to discharge the armed forces is not to discharge them from the army and leave them as unemployed vagrants; we are going to transform them into workers and, thus, to carry out our policy of promoting industrial construction by military force."[88] This policy was eventually carried out by both the Communists and the Nationalists in Mainland China, and in Taiwan separately after 1949.

5. Jiang Baili and His Military Thought

Generally speaking, there were no significant breakthroughs in the development of modern Chinese military thought in the early Republican period. One of the few exceptions was General Jiang Baili. He not only introduced the contemporary foreign military theories and systems to China, but also developed his own theory based on the particular circumstances of Chinese society. If his achievement was not as great as those of the prominent strategists, he could still be seen as a pioneer in the field of modern Chinese military theories.

A. The Socio-Political Background of Jiang

Jiang Baili was born in Haiyan County of Zhejiang Province in 1882. He spent his childhhood and youth studying Chinese classics and passed the *Siucai* degree of the Imperial examination in 1898 at the age of 17. It was only after he began studying at a public school for privileged children that he began to understand the feelings of national humiliation that arose from China's defeat in the Sino-Japanese War of 1894 and the Allied Expeditionary War of 1900. Jiang subsequently became pro-revolutionary. He was, therefore, expelled from the school. He then left China for Japan in 1901.[89]

Like many Chinese students, Jiang wanted to get into a military academy. After taking some preparatory military courses in Chengcheng school in 1901 and serving as a non-commissioned officer in the Japanese army, he was eventually admitted to the Japanese Academy in 1904.

He finished at the top of his class in December 1905, and was personally awarded a military sword by the Japanese Emperor. This gained him fame among the Chinese community in both Japan and China.

After returning to China, he was invited to serve as the Chief of Staff of the Viceroy of Manchuria, Zhao Erxun, who had sponsored Jiang's registration in the Japanese Military Academy. Only a few months later, however, he was sent by the Viceroy to continue his study of military science in Germany.[90] Instead of joining a military academy, however, he joined the German army and served as a trainee until 1910.

During his stay in Germany, Jiang spent much time studying Western literature, history, and philosophy. And so, upon returning, he was very familiar not only with European military science, but also with Western culture, history, and the socio-political situation. His expertise in these fields helped him greatly when he was later appointed Jiang Jieshi's personal envoy to Europe for diplomatic and military missions during the Second World War.

After returning to China, he accepted a position of battalion commander in the Palace Guard for a few months. He then joined his old employer and sponsor, Viceroy Zhao, to resume his position as chief of staff.[91] However, on the eve of the 1911 Revolution, Jiang was expelled from Manchuria by the anti-Xinjun forces, the *Xunfang Jun*, and was accused of a pro-revolutionary attitude. In fact, Jiang was still not a revolutionary. After the establishment of the Republic, he only passively accepted it but did not join it. Indeed, a few months after the onset of the Revolution, he returned to Beijing to join Yuan Shikai, after Yuan assumed the Provisional Presidency in early 1912. Jiang accepted his offer to be the Commandant of Baoding Military Academy in December of the same year. However, he tried to commit suicide after six months on the job because he failed to get the necessary support from the Beijing government.[92] He survived but left the Academy. He remained a councillor of the President until 1918, except for a brief period in 1916 when he joined the Southern revolutionary forces against Yuan Shikai for his betrayal of the Republic.[93]

In 1918, he was invited to join a fact-finding tour of post-war Europe. This trip gave him the opportunity to familiarize himself with developments in Western military thought since his last visit.

From 1918 to 1930, China was usually engulfed by civil wars. Instead of joining any warlord, however, Jiang spent most of his time writing military essays. He continued this work until the mid-1920s, when some warlords invited him to work for them. He accepted the position of chief of staff for General Wu Peifu in 1925. However, Jiang left after only a few months.

It seems that he never seriously thought of joining the Nationalist army, even after he was personally received by Jiang Jieshi in 1927.[94] He was subsequently jailed by Jiang Jieshi in 1930 for a few years for his relationship with a rebelling general, Tang Shengzhi. During this period in jail, he committed himself to writing. He published "A Historical Study of the Basic Principles of Economics of National Defence" in 1934. Perhaps because of this work, he was then appointed as a senior advisor in the Commission of Military Affairs by Jiang Jieshi. After this he began his career under the Guomindang regime and devoted himself to the war against Japan.

Since 1936, he was twice assigned by Jiang Jieshi to travel in Europe. One occasion was to investigate the systems of military mobilization in 1936; the other occasion was a diplomatic trip, which tried to stop the emerging alliance of Germany, Italy and Japan in 1937. History bears testimony that he did not successfully complete this mission. However, he once again seized the opportunity to broaden his military knowledge, which enabled him to publish more military papers upon his return to China.

1938 was important in Jiang's life. Among other things, he was appointed as the acting commandant of the College of the Army, while maintaining his position of senior advicer to the Commission of Military Affairs. He worked very hard and travelled a great deal; in three months, he published eight essays. However, his hectic schedule caused his health to suffer, and he died at 57 of a heart attack in Yishan, a mountainous town in Guangxi province in Southwest China.

B. The Military Thought of Jiang Beili

In *The Life of Jiang Baili 's Old Age and His Military Thought*, Prof. Xue Guangqian divided the development of Jiang's military thought into four stages:

The first stage consisted of the period in which he studied military science, from 1901 to 1910. Like many young military leaders of his time, he was a national militarist, and was devoted to building a strong national defense.

The second stage lasted from 1912 to 1930. During this period, he planned to devote his life to military education so that he could train military leaders for his country. He advocated the popular demands of abolishing the system of viceroyship and discharging the armed forces; he wrote articles promoting the mass militia system, conscription system, and the traditional system of *Yubing Yunong*.

The third stage lasted from the Manchuria Incident of September 18, 1931 to the Marco Polo Bridge Incident of July 7, 1937, which formally began the Sino-Japanese War. To meet the urgent needs of the war, he concentrated on developing his concept of the economics of national defence. He eventually developed a basic military principle based on the relationship between the national economic system and the requirements of war.

The last stage was from 1937 to his death in 1938. All his efforts in this period were focused on encouraging the Chinese to continue fighting. His method consisted of predictions of China's inevitable victory.[95]

Although Jiang had published quite a few papers during the first stage, most of them referred to current popular ideas such as national militarism and the advocacy of building a strong armed force. They do not demonstrate a unique military thought. Even many of his military works which were published during the second stage cannot definitely be said to contain Jiang's own thought, because several important articles were actually from "The Military Plan" of Cai E, which was discussed in earlier sections. Several different sources suggested that Cai had sent the first draft of "The Military Plan" to Jiang for his comments and editing in 1913.[96] Jiang might have added some of his own ideas to this paper, but the original inspiration was Cai's, and so it would be incorrect to attribute the theories in these works to Jiang.[97]

It is obvious that Jiang's important military works were published during the third period of his life. For example, his theory on the economic foundation of the national defence was first published in the mid-1930s. His "Mobilization" clearly expressed his thoughts on the economic problems involved with mobilization and war, it was developed on his European fact-finding tour in 1936. His discussion of the roles of economics in war has been seen by some scholars as a theory for national defence, instead of a military thought.[98] However, in general terms, these works are still treated as military thoughts by scholars such as Prof. Xue and Dr. Wang. A very significant aspect of Jiang's military thought would be excluded if these treatises on the economics of national defence were omitted.

(a) The Unification of Living Means with the Requirement of War

In "The Introduction (1) to the Treatise of National Defence", Jiang wrote: " From the history of the prosperity and peril of nations, I have found a basic principle. It is, when both the means of living and the requirements of war are correlated with each other, a nation would be strong; when they are irrelevant, weak; contradictory to each other, in danger of death. "[99] The same principle was again presented in the paper "A Historical Study of the Basic Principle of the Economics of National Defence."[100] To Jiang, the unification of the means of living and requirements of war can be achieved in two ways: one is by means of instruments or tools, and the other is by the socio-economic system. The horse for the Mongols, and ships for the European, are examples of simultaneous tools for both living and war. The modern mobilization system in the Western world and the "nine squares" system of land ownership in the Zhou dynasty of China are examples of the second method.[101]

The Mongols had once established their empire with their powerful cavalry, in which the horse was essential. More currently, ships, to a maritime country, are a means of living, but have been transformed into a powerful weapon by the Europeans, and thus helped them dominate the world for almost two centuries.

The mobilization system developed in the First World War not only related to military activites but to economic ones as well. And finally, the Nine Squares system of ancient China was the basic socio-economic system of the Zhou dynasty, and it was also the basic unit of defence. The Nine Squares system was possibly the earliest example of the system of *Yubing Yunong*, which trained and enlisted all of the qualified male peasants in the reserve force.[102] Also, according to Jiang Baili, it was designed as a square formation to block the assault of the cavalry and chariots.

Based on these examples, he concluded that: "to unify the means of living with the requirement of war is the essence of the economics of national defence."[103]

(b) *The Economics of National Defence:* In "The New Trend of the Development of the World Military Situation", Jiang, based on the experience of the World War I, indicated that economic power is actually a nation's fighting power; the two cannot be separated. If a country wants to reinforce its fighting power, it must carry out an economic policy of self-sufficiency.[104]

The economic power of a country consists of three elements: manpower, resources and organization. There are very few countries in the world that are completely self-sufficient in all these areas. Based on the German experience, Jiang believed that while the government should minimize any reliance on foreign countries, it should spare no effort to build its manufacturing industries with native labour and with whatever resources it may have.[105] By doing so, the country would be able to strengthen its national power and thus establish its economy of national defence.

To solve the shortage of manpower, Jiang felt a country should rely on an effective conscription system. Under such a system, a country can use a limited budget to train many draftees during peacetime. This is also based on the system implemented in Germany before and during the First World War.[106] Then, under the general mobilization system, the Germans were able to mobilize millions of soldiers overnight, with its regular standing army serving as a core.

(c) *The Mobilization System:* From the fall of 1935 to November of 1936, Jiang travelled in Italy, France, Germany, Great Britain, and the United States to study their mobilization systems. Upon returning to China, he wrote several reports about their systems.

Of the three aforementioned elements of national power, Jiang thought that the Chinese were particularly deficient in organizational skill. In his report to the government in "The Outline of General Mobilization No. 2", he thought that a mobilization system could help the Chinese improve their organizational skills. Indeed, he wrote:

From my investigation tour, one thing that I have to report to
you is the cultivation of the ability of our national organization.
. .The best display of this ability is the national general
mobilization system. . .If (we) can develop [our] national
ability of organization, [we] are likely to build up [our]
national defence. [107]

To further support his concept of mobilization, he quoted an old
Chinese military principle: "Perhaps a country will never use its armed forces
for one hundred years, but it should not leave it unprepared for any single
day." To Jiang, the word "prepared" (*Bei*) also has a different meaning; it
either means "getting ready" or means "perfect" (*Wanbei*). [108] Based on the
first meaning, a country must always have its armed forces ready to cope with
any situation, thereby increasing the chances of winning; in accordance to the
second meaning, everything must be done perfectly. To Jiang, the word
"*everything*" is wide-ranging in scope, and is not limited to "*everything
military*". Therefore, the term general mobilization was used in lieu of
military mobilization. Jiang wrote:

Military mobilization, which is primarily aimed at the military
forces, draws part of the resources from the society and
organizes them into a national force in order to defend the
country; general mobilization, however, is aimed at the whole
country. It unifies everything in the country and transforms
them into the power of the nation. When a country possesses
this power, it would be able to defend itself and, thus, its
citizens may survive [the war]. [109]

(d) *Protracted Warfare and Quick Decision:* From the previous
discussion, it is obvious that under the requirement of self-sufficiency, the
economics of national defence requires a long-term arrangement; a country
can only achieve its goals by a persistent and long term effort. Consequently,
a country needs a strategy with a protracted approach, in which total
preparation is completed in a step-by-step, year-by-year process.

The requirements of mobilization, both military and general, however, are totally different from this. Mobilization requires rapid action to
meet the necessity of war. Based on this fact, Jiang, after his trip to Europe
in 1936, concluded that, in the situation of a general war (*Quantixing
Zhanzheng*), the national defence should be arranged in such a way to
emphasize self-sufficency. This requires long-term or protracted preparation. However, where operations are concerned, quick decisions are needed. [110]
The former case refers to a country's political strategy or grand strategy,
whereas the latter refers to a country's military strategy. Jiang wrote: "From
the strategic point of view, a country should make quick decisions, not

protracted ones, in order to avoid the heavy burden on the national economy of a protracted war. Quick is the end, while protraction the means."[111]

To achieve the goal of quick decision in operations, Jiang emphasized the concept of mobile warfare, in which one should initiate attacks, rather than maintain fixed positions.[112] Jiang's concept of mobile warfare automatically requires an increase in the mobility of the armed forces. Jiang wrote:

> Although we need protracted warfare, its preliminary require-
> ment is to increase the mobility of our military force, because
> we have to achieve our goal of protracted warfare by means of
> quick decision.[113]

Contrasting Jiang's protracted warfare with Zuo Zongtang's strategy of slow movements and quick decisions helps to illustrate the point. Jiang's protracted warfare refers to a national policy or grand strategy rather than a military strategy. While Jiang's protracted warfare refers to socio-economic preparation before war, Zuo's slow movements refers to troop movements in war areas. It is only a military strategy.

As for quick decisions, while Zuo refers to individual operations or campaigns at a tactical level, Jiang discusses all military actions, at both a tactical and strategic level.

During the Sino-Japanese War, the Chinese often referred to their struggle as a Protracted Resistance War, which probably refers to both the grand strategy as well as the military strategy.

Finally, Jiang's mobile warfare relies on modern equipment, such as tanks, trucks and self-propelled artillery to increase the mobility of the armed force. It is, therefore, different from the well-known strategy of the People's Liberation Army during the Sino-Japanese War and the Civil War, which emphasized the strategy of maneuvering the enemy out of position and attacking him while he is moving.

(e) *New Guerrilla Warfare:* Ever since guerrilla warfare was used in the Russian Civil War, it had become a popular strategy used in situations where a weak force faced a stronger power. After Jiang read a work on guerrilla warfare written by a German, Major Heinz, he introduced these ideas to China on the eve of the Sino-Japanese war.

According to Major Heinz, there are two kinds of guerrilla warfare. He distinguished an older type which was used in the Russian Civil War that emphasizes attacks with a relatively large guerrilla force on the enemy in the occupied regions in order to cause political instability. To Heinz, this tactic is likely to result in heavy loss of life and in enemy retaliation against the local people.[114] Therefore, he suggested a new guerrilla strategy, by which the guerrilla force acts in smaller teams - half a dozen members - armed with time bombs, incendiary bombs, poison, chemical weapons and silenced pistols.

The focus of these smaller guerrilla forces was to disrupt supply centres instead of killing people.[115] To Heinz, the "old type" of guerrilla warfare would only inflict damage on a weak and badly organized internal enemy. If the enemy is strong and well-organized, and if it is a powerful external enemy, Heinz felt that the "old type" of guerrilla warfare would not be very successful.

Jiang was obviously convinced by Heinz. However, he still believed that the "old type" of guerrilla warfare would still be useful in certain circumstances in the Chinese situation. Indeed, Jiang wrote:

> The bad transportation conditions of North China make it possible to apply the old guerrilla warfare of the Soviet Union. The new guerrilla warfare should be applied only to South China and the seashore areas.[116]

In modern guerrilla warfare, however, there is no distinction between the so called "old method" and the new one. The two concepts have been combined by modern guerrillas.

(f) *The Air Force:* Jiang's major ideas concerning the role of the air force in modern war were demonstrated in a long article "The Foundation of the Power of Air Force".

Although air force had been introduced in World War I, the role of the air force was still a new subject for most military strategists in the post-war years. The roles of the new force in future war, its status in the whole military system, and its organization and command were all favourite subjects of discussion. Giulio Douhet published his paper "The Command of the Air" in 1922, but it was only recognized as the most influential theory concerning the air force almost ten years after publication. Like most European military leaders, Jiang Baili eventually embraced this theory. When he returned to China from his European trip, he introduced the Chinese translation of *An Introduction to Douhet's Theory*, which was written by Marshal Badon of France. In this work, the Marshal highly praised "The Command of the Air" as a revolutionary military theory that would definitely affect the way future wars would be fought.[117]

As discussed above, Jiang often paid particular attention to the economic foundations of national defence; he did so also with the air force. Whenever he discussed the air force, he emphasized not only the resources, industrial capacity and high technology necessary in developing a strong modern air force, but also the possible effects of the high speeds, long-range capability, and huge destructive powers of airplanes on the economy of a country at war. The rapid pace of changes in technology would make it prohitively expensive for underdeveloped countries to compete with the industrialized nations in the air. Consequently, it would be more likely for these underdeveloped countries to be exposed to the air raids of an enemy in war. However, the damage sustained by underdeveloped countries during air raids would be much less than that of the industrial countries.[118]

Referring to the Chinese situation, he made two suggestions about the organization of the Chinese air force, both of which are basically in accordance with Douhet's theories. First of all, the airforce should be independent from the army and navy, and be able to fulfil its responsibilites independently, and be under the command of its own commanders. Air force commanders also should be allowed to command the air defence forces and air communication units in order to achieve close cooperation to meet the needs of air defence[119].

According to Jiang, while an important function of the air force is to support the army and navy in operations, the air force also has to carry out independent operations. This function became increasingly important and began to take priority over other duties by the 1930s. Because of this development, Jiang preferred to have the air force organized in a manner which could most effectively facilitate its potential power of attack.[120]

The Chinese air force in the 1930s was still very small; there were no bombers at all. Although it was independent in organization, its basic function was air defence and providing support for the ground forces. Consequently, the air force itself was unlikely to act independently. The air force was, in fact, assigned to particular individual theatres of operation. Jiang's suggestions were, therefore, not immediately adopted by the government.[121]

Jiang also discussed many other relevant military topics such as the conscription system and disarmament. The former is, to a considerable degree, a copy of part of Cai E's "The Military Plan", which was discussed in section 3. With regard to the disarmament problem, Jiang perhaps contributed more than any of his contemporaries by paying particular attention to the procedure of demobilization and the necessity of making arrangements for living and working for the discharged soldiers. Unfortunately, China's socio-economic condition was so bad at the time that his proposals were unlikely to be put into practice. Many problems could have been avoided, however, had Chinese leaders considered Jiang's suggestions when the Sino-Japanese War came to an end in 1945. Nevertheless, his writings on this subject have had some influence. Indeed, since the end of the Chinese civil war in 1949, both the People's Republic and Taiwan have carried out policies of demobilization of the armed forces based on principles similiar to Jiang's.

Although Jiang is recognized as a prominent military thinker of China, his achievement, however, is primarily limited to the introduction of new ideas to China. Jiang was different from many other military leaders of that time. He was a well-educated man familiar with both Oriental and Western culture. With his unusual talent, scholarly quality, and, above all, his opportunities of conducting study tours in foreign countries, he was able to do some comparative and analytical works in his writings. By doing so, he showed the Chinese a clear picture of the situation, the trend of development, and, thus, the rational basis of the topics of his discussion. Furthermore, Jiang was not satisfied in simply copying foreign systems, but tried to adapt them to the Chinese situation. This gave people the impression that he had to some extent made a breakthrough over the long history (dating to the 1850s) of copying the ideas of foreign countries.

Jiang perhaps could have made a greater contribution to modern military thought. He was confident in his own abilities to achieve greatness but he did not fully attain it. He did not leave behind a systematic work as many believed he could have. His early death could partly be responsible for this failure. Another reason is perhaps that he failed to concentrate on a selected subject. He unnecessarily split his limited time and energy between too many things. As Dr. Wang, the author of *General Jiang Baili and His Military Thought*, said, had he concentrated on one subject his achievement would have been far more considerable. [122]

6. Conclusion

From the 1911 Revolution up to the death of Jiang Baili, China saw incessant warlord wars, reunification and the early stages of a national liberation war - the Sino-Japanese war. During this turbulent period, the more enlightened younger generation was able to gradually replace the old conservatives, who were leftovers from the Qing dynasty. And although the continuous civil wars caused the process of military modernization to be delayed and even to regress, this period, however, did leave behind a positive influence on Chinese military modernization. The development of modern Chinese military thought actually began at this time. The pioneers were mostly from the aforementioned young generation, who either attended foreign schools or who were educated by the Revolution. They not only vehemently protested against the corrupt warlords, but also began introducing new concepts, such as conscription and militarization, which they obtained from the West. However, the most signicant events of this period, with regard to modern Chinese military thought, are the rise of revolutionary forces and the politicization of the armed forces. This last change was initiated by Dr. Sun Yatsen, but was later adopted on a huge scale by both the Guomindang and the Communists. This change is simply a radical reaction on the part of the revolutionaries to the corrupt warlord forces.

In addition, Dr. Sun's industrial development project and General Jiang Baili's theories on mobilization and the economics of national defence both integrated economic development and national defence strategy. Though their ideas were not carried out in their lifetime, the effect of their ideas on modern Chinese military systems is clear. In the post-war years, both mainland China and Taiwan have been doing their best to carry out Sun's and Jiang's plans.

Footnotes

1. National Council of Military Science of China, *Modern Chinese History of War* (Beijing: Military Science Press, 1985), Vol. 3, pp. 108-135. In discussing the War of Bailong Rebellion of 1912, the authors particularly pointed out the major reasons for failure as the lack of political programs and the asking for leave of absence of the peasant soldiers. In *The Soong Dynasty* (New York: Harper & Row, 1985), the author, Sterling Seagrave, had a comment on Dr. Sun Yatsen. To him, Sun was claimed as the father of the Republic of China not because he was greater than many of his collegues who were killed in the uprisings. Sun's quirks and levitation kept him slightly disengaged, so he always survived and his leadership endured. And Sun was not personally involved in many military actions in the 11 uprisings. See pp. 83-85. The comment on Sun may not be completely correct, but the argument to some extent is convincing. According to *The Personal Records of President Jiang Jieshi* (Taipei: The Centre Daily News, 1976), (hereafter referred to as *Personal Records of Jiang*), Sun was personally involved in two out of eleven uprisings, once in Guangzhou (1895) and another one in Zhennanguan (1907). See Vol. 2, pp. 97 & 192.

2. *Personal Records of Jiang*, op. cit., Vol. 2, pp. 98 & 134-35.

3. Based on Jiang's records, since the sixth uprising, there were more and more rebels from the Qing army involved in the uprisings. See *Personal Record of Jiang*, Vol. 5, pp. 180-85. Also see Deng Yibing, "The Xunfang Dui of the Last Years of Qing Dynasty and the 1911 Revolution", *The Front of Social Science* (Shehui Kexue Zhanxian), No. 4, 1983, pp. 73-79.

4. Lei, Bailun, *Chinese Culture and Chinese Soldiers* (Taipei: Wannianqing, 1971), pp. 34 & 137-142.

5. Li, Zhen, *The History of Chinese Military Education* (Taipei: Zhongyang Winwu Gongyingshei, 1983), pp. 576-77.

6. Ibid. Also see Zhang Jungu, *The Biography of Li Yuanhong* (Taipei: Zhong Wai Press, 1971), p. 23.

7. Jiang, *Personal Records of Jiang*, Vol. 3, pp. 63-67.

8. Ibid., pp. 78-87, and pp. 154-160.

9. When Sun was the provisional president, the positon was close to the system of the U.S.A., but the revolutionaries could not trust Yuan Shikai and wanted to restrict his power by a parliamentary system. See Liu Yangyang, "A Comment on Huang Xing's Thought and Activities", in *One Hundred Subjects of Modern Chinese History* (Changsa, Hunan: Hunan People's Press, 1983), Vol. 2, p. 924, (hereafter referred to as *One Hundred Subjects*).

10. Zhu, Zongzhen, "The Second Revolution", in *One Hundred Subjects, op. cit.*, Vol. 2, pp. 1009-10. Also see Hu Baili, "The Founding and Collapse of Yuan Shikai's Dictator Rule", op. cit., Vol. 2, pp. 1043-47.

11. Hu, Baili, "The Founding and Collapse of Yuan Shikai's Dictator Rule", *op. cit.*, pp. 1053-55.

12. *Ibid.*, pp. 1055-56.

13. Pan, Rong, "The Campaign for Defending the Provisional Constitution", *One Hundred Subjects, op. cit.*, Vol. 2, pp. 1069-70.

14. Chen Jionming was the Commander-in-Chief of the Guangdong Army, the Governor of Guangdong Province, and the Minister of Army of the national government (in Guangzhou). He had been trusted by Sun as his main force in the War of Northern Expedition. He refused to supply Sun's army who was fighting at the front, but made a secret truce with Wu Peifu, the Commander of the Beiyang Army. When Sun tried to persuade him to support the Expedition, he refused to see Sun but carried out a coup and shelled Sun's official residence in Guangzhou in early morning of June 16, 1922. See *Personal Records of Jiang, op. cit.*, Vol. 5, pp. 175-80.

15. Li Yuanhong was born in 1864 in Huangpi County, Hubei Province. He was a graduate of the Navy Cadre School and started his earlier career as a navy officer in the Qing navy. He experienced the Sino-Japanese War of 1894 and tried to kill himself by jumping into the ocean when his warship was forced to surrender to the enemy in the wake of Chinese defeat. He was rescued by his soldiers and later was transferred to the army and worked as a staff member of Zhang Zhidong in Hubei Province. He had been sent to Japan to inspect its military system. Consequently, he became the most knowledgeable military officer among Zhang's staffs and was later appointed to train a unit of the New Army (brigade). He was highly respected by his men as an uncorrupted and competent military commander prior to the 1911 Revolution.

16. Yi, Guogan, ed., *The Official Documents of Vice-President Li: A Collection of Documents of Modern Chinese History* (Taipei: Wenxing, 1915), pp. 124-125.

17. *Ibid.*, pp. 125-126. See Yuan Shikai's telegram of April 16, 1912 in responding Li's.

18. *Ibid.*

19. *Ibid.*, p. 125.

20. See Li's telegram to the President and the government organizations outside Beijing (the Capital), April 14, 1912. *Ibid.*, p. 29. The candidate for the civilian governor (*Minzheng Zhang*), hand-picked

by Li from his own staff, was Fan Zengxiang.

21. The Telegram to the President (Yuan). *Ibid.*, p. 125.

22. In 1922, When he was asked to assume the presidency again, he publicly announced that should the military leaders agree with his policy of "abolishing the Viceroyship and demobilizing the armed forces", he would consider the office, otherwise he was not going to accept the offer. The generals vaguely agreed but nobody wanted to fullfil it after he took over the presidency. Quoted from Xiao Zhizhi and Ren Zequan, "A Preliminary Discussion of the Transformation of Li Yuanhong after the 1911 Revolution", *One Hundred Subjects, op. cit.*, Vol. 2, p. 982.

23. *Ibid.* Sun's telegram further asked the national government to transform the armed forces into workers and asked the Zhili fraction of the Beiyang Army to take a leadership in carrying out this policy.

24. Liu, Yangyang, "A Comment on Huang Xing's Thought and His Activities", *One Hundred Subjects, op. cit.*, Vol. 2, pp. 924-25. The cooperation between Sun and Huang once collapsed in 1914 when Sun reorganized the Goumindang into Zhonghua Gemingdang and insisted that "every member must pledge to sacrifice his life and freedom to follow Dr. Sun in order to restart the revolution". He disagreed with the wording and refused to join the Party. However, he did not oppose Sun beyond this. Later, when Sun started his movement against Yuan, Huang still stood by Sun's side and worked together in order to overthrow Yuan. See pp. 943-44.

25. Huang, Keqiang, *The Works of Huang Keqiang* (Taipei: the Commission of Party History of the Goumindang , 1967), p. 62. See "A Proposal on Military Education for all National Schools: A Farewell Speech to the Members of Parliament from Southern Provinces on July 16, 1914".

26. See "The Telegrams to the Vice-President and Governors on Removing the District Military Administration", in *The Works of Huang Keqiang, op. cit.*, pp. 410-11.

27. See "The Telegram to Yuan Shikai, Li Yuanhong, and Provincial Government in Reporting the Dissolution of the 3rd Brigade (May 1912)", *Ibid.*, p. 443; "The Telegram to the President and Other Officers for the Compliment of Division Commanders Zhu Qianzi, and Liu Yi for Their Voluntarily Dissolving Their Head-Quarters (May 1912)", p. 446; "The Telegram to the President and Other Leaders for the Compliment of Division Commander Du Huaichuan and Brigade Commander Yuan Huatong for Voluntarily Dissolving Their Head-quarters (May 1912)", p. 447; and "The Telegram to Yuan Shikai Asking for the Permission of Dismantling the Rear Office of Nanjing

(May 13, 1912)", p. 444.

28   See Huang Xing's telegrams to Yuan Shikai on the armed robberies in Nanjing in April 1912, *Ibid.*, p. 427. Also see the Telegram to Cheng Dequan in Suzhou to solve the discharged soldiers' problems carefully, April 1912, p. 430. Both in *The Works of Huang Keqiang.*

29.   See "The Telegram to Cheng Dequan", *Ibid.*, p. 430.

30.   See "The Telegram to Minli Newspaper Asking It to Send Telegrams Out in Order to Stop Zhang Zun's Enrolling of New Soldiers (May 16, 1910)", *Ibid.*, p. 446.

31.   Liu, Dawu, "The Chronicle of Cai Songpo," ed. by Liu Dawu, *The Posthumous Works of Mr. Cai Songpo* (Taipei: Wenxing Press, 1962), pp. 5-36. (Hereafter referred to as *Works of Cai.*)

32.   Cai, Songpo, "The Essay of National Militarism", *Works of Cai, op. cit.*, p. 64.

33   *Ibid.*, pp. 55 & 57.

34   *Ibid.*

35.   Idem, "Quotations of Zeng and Hu Regarding the Administration of the Armed Forces", *Works of Cai, op. cit.*, pp. 38-39.

36.   *Ibid.*, p. 40.

37   Idem, "Military Plan", *Works of Cai, op. cit.*, p. 65.

38   *Ibid.*, p. 68.

39   *Ibid.*

40   *Ibid.*, pp. 70-71.

41   *Ibid.*, p. 83.

42   *Ibid.*, pp. 84-85. The definition of discipline is quoted from the Japanese Infantry Drill Regulations and Charles Darwin's works.

43   *Ibid.*, p. 86.

44   Cai, "The Quotation of Zeng and Hu", *Works of Cai, op. cit.*, p. 52.

45   *Ibid.*

46   *Ibid.*

47   *Ibid.*

48.   The Introduction by Jiang Jieshi, in "The Quotation of Zeng and Hu", *Works of Cai, op. cit.*, p. 35.

49   See "The Autobiography of Dr. Sun Yatsen (1897)", *The Works of Dr. Sun Yatsen* (Guofu Quanshu)(Taipei: Institute of National Defence, 1963), pp. 388-89. (Hereafter referred to as *Works of Sun.*) Also see "Being Taken Hostage by the Chinese Embassy in London: a Memoir of Dr. Sun Yatsen", *Ibid.*, pp. 373-74.

50.   According to all official documents, it shows that Dr. Sun Yatsen had personally founded the first revolutionary organization--Xingzhonghui in Hawaii in 1894 and in Hong Kong in 1895. However, based on the information revealed in Sun's own work, "Being Taken Hostage in the Chinese Embassy in London", it seems that around 1892, there was a

Xingzhonghui in China. The headquarters was in Shanghai, but its major operation was in Guangzhou. He joined the organization as a member not a founder. Nevertheless, there is no information to show who was the leader at that time and what happened to that person or those people later. In the beginning, the Xingzhonghui was aimed at promoting Chinese political reforms by peaceful methods such as appealing to the government, etc. It turned to armed rebellion only after the defeat of China in the Sino-Japanese War of 1894. This is quite different from the official documents. See "Being Taken Hostage", *op. cit.*, pp. 373-75.

51. "A Proposal of The International Development of Chinese Industry Plan", *Works of Sun, op. cit.*, pp. 40-41.

52. The leaders of the Western countries who received a copy of this proposal and who were invited to join the development of a Chinese industry plan praised it highly but did not make any commitment. See the letters received from the Western leaders in *Works of Sun, op. cit.*, pp. 114-117.

53 See "Sun Wen Xue Shuo", *Works of Sun, op. cit.*, Ch. 5-8 pp. 18-38.

54. The Soviet Union had sent Mikhail Borodin to serve as Dr. Sun Yatsen's adviser and had stayed in Guangzhou to help Sun in reorganizing the Guomindang in 1923-24. Meanwhile, the Soviet Union also sent G. Maring and Adolf Joffe to Guangzhou and Shanghai in 1921 and 1922 to persuade Sun to cooperate with the newly established Chinese Communist Party. A Sun-Joffe Agreement permitted the Chinese Commuinist Party to join the Guomindang but still keep their own independent party identity. This accord was approved by the First Congress of the Guomindang in January 1924. See Lucien Bianco, *Origins of the Chinese Revolution, 1915-1949*, trans. by Murrid Bell (Stanford, CA: Stanford University Press, 1971), pp. 54-55 notes. Also see Jiang Jieshi, *Soviet Russia in China* (New York: Farrar, Straus and Cudahy, 1957), pp. 16-17.

55. Several months after the Sun-Joffe Agreement was signed, Dr. Sun sent Jiang Jieshi as his personal representative to visit the Soviet Union in August 1923. He spent three months in the Soviet Union to investigate their military, party and political system. After his return to China, within a few months, he was appointed to the president of Huangpu Military Academy. See Jiang, *The Soviet Russia in China, op. cit.*, pp. 19-24.

56. National Defence Planning--a letter to Leo Zhongkai in 1921. See *Works of Sun, op. cit.*, pp 169-70.

57. See the Preface to "A Proposal of International Development of Chinese Industry Plan", *op. cit.*, p. 39.

58. The inland ports are mostly designed to be constructed along the Yantze

River and Zhu River in Guangdong Province. They are, in Sun's plan, to be dredged in order to improve their navigation capacity, which is the central subject of the second and third plans. See *Works of Sun, op. cit.*, pp. 50-87.

59. The total mileage is caculated from the figures given on page 46 in the first plan.

60. See the fourth plan, in *Works of Sun, op. cit.*, pp. 91-93.

61. See the third plan, in *Works of Sun, op. cit.*, pp. 69-80.

62. See the fourth plan, section 5, in *Work of Sun, op. cit.*, pp. 69-80.

63 *Ibid.*, section 3, pp. 93-97.

64 *Ibid.*, section 4, pp. 97-100.

65 See the fifth plan, section 4: the industry of transportion, *Works of Sun, op. cit.*, p. 108; and the sixth plan, pp. 109-110.

66 Yao, Weiyuan and Xiao, Zhizhi, "The Great Contribution of Dr. Sun Yatsen to the 1911 Revolution", *One Hundred Subjects, op. cit.*, p. 915. The school was named Qingsan Military School.

67 "The Responsibility of Saving the Country and the People Is Laid on the Revolutionary Army", *Works of Sun, op. cit.*, p. 968.

68 "The Foundation of the Revolutionary Army Is Knowledge", *Works of Sun, op. cit.*, p. 993.

69 Sun, "The Victory of the Armed Forces and the Struggle of the Party Members,"--a speech to the staffs of the headquarters in Guangzhou on Dec. 9, 1923. See *Works of Sun, op. cit.*, pp. 944-45.

70. "A Letter to Jiang Jaishi for Setting Up a Revolutionary Committee", *Works of Sun, op. cit.*, p. 845.

71 Sun, "The Reasons of the Past Failure of the Guomindang and the Future Directions of Effort", *Works of Sun, op. cit.*, p. 939.

72 Idem, "A Letter to Jiang Jieshi Instructing Him about the Distribution of Weapons and Military Training etc. in the Way of North Expedition", (1924) *Works of Sun, op. cit.*, p. 844.

73. Idem, "The Revolutionary Army Must Pit One Against One Hundred", a speech on the ceremony of awards to the bodyguards of the Guanyinsan Incident in 1924, in *Works of Sun, op. cit.*, pp. 950-951.

74 Idem, "The Spirit Education of the Military", a speech to the Jiangxi and Guangdong armies in Guilin in January 1922, in *Works of Sun, op. cit.*, p. 915.

75 *Ibid.*, p. 916.

76 *Ibid.*

77 *Ibid.*, p. 907.

78 *Ibid*

79 *Ibid.*, p. 908.

80 *Ibid.*

81. Mao, Zedong, "Reactionaries and Atom Bombs Are Paper Tigers", an

interview with Anne Louisse Strong, August 1946. See *Selected Works of Mao Tse-tung* (Peking: Foreign Languages Press, 1969), Vol. IV, pp. 97-101. (Hereafter referred to as *Works of Mao.*).

82.   Sun, "The method of Struggle of the Guomindang Should not Completely Rely on Military, But Should Concurrently Emphasize Propaganda", a speech to Party members in Guangzhou, on Dec. 30, 1923. See *Works of Sun, op. cit.*, p. 950.

83.   *Ibid.*

84.   *Ibid.*, p. 950-51.

85   *Ibid.*, p. 951.

86.   See Mao, "On Correcting mistaken Ideas in the Party", (Dec. 1929) *Works of Mao, op. cit.*, p. 105.

87.   Sun, "An Introduction to the Beginner of War by Zhou Yingsi", (June 1914) *Works of Sun, op. cit.*, p. 577.

88.   Idem, "To Save Guomindang is to Start from Discharging and Banning the Military Force", a speech to the military and civilians in Guangzhou in February 1923, in *Works of Sun, op. cit.*, p. 923; and "The Discharge of the Military Forces and the construction of Road", a speech to the business leaders in Hong Kong on Feb. 20, 1923. See *Works of Sun, op. cit.*, p. 922.

89.   In this travel, he received financial assistance from two officials who were Fang Youting, the magistrate of Tong-xiang County, and Lin Dichen, the prefect of Hangzhou Prefecture. See Tao, Juyin, *The Biography of Jiang Baili* (Beijing:Zhonghua, 1985), pp. 3-4.

90.   According to Tao Juyin's record, Jiang's decision to go to Germany after only a few months on the job was due to his former teacher's suggestion in order to avoid a possible risk of conflict between the old army (Xunfang Jun) and the New Army (Xin Jun), because it was said that he was the target of Zhang Zuolin. Ibid., p. 12.

91.   Wang, Ranzhi, *General Jiang Baili and His Military Thought* (Taipei: Shuaizheng Press, 1975), p. 28. (Hereafter referred to as *Jiang Baili.*)

92.   The true reason for his suicide is still a mystery because it is unlikely that he would kill himself solely for a budget problem. Whatever the reason, it is certain that he was too emotional as a commandant of a military school such as Baoding.

93.   His involvement in the anti-Yuan movement was more for personal friendship rather than pro-revolution. He was a classmate of Cai E in the Japanese Military School and a close friend. See Wang Ranzhi, *Jiang Baili, op. cit.*, p. 21.

94.   Before the beginning of the Northern Expedition, he was selected by Xiang Jun to go to Guangzhou to see Jiang Jieshi to discuss military cooperation problems, but he was in Shanghai and did not go. Liu Wendao, another representative, met with Jiang, who personally

invited Jiang Baili to join the Revolutionary force, but it did not work out. Later when some military leader talked privately about the possibility of having him take over the post of Chief of Staff of the Revolutionary, he rejected this idea. See Tao Juyin, *The Biography of Jiang Baili, op. cit.*, p. 64.

95. Xue, Guangqian, *The Life of Jiang Baili's Old Age and His Military Thought* (Taipei: Zhuanji Wenzue Press, 1969), pp. 76-77.

96. Mao, Zhuqing, ed., *The Works of Cai E* (Zhangsa: People's Press of Hunan, 1983), p. 300.

97. Shen, Yunlong, ed., *The Essays of Jiang Baili* (Fang-zhen), (Taipei: Institution of National Defence, 1972), pp. 72-85, including the articles such as "Political Strategy and Military Strategy (Zheng Lue Yu Zhan Lue)", "National Power, Military Power, and Armed Froces (Guo Li, Wu Li, and Bing Li)", and "The Main Idea of Military Education (Jun Shi Jiao Yu Zhi Yao Zhi)", are exactly the same as in "The Military Plan", *Works of Cai E, op. cit.*, pp.301-306, 330-338.

98. His major works on this subject were given the title "Treatise of National Defence" by himself and by editors who were in charge of editing his posthumous works. See Jiang Fucong and Xue Guangqian, eds. *The Works of Jiang Baili, op. cit.*, Vol. 2, Also see Shen, *The Essays of Jiang Baili, op. cit.*, pp.72-85.

99. Jiang & Xue, eds., *The Works of Jiang Baili, op. cit.*, Vol. 2, p. 149.

100. *Ibid.*, p. 204.

101. *Ibid.*

102. Jiang, Baili, "The Introduction to the Treatise of National Defence (1)", *Works of Jiang Baili, op. cit.*, Vol. 2, p. 148.

103. Jiang, Baili, "The Introduction to the Treatise of National Defence (2)", *The Works of Jiang Baili, op. cit.*, Vol. 2, p. 155.

104. Idem, "The New Trend of the Development of the World Military Situation", *The Works of Jiang Baili, op. cit.*, Vol. 2, p. 167.

105. *Ibid.* p. 168.

106. Idem, "The Interpretation of Conscription System", *The Works of Jiang Baili, op. cit.*, Vol. 2, pp.230-31.

107. Idem, "The Outline of General Mobilization: Report No. 2", and Annex I of "The New Theory of Everyone a Soldier", *The Works of Jiang Baili, op. cit.*, Vol. 4, p. 268.

108. Idem, "The Indication of the Outlines of the Meaning of General Mobilization and Its Practical Method", and Annex I of "The New Theory of Everyone a Soldier", *The Works of Jiang Baili, op. cit.*, Vol. 4, pp. 280-81.

109. *Ibid.*, p. 184.

110. Idem, "The New Trend of the World Military," *The Works of Jiang Baili, op. cit.*, Vol. 2, p. 169.

111. *Ibid.*, p. 306.
112. *Ibid.*
113. *Ibid.*, p. 307.
114. Idem, "The Outline of New Guerrilla Warfare", the attached Chinese version of "The Method of New Guerrilla Warfare, by Major Heinz", *The Works of Jiang Baili, op. cit.*, Vol. 4, pp. 294-299.
115. *Ibid.*, p. 299.
116. Jiang, Baili, "The Outline of New Guerrilla Warfare", *The Works of Jiang Baili, op. cit.*, Vol. 4, p. 294.
117. Idem, "Introducing Marshal Badon's Preface to the Military Theory of the Command of the Air Written by Giulio Douhet", *The Works of Jiang Baili, op. cit.*, Vol. 2, p. 194.
118. Idem, "The Foundation of the Power of Modern Air Force", *The Works of Jiang Baili, op. cit.*, Vol. 4, pp. 315-25.
119. *Ibid.*, pp. 341-42.
120. *Ibid.*, pp. 346-47.
121. Wang, Ranzhi, *Jiang Baili, op. cit.*, p. 125.
122. *Ibid.*, pp. 59-60.

Chapter 5

Jiang Jieshi's Military Thought

The civil wars among the warlords in the 1920's almost ruined the country and brought it to the edge of collapse. However, a dramatic event occurred in the Goumindang in 1924 that changed the trend of Chinese political development within a few years, and significantly affected the Chinese military system.

As mentioned in last chapter, the Guomindang called its first National Congress at the beginning of 1924, at which the Party, among other things, decided to establish its own military academy in order to build up a revolutionary force similar to that of the Soviet Union.[1] Following the close of the Congress, Jiang Jieshi, a young general and confidant of Dr. Sun Yatsen, was appointed as the commandant of the school in March of 1924. From that point on Jiang became a rising star of the Chinese revolution. He very quickly claimed the leadership of the Party within a few years, after successfully defeating the warlords with his new revolutionary forces. He then unified China under a central government, at least nominally. Jiang proceeded to dominate Chinese political development for 25 years until 1949, when he was driven out of the mainland. He settled in Taiwan, where he continued to control the island under a personal dictatorship for another 25 years until his death in 1975.

During his long reins in both China and Taiwan, the Chinese military position was significantly strengthened, and he brought the military modernization of China one more step ahead. Indeed, his achievements cannot be totally discredited due to his defeat in the civil war against the CCP. Therefore, it would be worthwhile to consider Jiang's military thought in order to bridge any gap that may exist between the early Republican period and the emergence of the concept of people's warfare developed by Mao Zedong during the period of civil war and national liberation war.

1. The Historical Background of Jiang's Thought

Jiang JieShi was born in 1887, eight years before the Sino-Japanese war and thirteen years before the Boxer Rebellion and the Allied Expedition against China. The humiliating defeat of China in these wars had affected most Chinese. And like most young Chinese of that time who had witnessed these incidents of national humiliation, Jiang became patriotic and national-istic.

Jiang spent most of his boyhood and teenage years in his home town, Xikou Township, Fenghwa County, Zhejiang Province. He studied the Chinese classics at private schools until the age of 17 when he was admitted to the Fung Lu school in Fenghwa county in 1903, at which time he began to aquire a more modern education. He was later encouraged by his teacher, Gu Qinglian, to study military science abroad in order to defend his country one day. Gu even taught him Sunzi's *The Art of War*. From Gu, Jiang also learned about the recent revolution instigated by Dr. Sun Yatsen. Under this strong political influence, Jiang's own personal career orientation was gradually developed. He decided to study abroad and commit himself to the revolution in the future.[2]

Jiang left China for Japan in 1906 but returned within a few months. Shortly after returning to China, he was accepted by the Chinese Baoding Military Academy. He entered the school in the summer of 1907. However, he only stayed there for a few months and left for Japan again in early 1908 when he was chosen to study military science in Japan with about 60 other students.

He was admitted to Zhenwu school when he arrived in Tokyo in 1908. He completed three years of preliminary military training and was sent in 1910 to a Japanese army unit to serve as a private, which was a requirement for any candidate to enrol in any Japanese military academy. Before completing the required one year tour of duty, however, the 1911 Revolution broke out in Wuchang and he immediately returned to China when he received a message from Chen Qimei, his close friend and an important leader of the Tongmonhui. From that point, Jiang began his long military career.[3]

While Jiang was still studying at Zhenwu school in Japan, Chen Qimei introduced him to Dr. Sun Yatsen in June of 1910. After this meeting, Sun told Chen that "he [Jiang] is invaluable to the Tongmonhui. He will one day, without doubt, become a revolutionary practitioner *(Geming Shixing Jia)*."[4]

Under Chen Qimei's arrangements, Jiang took part in the successful operation of attacking the headoffice of the Xunfu of Zhejiang province in Hangzhou. He was later appointed the commander of a newly established army regiment by Chen, but he resigned after a few months in order to further his military studies in Germany. He never travelled to Germany, however. He was swept up in the Second Revolution in 1913. After the failure of the Second Revolution, Jiang took refuge in Japan with other revolutionary leaders and from that point onwards, his relationship with Dr. Sun became closer and he was able to receive instruction from Sun personally. He eventually became a confidant of Sun.

Following Yuan Shihkai's death, a Northern Expedition led by Dr. Sun Yatsen in the Guangdong area against the northern warlords began in 1917. However, internal disputes doomed the operation. Even Sun's own life was once endangered in the rebellion of Chen Jionming. During this difficult period, Jiang showed his personal loyalty to Sun when he rushed to Guangdong to stand by Sun through the ordeal of Chen's rebellion in June, 1922.[5]

After the rebellion was suppressed in 1923, it became obvious that none of the existing military forces under the revolutionary command could be trusted. Sun had to build up his own armed force in order to fulfil the revolutionary goals. For this reason, he decided to establish an army school to train military cadres. He assigned Jiang to head a tour on his behalf to the Soviet Union in August of 1923 to study the Soviet military system. Jiang spent three months there and submitted a report to Sun upon his return.[6]

Only one year after Jiang became commandant of the Huangpu Military academy, Sun suddenly died during a visit to Beijing to negotiate a peaceful unification of China with the Northern government. The death of Sun left the leadership of the Guomindang in disarray. This gave Jiang the opportunity to manipulate different factions of the party in order to gain the leadership for himself. Cooperating with the Guangxi army, he was able to unify Guangdong and Guangxi provinces within two years. In 1927, Jiang headed the Northern Expedition and was ready to unify the country by force.

Under China's traditional political culture, the ideal political leaders were required to achieve the status of Shengjun or the Platonic idea of philosopher king. Being a Shengjun, the ruler must be great in every respect. He must be able to set up an immortal model of morality, merit and scholarliness. To apply this idea to modern Chinese politics, a political leader is often an image of an Almighty God. He is not only a statesman, but also a political scientist, military strategist, economist and philosopher. This traditional idea has been more or less reflected in the roles of Dr. Sun Yatsen, Jiang Jieshi, and Mao Zedong. To fulfil these roles, Jiang, in his fifty years of political domination, left behind volumes of publications covering a broad spectrum of topics, including politics, military science and philosophy. His works contained both his own ideas and those of other people.

Jiang was a faithful adherent of Wang Yangming, a philosopher who lived during the Ming dynasty. Jiang believed that if China wanted to defeat Japanese imperialism, the Chinese would have to defeat the spirit of Bushido, which is based on the philosophy of Wang. Therefore, he suggested that everyone study Wang's philosophy and practice it. He instructed his officers to behave in accordance with their conscience *(Zhi Liang Zhi)*.[7]

In addition, because of his Japanese education, his early military writings showed strong Japanese characteristics. However, because of the military aid of the United States in later years, Western military theories have left their imprint on his later writings.

As a follower of Dr. Sun Yatsen, Jiang was certainly affected by him. He followed Sun's policy and thus also wanted to train a revolutionary force which would be consumed with revolutionary spirit, and which would have the courage to fight against a numerically superior enemy because each soldier would be willing to die for the cause of the Revolution.

2. Jiang's Thought Concerning Army Building

A country cannot survive for long without a military force to defend itself, and the armed forces are the core of any national defence. Therefore, the building of an armed force is often a country's top priority.

As far as army building is concerned, some questions inevitably arise: what are the goals of a country's armed force? What kind of armed force does a country need in order to fulfil these particular goals? And how should this force be constructed?

A. The Establishment of the Huangpu Military Academy

Once in Taiwan, Jiang restated his ideas of army building. He said when he was young, he had dreamed of creating a military school to train ambitious Chinese youths in accordance with his own ideas. This military school should not only be able to build up a modernized military force in order to complete the Northern Expedition, but also be able to build a modern country.[8]

From his report to Dr. Sun Yatsen, which he presented upon returning from the Soviety Union, one can realize how strongly he believed in establishing a military school. Jiang wrote:

Before the country can be prosperous and strong, we must unify it; to unify it, we must eliminate the warloads; to eliminate the war-lords, we must build up and strengthen our armed forces. Conse-quently, the unification and strengthening of our country depends on the establishment of a military school.[9]

Although he mentioned that his final goal of establishing the military school was building a prosperous and strong country, his immediate goal, however, was carrying out the aims of theRevolution. Therefore, the armed force to be built should be a revolutionary force and be controlled by the Party. It would be a Party force (Dangjun) and would fight for the cause of the Revolution. When the school was set up in 1924, its official name was The Army Academy of the Chinese National Party (Zhongguo Guomindang Lujun Junguan Xuexiao).[10] It was also known as Huangpu Military Academy, a name which referred to its location on Huangpu Island, about ten kilometers from Guangzhou, down the Zhu River. [11]

Jiang was not the first person in modern Chinese history to build a military school. As mentioned in Chapter 3, under the influence of the *Yangwu* Movement, Li Hongzhang and Zuo Zongtang had started to open military schools. Similar schools were also set up by other viceroys in Nanjing, Wuchang and Guangzhou.[12] After the Sino-Japanese War and the Boxer Rebellion, the Imperial Government asked the regional governments to train their New Army and ordered the provinces to establish their own military schools. However, while the whole country was feverishly building military schools and establishing armed forces, the government did not set up proper guidelines. This failure may have caused further localization of the Chinese military forces and may have promoted the emergence of separatist warlord regimes in the 1920s.

It was about 1906 when the Manchu government made its last effort to centralize its military force; it also started to regulate the military school system. A three-level military education system was designed. Army "primary schools" were set up in every provincial capital. Three army "secondary schools" were built in Qinghe Zhen of Hebei, Wuchang of Hunan, and Nanjing of Jiangsu. An army academy (*Bingguan Xuetang*) and an army university were built in Baoding of Hebei. These schools were permanently shut down after the 1911 Revolution, except for the Baoding Military Academy and the Army University, which were both later reopened in 1912[13].

Many modern Chinese military leaders in the Guomindang were actually trained at the Baoding Military Academy or other military schools operated by the provincial governments.

When the Huangpu Academy was established, it had, in contrast to the old Imperial schools, very little in weapons and equipment. What the Huangpu cadres did have was a willingness to fight their way through any opposition to unify the country. Therefore, Huangpu particularly emphasized the importance of spirit to overcome any material disadvantages.[14]

B. The Establishment of the Party Military Forces and Their Political System

The establishment of Huangpu Military Academy was aimed at completing the unfinished revolution. But how can one create a revolutionary armed force? According to Jiang: "only those soldiers who fully understand the Party's theory (*Dang Yi*) can obey the command of the Party; and only those cadres who believe in the Party's *Zhuyi* (ism) can create a revolution-ary force."[15]

In order to guarantee that the armed forces would obey the order of the Party and fight for the cause of the revolution, it is essential for the Party to control the forces organizationally as well as ideologically. To achieve this goal, the Guomindang adopted the political commissar system of the Soviet Red Army. When Jiang Jieshi was appointed as the commandant of the Huangpu Academy in 1924, the Central Committee of the Guomindang concurrently appointed Leo Zhongkai as the Party representative to the Academy. A political department was established, which was in charge of arranging political courses, handling propaganda, and managing other politi-cal activities in order to transform the cadets into fervent revolutionaries. Cadets and officers were all recruited as Party members.

Under the Guomindang command, the local army started its Eastern Expedition against Chen Jiongming in 1925. The cadets of Huangpu Academy were organized into "a school army" (*xiaojun*) and were later transformed into a Party army (*Dangjun*) in order to join the expedition. Party organizations were also established along with the Party army. Leo Zhongkai became the Party representative to the Party army and directed the army's political activity.[16] A similar system was set up down to the company level, in charge of political works.

In 1926, when the Guomindang was preparing for the Northern Expe-dition, and based on the experience of the Eastern Expedition, it enacted two rules to regulate the political works of the armed forces. One was called "The Regulations Regarding the Party Representatives of the National Revolution-ary Armies"; the other was "The Regulations of the Organization of the Department of Political Training". After that, the political work system was formally installed in all of the military units under the Guomindang com-mand.[17]

In a speech to the propaganda teams of the Department of Political Training in Xuzhou, Jiang revealed his ideas concerning the political works in the army. These fucntions were primarily limited to propaganda and/or political education. He asked the political workers to set a good model for the soldiers in order to gain their trust.[18] It seems that the political workers were asked to serve as teachers for the soldiers.

The political work system in the Guomindang Army did not last long; it collapsed in 1928 after the Jinan Incident of May 3, 1928. Jiang discharged all of the political workers and dismantled the organization from the regiment level down to the company level. The same happened later at the division level. The political work system was only kept intact at the army corps level.[19]

The reasons for this dramatic change, according to the author of *The History of Political Warfare in the National Revolutionary Army*, were twofold: the poor performance of the political workers and financial hardship.[20] Another possible reason for this change was the deterioration of the relationship between the commanders and the political workers. As Jiang said to the political workers in 1929, almost all of the Party representatives and other political workers had been either Communists or influenced by the Communists. After the Communists were expelled from the Party, the political workers in the army were no longer able to gain the trust of the soldiers. In addition, the commanders and soldiers had, from the beginning, been cynical of the Party representatives and political workers. It was only fear that kept the soldiers from criticizing the Party representatives. However, with the purge of the Communists from the Party, they began to defy the political workers and the entire system.[21] The cynical attitude of the soldiers toward the political workers, in fact, had little to do with any reputed connections between political workers and communists, but with their expanding power, which may have impeded the freedom of the commanders. As Jiang said:

> The most important reason is primarily due to the control and intervention of the Party and political workers over all of the military affairs that deprived the freedom of military commanders, and thus caused the conflict between them.[22]

When the system was initiated in the armed forces, most leaders in the Guomindang did not realize the importance of it and did not commit themselves to this work;[23] meanwhile, the Communists in the Guomindang were very conscious about it. They positively committed themselves to it and formed the majority of the Party representatives and political workers. After they were purged, the Guomindang did not have enough qualified people to fill the positions. The people who replaced the Communists in taking over the political works did not know how to perform their duties. They even abused their powers for the sake of personal interest. Consequently, the system was ruined.[24]

The system was later reinstated and strengthened in order to fight the Comnmunists in the Civil War of the 1930s. However, it could not compete with that of the PLA until the 1950s when the Guomindang moved to Taiwan and Jiang Jingguo, the elder son of Jiang Jieshi, was appointed the director of the General Department of Political Warfare. Jiang Jingguo did much better than his predecessors, not necessarily because he was better qualified than them, but because he was the only person who had the power to overcome the possible opposition within the armed forces. As a professional soldier and an ambitious political leader, Jiang Jieshi was always vigilant in protecting his powers. As Commander-in-Chief of the Guomindang forces, he prefered to control the armed forces by emphasizing personal loyalty rather than the political work system. Consequently, there were no powerful Party representatives, like those in the PLA, who were permitted to overrule the decisions of the commanders. Nevertheless, when the Guomindang was defeated in the Civil War and was forced to move to Taiwan, the situation was so bad that Jiang had to strengthen the political works of the armed forces in order to avoid any possible penetration by the Communist insurgents. Under Jiang Jingguo's leadership, the political work system was permitted to extend its powers to fulfil its needs. The political control of the armed forces in Taiwan will be further discussed. For the time being, however, it is necessary for us to analyze the spirit of the revolutionary forces.

C. Revolutionary Spirit and its Source

In addition to organizational control over the armed forces through the political work systems, the most significant control an army has over its soldiers is likely to be achieved by means of political indoctrination in order to transform their perception of the world. By doing so, the Party leaders and military commanders would expect to strengthen the resolve of the soldiers to fight for the cause of revolution. From Jiang's speeches to the Huangpu cadets, one would likely realize that Jiang had particularly emphasized the spirit factor in war. According to him, a revolutionary army has to rely on its special revolutionary spirit to defeat the enemy. "Should it not have this spirit, it cannot win the war, and, thus, it would no longer be a revolutionary force."[25]

An army is judged to be a revolutionary army on the basis of its spirit. If it has revolutionary spirit, it is a revolutionary force; otherwise, it is not. Jiang thought that spirit consisted of the following traits:

(a) *Courage to Die*

According to Jiang, the physical expression of revolutionary spirit is taking risk. Jiang said, "If one does not dare to take risks, there is no other way to show one's spirit. Only when one dares to fight to death against the enemy, one can expect to win the battle."[26]

Whether one dares to risk one's life depends on what perception one holds of the problem of life and death. Jiang talked of this problem repeatedly to his cadets. When he made his first public speech as the commandant of the Huangpu Military Academy, he emphatically explained his perception. He asked every cadet to set up a correct perception of his purpose of life. He said: "the purpose of one's life should not revolve around himself, but should promote the life of mankind."[27]

With a correct perception of life, one is likely to understand the value of life and death. Jiang told his students in the same speech:

> The duty of a soldier can only be expressed with the word "death"; so is the purpose of a soldier's life. . .If one does not understand this problem and only desires to preserve his own life by sacrificing justice, he would not only be disqualified as a soldier but even be disqualified as a person at all. . .Our life should not be limited to this world, it should survive forever. . .Our real lives should continue for a thousand years after our death. If our lives can be carried on by the generations of the future, we should no longer concern ourselves with our physical demise.[28]

An old Chinese said that everybody has to die one day. If one's death can benefit the world, it would seem to be as heavy as Taishan Mountain; on the contrary, if one's death has nothing to do with the society, it would be as light as a feather. Jiang's words contain the same philosophy. Besides this perception, Jiang's explanation of death implies a further meaning. From a commander's point of view, if his soldiers are no longer concerned with their own lives and are prepared to die in any decisive battle, they would probably form an invincible army. A revolutionary force, which is often inadequately armed, has to rely on their superior morale or spirit to overcome their disadvantage. Jiang's words were unmistakably aimed at this point.

(b) *Pitting One Against Ten*

Jiang preached a similar strategy as Dr. Sun Yatsen to his cadets. He said:

> This Academy is different from other military schools. This is the military school of a revolutionary party. As our Zongli [Sun] often said: "to be a revolutionary army, each soldier has to be able to fight one hundred enemy soldiers." To me, it seems that if a revolutionary soldier can hold his rifle firmly and shoot at the target accurately, he can not only fight one hundred but also possibly fight one thousand and even ten thousand enemies. . .How is this possible?. . .Fear no death.[29]

From this quotation, one is likely to find that the essential method of pitting one against one hundred is to master marksmanship, and to be calm when encountering the enemy in the field. However, on other occasions, he suggested a three-step method to further the success of his revolutionary strategy: the first is by the spirit of unity. According to Jiang, because of disadvantages in number and equipment, the revolutionary forces have to express a highly united effort in fighting, otherwise it would be difficult for them to win. A second strategy is to concentrate one's own force on one chosen front. By so doing, the revolutionary force is likely to transform its inferior position into a superior one, and thus, to win the battle easily.

171

Following the initial victory, it could extend its victory by attacking on the enemy's flank or rear. The last strategy suggested by Jiang is "courage to take the risks,"[30] which is simply a repetition of the principle of "fearing no death". His philosophy is that if one does not fear the enemy, the enemy would begin to fear him; if one feels scared by the enemy, the enemy would gain courage.[31]

(c) *The Emphasis on Discipline*

Discipline is an essential source of power for a military force. Without discipline, a military unit would become an armed gang. Without discipline, it cannot fight effectively when it meets a strong enemy in battle. "Strictness" has long been accepted as one of the five military virtues by the Chinese military leaders. No prominent commander in Chinese history has ever lost his reputation as a strict commander. People tend to equate discipline with penalties, and strictness with cruelty and harshness. Therefore, discipline has always been closely related to military criminal codes. The word "discipline" in Chinese is a compound word "Jileu" which contains two elements: "Ji" may be interpreted as discipline, while "Leu" means regulations or laws. Consequently, military discipline is often equal to "Junleu", that is, military law or military criminal codes. However, the concept of discipline should not be limited only to penalties, above all in the modern age.

Cai E argued in his "military plan", for example, that neither morality nor threats of penalites can hold soldiers firmly for long in a difficult battle. Feelings of patriotism would be overwhelmed when the situation becomes too difficult; penalties cannot stop soldiers from fleeing under the strong pressure of the enemy. He therefore quoted Darvin's theory, which holds that faith can keep soldiers together in a difficult situation in battle. With faith, the soldiers would believe that their commanders will lead them to victory and they will never be left behind by their superiors. This mutual trust, therefore, is the core of military discipline.[32]

Cai E's idea of military discipline is highly applicable to the revolutionary force, because most revolutionaries are motivated by a faith which makes them willing to risk their lives without any regret.

However, while faith is important to an armed force, nobody would totally deny the role of law in maintaining the proper function of military discipline. Even Cai could not totally reject this either.

Jiang's idea is similar to Cai E's. He said : "soldiers have to obey their superiors and should never lose their faith in the officers. If anyone fails to do so, it must be that he does not understand the Party theory and thus is not a true revolutionary party member."[33] To Jiang, the source of discipline is faith which includes believing in one's superiors, trusting one's subordinates and believing one's self to be a good revolutionary soldier who is fighting for the Party.[34]

It seems that Jiang's concept of faith includes some moral principles. He regarded the success of the Party and the prosperity of the country as a moral responsibility of the cadets and, therefore, required them to endure any hardship, to work hard, to behave themselves , and to study every possible method in order to fulfil their revolutionary responsibility.[35]

However, to Jiang Jieshi, the weight of penalties on the effect of military dicipline seemed more important than morality and faith. As early as 1924, only a few months after the Huangpu Military Academy was created, a law of joint liability (*Lianzuo Fa*) was promulgated. It required the punishment of those who are related to the offenders. From the corps down to the squad, if the commander of a unit gives up his position without receiving proper orders, he would be executed . On the contrary, if a unit gives up its position and leaves its commander behind to be killed by the enemy, all of the commander's immediate subordinates would be punished with death. In the case when a squad leader is left behind and, thus, killed, all his soldiers would be executed.[36] Jiang told the cadets:

> As soon as the Lianzuo Fa is effective, everyone in the army
> will always feel that there is a knife hanging over his head and
> a rope tied to his feet; everybody will be mutually supervised
> and bound together at all levels and nobody will dare to desert
> his position in time of war.[37]

The concept of Lianzuo Fa has had a long history in Chinese military thought. It was first found in the book of Weiliaozi. As an essential instrument of military discipline which guarantees the execution of military orders, the death penalty has often been used by military commanders and, thus, it has made the traditional military virtue of strictness seem cruel and brutal.

Logically, the members of a revolutionary force are all volunteers; their involvment in fighting is motivated by the idea of revolution. If a revolutionary force needs the death penalty to keep its soldiers fighting, it would no longer deserve the title of a revolutionary force. The revolution itself would soon collapse, as its members begin losing their enthusiasm for revolution.

The Party military force and its overemphasis on the power of revolutionary spirit have had a complicated effect on Chinese political development in the following decades.

While the Guomindang's armed forces defeated the local military forces and unified the country, they did not totally remove the problem of personal military forces. Indeed, the party force still primarily owes its loyalty to the party leader.

It is conceivable that a party in power will tend to use its own forces to suppress its political opponents. On the other hand, when a party forms the opposition, it would likely use its own forces to gain power. These power conflicts occurred in China, but are by no means limited to China. If a country has two or more parties each with their own armed force, the country would be consumed by long and intermittent civil wars, as is the case in present-day Lebanon. In these cases, a democratic system cannot develop smoothly. In addition, political parties with their own armed forces inevitably tend to establish authoritarian or even totalitarian regimes.

Revolution is basically a dramatic political change which takes place within a relatively short period of time with or without bloodshed. Should a revolution be prolonged for decades, its goal may also be changed. The same slogans may no longer mean the same thing. By the same token, the revolutionary spirit, which was interpreted as "courage to die" by Jiang Jieshi, cannot be continuously relied upon. The Eastern Campaign (against Chen Jiongming) and the Northern Expedition both were often cited as examples where a small force of soldiers filled with revolutionary spirit had defeated a numerically superior enemy. However, from Jiang's own speech, one can see that only five years after the establishment of Huangpu, the revolutionary spirit of the army had already begun to fade. As Jiang said in 1929, "the Party army now only has the empty name of 'revolutionary force'; its previous spirit and charactersitics are all gone. Corruption, demoralization, and lack of discipline now run rampant in the army."[38]

While revolutionary spirit cannot be always relied upon in war, morale is still an important factor which can affect the outcome of war. Nevertheless, it cannot be based primarily on the appeal of political theories and the perception of life and death. It has to come from the training, organization, command, and the natural and material conditions of the forces at a particular time.

3. Jiang's Perception of War

When the Northern Expedition started in 1926, the Guomindang army had greatly expanded. After the victorious conclusion of the campaign, the number of soldiers bearing arms totaled 2.2 million, without counting the regional forces, such as those of Manchuria, Sichuan, and Yunnan.[39] This expansion made the organization of the revolutionary army very complicated; the new soldiers were primarily recruited from the defeated warlord forces, and were in most cases, undisciplined, corrupt, and untrained. As the core of the revolutionary army, the graduates of the Huangpu Military Academy were quickly promoted to higher positions; however, in many cases, they were unable to properly lead, as they also became corrupt. Indeed, the Guomindang army, as Jiang claimed, retained nothing of its old revolutionary spirit and motivation. Something had to be done quickly to prepare the armed forces for the much tougher struggles ahead of them, including the civil wars against the Communists and the approaching Sino-Japanese war. This need became even more urgent when Jiang was defeated by the Communists and forced to retreat to Taiwan.

Among other approaches, Jiang's primary formula for improving the quality of the officers was to upgrade their military education. Many of his writings are actually the texts of his lectures to students; therefore, the contents of his works are sometimes more like the notes of a professor rather than the works of a great strategist.

A.   The Philosophical Perception of War

Although Jiang talked a lot about revolutionary philosophy, it would be an exaggeration for one to say that Jiang had developed a systematic theory of war. Most of his ideas on military philosophy were contained in his comments regarding military training. His discussion of military philosophy, therefore, was related to the current military situation rather than abstract theories.

According to Jiang's observation, Japan's status as a world power was not achieved by learning Western scientific knowledge, but by following Wang Yangming's philosophy of "behaving in accordance with one's conscience" (*Zhi Liang Zhi*), which is the core of the theory of "uniting knowledge with action."[40]

To Jiang, the Japanese national spirit is Bushido, which, in turn, is based on the philosophy of Wang Yangming. In following Wang's philosophy, the Japanese were able to put theories to work, while the Chinese on the other hand discussed empty theories which were devoid of actions. Consequently, China fell prey to Japan and the Western countries in the 19th century. Jiang quoted Sun Yatsen's maxim, and told his officers that "to learn the theory behind a project sometimes is more difficult than to implement the project itself." Therefore, he encouraged them to devote themselves to the cause of revolution in accordance with Dr. Sun's scheme of nation-building and *San Min Zhu Yi*.[41]

After the Goumindang armed forces moved to Taiwan following their collapse on mainland China in 1949, Jiang attributed their failure to the military education of his officers. Subsequently, he often reminded his officers that the most serious problem in war was not necessarily the strength of the enemy, but the lack of adequate spirit, knowledge and ideas of one's own forces.[42] With this thought, Jiang committed himself to improving the military education system ,and devoted himself to giving lectures on military problems such as military philosophy, science, and art.

(a) *The Nature of War: Benevolence and Mercilessness*

What is military philosophy? Jiang did not bother to define the term as a scholar might, but simply said: "military philosophy is the philosophy of war; it is the study of self-cultivation of military spirit and virtues. By accomplishing this, one would have a clear idea about war, would never be indecisive in war, and would never place the value of his own life above his duty and honour during critical moments."[43] Therefore, the primary issue of the philosophy of war, to Jiang, is the problem of life and death. Jiang believed that the purpose of one's life is to promote the general welfare of the society rather than only one's own interest. Based on this perception, one should have the courage to die in order to save one's country and people.

Among the numerous precepts of his philosophy of war, Jiang particularly singled out two principles as the most important issues: "benevolence" and "mercilessness". The former should be applied to one's own people, while the latter, to the enemy in war. Indeed, Jiang said, "If we show mercy to the enemy, it would be like dealing cruelly with our own comrades."[44] To further interpret the relationship of these two antonyms, Jiang said:

> . . .the substance of war is benevolence, but to apply it requires cruelty; while the purpose of war is peace, the means used in war are cruel and brutal. To achieve the goal of long-term or permanent peace, it is necessary to suffer temporary tragedies.
> . .We have to be more brutal than the enemy in order to overwhelm him and to win the war. This is the only way to eliminate war and to achieve the goal of peace."[45]

The traditional Chinese philosophy has consistently emphasized the objective value of death and life, above all when it refers to soldiers in war. The Chinese have always honoured soldiers who died in war, and have condemned those who shamelessly surrendered in order to save their own lives. However, Jiang's faith in this precept and in the principle of mercilessness to the enemy was not only a product of logic, but also a painful lesson from experiences in fighting the Communists. Jiang wanted to apply the principle of mercilessness to battlefield operations in order to overcome the psychological weakness of his armed forces. To Jiang, in learning the revolutionary philosophy, one should focus on Dr. Sun Yatsen's theory and Jiang's own philosophy. As we said before, Dr. Sun's theory can be summarized as "knowing is more diffult than doing", and Jiang's theory can be simplified to "doing one's best to practice" (*Lixing Zhexue*).[46] In other words, the Generallissimo wished that his officers would carry out whatever they learned from him.

(b)   *The Virtures of the Commander and their Functions in War*
When a military commander has had the correct perception of life and death, has learned to be merciless to the enemy and benevolent to his own people, and is determined to carry out these principles without any reservation, he still must learn to cultivate in himself the traditional virtues of determination, calmness, repose, and deliberation in order to be a successful commander. According to the Great Learning (Daxue), this process is as follows:

The point where to rest being known, the object of pursuit is then determined; and that being determined, a calm unperturbedness may be attained to. To that calmness there will succeed a tranquil repose. In that repose there may be careful deliberation, and the deliberation will be followed by the attainment of the desired end.[47]

In expounding on this process, Jiang particularly emphasized the starting point of "knowing where to rest". Quoting from Zhu Xi, Jiang believed that "the best goal for one to pursue" should be "where for one to rest". To a revolutionary military leader, the implementation of the Three People's Principles in China (*San Min Zhu Yi*) should be the final and best goal of all his followers.[48] After choosing this goal, one should pursue it without wavering. By doing so, one would then be able to achieve calmness and, in turn, repose. Consequently, one is unlikely to miss the correct way when one starts to deliberate anything. The desired end would then be attained.

Jiang further linked this procedure to Sunzi's theory. He thought that the cultivation of determination was similar to the control of the moral factor (Zhiqi); calmness was similar to the control of the mental factor (Zhixin); repose similar to the physical factor (Zhili); and, deliberation, similar to planning and strategy, which is the key to final victory or defeat in battle. If a commander can follow this procedure of self-cultivation in war, he would be able to attain victory.[49]

The ideal realm that Jiang wished his generals to reach through their conscious effort of self-cultivation was described using four philosophical words: danger, minuteness, precision, and one. They are from the Classic Book (Shujing), which contains the legendary instructions handed from Emperor Yao to Emperor Shun, and from Shun to Emperor Yu. The original words read:

While the mind of a human being tends to be dangerous, the principle of nature is often minute. Watch your mind carefully and stick to the right course sturdily in order to be able to attain the principle of the gold mean.[50]

The major point of this quotation is that the minds of people tend to deviate from the guidance of one's reason because of desires, and thus, is likely to fall into danger; the principle of nature is often obscure and looks remote and minute. Should one wish to hold the doctrine of the gold mean, which is the supreme law of the universe, one has to watch one's mind closely and maintain the right course constantly without any inclination to deviate. However, when Jiang applied these principles to the self-cultivation of military leaders, he interpreted them in a completely different way. For example, he urged the commanders to always be conscious of the potential "dangers" in operations, and to pay full attention to them; by doing so, one will not be caught unprepared by the enemy. As to the meaning of "minuteness", he said that the quantity of information about the enemy is usually very minute; one must look at extremely vague and insignificant information to catch slivers of opportunity in order to win battles. The term "precision" is primarily applied to calculation and planning. If one is more careful and precise in calculation, one's planning will be more accurate and detailed. The word "one" is interpreted as "concentration". "While we concentrate, the enemy divides." "While we are concentrated on one point, the enemy is divided into ten positions. It would be like pitting ten against one."[51]

If a commander can cultivate these virtues of danger, minuteness, precision, and one, he would likely be able to estimate the enemy situation as accurately as that of a god, and would miss no target with his strategy.[52]

Philosophical education, as mentioned above, may help a commander firmly sustain himself during difficult moments without wavering, and calculate the situation calmly and carefully in order to reach a correct decision and strategy; meanwhile, with his calmness and repose, he may also influence the morale of his troops and help them maintain the confidence of final victory in battle. However, modern war is scientific by nature. While an army may not be able to use its weapons and equipment effectively without a strong fighting spirit, it would incorrect to say that an ill-equipped army can defeat a properly trained and equipped enemy relying solely on high morale. Jiang realized this fact. He also understood that his soldiers lacked the necessary scientific backround to efficiently wage modern war. Therefore, science in general and military science in particular was, next to military philosophy and art, foremost on Jiang's agenda.

B. The Scientific Perception of War

To Jiang, science is necessary to the military on two different levels: the technical and the command levels. The former involves weaponry, equipment, and operations. Therefore, it is directly related to soldiers and low-ranking officers; the command level deals with organization, information, planning, and commanding, and therefore, is basically applied to commanders and/or staff officers. As Jiang said: "if a soldier does not have scientific knowledge, he would not be able to use modern machines and weapons; if a general does not understand science, he could not command modernized armed forces and, thus could not handle a scientific war."[53]

The underlying reason for Jiang's focus on this subject was the low quality of his commanding officers in the earlier years. Jiang believed that in his military forces, the low-ranking cadets were better educated than those of the middle ranks who were, nevertheless, more competent than the generals.[54] However, all great commanders, as he quoted from Napoleon, have seen war as a true science.

When he discussed the subject of the philosophy of war, he had mentioned that information about the enemy is often obscure and minute in quantity, and thus, the commanders must do their best to analyze all bits of information carefully and precisely in order to discover which is correct and useful; they then must make correct decisions and chose proper strategies. This is actually the basic topic which military science is concerned with. Jiang, therefore, saw a strong correlation in roles between military science and military philosophy. Indeed, Jiang claimed that the essence of science is to search for truth and to verify the absolute accuracy of the matter in question. From a military point of view, therefore, science is superior to philosophy in the realm of facts and precision. Jiang, however, believed that philosophy is more important than science when military education is concerned. This indicates that Jiang, like many Chinese strategists, emphasized the spiritual factor over material ones in war.[55]

Scientific methods applied to the military at the command level are aimed at planning and coordinating actions. While planning refers to preparations for a campaign, and includes estimating the enemy, co-ordinating refers to operations. Both require precision and cooperation, which are based on good organization. Therefore, Jiang said: "when we talk about military science, the only key point is 'organization', which is to achieve a high level of cooperation in operation."[56]

Although the aims of military science are to achieve precision and accuracy, it is, however, incorrect to equate it with mathematics. Jiang said:

Of course, we should follow the maxim of Sunzi that "with many calculations, one can win; with few, one cannot". But we must also realize Zeng Guofan's point that 'if one cannot fight, one is destined to be defeated even if calculation shows that one can win'. Therefore, when we talk about science, we should not overemphasize the mathematical nature; a military plan cannot be displayed in equations.[57]

C. The Artistic Perception of War

In the Western world, military strategists argue heatedly over the artistic nature of war. Some of them, like Henri Jomini, tended to emphasize the artistic aspect of war, while others dwelt on the scientific characteristics. However, nobody absolutely advocates one aspect and completely rejects the other. In discussing this subject, Jiang had extensively quoted the argument of Western strategists, and arrived at his own conclusion that "although the command of war is an art, science is still the basis of war and of military education."[58] However, he warned his officers that they should not overindulge themselves in purely scientific education and forget the essence of war; they should not, above all, see war as a pure science and thus believe that they can win two or more campaigns by following the same principles and rules.[59]

It seems that Jiang likened the relationships between military philosophy, science, and art to a triangle. Military philosophy, to Jiang, is at the bottom of the triangle because it is the foundation of all millitary education and, therefore, is the means by which a commander can hold together his army. Furthermore, military philosophy is the sole source of spirit, which is the determinant factor in war. Military science is a further development of philosophy in that it pursues precision and accuracy; it is the basis of all planning and coordinated actions of operation. However, military science is tainted with materialism. Thus, when adapting to Chinese tradition and the Chinese socio-economic situation, Jiang, though he did stress the importance of the scientific method, always reserved the primary roles for military philosophy and art.

In dealing with the subject of art in war, Jiang simply defined it as what is used to defeat the enemy in war. Art can be applied at two different levels: one refers to the direction of military operations and the maneuvering of troops in war; the other emphasizes the personality and the moral cultivation of the commander, which may help him command the respect of his subordinates.[60]

In applying military art to operations, Jiang quoted Sunzi's principle of deception, and the alternate uses of extrodinary and normal forces in war as the best explanation. "When these principles are applied, though there is only the choice of *Qi* and *Zheng*, the extent to which each principle is applied is as subtle as the changes of the five tones, the five colours, and the five flavours. There are endless areas of subjectivity with regard to those two principles. Nobody can exhaust them in use."[61] However, in using these principles, the talents and skills of the individual commanders are required to interpret the current circumstances correctly. No regular principles and rules can be followed. Therefore, the emphasis on using personal talent in war is the basic argument for the importance of art in war.

Jiang believed that one cannot achieve the highest level of art in war by only studying war history and other military books; one has to further rely on spiritual accomplishments. He, therefore, linked the artistry of war to military philosophy again. He said:

> If one can truly think and implement from the basis of philosophy and can reach the perfection of artistic accomplishment, with one's noble mind, supreme courage and talent, one would be able to attain the magic effect of the spirit and the artistic cultivation as well. This is known as understanding the root, which is the supreme knowledge.[62]

According to Jiang, the art of war is not independent of military science; they are a unified system. However, they are at different levels of development. The art of war is the result of the further development of military science. If there is a deficient background in science, one is unable to reach the perfect realm of art. On the contrary, if one has mastered the scientific method, one is likely to attain the stage of art by bringing one's skill of using scientific knowledge to perfection. [63]

Although military philosophy, science, and art are all vital in strengthening the ability of a commander in conducting war, the use of military forces is often thought by many strategists as primarily referring to an art, which includes manoeuvering troops, making strategies, and choosing tactics. If a commander is able to choose his strategy and tactics properly in accordance with the situation and implement them perfectly, he is likely to win the battle.

The following part will be committed to discussing the basic ideas of Jiang's strategies and tactics, and the principles of war.

4. The Art of Manoeuvring Troops

From the discussion above, it is clear that although Jiang recognized the importance of scientific knowledge, he tended to emphasize the art of manoeuvring troops in operation. This primarily includes command, staff, rear service, and the choice of strategy and tactics such as offence and defence, advance and retreat, *Qi* and *Zheng, Xu* and *Shi*, close and remote, the main force and reserves, and communication. [64]

A.   Jiang on Strategy and Tactics

Since he assumed the position of commander-in-chief of the Guomindang armed forces in the middle of the 1920's, Jiang personally directed his forces in almost all of their major campaigns, up to the time of his death in 1975. He did not have time to discuss strategic problems systematically until he settled in Taiwan after 1949, where he was able to rebuild military academies and improve his military training system.   Jiang personally lectured on strategies and tactics based on his own experience and based on studies of modern foreign military strategies. His concepts of strategies and tactics before 1949 were primarily revealed in his comments on the results of particular military campaigns.   Subsequently, his concepts are specific instructions and comments of a commander-in-chief rather than a theoretical analysis. However, when he lectured at the military academies in Taiwan, he often spoke like an old professor.   It seemed that Jiang wished to pass on his own ideas to his officer cadets, so that one day they may reconquer China using the grand strategies laid by Jiang. Therefore, some of his lectures on strategies and tactics are still classified as confidential and are inaccessible to researchers. [65]

In an important speech on strategy, Jiang made a systematic analysis of the development of strategic concepts in the Soviet Union and in the Western countries.   Jiang began his analysis by tracing modern concepts back to Machiavelli, Frederick the Great, Napoleon, Jomini, and Clausewitz. He then analyzed modern strategists and their concepts, before making his own definitions of strategy.[66] Though he criticized the current Western strategic concepts in dealing with the global strategies of the Soviet Union, Jiang's concepts still demonstrate the effects of strong Western influence; Soviet influence, on the other hand, is less apparent. Only in one aspect is Soviet influence predominant; Jiang's ideas on political warfare were influenced both by the Soviet example and by his own experiences.

Based on the current international situation and the political needs of the Guomindang government in Taiwan, Jiang gave a definition of strategy as follows:

> Strategy is the art of creating and utilizing advantageous situations to achieve the goals of war, campaigns, or decisive battles, of a nation or of a group of nations in order to increase the probability of success and the final victory.[67]

(a) *Grand Strategy*

According to Jiang's definition, "grand strategy is the strategy of allied nations. It is based on their mutual interest to promote cooperation in order to take unified steps and achieve their common goals with their joint forces." The confirmation of the common enemy, the methods of dealing with him, the priority of targets, and the possible actions are all the primary concerns of grand strategy.[68]

(b) *National Strategy*

"National strategy is the art of building and using the national powers, and of developing united forces in order to achieve the national goals."[69]

National strategy, according to Jiang, includes the guidance of the government in matters of politics, economics, society, culture, psychology, and military affairs. National strategy can be further divided into political strategy, economic strategy, psychological strategy and military strategy.

Jiang Jieshi suggested that modern war is a general war (Zongti Zhan) which includes political, economic, cultural, and military warfare; it cannot be won by military force only. Based on this concept, he particularly emphasized the importance of unity of different sections of the country. The political strategy has to support military strategy, while the military strategy should obey the political strategy; otherwise, the country would likely suffer defeats. Jiang believed that political strategy included two levels. One of these refers to "the decision of the political leaders on the following questions: whether the country should go to war, whether war can be avoided, when would the opportunity be best for the country to enter the war, and what actions should be taken to achieve the necessary goals." The second level of political strategy refers to "spiritual factors of one's armed forces in operation, and the situation of the enemy with regard to national will, military organization, standing army and reserves, resources, and his political system. "[70] This second level is perhaps more military nature than the first level of political strategy.

To coordinate the actions of various sections of the government and to avoid the possible conflict and contradictions among the political and military leaders, Jiang insisted that a comprehensive norm should be established among the leaders in order to unify the political and military strategies. This norm can be achieved by respecting the following guidelines:

(1) The choice of an important military strategy should be in accordance with the national political goals and the principles of political strategy.

(2) Although the military leaders are not permitted to decide strategies by themselves, they should have the right to choose tactics without any intervention from political leaders.

(3) Because political leaders are in charge of directing wars and are responsible for strategic problems, they should fully understand the principles of war and provide active leadership in war. However, they should not intervene in operations. "Everything beyond the gates of the capital is under the command of the general."

(4) The military leaders should cooperate with the political leaders in deciding strategic matters.[71]

As a professional soldier, Jiang paid particular attention to the possible conflict between politicians and generals. Therefore, he emphasized the close cooperation between them. Meanwhile, Jiang repeatedly stressed the importance that politicians remove themselves from the decision-making process on an operational and tactical level.

(c) *Military Strategy*

Military strategy is the most important pillar in supporting the national strategy. It refers to the general ideas of military action in wartime, building of armed forces and war preparation based on perceived needs and manpower available, mobilization system and its required speed and forms, etc. Under the concept of general war, Jiang treated military warfare equally as political warfare, economic warfare, and psychological warfare. Each of them is rated at 25 per cent of the total in peacetime. However, military is raised to 30 per cent of the total in wartime, so is the military strategy in comparing to political strategy, economic strategy and psychiological strategy.[72]

(d) *Field Strategy*

Field strategy is also called regional strategy in the American military forces, because it is primarily used to guide the military operations in different regions. However, because regional strategy also partially falls within the juristiction of the Department of the General Staff and the headquarters of the army, navy, and airforce, Jiang preferred the name field strategy.

The concept of field strategy to many people is not always clear; it is often confused with tactics and operation. They are actually very different. "The field strategy", according to Jiang, "is the art of creating and using opportunities prior to the establishment of battlelines, while tactics is the art of directing the armed forces to move and fight after the battlelines have been established."[73] Furthermore, "while operation is to guide the disposition and actions of one's own forces during a battle in order to win, field strategy is to direct the dispositions and actions of one's forces prior to the battle."[74] The major point of field strategy is the calculation and use of time, space and the forces in battle.

The purpose of choosing a particular strategy is to win the war, and thus, it must closely adapt to any changes in the enemy's disposition. There are basic principles that regulate the application of strategy and operations. They are generally called the principles of war by strategists.

B. Jiang's Ten Principles of War

Although commanding troops in operation is primarily regarded by most strategists as an art, all strategists also agree that war has its own objective regulations. Therefore, a commander is still bound to follow some important principles in using his forces.

The Western principles of war can be traced back several centuries to Napoleon, Jomini, and Clausewitz. Under the influence of Western military thought, Chinese leaders have adopted a similar set of principles in the process of military modernization. Both Mao Zedong and Jiang Jieshi had developed their own principles of war. While Mao's well-known principles were produced during the days of the civil war of the 1940s, Jiang's were formulated about ten years later. Jiang's principles were originally written by the College of the Army, but were later amended and approved by Jiang.[75] Jiang began discussing these principles in detail with his students at the College ten years after their formulation.[76]

He did not deny the influence of foreign ideas on the development of his ten principles, but he did emphasize his own experience as well.[77] His ten principles are as follows: (1) target and major point, (2) initiative and flexibility, (3) offense and preparation, (4) organization and duty, (5) unity and cooperation, (6) concentration and thrift, (7) maneuver and speed, (8) raids and deception, (9) safety and information, and (10) morale and discipline.[78]

Each of these principles consists of two parts. The first part is no different from the traditional principles well known to the Western world; the second part, however, was added by Jiang. The target and major point, for example, displays two mutually interacting concepts. When the term "target" is combined with "major point", the principle reminds the commanders that when they choose their target of operation, it is crucial that they only have one major point or focus, though they may have more than one target. All other targets are relegated to a secondary priority. The "major point", therefore, not only refers to the choice of target but the disposition of forces. "Initiative" is the basic principle of operation in any circumstance, but Jiang believed that "flexibility" is the essence of initiative. Therefore, he combined initiative and flexibility as a single principle.[79]

Although he listed ten principles, the extremely important ones, which refer to the manoeuvering of troops, constitute no more than half of his ten principles. For example, Jiang pointed out that the basic principle in any future war against mainland China would be flexibiliity, manoeuver, concentration, and safety.[80] On another occasion, he singled out the absolute offence, exterior line operation, preponderance of force at the crucial point, flank and rear attacks, and annihilation as the great rules of operation, which may help to achieve the goal of initiative.[81]

Similarly, General Jiang Weiguo, the younger son of the Generalissimo, felt that his father's ten principles revolve around a few important ones. Indeed, he said his father's thought on commanding troops could be generalized into six principles: annihilation, offence, concentration, manoeuver, hitting the weak points (Ji Xia), and political warfare.[82] He also claimed that his father's last principle, that of morale and discipline, is unique in the world.[83] This principle will be discussed later in the book.

Generally speaking, Jiang's principles of operation are quite similar to the modern Western military principles. Even political warfare is not Chinese in origin; it was introduced from the Soviet Union.

In his ten principles, Jiang particularly emphasized the principle of offence in the projected operations against the mainland. Although "offence" has long been advocated by modern strategists as a major principle of war, Jiang, however, was not just parroting Western strategists when he advocated offence. He derived this conclusion from his own experiences in war. Furthermore, the contemporary situation he faced in the 1960s left him with no choice but to take the offence if he wished to retake China.

During his military career, Jiang had won many campaigns against numerically superior enemies by using the principle of absolute offence. In the wars against Chen Jiongming, for example, Jiang defeated the enemy with a much samller force by offensive strategy. He almost repeated the feat with similar methods during the Northern Expedition of 1927 against the warlords. He started the Expedition with less than one hundred thousand men, but defeated the warlord forces one by one in attack, which numbered over one million soldiers in total. Jiang was able to unify the country within two years.[84]   However, when he started the "encirclement and suppression" campaigns against the Red Army in Jiangxi Province in 1930, he had a numerically superior force and yet was only able to win an incomplete victory after suffering four defeats. He was also in a numerically superior situation in 1946, but suffered disastrous defeats and was eventually forced to flee to Taiwan within four years.[85]

From these experiences, Jiang realized that numbers are not the determinant factor in war, and that an offensive strategy is probably the method for a numerically inferior force to keep its initiative and win the war. Consequently, he reminded his officers to take an absolute offensive strategy in the future war against the CCP on mainland China. He said:

> All in all, in the operation of the counter-offence war against the Communists, we have to emphasize the spirit of initiative, manoeuver, and mobility. . .in every campaign. Attacks from the front and flank, outflanking attack, (and) unstopping attacks. . .(we must) continously attack with a lightning surprise force, as a rolling stone down the mountain of ten thousand feet.[86]

C. The Triangle Formation--Jiang's Tactics

In his discussion of tactics, Jiang primarily concentrated on analyzing his enemy's tactics. He tried to find an effective way to deal with them or to avoid being caught by them. During the "encirclement and suppression" campaign against the Red Army in the 1930s, for example, after suffering repeated defeats, he began to adopt Zeng Guofan's tactics. To Jiang, the situation in the 1930s was similar to that in the 1850s, when Zeng was fighting against the Taiping Army. [87] Jiang began adopting a fortification tactic, in which he used fortified positions to completely block the supply lines of the Red Army, thereby forcing them to abandon their base.

During the Sino-Japanese War and the following Civil War against the CCP, the Nationalist Army was often under attack and suffered heavy losses. Jiang spent much time discussing the enemy's tactics and he encouraged his officers to learn from the enemy. This type of discussion occurred even more frequently after the Guomindang had settled in Taiwan. For example, he made at least two speeches referring to the tactics of the PLA, above all, those of Marshal Lin Biao.[88]

The Triangle formation tactic is regarded in Taiwan as Jiang's unique contribution to military tactics. It is also known as the Triangle Attack Formation because it functions more effectively when used in attacks.[89]

(a) *The Undefeatable Tactic*

According to Jiang, this formation is almost an undefeatable tactic; it can deal with any enemy disposition. Jiang said:

> From my personal study and experience, I found that the principle of the triangle can be applied as a basic tactical principle to deal with all dispositions of the enemy .... I believe that no matter what progress the world may see, no matter how advanced weapons may become, and no matter how the art of war may change, this tactical principle will last forever.[90]

To emphasize the unlimited power of the formation, the late General-issimo went further to say that the trinagle formation can be used to defeat Marshal Lin Biao's tactic of "one point and two aspects"(Yidian Liangmian), which was known as a tactic of attack. Jiang even listed all forms of the triangle formation to show that "it can be developed into countless disposi-tions in order to overcome any kind of tactic used by the bandit (the PLA)."[91]

As the originator of the triangle formation in China, Jiang did not clearly define the application of the form. This work was left to his son, Weiguo. He clarified the concept and even interpreted the limitation of its application. He wrote:

> When our leader (the Generalissimo) talked about the triangle, he was referring to the three angles of a triangle, not the three sides. The three angles refer to the proximate locations of the three units of our force. They are not fixed at three points, nor have to be in a shape of triangle, above all, not the shape of an equilateral triangle. The disposition can be changed in accor-dance with the situation of the enemy, our force, the weather, and the terrain in order to keep the initiative and to maintain flexibility in the use of our troops.[92]

(b) *The Limitation of its Application*

Although the Generalissimo emphasized the unlimited applicability of his triangle formation, and although General Jiang Weiguo tried to stress its flexibility to deal with otherwise troublesome counter-formations, in fact, the triangle formation is not applicable to all situations. Even Jiang Weiguo recognized this fact in his discussions of his father's military thought.

According to Jiang Weiguo, although the formation could be used in defensive situations, it was primarily designed for offence.

Furthermore, the formation was designed primarily to apply at the tactical level. The biggest tactical unit of the Nationalist Army in Taiwan is the regiment. Therefore, this formation can only be applied up to the regimental level. According to Jiang Weiguo, even the Generalissimo had made it clear that it should be applied primarily to the battalion and regiment level; a division can try to apply it whenever possible, but it would make no sense to apply it to larger units.[93]

Also, the formation was designed for the army and not for the air force and navy. Although General Jiang Weiguo mentioned that the navy and air force could use the formation, he did say that they should not be bound by it. Furthermore, when applying the formation to the army, it should not replace other tactics but serve as their foundation.[94]

The essence of the triangle formation is that in operation, above all in attacks, the location of the three organic units of the army are usually at three points which can be formed into different shapes of triangles such as the isosceles triangle, scalene triangle, right-angled triangle, obtuse triangle, and acute triangle, as the Generalissimo described them in his own words.[95] If any general were to take Jiang's words seriously and insist on deploying his force in accordance with the triangle shapes, one would inevitably be found in a dilemma, because on some occasions, a commander may have to put his forces in depth formation or line formation. If a depth formation is required, a commander needs to place his force on a narrow front, one unit after another; if a line formation is called for, however, he may have to arrange them into line to cover a large front. The triangle formation would fit none of these cases. To solve this dilemma, the younger Jiang particularly reminded his officers that they should not be restricted by the term "triangle formation". They could arrange their forces into whatever shape they require based on the actual situation of the enemy, the terrain, and their own objectives. This qualification pointedly included the depth and line formation of all of the three units as possible options.[96]

In order to accommodate the triangle tactic, the Nationalist army has long been organized along a 3-3 system, which subdivides each unit into three organic subunits. According to General Jiang, however, even the armored divisions, which are not organized along the 3-3 system, can also apply the triangle attack formations without any substantial difficulties.[97]

The only test of the triangle formation, the analysis of strategists aside, is war. Even if the formation is judged to be useful, it would be incredibly naive of any commander to trust the formation to win any and all campaigns in all circumstances. It is only a basic formation, and not some magic super-tactic.

5. The Ideas of Political Warfare

As mentioned earlier, the political work system was renounced in the late 1920s and was reinstalled in the early 1930s when the "encirclement and suppression" campaign against the Red Army in Jiangxi Province was initiated. The system was gradually extended to all of the armed forces including the old warlord forces, which were integrated into the Nationalist army after the unification of the country.

Following the surrender of Japan in the Second World War, Chinese public opinion and the American government brought the leadership of both the Guomindang and the Communists together to commence negotiations about the future of China. During this period, the military-political system of the Guomindang became a major target of criticism for Communists and non-Communists alike. Opponents asked the Guomindang to withdraw from the armed forces, allowing the forces to be the military force of the nation instead of the Party. This demand received the support of the United States and, thus, the Nationalist government was forced to remove the political work system from the armed forces in 1946. In its place, a bureau of information was established to handle political education and propaganda.[98] The collapse of the peace talks and their subsequent military losses in the ensuing civil war made the Guomindang decide to restore the political work system in 1947. The system was not affected to any great extent by this process. Only in 1950 was a major reform initiated in the system, after the Guomindang regime settled in Taiwan and started to reorganize its armed forces. Under the leadership of Jiang Jingguo, the role of the political work system in the armed forces was greatly expanded.[99]

A. Jiang Jingguo and His Reform of the Political Work System

Jiang Jingguo, the elder son of the Gerneralissimo, left China in the 1920s to study in the Soviet Union. He stayed there for more than ten years, until the late 1930s, when the Sino-Japanese war began.

After a few years of working at the local level in Jiangxi Province, he was appointed both the director of the Department of Political Works of the Youth Army and the director of the Institute of Political Training for the Military Political Workers of the Youth Army in 1944. Although the Youth Army was never sent to the field during the war, Jiang Jingguo greatly benefited from his short career as a leader of military political workers.

In 1949, the Generalissimo appointed a committee to review the situation of the armed forces and to make recommendations for reform. When a proposal was submitted, he immediately appointed his son, Jiang Jingguo, to the directorship of the General Department of Political Works in 1950, and asked him to initiate reforms.[100]

As mentioned before, under the old system, the major function of the political work system was political education and propaganda. The new organization inherited all the functions of the old system. In addition, it also became responsible for other duties, such as maintaining the security of the forces, and later organizing the administration in the war zone (Zhandi Zhengwu) and the political work system of guerrilla forces. It was later charged with the responsibility of organizing discharged soldiers for reclaiming land and other economic activities.[101]

In 1954, after two terms in this job, Jingguo was appointed the Vice-Secretary General of the National Security Council and became responsible for supervising the intelligence activities of the Taiwan government. In this position, Jingguo still retained control over military political works.

In 1963, the General Department of Political Works became "The General Department of Political Warfare of the Ministry of National Defence". The political work system, at all levels, also assumed this new name. Furthermore, the political workers were offered for the first time in the history of the Nationalist Army the formal title of officer of political warfare (Zhengzhi Zuozhan Junguan).[102]

With their new title and rank, the political workers could then be appointed commanding officers in the armed forces. This development helped Jiang and his political supporters expand their powers in the armed forces.

In addition, after Jiang Jingguo left the Directorship, the government appointed some high military commanders to the directorship of the General Department of Political Warfare. Furthermore, the political work officers at each level of the armed forces were required to serve as the chief of staff for military commanders with regard to political affairs. These events, to a large extent, deflated the hostile feelings of the military officer group towards the political officers. The result was that Jiang once again consolidated his political control over the armed forces.[103]

After the death of his father, Jiang Jingguo assumed the presidency within two years. He extended his power to all areas of the military. While he still relied on the political workers to control the armed forces, he was very cautious that the officer group of the political warfare organization did not become too powerful. Jiang subsequently began curbing their powers.[104]

B. Jiang's Idea of Political Warfare

As mentioned earlier, the Generalissimo had said that modern war consists equally of military, political, economic, and psychological elements. In reality, however, he believed that the military is the most important of the four elements of modern war.

In discussing the concept of politics, he created two scales. From a strict point of view, politics refers to national politics and international politics. From a broader point of view, however, politics, in terms of war, includes everthing except the military. It includes economic, psychological and social elements. This definition is based on his concept of Total War, by which he meant a war in which everyone and everything in the country would be directly or indirectly involved.

Based on this concept, the Generalissimo developed his theory of political warfare.

(a) *The Definition of Political Warfare*

According to Jiang, political warfare consists of psychological, organizational, and mass warfare, and intelligence and strategem operations. Operations in diplomacy, economy and society can also be categorized as political warfare. Consequently, Jiang proposed a definition as follows: "all operations except those directly using armed forces against the enemy may be seen as political warfare. "[105]

To emphasize the importance of political warfare, Jiang further stated that "all modern wars, limited or total, with conventional or nuclear weapons, involve psychological or spiritual warfare; only when one wins the psychological battle, operations with weapons can be effective; therefore, a modern war is actually political warfare. "[106] He particularly emphasized the interrelationship of the multiple operations of political warfare. Jiang said:

> An ideological operation can only be carried out through psychological warfare, while a stratagem operation can happen only when there is enough information. As for organizational warfare, it is completely based on the result of mass war. Therefore, when ideological warfare is the substance, a psychological operation serves as its instrument; when stratagem warfare is the purpose, an intelligence operation is used as the means; and when mass warfare is the core of the organizational operation, it serves as the essential instrument of ideological and stratagem warfare. "[107]

While the wars of ideology, stratagem, and organization are primarily used as a guide at the strategic level, those of psychology, intelligence, and the masses are carried out at the tactical level. They can be waged at any time and any place, by anybody with any method; they can be carried out in a normal way or using extrordinary methods, either directly and publicly or invisibly and secretly. These sorts of wars are "basically battles of wits, but they do not exclude the battle of forces, because they may rely either on showing force without fighting, or on insurrection and armed violence. "[108]

Political operations are always occurring; they start before a military campaign begins and continue after the battle is over. Political warfare uses psychological warfare, guerrilla warfare and sabotage on the enemy's rear or front; it can also occur in newly conquered areas to stop the enemy's guerrilla band from committing violence. Political warfare does not rely on force, but only on wisdom and intelligence. According to Jiang, it constitutes the most delicate and supreme art of war.[109]

(b) *Mass Warfare*

Based on Jiang's interpretation of the mutual effects of the six important types of political warfare, it is clear that the major focus of the operation is aimed at mass warfare because all of the six, except for stratagem operations, are either waged among the masses or through them. The purpose of propaganda and psychological warfare, for example, is basically to affect the masses, while the work of intelligence is accomplished through the masses. As for organizational warfare, it is primarily designed to mobilize the masses to fight for the cause. Therefore, mass warfare is the centre of political warfare.

Mass movement is the essential work of mass warfare, which has to be achieved by means of mass mobilization and organization. Prior to getting the masses organized, they have to be mobilized with propaganda or persuasion.

In discussing mass mobilization and organization, Jiang mentioned two principles which, to a large degree, are similar to those of the CCP.

The first principle is "to go to the masses". Jiang said "this is the order of the Party and its will. . .It is the initial step of organizational work."[110]

The well-known mass line of the Communists consists of two parts: coming from the masses and going back to the masses. It has been designed by the Communists as an ideal process of policy making. Prior to the development of a policy, the party leaders go to the masses to collect information or to listen to the opinions of the local people; this is the process of input. After carefully weighing the different opinions of the masses, the party committee makes its initial policy, and then returns to the masses in order to discuss the resolution. If there is any significant reaction to the proposal, the party evaluates the reactions of the masses to make necessary amendments. After this stage, the party uses propaganda to popularize the amended resolution among the masses. The final resolution is then embraced by the masses and carried out by them.

Though Jiang did not say how "going to the masses" fits into an overall scheme of policy making, he did say that "the activity of the party among the masses is not limited to appealing to them only but should also be able to get the necessary information from them."[111] If so, Jiang had a mass line in mind as well.

The second principle is the united front. The CCP called it "Tongyi Zhanxian", whereas the Guomindang called it the "Lianhe Zhanxian". In fact, the two parties are describing the same thing.

If one believes that the principle of "going to the masses" is designed to organize the ordinary people, the united front is then a device to organize the special socio-political groups. According to the Generalissimo, the united front is basically aimed at political organizations or parties who are either neutral in the conflict between the Guomindang and the CCP or are anti-Communist but independent of the Guomindang. To transform their neutrality into anti-Communism and then to draw them under the leadership of the Guomindang are the essential goals of the united front.[112]

"Neutralism", as a strategy, can be used in political warfare for different purposes. If there are those who are hostile to the Guomindang or pro-Communist, the party may first try to persuade them to maintain neutrality, in order to avoid making more enemies.

If the group in question takes a neutral stand, the party would then use every possible method to pursue them to be pro-Nationalist. In addition, when the party is in a defensive posture, the party organization should use the neutral strategy to protect its base among the masses.[113] This strategy is very similar to that used by the CCP.

In mass movement, Jiang realized that the movement should not be used as an instrument but be sincerely aimed at promoting the interest of the masses. In the past, mass movement had often been seen as a public spectacle, controlled by a handful professionals who were specialized in agitating the people by demagogy. Therefore, the end of the show also marked the end of the movement. Subsequently, Jiang asked the Guomindang to change its approach. The party should realize that the masses are the essential targets of the revolution and nation-building. There is no purpose beyond the interest of the masses.[114]

(c) *Political Warfare in the Enemy Area*

In the late 1950s, the Guomindang government announced that "its strategic principle in the counter-offensive war against the Communist regime on mainland China would be primarily a political one; the military would only play an assisting role". "The major battlefield would be on mainland China, not in the Taiwan Strait which would only be a field in supporting the campaigns on the mainland."[115]

Based on this perspective, Jiang further declared that his revolutionary war against the Communists in the future would be conducted from within the enemy and/or at its rear. He insisted that his method was to concentrate 70 per cent of his effort on enemy occupied areas, and only use the other 30 per cent on frontal campaigns. He even imagined that through a successful campaign behind the enemy, he would not only be able to get supplies of food from the enemy but also weapons and ammunition. In Jiang's eyes, this would guarantee final victory in a protracted war against the Communists.[116]

From this strategic view, Jiang identified the supreme principle behind his tactics against the Communist as attacking the enemy from its flank or rear. Jiang wanted to distract the enemy's power by attack from behind and from the flanks, then destroy its foundation, and disrupt its communication lines.[117]

Generally speaking, Jiang's ideas on waging political warfare behind the enemy lines were a product of his situation. The disparity of military power between him and the Communists, and the lack of positive support for the military campaign against China from the U.S.A. and other non-Communist countries, forced him to emphasize political warfare from the inside of the mainland without formally initiating military campaigns.

(d) *Military Administration in the War Area*

The last point of Jiang's concept of political warfare which is worth mentioning here is military administration in the war area.

Military administration may have existed for a long time in history. However, as a consciously signficant issue in war, it is a relatively new development and a product of the modern age. The most famous and successful military administration of a war area in modern history is the military administration of Germany and Japan, established by the Allied Powers, after the end of the Second World War. The purpose of the administration was to help restore the local administrative and social order, arrest and try war criminals, and protect the society from acts of sabotage.

In modern China, after the CCP defeated the Guomindang in the civil war, it also carried out military administration of the newly conquered areas, above all, after conquering the large cities. They called the system *Junguan* or "military rule". The Guomindang, however, never seriously considered the issue of military administration of conquered areas until the 1950s, when it began considering the possibility of a counter-attack on the Communist mainland. Military administration, then, was relegated to the General Department of Political Works.[118]

Using the principle of political warfare, Jiang defined the military administration of a war zone as follows:

> The military administration in the war areas is classified as a political operation. Everyone realizes that victory in a military campaign is only the initial step; the success of military administration is the real and final victory. Therefore, the military administration is more important than the military operation itself.[119]

As military administration is part of the responsibility of the political work system, it is, therefore, a duty of the political workers. They are asked not only to serve as local government and party officials in the restored areas, but also the major personnel in organizational, cultural, and economic works in the social reconstruction period.[120]

Based on this concept, when the military campaign is over, the first thing for the political workers to do is to set up a local regime and restore social order. Following this, the local government begins rooting out any hidden enemy elements and other trouble-makers. After restoring the local order, the administration would then start social and economic construction in order to support further military campaigns.

6. Conclusion--Jiang's Effect on Chinese Military Modernization

Jiang Jieshi was a professional soldier and had been involved in almost every major war in China's modern history. He led the Nationalist Army in unifying China and in resisting the Japanese, but lost to Mao Zedong in the Civil War. His personal losses and successes have greatly affected the development of modern Chinese political history. It is difficult to give an objective assessment of the man because there are too many biases that distort the perspectives of the commentator.

In the context of modern Chinese history, Jiang has been a key figure in the process of Chinese military modernization. Since the *Yangwu* Movement in the middle of the 19th century, the Chinese reformers had tried different ways to modernize the Chinese military system, but nothing significant was achieved until the beginning of this century, when Yuan Shikai started to adopt the Western military method to train the new army. This was really a great leap forward in the process of modernization.

After unifying China from the fragmented warlord rule, Jiang was in a very good position to continue Chinese military modernization and to create a unique Chinese military force. However, he met with only limited success. The most important reason for this unsatisfactory result was the endless political and military turbulence of the time. Since the victorious close of the Northern Expedition in 1928, China experienced about twenty military rebellions, civil wars, and foreign intrusions in less than ten years. Some of these struggles lasted several months, some even lasted several years. Some of them affected a wide geographic area, spanning several provinces. These internal struggles only halted when the country was forced to enter a general war against Japan, after the Marco Polo bridge incident of July 7, 1937. The eight years of the Sino-Japanese war and the four subsequent years of civil war between the communists and the Guomindang prevented Jiang from completing his planned military reforms.

The continuous wars caused China's already serious financial situation to slip to the brink of bankruptcy. It was said that in 1928, eighty percent of the national budget was spent on the military.[121] There were about three million men in uniform to support, and this number grew after the Sino-Japanese war and the Civil War.

The numerical growth of the armed forces was not matched by a compatible military industry, which could maintain a proper fighting ability in the men. To solve this problem, the military could not help but purchase weapons from international dealers or accept aid from foreign powers. And with the influx of foreign weapons, there was also an influx of military advisers, who were invited to China to help in using these imported weapons. The imported weapons caused difficulty in efforts to standardize weapons for Chinese soldiers. And the influence of foreign military advisers may have also complicated the situation and delayed the success of military modernization. These advisers introduced different models of organization at different stages to the Chinese armed forces. However, the Chinese never mastered any one of the models. While strategic and tactical training was concerned, the Chinese mostly copied the Western countries without properly adapting to the Chinese situation. Meanwhile, the traditional Chinese art of war was, to some extent, ignored by the young officers. Consequently, the national military force was not much better than the armed forces of newly independent countries, which usually do not receive proper military training on strategy and tactics from their former suzerain.[122]

no choice for them but to rely on the support of the Americans, politically and militarily. The Guomindang armed forces then began standardizing their weapons, using American weapons. Furthermore, they adopted the American model of military organization and training. A complete military education system was established. Officers began undergoing retraining programs. These trends improved the Nationalist armed forces considerably with regard to strategic and tactical matters.

Furthermore, after the first Chinese atomic test in 1964, Jiang decided to set up his own research project in order to develop modern weapons, including nuclear weapons, rockets and electronic systems in 1965. He concentrated the efforts of ten thousand scientists and technicians on this project, and poured hundreds of millions of dollars annually into the project.[123]

According to news reports, after twenty years of intense work, the Taiwanese have made some impressive achievements. Various types of rockets have been successfully developed. Furthermore, the Taiwanese now have one of the top five training planes in their air force. This plane has been recently developed into a fighter, the A3. Taiwanese shipyards are turning out advanced warships ro replace their obsolete vessels.[124] They have even built a powerful intermediate tank for their army, which is now known as the M48H tank.[125]

As a sign of Guomindang progress and as a tribute to the late Generalissimo's leadership, the Chief of Staff of the Guomindang Armed forces has recently put a set of Taiwan-developed jet engines for their TFE-1042 fighters in front of Jiang Jieshi's grave.[126]

These achievements in weaponry may not be great enough to compete with the superpowers and consequently completely free Taiwan from foreign suppliers, nor will they be sufficient to protect Taiwan from an invasion by the Communists. However, from a historical point of view, one cannot help but agree that the Chinese, including Taiwan and mainland China, have eventually made a breakthrough in military industry since the *Yangwu* movement began in the 1860s. Jiang had more or less contributed to this achievement.

As the commander-in-chief of the Nationalist army, Jiang was logically in the best position to make impressive achievements in military thought. However, although he did leave behind a great deal of work, Jiang's works are not as analytical and convincing as one would expect from a great treatise. Jiang's thoughts are not strictly arranged in logical structures. Many of his early discussions are comments referring to particular problems and do not contain any general principles. The works produced in Taiwan, however, show that Jiang had committed himself to military writings in his later life, above all, on military philosophy. Some of these works atttempted to propose certain general principles, while the others aimed at solving individual issues. Nevertheless, most of them demonstrated a traditional orientation. Many of his discussions on philosophy, strategy, and tactics look like the teaching manuals for an introductory course prepared by a professor. They did not present the necessary insight of a great strategist on the subject in question. They are, in many cases, full of common sense and basic knowledge. He devoted much time to philosophical subjects in order to improve the self-cultivation of his officers. However, he may have exaggerated the effect of philosophy on the ability of a military commander in directing war. He talked about a counter offensive war against the Communists in the future, but there was no strong evidence to show that his perception of war had changed very much. Indeed, his favourite tactics and strategies were still propounded as if he were dealing with the same enemy that would use their same tactics.

No matter how long Jiang and his military force had indiscriminately copied foreign military systems, and despite the fact that his military thought lacked imagination regarding potential changes in accordance with the developing technologies, he still made contributions to Chinese military modernization. After several decades of accepting military assistance from the Americans in weapons and training, Jiang and his generals gradually reached a stage of maturity. They have mastered Western military philosophy and its relevant factors that affect the result of its application. With this achievement, they are unquestionably capable of departing from this "copying stage" and can now consciously search for their own breakthroughs in this area. Indeed, Jiang had even started to criticize the weakness of the strategies of his former patron, the Americans. Therefore, after reviewing the development of Jiang's military thought and those of previous stages, we can say that Jiang had led the Nationalist forces from a stage where they could only copy foreign systems to a new stage where the forces can find their own unique way to adapt to a particular situation.

Footnotes

1. G. Maring was a Dutchman; he single-handedly promoted the establishment of the Chinese Commuinist Party in 1921 and then persuaded Dr. Sun Yatsen in the same year to reorganize the Guomindang, to establish a military school in order to create a revolutionary force, and to cooperate with the CCP. See *The Personal Records of President Jiang Jieshi* (Taipei: Central Daily New, 1976), Vol. 5, p. 251. (Hereafter referred to as Personal Records of Jiang.)

2. See *Personal Records of Jiang, op. cit.*, Vol. 2, p. 35.

3. *Ibid.*, pp. 262-63.

4. *Ibid.*, p. 62. Dr. Sun classified the talent of persons into three categories: the first is theorist or inventors; the second, propagandists, who spread the theories of the inventors to the public; and the third, the practitioners who carry out the theories or the orders of the leaders. This theory was developed in the 1920s in "The Theory of Dr. Sun Yatsen," see *Works of Sun.*

5. As mentioned in the last chapter which discussed Dr. Sun Yatsen's military thought, Chen Jiongming's rebellion had a serious impact on Sun and the Guomindang's revolutionary activity. The rebellion occurried on June 16, 1922, Sun barely escaped death and took refugee on a warship, Chuyu, and, later, on Yungfeng. Jiang was called by Sun on June 18, 1922, and presented himself to the scene on June 29, 1922, and accompanied with Sun on Yungfeng warship for 42 days until Sun left the ship for Shanghai. The rebellion was suppressed by Xu Chongzhi's *Yuejun* (Guangdong Army) and Liu Zhenhuan's *Guijun* (Guangxi Army) in middle of January, 1923. It was exactly 7 months since the rebellion was started. See *Personal Records of Jiang, op. cit.*, Vol. 5, pp. 177-198.

6. Jiang began his tour from Shanghai on August 16, 1923 accompaned by Shen Dingyi, Zhang Tailei, and Wang Dengyun. He travelled by ship and train, and arrived at Moscow on September 2, 1922. His visit to the Soviet Union was not limited to observing its military system but also the socio-political situation. He was highly impressed by the military and education systems, but criticized socio-economic system. He, above all, was cynical about the possible Soviet policy toward China. He even reported to Dr. Sun about his personal concern, but it is said that Sun thought that he had been overly worried about it. See *Personal Records of Jiang, op. cit.*, Vol. 5, pp. 206-213.

   What is most important is that Jiang learned about the relationship between the party and the army in the Soviet Union, and felt that this system could guarantee the party control over the armed forces; this personal impression definitely affected his decission to have party commissioner and political work systems in the coming Huangpu Military Academy and the Guomindang Revolutionary Army. See *Personal Records of Jiang, op. cit.*, Vol. 5, p. 206.

7. Jiang, Jieshi, "Philosophy and Science", in *The Collections of President Jiang's Speeches and Essays* (Taipei: Zhongyang Wenwu Gongyingshe, 1977), p. 128.

8. Idem, "A Criticism of the Past Military Education and the Purpose of Opening the Advanced Class", a speech in 1951, quoted from *Personal Records of Jiang, op. cit.*, Vol. 5, p. 220.

9. Quoted from Jiang, Weiguo, *The Special Essays of T.V. Broadcast Program on President Jiang's Military Thought* (Taipei:Ministry of Education, 1979), Part II, p. 106. (Hereafter referred to as *Broadcast Program.*)

10 Li, Zhen, *The History of Chinese Military Education* (Taipei:Zhongyang Wenwu Gongyingshe, 1983), p. 605.

11. *Personal Records of Jiang, op. cit.*, Vol. 5, pp. 220-21. The Huangpu Military Academy was closed in 1930. Before 1930, the Party had already established a Central Military and Political School in Nanjing, the Capital city, to replace it. Prior to its formal close, the school had experienced a lot of internal incidents caused by power struggles of party factions. The struggle became even worse after Jiang Jieshi, the president of the Academy, was occupied by his duty of the Commander-in-Chief of the Northern Expedition Army and left the school behind to other people. Even the name of the school had changed three times before its close. See Li Zhen's *The History of Chinese Military Education, op. cit.*, pp. 614-78.

12. Li, Zhen, *The History of Chinese Military Education, op. cit.*, pp. 578-81.

13. The Baoding Military Academy and the Army University were in operation until 1927 by the Beijing warlord regimes. When the Guomindang-led Northern Expedition marched to the North and overthrew the warlords, the Baoding Academy was shutdown again. However, the Army University was later reinstalled in 1928 when the Guomindang unified China.

14. Li, Zhen, *The History of Chinese Military Education, op. cit.*, p. 206.

15. Jiang's report to Sun is quoted in Jiang Weiguo's *Broadcast Program, op. cit.*, p. 106

16. Bai, Guangya, ed., *The History of Political Warfare in the National Army* (Taipei: Zhenggong Ganbo Xuexiao, 1970), pp. 9-15.

17. *Ibid.*, pp. 13-14.

18. Jiang, "The Duty of the Political Workers in the Armed Forces", *The Works of President Jiang* (Taipei: Institute of National Defence Study, 1963), Vol. 1, pp. 492-94. (Hereafter referred to as *Works of Jiang.*)

19. Bai, Guangya, *The History of Political Warfare in the National Army, op. cit.*, p. 31.
20. *Ibid.*
21. Jiang, "The Political Works of the Army in the Future", a speech to the political workers in 1929, in *Works of Jiang, op. cit.*, Vol. 1, p. 533.
22. *Ibid.*
23. This may include Jiang himself in it. For example, he discussed little about political works of the armed forces in his works.
24. Jiang, "The Political Works of the Army in the Future", *Works of Jiang, op. cit.*, Vol. 1, p. 533.
25. Idem, "The Special Spirit and Tactics of the Revolutionary Army", a speech in Huangpu on Nov. 9, 1924. See *Works of Jiang, op. cit.*, Vol. 1, p. 441.
26. *Ibid.*
27. Idem, "The Mission of the (Huangpu) Army Academy and the Life of a Revolutionary", (May 8, 1924), in *Works of Jiang, op. cit.*, Vol. 1, p. 392.
28. *Ibid.*
29. Idem, "The Necessity of Overcoming the Hardship and Tiredness and Going to Death as a Hero", a speech to the Huangpu cadets on May 21, 1924, in *Works of Jiang, op. cit.*, Vol. 1, p. 399.
30. Idem, "The Special Spirit and Tactics of the Revolutionary Army", *Works of Jiang, op. cit.*, Vol. 1, pp. 440-41.
31. Idem, "The Basic Spirit of the Revolutionary Forces Is to Die for the Revolutionary Programs", a speech to Huangpu cadets on Nov. 29, 1924, in *Works of Jiang, op. cit.*, Vol. 1, p. 443.
32. Cai, E, "The Military Plan", *The Posthumous Works of Mr. Cai Songpo* (Taipei: Wenxing Press, 1962), p. 334.
33. Jiang, "The Special Spirit and Tactics of the Revolutionary Army", *Works of Jiang, op. cit.*, Vol. 1, p. 439.
34. Idem, "Talking about Discipline", a speech to the Huangpu cadets in 1924, in *Works of Jiang, op. cit.*, Vol. 1, p. 408.
35. *Ibid.*, p. 439.
36. See the Article 3, the *Lianzuo Fa* of the Revolutionary Army, attached to the "To Overwhelm the Enemy with Our Determined Action of Death Is the Key to Victory", a speech of Jiang to the Huangpu cadets on December 28, 1924, in *Works of Jiang, op. cit.*, Vol. 1, p. 451.
37. *Ibid.*
38. Jiang, "The Political Works of the Army in the Future", in *Works of Jiang, op. cit.*, Vol.1, p. 533.
39. Jiang, *Personal Records of Jiang, op. cit.*, Vol. 7, p. 119.
40. Jiang, "An Account in His Own Words of Studying of the Revolutionary Philosophy", *Works of Jiang, op. cit.*, Vol. 1, p. 578.

41. Idem, "A Digest of Philosophy for the Revolutionary Soldiers", a speech to the officer group on July 23, 1934, in *Works of Jiang, op. cit.*, Vol. 1, pp. 778-780.

42. Idem, "The Comment on and Criteria of Military Education and Training", a speech to the military education and training meeting of the Nationalist Army in September of 1968, in *The Collection of Military Speeches of President Jiang* (Taipei: the Editorial Committee of the Zhongxing Speeches Collections of President Jiang, 1971), Vol. 4, pp. 1529-30. Also see "The Importance of Military Philosophy to the Military Commanders", a speech to the students of Command and General Staff College on March 12, 1957, in the same book, Vol. 3, p. 1341. (Hereafter referred to as *Military Speeches of Jiang.*)

43. Idem, "An Instruction to Military Education and Its Systems", in *Military Speeches of Jiang, op. cit.*, Vol. 3, p. 1432.

44. Idem, "The Importance of Military Philosophy to the High Commanders", *Military Speeches of Jiang, op. cit.*, Vol. 3, p. 1357.

45. Idem, "The Meaning and Effect of Military Discipline and the Key Issues of the Philosophy of War", a speech on September 10, 1951, in *Works of Jiang, op. cit.*, Vol. 2, p. 1803.

46. Idem, "The Foundation of the Revolutionary Education -- the Rudiments of Revolutionary Philosophy", a series of lectures from July 5 to 12, 1954, to the students of the Institute of Revolutionary Practice, in *Military Speeches of Jiang, op. cit.*, Vol. 3, p. 1381.

47. "The Great Learning", the Text of Confucius, in *The Four Books*, with English translation and notes by James Legge (Taipei:Culture, 1981), p. 3.

48. Jiang, "An Interpretation of Sunzi's Art of War, the Ancient Principles of Operation, and the Meaning of Artistic Perception of Modern War", a speech to the students of the Command and General Staff College on June 1, 1953, Part I & II, in *Military Speeches of Jiang, op. cit.*, Vol. 4, pp. 1700-1702.

49. *Ibid.*, pp. 1703-05.

50. Quoted by Jiang. See *Military Speeches of Jiang, op. cit.*, Vol. 4, p. 1699.

51. *Ibid.*, pp. 1706-07.

52. *Ibid.*, p. 1707.

53. Jiang, "An Interpretation of Sunzi's Art of War, the Ancient Principles of Operation, and the Meaning of Artistic Perception of Modern War", op. cit., Vol. 4, p. 1685.

54. Idem, "Some Basic Problems of the Military Education", *Military Speeches of Jiang, op. cit.*, Vol. 4, p. 1564.

55. Idem, "An Instruction on Military Education and Its Systems", *Military Speeches of Jiang, op. cit.*, Vol. 3, pp. 1438-39

56. *Ibid.*, p. 1439.
57. Idem, "An Interpretation of Sunzi's Art of War, the Ancient Principles of Operation, and the Meaning of Artistic Perception of Modern War", *op. cit.*, Vol. 4, p. 1685.
58. Idem, "The Aim and Purpose of Military Education", in *Military Speeches of Jiang, op. cit.*, Vol. 3, p. 1265.
59. *Ibid.*
60. *Ibid.*, pp. 1259-63.
61. These principles are from Sunzi's *The Art of War*, Ch. 1, Estimates, and Ch. 5, Energy. Jiang discussed that in "The Aims and Purposes of Military Education," in *Military Speeches of Jiang, op. cit.*, Vol. 3, pp. 1260-66. Also see Jiang's "The Interpretation of Sunzi's Art of War, the Ancient Principles of Operation, and the Meaning of Artistic Perception of Modern War", in the same book, Vol. 4, p. 1686.
62. Jiang, "The Aim and Purposes of Military Education", *Military Speeches of Jiang, op. cit.*, Vol. 3, p. 1263.
63. Idem, "An Interpretation of Sunzi's Art of War, the Ancient Principles of Operation, and the Meaning of Artistic Perception of Modern War", *Military Speeches of Jiang, op. cit.*, Vol. 4, pp.1687-88.
64. Jiang, "The Main Points of Leading, Training, and Manoeuvring Military Forces", *Military Speeches of Jiang, op. cit.*, Vol. 4, p. 1509.
65. *Military Speeches of Jiang* has printed the following words in the inside of the cover page: "These speeches are military secrets, please keep in confidential files". Jiang Weikuo, his younger son, even publicly announced on the T.V. broadcast that he could not reveal more than what he had said about his father's military thought on the manoeuvring of troops, because they were military secrets. It was many years after the death of the Generalissimo. See Jiang Weikuo, *Broadcast Program, op. cit.*, p. 45.
66. Jiang, "The Importance of Studying of Strategies in Military Education", a speech on the opening ceremony of the Joint University of the Armed Forces on June 30, 1969, in *Military Speeches of Jiang, op. cit.*, Vol. 3, pp. 1179-1201.
67. *Ibid.*, p. 1206.
68. *Ibid.*, pp. 1201-02.
69. *Ibid.*, p. 1202.
70. Idem, "The Major Points of the Study of National Defence", a speech on the opening ceremony of the Institute of National Defence on April 15, 1959, in *Military Speeches of Jiang, op. cit.*, Vol. 3, p. 1320.
71. *Ibid.*, pp. 1315-16.
72. Idem, "The Importance of Studying of Strategies in Military Education", *op. cit.*, Vol. 3, pp. 1204-05.
73. *Ibid.*, p. 1205.

74. *Ibid.*, p. 1206.

75. Jiang, "Directive on the Decision of the Principles of War", Feb. 15, 1959, in *Works of Jiang, op. cit.*, Vol. 2, p. 2612.

76. Idem, "The Importance of Studying of Strategies in Military Education", *op. cit.*, Vol. 3, pp. 1188-92.

77. *Ibid.*, p. 1189.

78. Jiang, "Directive on the Decision of the Principles of War", *op. cit.*, Vol. 2, p. 2612.

79. *Ibid.*

80. Jiang, "The Importance of Studying of Strategies in Military Education", *op. cit.*, Vol. 3, p. 1207.

81. Idem, "Carrying Out the Determination and Action of the Counter-attack for National Restoration", a directive to the Army High Cadres on January 28, 1965, in *Military Speeches of Jiang, op. cit.*, Vol. 4, p. 1647.

82. Jiang, Weiguo, *Broadcast Program,* op. cit., p. 37.

83. *Ibid.*, p. 33.

84. According to *Personal Records of Jiang, op. cit.,* Vol. 6, p. 13, when the first war against Chen Jiongming occurred in February, 1925, the enemy army consisted of about one hundred thousand men, and while there was no figure about the total number of the *Yuejun* (Guangdong Army), the Huangpu Cadet Army was only about two thousand and was under Jiang's direct command. In the Campaign of Mian Hu, which was a decisive operation, the Huangpu army defeated an enemy no less than ten times larger than itself. The second war against Chen began in late September of the same year; the enemy was no less than thirty thousand and Jiang's army consisted of three columns about the same number. Jiang was the Commander-in-Chief, and he easily defeated the enemy. In both campaigns, Jiang used offensive strategy and won the victory.

    The Northern Expedition Army was about one hundred thousand, and the warlard forces were more than ten times larger. See the same book, Vol. 6, p. 97.

85. Jiang mobilized 44,000 men to fight about the same numbner of the Red Army in the first campaign in Jiangxi in 1930, but he was defeated. In the second campaign, Jiang's force was at least twice as large as the enemy, but he still suffered a heavy loss. The last campaign started in 1933, he personally commanded a 800,000 men to engage about 150,000 enemy. Jiang used a fortification strategy to block all the transportation to the CCP-occupied area. It eventually forced the Red Army to give up their base, break out of the encirclement, and start their long march of 25,000 Li toward the Northwest. See *Personal Records of Jiang, op. cit.,* Vol. 7, pp. 172-73, and Vol. 9, pp. 122-154.

As to the last civil war in 1946, the Nationalist armed forces consisted of about 5 million men plus air force and navy at the beginning of war, while the People's Liberation Army was only about a million with more than two million militia. Jiang adopted a frontal offence in the first year but suffered losses. In the second year, he was forced to limit his offence on several major fronts but still suffered heavy losses. In the third year, when he was forced to change strategy from offence to defence, his front was soon broken and started to collapse.

86. Jiang, "Carrying Out the Determination and Action of the Counterattack for National Restoration", a directive to the army high cadres on January 18, 1965, in *Military Speeches of Jiang, op. cit.*, Vol. 4, p. 1647.

87. Jiang, "The Hand Book of Suppressing the Bandit (Jiaofi Shao Ben)", 1933, in *Works of Jiang, op. cit.*, Vol. 1, pp. 184-193. In this hand book, Jiang clearly figured out the tactics of fortification and also decided to copy Zeng Guofan's method in many aspects such as writing songs for the soldiers in order to remind them what they should do, etc.

Also see "The Study of the Skills of Suppressing the Bandit", April 25, 1933, in *Works of Jiang, op. cit.*, Vol. 1, p. 616. In this speech, he interpreted Zeng's principle of "those who take a position of defence are the master of the field and those who take attacks are the guest of it". He said Zeng used this strategy successfully in the war against the Taiping Army, and, thus, asked his officers to learn this strategy. In the same speech, he determined to emphasize political warfare. He said in this campaign, 70 per cent of the efforts should be put on politics which includes organizing the local people with *Baojia* System and economic blockade, etc.; military works only accounted for 30 per cent.

88. Jiang, "A Comment on and Criteria of the Military Education and Training", a speech on the Military Education and Training Conference on September, 1968, in *Military Speeches of Jiang, op. cit.*, Vol. 4, pp.1527-59. In this speech, Jiang discussed the PLA's tactics in general and Lin Biao's tactics in particular. His recommendation was to use his triangle formation to overcome these tactics. See p. 1545.

89. Jiang Weiguo, *Broadcast Program*, op. cit., p. 56. He did not exclude its use for defence, but made it clear that it was primarily designed for offence.

90. *Ibid*

91. Jiang, "A Comment on and Criteria of the Military Education and Training", *op. cit.*, Vol. 4, p. 1545.

92. Jiang Weiguo, *Broadcast Program, op. cit.*, p. 53.

93. *Ibid.*, pp. 58-9.

94. *Ibid.*, p. 53.
95. Jiang, "A Comment on the Army Manoeuvre of Shanglin," Feb. 8, 1965, in *Military Speeches of Jiang, op. cit.*, Vol. 4, p. 1593. Also see "A Comment on and Criteria of the Military Education and Training", in same book, p. 1545.
96. Jiang Weiguo, *Broadcast Program,* op. cit., p. 53.
97. *Ibid.*, pp. 54-55.
98. Bai Guangya, *The History of Political Warfares of the Nationalist Army, op. cit.*, p. 72.
99. Based on the history of political warfare, it seems that the major functions of the military political work system in the Nationalist military before 1950s were propaganda and political education. The former was primarily aimed at the public, while the latter was given to the soldiers. When the political work system was changed to the Bureau of Information, the major functions of the information officers in the armed forces were still the same. See the description of the duties of the Bureau of Information in the Regulation of the Organization of the Department of National Defence, *Ibid.*, p. 73.
100. In October 1949, Jiang Jieshi appointed a committee led by Huang Shaogu and Gu Zhenggong. They submitted "A Proposal of Establishment of the Political Work System of the National Armed Forces", in November of the same year, which was adopted by the Military Conference later. On April 1, 1950, the Ministry of National Defence ordered the armed forces to start the new system, which was named "The Department of Political Works of the Ministry of National Defence". It was later changed to "The General Department of Political Works of the Ministry of National Defence". *Ibid.*, pp. 88-89.
101. *Ibid.*, pp. 89-90.
102. *Ibid.*, pp. 91-93.
103. *Ibid.*, p. 93.
104. The dismissal of General Wang Sheng may be seen as a typical example of Jiang's use of balance of power. Wang had been his close follower and supporter since the early 1940s until his dismissal in the 1980s. During this period, Wang had been the commandant of the College of Political Cadres for a long time; he had also been the director of the General Department of Political Warfare. His former students had developed a strong political force behind him. He became so powerful that many people were guessing that he one day might use his power to influence the political succession of Taiwan after Jiang Jingguo's death. Consequently, Jiang dismissed him and assigned him to be the ambassador in Uruguay.

105. Jiang, "The Major Points of Political Warfare", April 4, 1957, quoted from *The Digest of the Instructions of the Late Leader on Political Warfare* (Lingxiu Zhengzhi Zuozhan Yixun Jilu) (Taipei: General Department of Political Warfare of Ministry of National Defence, 1975), p. 25. (Hereafter referred to as *Digest of Political Warfare*.)

106. Jiang, "The Duties and Qualifications of the Military Political Workers", in *Digest of Political Warfare, op. cit.*, p. 29.

107. Idem, "A Critical Comment on the Political Works", June 10, 1963, in *Digest of Political Warfare, op. cit.*, p. 30.

108. *Ibid.*

109. *Ibid.*

110. Idem, "The Establishment and Utility of the Party Organization", October, 1953, in *Digest of Political Warfare, op. cit.*, p. 43.

111. *Ibid.*

112. *Ibid.*, p. 45.

113. *Ibid.*, p. 63.

114. Jiang, "What Is Called as a Scientific and Masses Age", in *Digest of Political Warfare, op. cit.*, pp.60-61.

115. Jiang, "A New Year Message to the Public in 1959", *Digest of Political Warfare, op. cit.*, p. 171.

116. Idem, "The Major Point of the Counter-Offensive War Direction", September 7, 1959, in *Digest of Political Warfare, op. cit.*, p. 272.

117. Idem, "An Instruction on the Main Point of the United Operation of the Party, Administration and the Armed Forces, and an Explanation of the Characteristics of the Counter-Offensive War", August 7, 1955, in *Digest of Political Warfare, op. cit.*, pp. 173-74.

118. Bai, *The History of Political Warfare of the National Army, op. cit.*, pp. 88-89.

119. Jiang, "The Spirit of the Counter-Offensive Operation and the Direction of Action", January 14, 1966, in *Digest of political Warfare, op. cit.*, p. 157.

120. *Ibid.*

121. Jiang, *Personal Record of Jiang, op. cit.*, Vol. 7, pp. 119-120.

122. There are two examples which may indicate this phenomenon: one is from Jiang's work, "To Strengthen the Fighting Power of the Counter-Offensive War and Create the Opportunity of National Restoration", a speech at the Army Training Conference of 1964, in *Military Speeches of Jiang*, Vol. 4, pp. 1649-1682. Jiang said that a foreign adviser told him after he worked several months in his army that the Nationalist forces were better than the Egyptian forces, which did not have a good strategic and tactical training under British assistance. He, showed, however, that while the Chinese force was better than the Egyptian force, it inherited a similar problem from the American advisers.

Another case was from a foreword written by B.H. Liddell Hart, a modern British strategist, in the English version of Sun Tzu, *The Art of War,* translated by Samuel B. Griffith. Hart said when he talked to a Chinese military attaché, a pupil of Jiang Jieshi, in the middle of Second World War in London, the attaché said that Sun Tzu's book was considered out of date by most of the younger officers and hardly worth of study in the era of mechanized weapons.

123. "The Achievement of the Zhongshan Academy of Science", in *The Overseas Digest Semimonthly,* Vol. 605 (October 1, 1988), pp. 119-20.
124. *Ibid.*
125. A Report on *The World Daily News,* Nov. 13, 1988.
126. See "The Important News of the Past 15 Days", in *The Overseas Digest Semimonthly,* Vol. 607 (November 1, 1988), p. 4.

CHAPTER 6

The Military Thought of Mao Zedong

The success of the Communist Revolution of 1917 in Russia had a tremendous impact on the Chinese intellectuals, who were wrestling with the problem of warlord fighting. The May 4th movement of 1919 further turned the attention of the Chinese to the outside world for possible new models of culture and politics. The rapid success of the Russian Revolution attracted the interest of the Chinese intellectuals, and soon, Marxism was accepted by them as a potential alternative model to the Chinese Revolution. Even Dr. Sun Yatsen was impressed by the Russian success, and sent General Jiang Jieshi to lead an investigation tour of the Soviet Union in 1923 and to further establish diplomatic relations. With this sort of encouragement and opportunity, the Communists did not hesitate in spreading Marxism to China. With the help of members of the Communist International (Comintern) such as Gregory Voitinsky, Henricus Sneevliet (alias Maring), a tiny group of Chinese intellectuals established the Chinese Communist Party (CCP) in May 1921, and held a meeting attended by twelve representatives in July of the same year in Shanghai. This meeting is now known as the first National Congress of the Party, and Mao Zedong was one of the twelve delegates.

Only two years after the Communist Party was established, once again with the assistance of Comintern representatives, the CCP began to cooperate with the Guomindang. The CCP members were permitted to join the Guomindang. In the first National Congress of the newly reorganized Guomindang held in January 1924, Mao and several leading Communist Party members were elected to the Central Committee. This cooperation did not last long, but it opened the Chinese political arena to the Communist Party.

After the collapse of cooperation between the CCP and Guomindang in 1927, however, the CCP members were ruthlessly purged from the Guomindang. Many CCP members were killed in the April Coup. Mao fled to Jinggangshan with a small peasant army and was later joined by Zhu De and other leaders. An armed independent Communist regime was soon established in the Jiangxi-Hunan border area. From then, Mao rose to the upper echelons of the CCP, and soon made his influence felt in China and in the world. In fighting against his sworn enemy, Jiang Jieshi, Mao dominated the Chinese political arena for fifty years. It was during his struggle against Jiang that his military thought began to develop.

The military struggles in China against both foreign imperialists and domestic adversaries brought Chinese military modernization several steps forward, completely moving beyond the stage of copying foreign systems. Much of the impetus was from the side of Mao and the CCP, who were isolated in the inland areas and were forced to fight for survival without receiving much outside assistance. Mao's thought was, consequently, less affected by foreign military ideas. Even so, Mao's military thought did use the basic ideology of Marxism, dialectical materialism, as an analytical method in developing his military strategy and tactics. Mao's military thought was also affected by the socio-political factors of that time.

1. The Socio-Political Background of Mao's Military Thought
A. Education and Political Activities in His Youth

Mao Zedong was born in 1893 to a peasant family in the county of Xiangtan, Hunan Province in central China. As a little boy, he experienced the humiliation of China's defeat in the Sino-Japanese war of 1894, the failure of Emperor Guangxu's reform of 1898, and the turmoil of the Boxer Rebellion and the Allied Expedition of 1900. These incidents of national humiliation caused him to join the revolutionary army to fight the Manchu regime, when the Revolution broke out in 1911. However, Mao differed from Jiang Jieshi in that he neither tried to pursue a military career by registering himself in any military academy nor stayed in the army for more than a few months. Instead, he entered the First Normal School of Changsha in 1913, in which he met his teacher and future father-in-law, Yang Changji. Yang not only taught him Chinese philosophy but also introduced him to Western philosophy, and most importantly, such Chinese periodicals as *Xin Qing Nian* (the New Youth), a popular magazine edited by Chen Duxiu, Dean of the College of Letters at Beijing University and subsequently the first leader of the Chinese Communist Party.[1]

After Yang had moved to Beijing University, he introduced Mao to Li Dazhao, the Head of the University Library and got him a job as an assistant librarian in 1919. Mao then began to read about anarchism and became involved in a study group of socialism sponsored by Li and Chen. This activity had a great influence on him, and led him to commit himself to the cause of the Communist revolution of China for the rest of his life.

After the May 4th movement, Mao began initiating socio-political activities, beginning in his home province of Hunan. He founded *Xiangjiang Pinglun,* a magazine which propagated the ideas of the May 4th movement. Mao also organized protest activities against the local warlord regimes and Japanese aggression in Changsha. In 1920, he organized a Communist group in Hunan and worked in the labour movement, which led him to participate in the First Congress of the Chinese Communist Party in 1921 in Shanghai.[2]

B. The Effect of Chinese Military Traditions on Mao

Before he had received any formal education beyond the public school level, Mao had often indulged in reading Chinese classic novels, through which he learned traditional Chinese military ideas and military history. His favourite novels were The Romance of the Three Kingdoms and *The Water Margin.*

The Romance of the Three Kingdoms is not only one of the best pieces of classic literature produced in China, but also a unique work that interpreted ancient Chinese military theory. The principles of *Qi* and *Zheng,* and *Xu* and *Shi,* which are the major principles in Sunzi's Art of War, are dialectically applied to the military actions in this book.[3] The normal application of the principle of *Xu* and *Shi,* for example, is that when one is "solid" *(Shi),* one should appear to look as if one were "void", and likewise, if one were "void", one should give the appearance of being "solid". The author not merely applied this principle to most campaigns in his book, but he took the deception one step further. He anticipated that an enemy could second guess his first deception, so he suggested that sometimes, "when one is solid, one should show that he is solid, and when void, show that he is void".[4]

It is said that Mao read the contents of *The Romance of the Three Kingdoms* as historical facts, and tolerated no questions about the authenticity of its events. Indeed, when his history teacher stated that it is a novel and not history, Mao tried to mobilize fellow students against him. He even appealed to the mayor of Changsha City, asking for the removal of the headmaster, who sided with the teacher.[5] This fact not only indicated Mao's stubborn personality but also impresses upon us the fact that Mao accepted the ideas of the book unquestioningly.

The influence of the novel *Shui Hu* or The *Water Margin* on Mao's military thought probably is only secondary to that of *The Romance of the Three Kingdoms.* He had, on several occasions, quoted examples from it in order to explain his own military strategies and tactics. The attacks on the Zhu

Village, for example, were mentioned as a typical model of how a commander in operation should choose proper tactics based upon the objective situation.[6]

Although Mao had claimed that he only went through Sunzi's *Art of War* once before starting his major military essay, thereby denying that the book had any significant effect on him, the prominence of the book in Chinese military thought caused its influence to be felt in more subtle ways. Indeed, the doctrines of Sunzi's military philosophy were not only carefully integrated by Luo Guanzhong into *The Romance of the Three Kingdoms,* but were also present in other history books and literature.[7] Anyone who ever read Mao would agree that Mao had an extensive knowledge of Chinese history and accepted his cultural heritage, if only selectively. The following quotation not only suggests Mao's attitude towards Chinese history and culture, but also indicates that he was even willing to adapt Marxism and Leninism to the specific circumstances of Chinese culture:

> . . .Our task is to study our historical heritage and use the Marxist method to sum it up critically. Our national history goes back several thousand years and has its own characteristics and innumerable treasures. . .Contemporary China has grown out of the China of the past; we are Marxist in our historical approach and must not lop off our history. We should sum up our history from Confucius to Sun Yatsen and take over this valuable legacy. . .We can put Marxism into practice only when it is integrated with the specific characteristics of our own country and when it acquires a definite national form.[8]

With such views on the ideas of the past, it is difficult for anybody to believe that Mao was not influenced by the theories of Sunzi and other ancient Chinese military strategists.

What Mao had inherited from traditional Chinese military philosophy is subject to debate, but most scholars would agree on two aspects: the emphasis on the human factor in war, and guerrilla and mobile warfare. The first principle not only made Mao's military strategies adaptable to the contemporary Chinese socio-economic condition but also gave him some theoretical support for mass political mobilization and the mass militia movement, as expounded in People's Warfare. The Communists thereby directly or indirectly involved everybody in the war effort.

Mao's guerrilla tactics and mobile warfare are primarily based on Sunzi's philosophy. As mentioned in Chapter II, Sunzi believed that all warfare is based on deception. Therefore, "when capable, feign incapacity; when active, inactivity. When he concentrates, prepare against him; where he is strong, avoid him. . .Pretend inferiority and encourage his arrogance. Keep him under strain and wear him down. . .Attack where he is unprepared; sally out when he does not expect you."[9]

A careful reader could easily find the similarity between Sunzi's words and Mao's sixteen-character formula of guerrilla tactics written in Jinggang-shan:

> The enemy advances, we retreat;
> the enemy camps, we harass;
> the enemy tires, we attack;
> the enemy retreats, we pursue.[10]

Like many other Chinese strategists, Mao also used the words "making disturbances in the east while attacking in the west, appearing now in the south and later in the north", to suggest the use of tactics to confuse the enemy. This is also the application of the principle of deception.[11]

In addition, Mao had drawn part of his military ideas from other Chinsese classics which have recorded many great military campaigns in ancient China. The war between the states of Qi and Lu in the Spring and Autumn (Chunqiu) era from Zuo Zhuan was one example used by Mao to indicate how a weak force can defeat a strong enemy.[12]

C. The Effect of Foreign Ideas - Marxism

Mao, without a doubt, was significantly affected by the theories of Marxism. The relevant question is what kind of influence have Marxist theories had on Mao's military thought. According to Stuart Schram, Mao was a relatively mediocre Marxist philosopher , who did not make any significant contribution on a high level of abstraction in terms of Marxist categories. However, it seems from Mao's works that Mao was simply lacking in interest in matters of pure theory; instead, he had a tendency to relate everything to the class struggle and to certain other values.[13]

Schram is probably correct in his comment on Mao's non-philosophical characteristics. In fact, Mao had made it very clear that he studied Marxism-Leninism only "to learn it as a science of revolution". By doing so, he not only wanted to learn from its extensive study of real life and revolutionary experience, "but wanted to study its standpoint and method in examining and solving problems."[14]

This attitude can also be found in one of the few philosophical essays he ever wrote, in which Mao particularly emphasized the application of the unity of opposites or the law of contradition to military strategy. As he wrote:

> In war, offence and defence, advance and retreat, victory and
> defeat are all mutually contradictory phenomena. One cannot
> exist without the other. The two aspects are at once in conflict
> and interdependent, and this constitutes the totality of a war,
> pushes its development forward and solves its problems.[15]

Based on this understanding, Mao, therefore, emphasized the particularity of contradiction in order to solve the particular revolutionary problem of China. When he criticized the dogmatists in the CCP, he emphasized the importance of "the study of the particularity of contradiction in the concrete things confronting us for guiding the course of revolutionary practice."[16]

From these examples, it is possible for one to say that the influence of Marxism-Leninism on Mao's military thought is primarily in its methodology. This statement can be confirmed by his essay "Problems of Strategy in China's Revolutionary War", in which he fully applied dialectical materialism to analyze the Chinese revolutionary war, from the law of war to strategy and tactics, from general principles to specific situations.[17] Similar examples can also be found in other essays such as "Problems of Strategy in Guerrilla War against Japan", "On Protracted War", and "Problems of War and Strategy".[18]

In addition to the methodological influence, Mao definitely had integrated Marx and Lenin's theory of guerrilla warfare and their militia system into his military thought. In his introduction to *Mao Tsetung on Guerrilla Warfare*, S. Griffith pointed out that Mao's strategic and tactical theories, in light of his principles of unity of opposites, seem to have adapted the ancient Chinese philosophical concept of Yin Yang, which are two opposite polarities and represent female and male, dark and light, cold and heat, recession and aggression.[19]

Generally speaking, Mao inherited concepts concerning the nature of war, the classification of war, and other things referring to the epistemology of war from Marxist thoery. However, Mao consistently accepted Clausewitz's definition of war, that is, the relationship between war and politics.[20]

D. The Effect of Economic Situation on Mao's Thought

Material conditions often determine the outcome of war. Sunzi already realized this fact as early as 500 B.C. He wrote: "an army which lacks heavy equipment, fodder, food and stores will be lost."[21] When an army is in operation, the problem of supply becomes even more complicated and expensive. Provisions have to be transported for a thousand miles to the field. Furthermoe, expenditures at home and in the field, wages and maintenance , and other expenses will "amount to one thousand pieces of gold a day. When this money is in hand, one hundred thousand troops may be raised."[22]

Due to the extension of the scale of war and the development of modern technology, a modern war has become extremely expensive, and the effect of material conditions on the outcome of war has become even more pronounced than before.

As a Marxist, Mao definitely recognized the fact that material conditions, to a large degree, can determine the outcome of war. However, for most of his career as a wartime commander, he was forced to fight while in the midst of extremely poor material conditions. In the anti-encirclement and suppression campaigns in the Jiangxi-Hunan border areas, for example, the infant Red Army was completely deprived of food and weapons by the Guomindang army. However, the Red Army still had to fight for its survival. A similar situation arose during the Sino-Japanese war in the border areas, where the Communist regimes and guerrilla bases were located. Communist supply lines were often blocked by the Guomindang and the Japanese army. To improve the food situation, Mao carried out a series of effective policies in the border areas. For example, he launched a social movement to mobilize the peasantry to raise grain production, and ordered the party to implement a policy of "better troops and simpler administration". This policy had the effect of reinforcing the armed forces by cutting administrative staff and expeditures. He also assigned the PLA to open up the wasteland for agriculture in order to supply their own food. At the same time, he used the traditional peasant mutual aid system in the North Shaanxi province to expand his force from the agricultural front. He called his approach "Laowu Jiehe", which in English means an approach which combines military missions with labour duties. By carrying out these policies, Mao not only virtually solved the food problems in the border areas, but to a considerable degree, consolidated the Communist regime and military forces there. However, to completely overcome the disparity in manpower and weapons between the PLA and the Guomindang Army, Mao also appealed to his own commanders to be innovative with military tactics and strategy. He recognized the determinant role of material conditions on the outcome of war, but he followed Chinese military tradition by emphasizing the human factor in war. Indeed, Mao wrote:

> Unquestionably, victory or defeat in war is determined mainly by the military, political. economic, and natural conditions of both sides. But not by these alone. It is also determined by each side's subjective ability in directing the war. In his endeavour to win a war, a military man cannot overstep the limitation imposed by the material conditions; within these limitations, however, he can and must strive for victory.[23]

In talking about the role of the human factor, Mao did not overemphasize the power of spirit as Jiang Jieshi did. Instead, he also tried to use proper strategies and tactics to overcome his material disadvantage. The strategies of guerrilla warfare and mobile warfare, the concentration of absolute superior force in campaigns, the emphasis on night operation, surprise attack, military democracy, the political work system in the armed forces, and the mobilization and arming of the masses in supporting the front are all designed to change the disadvantageous situation of the Red Army. These all constitute the essence of people's warfare.

E. Mao's Personality and his Military Thought

Schram says that when one considers Mao's thought, one has to integrate the current ideas of foreign countries, the national traditions of China, and Mao's particular personality.[24]

Mao's biographers and other sinologists often describe stories of Mao's youth, which suggest that some elements of his later thought, including his military thought, can be traced back to some of his childhood behaviour. Indeed, Mao knew how to use the concept of united front in his family to unify his mother and brothers and sisters against his authoritarian father; he also knew how to use the strategy of threats in order to make compromises with his father. His particular dislike of farm work and his passion for histories such as *The Romance of the Three Kingdoms* are all examples of an early childhood inclination that manifests itself in latter life.[25]

Some sinologists have read different conclusions from these stories, but it is difficult to deny the suggestion that Mao had already shown a strong tendency to oberve and analyze the objective environment around him and tended to manipulate it with his own strategies even as a little boy. Therefore, it may not be wrong to say that Mao was by nature a strategist. The ancient Chinese military traditions such as those revealed in *The Romance of the Three Kingdoms,* and the methodology learned from dialectical materialism only helped him to develop his potential gift to a prominent status.

2. Mao's Epistemology of War

In a prolonged period of war and turbulence, people often suffer terribly, and subsequently, question the motives behind the war. Furthermore, they may ask: Who is involved? What is the nature of war? These are questions concerning the epistemology of war. The strategist and political leaders deal with the same questions, but for different reasons. They have to deal with war, and they must try to win. Consequently, it is necessary for them to use their insight to make a comprehensive analysis in order to design their own strategy. For this reason, we will discuss Mao's epistemology of war.

A. The Cause of War

As mentioned above, Mao believed that war is the continuation of politics. However, war has its own characteristics, and it cannot be equated with politics in general. Therefore, he believed that "war is the continuation of politics by other means." To specify the term "other means", Mao said: "when politics develops to a certain stage beyond which it cannot proceed by the usual means, war breaks out to sweep the obstacles from the way."[26] He did not limit war to direct military conflicts, but emphasized the point that the use of weapons was only the final means of solving problems. Consequently, Mao wrote that "politics is war without bloodshed while war is politics with bloodshed."[27]

The concept of "war serving as a means of politics to achieve the political goals" was introduced by Clausewitz and was repeatedly quoted by Lenin and other Communist theoreticians. Mao, in turn, inherited this concept from Lenin. However, a similar idea had existed in ancient China long before it was discussed by Clausewitz and Lenin.

According to Simafa, war is an expedient means by which a ruler can govern his country. It would be used when the normal way has failed to achieve his political goals. The normal way involves governing based on the precept of benevolence. In a time of revolt or social chaos in the country, the ruler is permitted to use his force to quell the disorder and to restore the social order.[28]

From Marx and Lenin's theory, it is obvious that war is the culmination of the dramatic development of social contradictions, which, according to dialectical materialism, exist in everything.[29]

Although the existence of contradiction is a universal phenomenon, its development is greatly accelerated in a society in which the concept of private property exists. Indeed, when people begin arguing over property, war is inevitable. Therefore, according to Lenin, private property is the source of war and it will always be the source of war whenever and wherever it exists.[30]

When the social contradiction reaches a certain stage, it becomes a struggle between different groups of people and dominates the development of human history. Marx calls this event class struggle. As he wrote in the Manifesto of the Communust Party:

> The history of all hitherto existing society is the history of class struggle. Freeman and slave, patrician and plebian, lord and serf, guildmaster and journeyman, in a word, oppressor and oppressed, stood in constant opposition to one another, carried on an uninterrupted, now hidden, now open fight, a fight that each time ended, either in a revolutionary reconstruction of society at large, or in the common ruin of the contending classes.[31]

Mao also went further to make a general statement about the nature and cause of war. He wrote:

> War is the highest form of struggle for resolving contradictions, when they have developed to a certain stage, between classes, nations, states, or political groups, and it has existed ever since the emergence of private property and classes.[32]

Although all Marxists believe that private property greatly promotes the development of contradictions in society, which will eventually culminate in class distinction, hostility and war, they did not suggest that private property is the sole cause of war. Many other reasons may also dramatize the development of contradictions and, in turn, bring people to war. The ancient Chinese military strategist Wuzi, for example, suggested that there are five motivations for a ruler to begin a war-the struggle for fame, advantage, the accumulation of animosity, internal disorder, and famine.[33] Some of these struggles are not directly motivated by economic or territorial gains, and so, Wuzi classified wars into righteous war, aggressive war, enraged war, and insurgent war. Wars to suppress violence and quell disorders are seen as righteous, and all others are unrighteous.[34] Mao reached a similar conclusion concerning the classification of war, albeit from a different perspective. He also divided wars into just and unjust wars.

B. Just and Unjust War

"History knows only two kinds of war, just and unjust." Mao wrote: "We support just wars and oppose unjust wars."[35] Mao's definition of just and unjust is based on whether a war is a revolutionary war or not, because, to him, all counter-revolutionary wars are unjust, and all revolutionary wars are just. Based on this assumption, Mao suggested that everybody should oppose counter-revolutionary wars and support revolutionary ones.[36]

The Marxists believe that the "state" is an organ of class rule, and an organ used for the oppression of one class by another, which "inevitably causes civil wars in every society when the class struggle is intensified to a particular stage."[37] The theory of the state as an oppressing instrument has been applied not only to civil wars but also to wars between countries, above all to the modern imperialist war, which, according to Lenin, is the method by which governments and the ruling classes of the great powers can plunder colonies, oppress other nations, and suppress the working class movement of other countries.[38]

Based on this theory, Marxists have regarded all civil wars against the government and all wars against imperialist aggression as revolutionary wars. The only point of difference among them is that some Marxists see wars against imperialists as national liberation or national wars.[39]

Following this line of thought, Mao further included class war, national revolutionary war, and counter-revolutionary war in his category. A revolutionary or counter-revolutionary class war is limited to civil war, while a revolutionary or counter-revolutionary national war refers to interstate conflicts.[40]

It seems that Mao did not try to label all civil wars as class conflicts. For example, he once said that the Northern Expedition War, the War of Agrarian Revolution, and the War of Resistance against Japan are all revolutionary wars, all directed against counter-revolutionaries by the revolutionary people.[41]

The Northern Expedition War against the warlords, conducted jointly by the CCP and the Guomindang, was labelled by Mao as a civil war but not a class war, at least not in the strict sense of class struggle. The Agrarian Revolutionary War conducted by the Communists against the Guomindang from 1927 to 1936 was seen by Mao as a revolutionary class war against the landlord class and the collaborator bourgeoisie.[42]

In supporting revolutionary war and opposing counter- revolutionary war, Mao is a little different from Lenin, who not only publicly declared his support of civil wars and national liberation wars in his own country, but also unequivocally supported the revolutionary wars waged by the working class in other countries. "In such a case", Lenin wrote, "a war on our part would be a legitimate and just war. It would be a war for socialism, for the liberation of other nations from the bourgeoisie."[43]

The so-called "legitimate and just" right of a socialist country to wage a war against the bourgeoisie of other countries in order to support the socialist cause may have been seen by the Soviet Union as a legitimate reason for intervening in the domestic affairs of other Communist countries in Eastern Europe. However, a comparable theory does not exist in Mao's thought. Though Mao had actually helped the Koreans and Vietnamese to wage wars against foreign invaders, China did not take military actions against other countries to intervene in their domestic politics as the Soviet Union has. Even the 1979 Sino-Vietnamese border war cannot be cited as an example of intervention. It may be seen either as a war supporting the liberation cause of the Cambodians or as a war between two hostile countries, as was the Sino-Indian war of 1962.

C. To Stop War by Means of War

Although the Communists justify revolutionary class war and national liberation wars, they believe that the elimination of war is possible. According to Mao, war could be brought to an end by the effort of people. "When human society advances to the point where classes and states are eliminated, there will be no more wars, counter-revolutionary or revolutionary, unjust or just; that will be the era of perpetual peace for mankind."[44]

Based on the common assumption of the inevitable connection of wars and class struggles within a country, Mao's statement concerning the elimination of war is actually similar to Lenin's. Lenin had stated that "war cannot be abolished unless classes are abolished and socialism is created."[45] "Only after we have overthrown, finally vanquished, and expropriated the bourgeoisie of the whole world, and not only in one country, will wars become impossible."[46] Any difference in perspective between Lenin and Mao on this issue exists only in degree, not in concept. Mao does not particularly point out the necessity of overthrowing the bourgeoisie in his major military writings of the 1930s.

A reason for Mao's conciliatory tone is that the circumstances facing him were different from those facing Lenin. Mao's statements on this issue, made in December of 1936 in Yanan, were designed to sell to the country the strategy of a united front against the Japanese and to search for the support of the national bourgeoisie. Subsequently, it was necessary for him to be more moderate to defuse the hostile feelings of class antagonism. Indeed, Mao badly needed a truce with the Guomindang in order to gain relief from their constant military pressure. His Red Army might have been destroyed if it were not for the Xian Incident of the same month.[47]

No matter how conciliatory Mao's words were, Mao, like Lenin, advocated the policy of stopping war by means of war. He wanted "to oppose war with war, to oppose counter-revolutionary war with revolutionary war, to oppose national counter-revolutionary war with national revolutionary war, and to oppose counter-revolutionary class war with revolutionary class war."[48] From a historical point of view, this is not only a Marxist policy, but also traditional Chinese military philosophy. For example, in Simafa, a well-known statement on this subject reads: "it is justifiable to kill those who have threatened the peace and safty of other people; it is also permissible to attack a state in order to liberate its people from a cruel tyranny. To stop a war by means of war is therefore acceptable."[49]

There is no evidence to indicate that Lenin had ever been influenced by Simafa's theory, but it is beyond question that there is a similarity between them. Both of them advocated liberation wars against other countries.

Whether war can be completely eliminated from human society depends on the elimination of social classes by abolishing private property and the dissolving of the state. The next logical question, therefore, is whether social classes can be totally eliminated from society, and whether war would automatically disappear from a classless society. Another question is whether people can maintain their civilized life without the state or a similar organization to fulfil the functions of the state. The answers to these questions are not known, and this work is not in a position to discuss these questions in any detail. It is proper, however, for us to reiterate what we have pointed out above. Private property is not the sole reason for the polarization of social contradictions, and it is not the only cause of the rise of classes and class struggle. The elimination of private property may not totally stop polarization into social classes and class hostility. As a matter of fact, social differentiation in the Communist countries still exists, and class hostility is still visible.

Lenin believed that the state will eventually disappear from human society after the proletariat has used it to overthrow the bourgeoisie and to take over all property. However, he opposed the anarchists' theory of abolishing the state overnight. He advocated a theory of the "withering-away" of the state, which suggests that the state should remain for as long as it is necessary until finally "it becomes superfluous in one sphere after another, and then ceases [to exist] by itself."[50]

As a matter of fact, the power of the state in socialist countries is incomparably stronger than in capitalist countries. Neither social antagonism (if not class antagonism) in socialist countries nor inter-state conflict among them has been eliminated or weakened significantly; on the contrary, it seems that antagonisms and conflicts are somewhat more enhanced in these countries. Therefore, it is unlikely that war would be completely eliminated in the event that Marxists ever gain control of the world.

D. The Laws of War and Its Development

While the ancient Chinese military strategists (Sunzi for instance) have already established the basis of using the scientific method in analyzing the situation of war, the Chinese military writers of later ages often give an impression that the traditional Chinese military strategists tended to perceive the maneuver of forces as a high form of art. Based on this perception, the Chinese term *Bing Fa* has been translated into "The Art of War", though the Chinese character "Fa" could be more properly translated as law, method, and way. Sunzi once said in his book that military devices "are the strategist's keys to victory. It is not possible to discuss them beforehand".[51] Many writers often used these words to support their conviction that directing wars involves a high level of artistry.

Sometimes, they even combined the Chinese character "Fa" with "Xin" into the phrase *Xin Fa,* which means an unteachable device that can only be understood by cold thinking or personal wit. Consequently, it has almost become a maxim that it is impossible to lay down rules for warfare until one encounters the enemy. This explanation can even be found in the works of modern military strategists in China.

This historical tendency was, however, repudiated by Mao. He particularly emphasized the objective laws of war and the scientific characteristics of strategy, campaigns, and tactics. Mao left no evidence to show that he ever thought that the conduct of war is an art. He defined the law of war clearly; he wrote: "All military laws and military theories which are in the nature of principles are the experience of past wars summed up by people in former days or in our own time"; they ". . .like the laws governing all other things, are reflections in our minds of objective realities. . ."[52]

In discussing how to study war, Mao categorically stated that "the laws of war are problems which anyone directing a war must study and solve."[53] "It is well known", he wrote, "that when you do anything, unless you understand its actual circumstances, its nature and its relations to other things, you will not know the laws governing it, or know how to do it, or be able to do it well."[54]

As mentioned in the previous section, Mao paid more attention to the particularity of contradictions than the universality of them. By the same token, he emphasized the specific laws of individual war. He believed that the

Chinese revolutionary war has its own specific laws which are different from the laws of war in general. Therefore, he told his military leaders that they must study not "only the laws of war in general, but the specific laws of revolutionary war, and the even more specific laws of revolutionary war in China."[55] Due to the different circumstances and nature of the particular war, the characteristics of the laws of each war may also be different from each other. Therefore, Mao opposed the idea of indiscriminately copying the military ideas of foreign countries and even those of ancient China. He warned his officers that doing so can be likened to cutting their toes off to fit small shoes, and such a practice would inevitably lead to defeat.[56] Mao even opposed copying the military manuals of the Soviet Union, because they embodied the specific characteristics of the civil wars and the Red Army of the Soviet Union only, which in many aspects are different from the Chinese circumstances.[57]

While he opposed the indiscriminate copying of previous experiences of other people, Mao did not suggest that other ideas are completely useless. On the contrary, Mao wanted his commanders to carefully select whatever was applicable from the military laws left behind by past strategists. He then wanted his commanders to integrate these ideas with their own, to come up with an approach for dealing with their unique situation.[58]

Testing the laws and experiences of other people from previous wars with one's own experience may allow one to further deduce some useful principles concerning the guidance of war. However, this process is still not sufficient because war is not immutable; it is always developing. According to Mao, the laws and experience gathered from previous wars may become obsolete because different laws for directing wars are determined by the different cirtcumstances of those wars--differences in their time, place and nature. With regard to the time factor, both war and its laws develop; each historical stage has its special characteristics, and the laws of war of that stage cannot be mechanically applied to another stage.[59]

The developmental theory of war is the key that not only persuaded Mao to depart from the stage of copying foreign countries but also infused Mao's thinking with the dynamics to break from the old traditions of Chinese military philosophy without totally rejecting the useful aspects. This is probably the major reason why Mao was able to develop a unique and successful theory of people's war to deal with his particular adversaries.

As mentioned in the previous section, the theory of development is part of dialectical materialism and has been used by both Marxists and non-Marxists in various diciplines. Mao applied it to guerrilla warfare, to the recruitment of the armed force from lower level to higher ones, and applied it to the choice of strategies and tactics in operation. It was a core idea that penetrated the whole system of Mao's military thought and made it more flexible and dynamic. It will be discussed in more detail later.

3. Army Building and the Basic Concept of People's Warfare

Most Western strategists who study Mao's military theory are often influenced by two works: one is Mao Zedong's *On Guerrilla Warfare,* the other is Marshal Lin Biao's *Long Live The People's War!* Both were translated by Samuel Graffith and became extremely popular in the mid-1960s when the Vietnam War and the Chinese Cultural Revolution were running high. Consequently, Mao's military theory has often been identified as either guerrilla warfare or people's warfare.

Admiral J.C. Wylie, the author of *Military Strategy: A General Theory of Power Control,* listed Mao's theory of war as one of the four recognized existing military theories in the modern world. The other three are the continental, maritime, and the air theories, which have been well known in the Western world for at least half a century. He named Mao's theory as "the wars of national liberation", which "is by far the most sophisticated of the current theories of war. It, more clearly than any other, states its purpose and sets forth the systems of measures for its accomplishment."[60] Wylie did not refer to Mao's theory as guerrilla warfare, because it is "too restrictive and misleading to use as a descriptive title."[61]

As a matter of fact, neither guerrilla warfare nor the wars of national liberation can cover the whole system of Mao's theory. Probably the title of "people's warfare" can better indicate the basic concept of the theory, because the core of Mao's theory is built on the basis of mobilizing, organizing, arming, and fighting with the whole people of the society.

Cai Xiaoqian, the author of *The Study of Mao Zedong's Military Thought and The People's Warfare,* divided the content of people's warfare into two parts: one is the strategic guidance of the people's warfare; the other, the measures or methods of war. While the former refers to the basic concept of the people's warfare as a grand strategy or political strategy, the latter deals with the military strategy and tactics applied to operations.[62]

According to Cai, the basic theory of people's warfare initially emerged in the late 1920s and early 1930s and was developed in the Sino-Japanese War and the Liberation War. As a grand strategy, the basic principle of people's war has not changed dramatically since it was developed in the Jiangxi-Hunan period. However, the tactics and military strategies at the operational level were further developed in the Sino-Japanese War. They not only promoted the roles of the guerrilla forces from tactical to strategic status, but consistently carried out a plan of transforming guerrilla warfare to mobile warfare and, in turn, to other orthodox wars by improving the organization, equipment, and training of the army.

People's warfare is also regarded as political warfare, because it paid particular attention to the political mobilization of the armed forces and the common people.

In the rest of this section, the discussion will concentrate on the development of the basic concept of people's warfare in the process of army building. Strategic and tactical problems and the political work system will be dealt with in the following sections.

While it is correct to say that Mao's people's warfare was primarily developed in the Jiangxi-Hunan border area, it would be a serious omission to not take account of his early writings: "The Analysis of the Classes in Chinese Society" and "The Report on an Investigation of the Peasant Movement in Hunan". Taking these works into account, one would realize that part of Mao's ideas of army building in the border area was, to a large extent, actually developed before he reached the border area. In other words, the theory of the people's warfare could be traced further back to these two articles.

A. The Analysis of Chinese Class Structure and Mao's Ideas of Military Establishment

(a) *The Revolutionary Alliance--The Peasant*

At the beginning of the analysis of the classes in Chinese society, Mao stated bluntly that to ensure the success of revolution, the Communists must pay attention to uniting with all real friends in order to attack their real enemies. To distinguish real friends from real enemies, "We must make a general analysis of the economic status of the various classes in Chinese society and their respective attitudes towards the revolution."[63]

Mao divided the Chinese population into five groups in accordance with their economic status. At the top of the five strata is the landlord and the collaborator class, which, to Mao, always sides with imperialism and constitutes an extreme counter-revolutionary group.

The middle bourgeoisie was seen as a class representing the capitalist relations of production in the Chinese town and country. They were inconsistent in their attitude toward the Chinese revolution.

The third class in Mao's classification is the petty bourgeoisie which includes the owner-peasants, the master handicraftsmen, the lower levels of the intellectuals, the government functionaries, office clerks, small lawyers, and the small traders, etc. To different degrees, this group of people supports the revolution.

Next to the petty bourgeoisie is the semi-proletariat, which includes the overwhelming majority of the semi-owner peasants, the poor peasants, the small handicraftmen, shop assistants, and the pedlars. They want social change in order to improve their status.

The last group in Mao's scheme is the proletariat, which is considered as the most progressive class in the society and, thus, is expected to serve as the leading force in the Chinese revolutionary movement. Its total number in the 1920s was no more than two million, who consisted of the core of Chinese industrial workers.[64]

To sum up his analysis, Mao concluded that their enemies are all those in league with imperialism--the warlords, the bureaucrats, the collaborator class, the big landlord class and the reactionary section of the intelligentsia. While the leading force in their revolution is the industrial proletariat, their close friends are the entire semi-proletariat and petty bourgeoisie. As for the vacillating middle bourgeoisie, the right-wing may become their enemy and the left-wing, their friend--but it is necessary for them to keep on guard and not let them create confusion within the revolutionary force.[65]

In this analysis, although Mao conferred the honourable title of "the leading force of the revolutionary movement" on the industrial workers, he saw the Chinese peasants (semi-proletariat) as its closest allies. He went a step further to confirm the most important revolutionary role of the peasant in the investigation of the peasant movement in Hunan Province.

(b) The Vanguard of Revolution--the Poor Peasant

Before the collapse of the cooperation between the CCP and the Guomindang in the early stage of the Northern Expedition, the Communists had been enthusiastically involved in the peasant movement wherever they were. Mao undertook an investigation tour of five counties of Hunan Province in order to assess the real situation and to respond to the complaints within and without the Party. His report further confirmed his conclusions in his analysis of the Chinese social classes that the peasants would be the reliable revolutionary force to be mobilized by the Party. Among other things, there are at least three points in the report that would dominate Mao's military and political strategies in the coming revolution.

First, he found that "the poor peasants have always been the main force in the bitter fight in the countryside. . .They are the most responsive to the Communist Party leadership. They are deadly enemies of the camp of the local tyrants and evil gentry and attack it without the slightest hesitation."[66]

According to Mao's survey in Changsha County, the poor peasants made up 70 percent of the total population in the countryside; they were the backbone of the peasant association and the vanguard in the overthrow of the feudal forces. "Without the poor peasants it would have been impossible to bring about the present revolutionary situation in the countryside. . .Without the poor peasants there would be no revolution." Consequently, he made it clear that whoever denies the role of the poor peasants would deny the revolution.[67]

Second, he found that after overthrowing the local feudal forces, that is the local tyrants and evil gentry, the peasant association had easily taken over the local political power below the county level and become the sole political authority at the district (Tu or Qu) and the township (Tuan or Cun). In the traditional Chinese society, the local political power below the county in the countryside used to be in the hands of the gentry and landlord classes.

According to Mao, the local gentry who ran these organs were the virtual monarchs of the countryside. After the peasants' revolt, however, the authority of the landlord class was generally struck down, and the organs of the rural administration easily collapsed in its wake.[68]

The quick destruction of the hostile local political authority with organized poor peasants and its replacement with the pro-Communist peasant association had probably helped Mao to develop his strategy of encircling the cities from the countryside, which became an important part of the people's warfare in defeating the Guomindang force in the civil wars later.

Third, the armed peasant was the biggest asset of the CCP. It made it possible for the Party to control the countryside and, thus, to achieve its strategic goals of encircling the cities from the countryside.

In the Chinese countryside, the armed forces used to be controlled by the local government, the landlords and the gentry; they were known as self-defence corps and local security guards. When the peasant associations took over the local government from the local gentry and landlords, they lost no time in gaining control of these armed forces and reorganized them in accordance with their own needs. These forces were not large in number but were equipped with rifles and other light weapons, and, thus, consisted of the elite armed force in the countryside.

In addition, the peasant associations further armed their members with spears and knives or whatever they could get in the countryside and organized them into spear corps. Compared to the elite armed self-defence corps, their weapons were rather primitive, but with their huge number, they became a significant armed force in supporting the peasant power in the countryside. They were able to keep all of the armed guards, the police, and the bailiffs of the county government out of the villages. Even when these officials had to go to the countryside, they trembled at the sight of the peasants' spears and did not dare to practise extortion.[69]

When Mao wrote this report in March of 1927, he probably did not expect an immediate collapse of the cooperation with the Guomindang; thus, he did not anticipate organizing his Red Army with these armed peasants in the near future. Nevertheless, this happened within a few months after the April Coup.

To Mao, the peasant movement in Hunan achieved many great things, which Dr. Sun Yatsen and his Guomindang had been fighting for several decades but failed to do. He even saw the change in the countryside under the peasant association as a great revolution that would sweep away the thousand-year-old system and turn the Chinese countryside upside down overnight. Based on what he saw and his imagination, he arrived at the following conclusion which obviously formed part of his own military and political strategies in the quickly approaching revolution.

> In a very short time, in China's central, southern, northern provinces, several hundred million peasants will rise like a mighty storm, like a hurricane, a force so swift and violent that no power, however great, will be able to hold it back. They will smash all the trammels that bind them and rush forward along the road to liberation. They will sweep all the imperialists, warlords, corrupted officials, local tyrants and the evil gentry into their graves. Every revolutionary party and every revolutionary comrade will be put to the test, to be accepted or rejected as they decide. There are three alternatives. To march at their head and lead them? To trail behind them, gesticulating and criticizing? Or to stand in their way and oppose them? Every Chinese is free to choose, but events will force you to make the choice quickly.[70]

Mao chose the first of the three alternatives he listed. He decided to lead the peasants on the march to the end of the revolution. The armed peasants became his major force and revolutionary vanguard and helped him and the CCP to gain power.

B. The Struggle in Jinggangshan and the Emergence of People's Warfare

The name of "people's war" first appeared in Mao's works written in the early 1940s before the Sino-Japanese War was over,[71] but its theory had long been developed when Mao started his armed struggle against the Guomindang in Jinggangshan in the Jiangxi-Hunan border area.

(a) The Coup d'Etat of April 1927 and the CCP Armed Revolt

Only one year after Dr. Sun Yatsen's death, the relationship between the Guomindang and the CCP deteriorated. The growth of Communist power within the Guomindang and its far-reaching peasant and worker movements scared the Guomindang, and the conflict between local governments, armies, and the Communist-led peasant-worker organizations happened spontaneously and intermittently.

When the Northern Expedition forces fought their way to the Yangtze River Valley, the Communist peasant-worker movements also extended to this area. The peasant movement in Hunan Province as stated in Mao's investigation report was only one example of many similar cases. The CCP's worker movement had even controlled Shanghai and armed the workers with modern weapons before the Gomindang army approached the city; their radical activities may have occasionally caused attacks on the foreigners and the Chinese merchants. Increasing chaos had raised fears of international intervention from the imperialist forces quartered in that area. This gave the Guomindang and Jiang Jieshi an excuse to undertake armed suppression of the worker organizations and their sponsors, the Communists.

The incident first happened in Nanjing on March 24, 1927, when troops marching into the city attacked the foreigners and their properties, for which the Communist political commissars were subsequently blamed. When more chaos happened and expanded to Shanghai, Jiang ordered an armed suppression in Shanghai on April 12 following the resolution of the Central Censorial Committee of the Guomindang a few days earlier.[72] This suppression was coordinated with a similar action by the warlord Zhang Zaolin in Beijing on April 6, in which one of the CCP founders Li Dazhao was hanged.[73]

The suppression of the Communist activities in Shanghai, Nanjing, and Beijing did not immediately cause the CCP to withdraw completely from the Guomindang. They took advantage of the internal split in the Guomindang to get protection from Wang Jingwei and his left-wing faction in Wuhan for almost four months until the end of July, when Wang decided to join the Guomindang right-wing to expel the CCP from the Party.[74]

The expulsion of the Communists from the Wuhan regime opened the way for Mao Zedong to stir up the peasant uprising which he had predicted would smash all trammels and wipe out all of their enemies.

After the Wuhan purge, the armed forces under the CCP influence concentrated on Nanchang, the capital city of Jiangxi Province and decided to launch an armed uprising against the Guomindang on August 1. A week later, an emergency meeting of the Party was held in Jiujiang and, among other things, the Party appointed Mao as the secretary of the Front Committee of the Autumn Harvest Uprising in order to help the Red Army to take Wuhan and other cities. The campaign failed and the Red Army suffered heavy losses. Mao was blamed for this failure and the violation of order, and was removed from his Party positions. However, before learning of his dismissal, he marched his remnant force to the border area of Jiangxi and Hunan and established his base and local Soviet in the nearby town of Jialing. He then formally started building up the Red Army to consolidate his independent regime in the Jinggangshan area.[75]

(b) The Establishment of Base Area and the Agrarian Revolution

When Mao arrived at the border area, he immediately decided to implement a series of mutually supplementary policies in order to create a nation-wide revolutionary upsurge. The policy was to establish a base area, set up a political power, deepen the agrarian revolution, and expand the people's armed force by a comprehensive process of buiding up the Red Guards from townships all the way up to the regular army. As soon as these tasks were completed, the independent political power would be spread to the whole country in a series of waves.[76]

The Establishment of Base Area: The survival of an independent political regime needs an armed force to support it. In regular warfare or guerrilla warfare, the armed forces always need a secure base to preserve themselves from immediate enemy attack. Without such a base, it will be difficult for them to carry out their missions. This is even more crucial for a guerrilla force to fulfil its strategic function behind the enemy lines. After Mao fled to the Jiangxi-Hunan border area from the defeat of the Autumn Harvest Uprising, he desperately needed a secure base in order to reorganize his forces and to start a new struggle. Therefore, Mao listed the establishment of a base area as his primary task.

Ten years after the Jinggangshan struggle, in discussing the establishment of base area in the Japanese occupied areas, Mao summarized his previous experience of the struggle by pointing out how to transform a guerrilla zone into a base area. He gave the fundamental condition as follows:

> ... When large numbers of enemy troops have been annihilated
> or defeated there, the puppet regime has been destroyed, the
> masses has been roused to activity, anti-Japanese mass organi-
> zations have been formed, people's local armed forces have
> been developed, and anti-Japanese political power has been
> established.[77]

When Mao started to establish the border political power, he definitely had already experienced a period of military struggle to destroy the old local regime and its military forces. Thereafter, he paid a lot of attention to deepening the agrarian revolution in order to expand political influence in the border area and, thus, consolidate his newly established independent power.

The Agrarian Revolution: The agrarian revolution is also known as land struggle or the distribution of land. Although this was an important political program for the Communist movement in the countryside, it was conveniently used by the Party as an important vehicle of political mobilization to rouse the peasants, organize them, and, thus, arm them in order to expand the Red Army. If there had been no distribution of land, the party might not have been able to achieve its goal of military cooperation from the peasants.

During the Sino-Japanese War, under the United Front, the policy of distributing land was replaced by the policy of "reduction of rent for land and of interest on loans". When the local Party in Jiangsu Province temporarily postponed this policy in their base area, the emthusiasm of the peasants in supporting the guerrilla force faded. Consequently, the Party was forced to reinstate it even at the risk of being denounced by the Guomindang regime.[78] Therefore, it is true to say that the immediate aim of the agrarian revolution was primarily military rather than political during the war years.

Land struggle and peasant mobilization were carried out by the party organization and local government with the help of the Red Army. Therefore, the local political power and party organization in the base area had to be set up prior to the land revolution.

(c) The Establishment of Political Power

Mao had repeatedly mentioned the necessity and possibility of establishing small armed independent political power centres in the border areas, even those completely surrounded by the enemy. In discussing why it is possible for the Red political power to exist in China for a long time, Mao listed five reasons, which formed the objective conditions or requirements for a border regime to survive. They are: first, an economically backward country being semi-colonial and under indirect imperialist rule; second, continual wars among the various factions of the ruling class, which will distract their forces from fighting the Red regimes; third, the consistent development of the nation-wide revolution; fourth, the existence of a regular Red Army of adequate strength to keep the base area free from the sabotage and attack of the enemy forces; and the last but not the least important is to have a party organization to provide the leadership.[79]

Two of the five conditions are more important than the others; they are the economic conditions and the strength of the Red Army.

When Mao discussed the economic situation, he emphasized the characteristics of backwardness and the localized agricultural economy. He meant that both the enemy and his forces had to rely heavily on the agricultural sector. Thus, if he was able to control a border area with adequate agricultural production, he would be able to survive for a long time when the enemy cut him off from city support. However, he did not ignore the serious situation under the tight blockade of the enemy. He never ceased to remind the Party to pay particular attention to solving economic problems in the border area.[80]

Since the struggle in the border area was primarily military, both the party and the masses had to be placed on a war footing. How to deal with the enemy was a central problem. According to Mao, an independent regime must be an armed one. Wherever such an area is located, it will be immediately occupied by the enemy if armed forces are lacking or inadequate, or if wrong tactics are used in dealing with the enemy.[81] People in the base area were usually armed, but the Red guards were only adequate in maintaining local order or suppressing the landlords, not in fighting the enemy's regular army. Therefore, it is virtually "impossible to create an independent regime. . . unless we have regular forces of adequate strength," Mao wrote.[82]

A strong regular armed force is crucial in ensuring the independent regime's survival, but the growth and expansion of the regular army have to rely on the support of the armed masses.

(d) The Armed Masses and the Expansion of the Red Army

Mobilizing and Arming the Masses: The Red Army of the Jiangxi-Hunan border area in the late 1920s was required to perform a lot of noncombatant works. Mao wrote:

> The Red Army is an armed body for carrying out the political tasks of revolution. . .The Red Army fights not merely for the sake of fighting but in order to conduct propaganda among the masses, organize them, arm them, and help them to establish revolutionary political power. Without these objectives, fighting loses its meaning, and the Red Army loses the reason for its existence.[83]

He used these words to criticize the so-called pure military viewpoints of the Red Army in the base area. However, he did not mean that the importance of the fighting role of the army could be ignored. In fact, what Mao wanted to do by particularly emphasizing the non-military role of the Red Army was to strengthen and expand the Red Army itself.

In mobilizing the masses, the regular army organized all of the people in the base area into different groups in accordance with their age, physical condition, political background, and military training, etc. Generally, all peasants were organized into Red Guard or insurrectionary detachments. Those who were 18 to 23 years old with the best class background were put into the young pioneers; those who were good in military training with the best class background were assigned to the model teams. People who were under 18 and over 40 years old and were not qualified to be Red Guards or insurrectionary detachments were usually organized into laundry teams or recreation teams and children's corps, etc. All of them were armed with whatever was available at that time and were assigned to exercise military and/or political functions in war time.[84]

This kind of mass mobilization activity continued and even expanded later in the Sino-Japanese War and the Communization Movement in the late 1950s when the Everybody A Soldier Movement was at its high point.[85] In puting these organizations together, the whole population of the border area and later even the whole country became an armed force.

The Three-Ladder Recruitment of the Red Army: Although the CCP established its own military schools in the border area in the 1930s to train military leaders, the most significant characteristic of the army building of the CCP was in its grassroots approach. Partly due to the special circumstances and partly due to his own populistic philosophy, Mao adopted a three-ladder military system which guaranteed the CCP armed struggle inexhaustible manpower in the war years. The three-ladder system consisted of the armed masses, the local Red Army troops, and the regular Red Army troops.

At the bottom of the three ladders was the armed masses which were organized into either the insurrectionary detachments or the Red Guards. The former were organized in the villages, and the latter at the district and county levels. While the Red Guards were armed with rifles and other modern weapons, most insurrectionary detachments of the workers and peasants were only equipped with spears and knives. They were indistinctly designated as local armed forces in the early stage of the Agrarian Revolution. During the war period, while the Red Guards were often assigned as a guerrilla band to fight the invading enemy forces, the insurrectionary detachment was primarily used to maintain social order and assist the Red Guards in battle.[86]

This system was further refined and made more consistent in accordance with a comprehensive process of development from the village to the whole border area. As Mao wrote:

> . . .expanding the people's armed forces by a comprehensive process of building up first the township Red Guards, then the district Red Guards, then the county Red Guards, then the local Red Army troops, all the way up to the regular Red Army troops.[87]

Under the three-ladder system, the Red Guards, which included both the previously named insurrectionary detachments and Red Guards, were no longer designated as local armed forces. Instead, there was a new organization called the "Local Red Army" between the Red Guards and the "Regular Red Army". The Red Guards which at different times had been designated the self-defence corps, militia, insurrectionary detachment of workers and peasants, model teams and young pioneers, etc. represented the basic armed forces of the masses, and were attached to the local governments of village, township, district, and county. They were in most cases on a part-time basis and were not supposed to depart completely from their primary role of production as farmers or workers.[88]

The "Local Red Army", which were developed as regional garrision forces in the later years, were basically assigned to defend an area where they were quartered, and, thus, were different from the main forces which could be used to strike in any region.[89]

While the Red Guards were primarily mobilized to consolidate the base area, their final goal was to provide an inexhaustible supply of manpower to expand the regular Red Army. This is one of the main purposes of the three-ladder system. Before China adopted the conscription system in the late 1950s, the Liberation Army had consistently relied upon this system to recruit its soldiers. Some selected members or units of the Red Guards, or of the militia as it was later known, were often mobilized to join the local Red Army from which the main Red Army often recruited its manpower. This ladder recruitment process was often referred to as "promotion", by which the Red Guards and the local Red Army could be promoted along the ladder step by step. Even after conscription was adopted in 1957, the conscript has often

om the basic militia unit, which has replaced the roles of the
Chinese society.[90]

the People and Fighting for the People
yzing the ways of handling the Sino-Japanese War by the
government, Mao distinguished the two lines between the
nd the CCP. He declared that there was "the Chinese people's
1 the CCP sought to unite all patriotic people to fight an "all-
ple's war leading to victory."[91]
gh Mao did not define the term of "the Chinese people's line",
le, however, that it is similar to the concept of mass line, which
olitical party or government adapts its policy in accordance with
the best interests of the masses and relies on them to carry out
he Communists have called their armed forces the people's army
ing for the interests of the broad masses and of the whole nation.
irpose of this army", Mao wrote, "is to stand firmly with the
ple and to serve them wholeheartedly".[92]
: Report on the Investigation of the Peasant Movement in Hunan,
Mao convinced himself that the revolutionary party has to understand the
power of the peasant movement and change its attitude towards it. Only thus
can the future of the revolution be assured. Later, he went further to say that
"the richest source of power to wage war lies in the masses of the people,"[93]
"the resolute rallying of the people on a broad scale is the only way to secure
inexhaustible resources to meet all the requests of the war."[94]When the Red
Army put itself among the people and is seen by the people as their own army,
it will be invincible.

Based on this realization, Mao directed his effort of army building to
mass mobilization and mass arming. It eventually developed into a three-
ladder military system. Under this system, as long as the three armed forces
can cooperate with each other in war, it would be "a real people's war. Only
by waging such a people's war can we defeat the national enemy".[95]

4. Strategies and Tactics of People's Warfare

While we have discussed Mao's basic concept of people's warfare and
his general guideline of directing a revolutionary war, his military strategies
and tactics particularly tailored to reflect the characteristics of the people's
armed forces in war are left untouched.

As mentioned before, according to Mao, the laws of war have their
particular characteristics and cannot be applied indiscriminately to other
wars, because different laws of different wars are determined by their
individual circumstances such as their times, places and nature. As regards the
time factor, "both war and its laws develop; each historical stage has its special
characteristics. Therefore, the laws of war in each stage have their special
characteristics and cannot be mechanically applied to another stage."[96]

Instead of spending too much time discussing Mao's strategy and tactics in detail, the analysis in this section will be directed to the particular factors that affected his choice of strategy and tactics and how he changed them at different stages to meet the new challenges of operation. Therefore, the analysis will try to answer such questions as: How did Mao define the concept of strategy, tactics, and campaign? What is their relationship? What is the basic assumption on which Mao designed his strategy and tactics in the Chinese revolutionary war? How did Mao change his disadvantage in strategy by means of tactics? And how did Mao guide the strategic and tactical change in accordance with the development of war? Mao had written down a set of military principles based on his personal experience of directing the Chinese revolutionary wars. To what extent can it be treated as a general law of war, or it is valid only in a limited sense?

A. Mao's Concept of Strategy, Tactics, and Campaign

Mao had analyzed the subject of strategy in great detail in one of his major military writings but stopped short of giving a precise definition. He simply said that "the task of science of strategy is to study those laws for directing a war that govern a war situation as a whole."[97]

In this simple definition, there are three conceptual terms. They are: science, laws of directing a war, and a war situation as a whole.

In discussing Mao's epistemology of war in the second section of this Chapter, we mentioned that Mao's attitude toward the problem of war tended to be scientific rather than artistic. The laws of war are "the reflections in our minds of objective realities."[98] According to Mao, everything outside our mind is objective reality, which, in terms of war, includes all aspects of the enemy situation and our own. One has to "familiarize oneself with all of these situations in order to discover the laws governing the action of both sides and to make use of these laws in our own operations."[99] "The only way to study the laws governing a war situation as a whole is to do some hard thinking. . .there is no other way."[100]

From these quotations, it is clear that Mao treated strategy as a science, which is to study the laws of war that "govern a war situation as a whole", not a part of it. The laws of war which govern a partial situation are studied as a science of campaigns or tactics.[101]

The "war situation as a whole" is the key point of the science of strategy which Mao had taken great pains to analyze. He said:

Wherever there is a war, there is a war situation as a whole.
The war situation as a whole may cover the entire world, may cover an entire country, or may cover an independent guerrilla zone or an independent major operational front. Any war situation which acquires a comprehensive consideration of its various aspects and stages forms a war situation as a whole.[102]

While "the war situation as a whole" can be applied to different levels such as the entire world, a whole country, a whole guerrilla zone, or an independent major operational front, the concept of strategy can be also classified into similar levels, and thus it is close to Jiang's classifications of strategy such as grand strategy, national strategy, military strategy, field strategy, etc.

What should be considered as the war situation as a whole? According to Mao, the problems of the grouping of military units and formations, the relations between campaigns, the relations between various operational stages, and the relations between our activities as a whole and the enemy's activities as a whole, are all the subjects that should be considered.[103] Besides, he listed no less than 15 items to indicate what should be considered by a commander at the strategic level. All in all, the primary consideration of strategy is focused on those facts which may have a serious effect on the final success or loss of the war as a whole.

When there is "a war situation as a whole", there must be a war situation as a part, which is governed by laws of wars referring to the science of campaigns or tactics as defined by Mao.

While he paid overwhelming attention to the former, Mao did not totally ignore the functions of the latter, that is the problems of campaign and tactics. On the contrary, he pointed out that the situation as a whole "cannot be detached from its parts and become independent from them, for it is made up of all its parts."[104] However, he did not treat all its parts as the same, because the effects of the individual parts are not the same.

Some defeats or failures in tactical operations or campaigns do not lead to deterioration in the war situation as a whole, because they are not decisive of significance. But the loss of most of the campaigns making the war situation as a whole, or of one or two decisive campaigns, immediately change the whole situation.[105]

B. Factors Used to Decide Strategies

In discussing the characteristics of Chinese revolutionary wars in order to discover the laws of war governing the actions of both sides, Mao used five factors to indicate his analytical process in choosing strategies in the Sino-Japanese War, which includes the situation of the enemy, that of oneself, the space or terrain, the time, and the nature of the war. All of them except the last one are typical factors used by military commanders in operation.

(a) The Situation of the Enemy

This not only refers to the advantages of the enemy but also his disadvantages. Japan, for example, was a powerful imperialist country in the

Sino-Japanese War; it had great military, economic, political, and organizational power but it was quantitatively inadequate. It "is a comparatively small country, deficient in manpower and in military, financial and material resources, and therefore, she cannot stand a long war.[106]

(b) The Situation of Oneself

In the war of resistance, China was said to be a semi-colonial and semi-feudal country. It was still a weak country and manifestly inferior to the enemy in military, economic, political, and organizational power. "Here again", Mao wrote, "one can find the basis for the inevitability of the war and the impossibility of quick victory for China.[107]

(c) The Space

While Japan is a small country without enough resources, China is a very big country with vast territory, rich resources, a large population and a plentiful supply of soldiers, and is capable of sustaining a long war.[108]

(d) The Time

According to Mao, China was still weak in the late 1930s, but with its cumulative development over the last hundred years, its liberation movement was different from any previous period. Though the domestic and foreign forces opposing it caused serious setbacks, at the same time they also tempered the Chinese people. Therefore, China on the eve of the Sino-Japanese War was more progressive than at any other period of her history. Based on this assumption, Mao believed that China's war of liberation would be protracted and would achieve final victory.[109]

(e) The Nature of War

In addition to the material conditions , Mao believed that there is a spiritual factor that has to be taken into account. Because the Sino-Japanese War was an imperialistic and aggressive war started by Japan, its reactionary and barbarous character would inevitably arouse the antagonism of the Chinese people and those of other countries. "Such is the law that, " Mao wrote, "an unjust cause finds meager support, and such is the consequence of the very nature of Japan's war." On the contrary, "there is a broad international support for China stemming from the progressive and the just character of her war." This was a big advantage to China.[110]

Based on this analysis, Mao concluded that the above mutually contradictory characteristics of the Sino-Japanese War had determined all of the political policies and military strategies and tactics of the two sides; they had determined "the protracted character of the war and its outcome, namely, that the final victory will go to China and not to Japan."[111]

This analysis and its conclusion not only served as the basis of the strategy of the "protracted war" against Japan, but also determined the strategic status of the guerrilla warfare in the Sino-Japanese war. According to Mao, the guerrilla warfare in a small country can only render direct support to the campaigns of the regular army over short distances; in other words, it would be only tactical not strategic support. On the other hand, if a country is strong, the invading enemy could be either quickly expelled or could not occupy extensive areas. However, when a country which is both large and weak such as China, is being attacked by a small and strong country such as Japan, the enemy is able to occupy vast areas of the big country but does not have sufficient soldiers to control them and has to leave many gaps in the occupied areas. Therefore, the anti-Japanese guerrilla warfare would no longer be limited to interior-line operations in supporting the regular troops; it could carry out independent operations on exterior-lines. In other words, guerrilla warfare can play a strategic role in operations.[112]

This analysis gave the CCP a theoretical background to develop guerrilla warfare in the occupied areas and shifted the role of the guerrilla forces from a tactical to a strategic status.

The Vietnam War, however, showed that the size of a country had become less important in determining the strategic or tactic role that a guerrilla force may play because the Vietnamese guerrilla force did not limit its role to the tactical level, although its territory is proportionally smaller than that of China.

C. The Dialectical Change of Balance of Forces

As mentioned before, materialist dialectics as an analytical method had a significant effect on Mao. He often said that one must see things from two aspects: "the problems of identity and struggle. . .In given conditions, each of the two contradictory aspects transforms itself into its opposite."[113]

It seems that from this theory of contradictory relations Mao developed his dialectical logic about the relationship between offence and defence, advance and retreat, victory and defeat, and strategy and tactic. To some extent, he integrated the traditional Chinese Yin Yang philosophy into the law of opposites and transferred their contradictory relationship into a mutual complementary one. By doing so, he was able to change the balance of forces from a disadvantageous one to his own advantage.

> An army operating on strategically interior-lines suffers from
> many disadvantages. . .But in campaigns and battles we can
> and absolutely must change this situation. We can turn a big
> encirclement and suppression campaign waged by the enemy
> against us into a number of small, separate campaigns of
> encirclement and suppression waged by us against the enemy.
> . .We can change the enemy's strategic superiority over us into
> our superiority over him in campaigns and battles. We can put
> the enemy who is in a strong position strategically into a weak

position in campaigns and battles. This is what we call exterior-line operation within interior-line operations, encirclement and suppression within encirclement and suppression, blockade within blockade, the offensive within the defensive, superiority within inferiority, strength within weakness, advantage within disadvantage, and initiative within passivity. The winning of victory in the strategic defensive depends basically on this measure--concentration of troops.[114]

There is nothing new about the principle of concentration of forces; the problem is how to apply it effectively to operations. The Chinese military leaders, for example, had talked about revolutionary tactics for decades by saying "pit one against ten, pit ten against one hundred," and even "pit one against one thousand or ten thousand," but no one treated it seriously and interpreted it a little further in order to put it into practice. Consequently, it became a slogan, looking great but doing no good in operation. However, under Mao, it became a highly practical tactic. He said:

Our strategy is "pit one against ten" and our tactics are "pit ten against one"--this is one of our fundamental principles for gaining mastery over the enemy.[115]

This is a typical example of Mao using a tactical method to break the enemy's strategic superiority.

Mao repeated this principle many times in his military writings. He often said: "to concentrate superior force to destroy the enemy one by one." "The effects of this method of fighting are, first, complete annihilation and, second, quick decision."[116]

What he said may not be really new to experienced commanders, but his successful combination of these principles and his insistence on carrying them out to the maxium limitation have had an astonishing effect on the result of operations. In talking about concentrating superior force, for example, he often said that "our army must concentrate an absolute superior force--six, five, four, or at least three times the enemy strength--and pick an opportune moment to encircle and wipe out one enemy brigade (or regiment) first."[117] In referring to annihilation, he insisted that "injuring all of a man's ten fingers is not as effective as chopping off one, and routing ten enemy divisions is not as effective as annihilating one of them."[118]

The sucessful application of these strategies and tactics was the determinant factor that helped the CCP win the Civil War in 1949.

D. Mao's Principles of Operation

Since the CCP started its armed rebellion on August 1, 1928 in Nanchang of Jiangxi, Mao had personally led its military struggles against both domestic and external adversaries for twenty years. When he entered the second year of the last civil war against the Guomindang army in 1947, he summed up all of his military experiences of the Chinese revolutionary war, above all those from the previous two years, and wrote down his well-known principles of operation for guiding the final stage of the civil war. If the principles mentioned in the previous section can be seen as Mao's application of general military doctrines to the particular Chinese conditions, the principles of operation to be introduced below represent a set of military principles derived from the particular Chinese experience of people's war which might be applied to other countries in similar circumstances.

An original version of the principles was drawn up by Mao on September 1, 1947 as a strategic directive of the Central Committee of the CCP to the army in the second year of the war. [119] It was refined and reported to the Central Committee four months later. The principles read as follows:

(1) Attack dispersed, isolated enemy forces first; attack concentrated, strong enemy forces later.

(2) Take small and medium cities and extensive rural areas first; take big cities later.

(3) Make wiping out the enemy's effective strength our main objective; do not make holding or seizing a city or place our main objective. Holding or seizing a city or place is the outcome of wiping out the enemy's effective strength, and often a city or place can be held or seized for good only after it has changed hands a number of times.

(4) In every battle, concentrate an absolutely superior force (two, three, four and sometimes even six or seven times the enemy's strength), encircle the enemy forces completely, strive to wipe them out thoroughly and do not let any escape from the net. In special circumstances, use the method of dealing crushing blows to the enemy, that is, concentrate all our strength to make a frontal attack and also to attack one or both of his flanks, with the aim of wiping out one part and routing another so that our army can swiftly move its troops to smash other enemy forces. Strive to avoid battles of attrition in which we lose more than we gain or only break even. In this way, although we are inferior as a whole (in terms of numbers), we are absolutely superior in every part and every specific campaign, and this ensures victory in the campaign. As time goes on, we shall become superior as a whole and eventually wipe out all the enemy.

(5)   Fight no battle unprepared, fight no battle you are not sure of winning; make every effort to be well prepared for each battle, make every effort to ensure victory in the given set of conditions as between the enemy and ourselves.

(6)   Give full play to our style of fighting--courage in battle, no fear of sacrifice, no fear of fatigue, and continuous fighting (that is, fighting successive battles in a short time without rest).

(7)   Strive to wipe out the enemy through mobile warfare. At the same time, pay attention to the tactics of positional attack and capture enemy fortified points and cities.

(8)   With regard to attacking cities, resolutely seize all enemy fortified points and cities which are weakly defended. Seize at opportune moments all enemy fortified points and cities defended with moderate strength, provided circumstances permit. As for strongly defended enemy fortified points and cities, wait till conditions are ripe and then take them.

(9)   Replenish our strength with all the arms and most of the personnel captured from the enemy. Our army's main sources of manpower and material are at the front.

(10)   Make good use of the intervals between campaigns to rest, train and consolidate our troops. Periods of rest, training and consolidation should in general not be very long, and the enemy should so far as possible be permitted no breathing space. [120]

As pointed out earlier, Mao's principles of operation have characteristics different from other military principles, which can be summed up as follows:

First, almost half of these principles refer to the strategy of avoiding the enemy's strong point and striking at his weak point, which is the most prominent doctrine in Sunzi's art of war. Mao applied it to the concrete situation in the Chinese revolutionary war.

Second, he emphasized the necessity of supplying his army from the enemy in the field. According to Sunzi, an army could rely for provisions on the enemy, but should carry their equipment from home. To Mao, not only provisions but weapons and personnel could be supplied from the enemy. It is a generally accepted principle that in modern war it is difficult to rely on looting to supply one's force, above all weapons and ammunition. However, to a revolutionary force, which usually does not have its own reliable supply in its early stage, it is still possible to supply itself from the enemy in the field.

Third, Mao did not mention his well-known strategy of encircling cities from the countryside in his operational principles. Instead, he advised his army to take the extensive rural areas and small and medium towns first. However, he made it clear in his other writing that, although it is difficult to oppose the city from the countryside, one can defeat the enemy from the countryside by encircling the cities and isolating them.[121]

The theory of opposing and encircling cities from the countryside became an internationally known strategy after Marshal Lin Biao published his article "Long Live the Victory of the People's War!" in the mid-1960s; Lin even went further to give this strategy an international significance. He saw the United States and other developed industrial countries in Western Europe and Japan as the cities of the world, while the numerous developing countries in Asia, Africa, and Latin America were the large countryside of the world. The revolutionary people in this large world countryside could defeat the U.S.A. and other big powers in the world cities by occupying the countryside.[122]

Finally, when Mao advised his army to concentrate four, five and sometimes even six to seven times the enemy's strength in order to wipe out one unit of the enemy, the reader may have the impression that he tended to overuse his force in the battlefield. Generally speaking, two to three times of the enemy's force should be enough to dominate the field and be able to wipe out his enemy. However, there are two points worth mentioning. First, the guerrilla bands or the revolutionary forces are usually not as well armed as their adversaries; therefore, they need to double or triple the usual standard of absolutely superior force in order to guarantee their victory. Secondly, this principle is closely related to his theory of paper tiger. According to Mao, "we must despise the enemy strategically and take full account of him tactically."[123] When he said to despise the enemy strategically he was referring to the enemy as a whole ruling class, which Mao believed was reactionary and thus a paper tiger. However, when one meets it on the battlefield, it may be a real tiger; therefore, one must take it seriously. Consequently, one must concentrate an absolutely superior force to deal with it one by one.[124]

E. The Development of Strategy and Tactics

As mentioned in the previous section, one characteristic of Mao's military theory is to recognize the constant change of laws of war in accordance with the development of the war situation. His comprehensive analysis of this problem is clearly expressed in the "Strategy in China's Revolutionary War". He believed that each historical stage has its special characteristics; hence the laws of war in each historical stage have their special characteristics and cannot be mechanically applied to another stage. Based on this understanding, Mao showed a flexibility in choosing strategy and tactics and kept them in constant development in accordance with changes in the objective situation.

(a) The Transformation of Guerrilla Force and Guerrilla War
Although the author does not equate people's warfare with guerrilla warfare, it is important to recognize that guerrilla warfare is almost the only strategy that a revolutionary force can take when it is forced to wage a war against a well-armed strong enemy. In reviewing the important roles of guerrilla warfare in the process of revolution, Lin Biao wrote:

> Guerrilla warfare is the only way to mobilize and apply the whole strength of the people against the enemy, the only way to expand our forces in the course of war, deplete and weaken the enemy, gradually change the balance of forces between the enemy and ourselves.[125]

From the experience of the Chinese revolutionary wars, there is no doubt that a guerrilla force was often brought into being in civil war as the pioneer of the revolutionary forces. However, when the revolutionary war proceeded to a higher stage, regular warfare emerged, and, in turn, the guerrilla units were transformed into regular forces in size as well as in organization. Otherwise, it might have been difficult to meet the needs of the war. This is why Mao insisted that "the guerrilla units and guerrilla warfare will not remain as they are but will develop to a higher stage and evolve gradually into regular units and regular warfare."[126]
The development and transformation of the guerrilla force and guerrilla warfare made Mao's theory significantly different from that of Marx and Lenin. According to Marx, guerrilla bands "are the only means by which a small nation can hope to maintain itself against an adversary superior in numbers and equipment. By their use a weaker force can overcome its stronger and better organized opponent."[127] Lenin believed guerrilla warfare was an unavoidable form of action at a time when the mass movement had matured to the point of insurrection and when the intervals between the big battles of the civil war were becoming shorter.[128] Neither Marx nor Lenin made it clear whether the guerrilla bands would and should be transformed deliberately into a regular armed force to make it able to wage a higher form of war.
In the initial stages of the CCP armed struggle, guerrilla warfare was primarily used at the tactical level, which could be identified with Mao's basic tactics of guerrilla warfare:

> The enemy advances, we retreat; the enemy camps, we harass;
> the enemy tires, we attack; the enemy retreats, we pursue.[129]

Before long, however, Mao started to transform the guerrilla forces. For this purpose, he argued strongly against the political ideology of roving rebel bands and insisted on establishing bases and expanding the Red Army.[130]

The transformation of guerrilla warfare into regular warfare in the early period of war "was of the Chinese type", as Mao described, "regular only in its concentration of forces for mobile warfare and in a certain degree of centralization and planning in command and organization. It still retained a guerrilla character in other respects."[131] In other words, the upgrading of the guerrilla band and guerrilla warfare still had to follow a step-by-step approach in accordance with the objective conditions.

(b) The Three-Stage Development of Strategy in a Protracted War

The strategy of protracted war emerged in China long before the beginning of the Sino-Japanese War; however, its prospects and the possible course of development remained vague until Mao's "On Protracted War" was released in early 1938. Mao assumed that the protracted war would pass through three stages of development and transformation of the balance of power, and it would end with the victory of China.

Japan's abrupt surrender after the Americans dropped atomic bombs on Nagasaki and Hiroshima left Mao's three stages of strategy transformation incomplete. However, it was later implemented and to a considerable degree confirmed in the last civil war against the Guomindang.

According to Mao, the first stage covers the period of the enemy's strategic offensive and the Chinese strategic defensive. As a weaker side, the Chinese should primarily adopt mobile warfare, supplemented with guerrilla and positional warfare. Due to the staunch resistance of the Chinese and the exhaustion of Japanese finances and economy, the momentum of the enemy attack would be checked in the middle of this stage and would be further cut in the concluding phase.

The second stage could be called a strategic stalemate. At the close of the first stage, "the enemy will be forced to fix certain terminal points to his strategic offensive owing to his shortage of troops and our firm resistance, and upon reaching them he will stop his strategic offensive and enter the stage of safeguarding his occupied area."[132]

Due to the over-extension and shortage of troops, the enemy could only control some strategic points and communication lines, and left the countryside unguarded. This gave the Chinese army a chance to penetrate and carry out guerrilla warfare. Therefore, at this stage, the Chinese "form of fighting will be primarily guerrilla warfare, supplemented by mobile warfare."[133] The guerrilla warfare fought at this stage was by regular armed forces; this was different from the guerrilla warfare of the Jiangxi-Hunan area in the early 1930s.

The increasing guerrilla activity in the enemy occupied area, according to Mao, will no longer be a tactical action, it becomes a strategic activity. The army enters the enemy rear area to establish guerrilla bases, mobilize and arm the peasants; it starts to contest guerrilla areas with the enemy. The duration of this stage will depend on the degree of change in the balance of forces between the two sides and on the changes in the international situation. According to Mao, it "will be the transitional stage of the entire war. . .China will in that stage gain the power to change from weakness to strength."[134]

The third stage will be the stage of the counter-offensive to recover the lost territories. When China turns the war to strategic offensive and exterior lines, "the primary form of fighting will be mobile warfare, but positional warfare will rise to importance. . ." The guerrilla warfare will again provide strategic support supplementing mobile and positional warfare, but it will no longer be the primary form as in the previous period.[135]

The development and transformation of strategy and tactics at each stage of the war will basically depend upon the change in the balance of force of both sides. The roles played by the guerrilla force, though still supplementary in nature, will be strategic rather than tactical only. The guerrilla bases and the armed peasants in the enemy area build-up in the earlier stage will play an important role in the counter-offensive fighting. However, Mao's theory of guerrilla warfare at the strategic level depends to a large extent on the size of the country. As mentioned above, if a country is small, there would not be enough room for the guerrilla force to manoeuver in the enemy occupied area.

(c) The Implementation of Mao's People's Warfare in the Civil War

The Civil War between the Guomindang and the CCP resumed immediately after the Sino-Japanese War. The Americans tried to negotiate a peaceful solution but that only postponed the total war for a few months. When it eventually became inevitable, Mao got to implement his theory of people's war, though it was not exactly as Mao predicted.[136]

At the beginning of the war, the military disparity between the Guomindang and the CCP was obvious. The CCP was in strategic defensive. However, the situation was different from both the first Civil War and the War of Resistance because the CCP had about a million men regular army and two-and-a-half million militia forces. So Mao was able to carry out mobile warfare at the beginning of the civil war as he imaged in the first stage of the War of Resistance. Guerrilla warfare became less important in his strategic planning.

> In the present civil war, as conditions have changed, so should the method of fighting. The concentration of our forces for mobile warfare should be primary, and the dispersal of our forces for guerrilla warfare should be supplementary.[137]

During the first stage of the civil war, the PLA was able to stop the Guomindang's strategic offensive in some area within one year; so, as early as February 1947, Mao was able to take the initiative on several fronts. This unexpected situation made it possible for Mao to bring the fighting to the

Guomindang's area in the middle of 1947 and to establish guerrilla bases in central China. The stage of strategic stalemate lasted only a short period of time before Mao launched his final counter-offensive.[138]

From September 1947 to October 1948, the Guomindang army suffered serious setbacks on several fronts and, thus, was forced to take a strategic defensive. The People's Liberation Army engaged the Guomindang army in a series of decisive campaigns in Manchuria, Xuzhou, and Beijing from late 1948 to early 1949 and wiped out almost all of them. Therefore, when the war entered its fourth year, the Guomindang regime started to collapse and was forced to retreat on all fronts until its total withdrawal from the mainland in early 1950. The civil war was basically closed except for Taiwan and several off shore islands which have remained under Guomindang control up to now.[139]

5.   The Political Work System and Politics Taking Command

It is commonly accepted that the People's Liberation Army is an armed force of the Communist Party of China and it served as an armed political work team in the Chinese revolutionary war. Therefore, when one comes to deal with the military political work system of the PLA and the Party supremacy over the military forces, one may ask why the Chinese Communists have developed this system? How has it worked in the armed forces? How has the PLA worked as an armed political work team? And finally, what would be the future of this system? In other words, what can be the potential change in the relationship between the PLA and the CCP? The analysis below will concentrate on these questions.

A. The Historical Background of the Political Work System

As mentioned in the second section of this chapter, according to Marxism, the arise of private property is the source of class antagonism which, in turn, gives rise to the state. Therefore, the state is the product and manifestation of the irreconcilability of class antagonisms; it is an organ of class rule and an organ for the oppression of one class by another.

To maintain effective class rule, violence becomes the indispensable instrument of the ruling class, which in an organized form is represented by the armed forces of the state.[140]

In the class struggle between the bourgeoisie and the proletariat, the goal of the Communists, as the revolutionary pioneers of the latter, is to raise the proletariat to the position of the ruling class and to use its political supremacy to wrest all capital from the bourgeoisie, and to centralize all instruments of production in the hands of the state.[141]

To achieve this goal, the proletariat must have their own armed forces in order to overthrew the bourgeoisie. Accordingly, Lenin insisted that the proletariat should be armed "for the purpose of vanquishing, expropriating and disarming the bourgeoisie. . .Only after the proletariat has disarmed the bourgeoisie will it be able. . .to throw all armaments on the scrap heap. . ."[142]

After the October Revolution of 1917, Lenin immediately established an over-all military political system in the armed forces. The political commissar represented the party in exercising political control over the military commanders. By so doing, it was able to transform the Tsarist Russian armed forces into a Red Army within a few years.

The Soviet achievement had a tremendous impact on the Guomindang of China. Dr. Sun Yatsen assigned General Jiang Jieshi to make an investigative tour of the Soviet Union in 1923 and later adopted a party representative system in the Huangpu Military Academy in 1924, which was extended to all of the revolutionary forces as mentioned in Chapter 5.

When the Guomindang established the Huangpu Military Academy, under the newly signed agreement of cooperation many CCP members such as Zhou Enlai and Ye Jiangying were also invited to work in Huangpu and other military units. Many of them were appointed as party representatives or political officers in the Guomindang army. Therefore, the party army system of the Guomindang had undoubtedly affected the CCP's military establishment.

The collapse of the cooperation between the Guomindang and the CCP, and the heavy loss of lives in the April 1928 Coup, made the CCP leaders decide to establish their own armed forces controlled by the Party. In the "Problems of War and Strategy", Mao wrote that in modern China "whoever has an army has power."[143] Political parties which did not have an army or did not want to have their own armies could not share any positions in the government. Mao concluded that:

> Parties which have guns have power, and those who have more guns have more power. Placed in such an environment, the party of the proletariat should see clearly to the heart of the matter.
> Communists do not fight for personal military power, but they must fight for military power for the Party, for military power for the people. . . . Every Communist must grasp the truth, "political power grows out of the barrel of a gun."[144]

What should be the relationship between the gun and the Party? Should the CCP let the military leaders take the command? Mao himself was not a soldier. Furthermore, the incessant civil wars among the warlords had ruined the image of the soldiers. It is inconceivable that the CCP would put the future of the Party in the hand of the warlords. Therefore, Mao insisted that: "our principle is that the Party commands the gun, and the gun must never be allowed to command the Party. Yet having guns, we can create Party organization."[145]

With this historical background, the military political work system was added to the Red Army at the very beginning. Mao himself assumed the political commissarship rather than the position of commander in the Jianggangshan period. He then created a model for the military political work system and for the relationship between the Party and armed forces.

B. Party Organization and Its Functions in the Army

With the military political work system, Mao not only achieved political control over the armed forces, but also transformed it into a political work team in order to carry out the Party's political programs in the war. This is the primary difference between the political work system of the PLA and that of its adversary, the Guomindang army.

(a) Party Organization in the Army

It is well known today that the Communist Party has a well-organized military political work system in the PLA. At the top is the Military Affairs Commission (MAC), which makes most specific policy decisions and is always chaired by the supreme leaders of the Party. Below the MAC is the General Political Department, which is responsible for ideology, discipline, morale and political education works of the armed forces. Its organization extends from the headquarters of the PLA down to the company level. At each level, it is headed by a political commissar or director or both. Generally speaking, there is both a full-time political commissar and a political director at the higher levels of the army unit, but below the regiment there is only a political director. While the commissar is the party leader of the unit and represents the party in supervising the armed forces, the political director is in charge of the day-to-day political work. In case there is no full-time political commissar, the political director would take his place.[146]

Below the company, the Party members are usually organized into Party cells and are led by the political director and the Party branch of the company.

During the early years of the revolutionary war, the power of the political commissar was on many occasions even greater than that of the commanders, because many commanders were promoted from the captured enemy soldiers. Therefore, Mao particularly emphasized the important roles of the Party representatives at the company level. He said: "Facts have shown that the better the company Party representative, the sounder the company, and that the company commander can hardly play this important political role."[147] The roles Mao wanted the Party representatives to play, include supervising political training of the soldiers, guiding the works of mass movements, and serving as the secretary of the Party branch, etc. Mao even said that it would be a gross error to believe that the commanders, above all those promoted from the captured enemy soldiers, can fulfil these roles without Party representatives.[148]

(b) Political Training in the Army

In the early stage of the Chinese revolution, the Red Army often suffered heavy casualties in fierce fighting and thus faced a serious shortage of manpower. To replenish their soldiers they were forced to recruit the lumpen-proletariat and the captured enemy soldiers; these people later even outnumbered the peasants and workers and became the major source of replacements. Mao realized that too many of these elements would not be good for the army and the Party but he did not have a choice. Mao's solution was to intensify political training in order to transform them into good soldiers and revolutionaries.[149] That is similar to Dr. Sun Yatsen's unsuccessful attempt to transform the warlord forces in Guangdong.

Political training includes political indoctrination or propaganda but is not limited to that; it is also concerned with the day-to-day material and spiritual lives of the soldiers. For example, under extreme economic situations, when there was no regular pay for the soldiers, military democracy and the abolition of corporal punishment gave the soldiers some personal dignity that they never enjoyed before, and, thus, they were willing to fight together with the Party. It seems that this training was very successful. As Mao wrote:

After receiving political education, the Red Army soldiers have become class-conscious, learned the essentials of distributing land, setting up political powers, arming the workers and peasants, etc., and they know they are fighting for themselves, for the working class, and the peasantry. Hence they can endure the hardships of the bitter struggle without complaint.[150]

(c) Political Control and the Supremacy of the Party

The purposes of political education in the army are two-fold:
(1)   to transform or improve the quality of the armed forces, and
(2)   to prevent deviation from the basic party line. Both were designed to ensure the supremacy of the Party leadership and Party control over the army. However, to prevent the possible deviation of the armed forces from the Party line, the Party may sometimes have to use other effective approaches such as criticism, the pressure of public opinion, and even the threat of punishment. It is said that in the Jiangxi-Hunan period many soldiers regarded military affairs and politics as opposed to each other and refused to recognize that military affairs are only one means of accomplishing political tasks; some of them even required the political workers in the army to subordinate themselves to the military commanders. Mao therefore believed that "if allowed to develop, this idea would involve the danger of estrangement from the masses, control of the government by the army and departure from the proletarian leadership--it would be to take the path of warlordism."[151]

To prevent the emergence of warlordism and possible deviation from the Party leadership, short of using purges, Mao suggested criticism within and without the Party to destroy this idea and check its potential development. The methods of correction are as follows:

(1)   raise the political level in the Party by means of education, destroy the theoretical roots of the purely military viewpoint;

(2)   intensify the political training of officers and men, and especially the education of the ex-prisoners;

(3)   mobilize the local Party organization to criticize the Party organizations in the Red Army, and use the organs of mass political power to criticize the Red Army itself in order to influence the Party organizations and the officers and men of the Red Army;

(4)   actively attend to and discuss military work--all the tasks must be discussed and decided upon by the Party before being carried out by the rank and file; and

(5)   draw up Red Army rules and regulations which clearly define its tasks, the relationship between its military and political apparatus. [152]

The political training used in correcting this potential danger is basically the same as mentioned earlier. Criticism or the pressures of public opinion have been developed into a unique method in China in general, and in the Party and the army in particular. Mao tried to rely on this mass line approach to solve almost every socio-political and military problem throughout his life. It had been seen as a "good prescription for all diseases" and became part of the established social system of China.

The involvement of Party Committee in the process of decision-making has greatly reinforced its control over the armed forces and ensured that the party line is closely followed. This method of political control has since been institutionalized.

If these methods are still ineffective in preventing deviation of the armed forces from the party line, a special purge accompanied by various socio-political movement would be necessary. The purge of Peng Dehuai and Lin Biao are recent examples of this kind.

C. The Political Roles of the PLA

Mao not only wanted to keep the armed forces under Party control, he but wanted to use the army as a reliable instrument to achieve socio-political goals. Instead of going into detail, we will summarize a few points as follows:

(a) Helping Set Up Local Party and Political Power

There is no question that an armed independent political power, such as those of the Red border areas in the 1930s, has to be supported by the armed forces in order to ensure its survival. What is unique in Mao's idea is that the Red Army was required not only to support an existing political power of the

CCP but to create one for the Party. It was even required by Mao to build up a Party organization at the local level when it conquered new territory which did not yet have a functioning Party organization. "The Red Army should shoulder such important tasks as. . .helping them to establish revolutionary political power and setting up Party organizations."[153]

(b) Political Work Team in Arms

A revolutionary is probably at the same time a fighter or soldier, but a soldier may not always be a revolutionary. However, under Mao Zedong's army building philosophy, the soldier of the Red Army must be a fighter, propagandist, political organizer, and information collector. Mao had harshly criticized the army man who believed that fighting is the only task of the Red Army and refused to do political work. He declared that "the Chinese Red Army is an armed body for carrying out the political tasks of the revolution. . .Without these objectives, fighting loses its meaning, and the Red Army loses the reason for its existence."[154]

Mao was firmly opposed to confining the role of the army to fighting, above all in the struggles of the Jinggangshan period. He wanted them to do propaganda work among the masses, organizing and arming them, because the mobilization of the people is the key to victory.

(c) Mass Mobilization by the Army

Mao stated that "the richest source of power to wage war lies in the masses of the people. . .The army must become one with the people so that they see it as their own army. Such an army will be invincible."[155] Political works of the army can help them to achieve this goal.

Mao defined the army's political works in three dimensions: the unity between the officers and men; the unity between the army and the people; and the disintegration of the enemy.[156] The first is an internal work of the army that can be omitted from our discussion; the third dimension belongs to propaganda in the battlefield and may also be omitted here. The second dimension can be accomplished chiefly by mass mobilization, which includes propaganda among the masses, and organizing and arming them.

To Mao an extensive mobilization can do more than enough to close the disparity in weaponry and other material conditions between the revolution- ary and his enemy. Mao wrote:

> This move (mobilization) is crucial; it is indeed of primary im-
> portance, while our inferiority in weapons and other things is
> only secondary. The mobilization of the common people
> throughout the country will create a vast sea in which to drown
> the enemy, create the conditions that will make up for our
> inferiority in arms and other things, and create the prerequisites
> for overcoming every difficulty in war.[157]

The function of mass mobilization includes two aspects: one is to arouse the people by telling them that the nation is in danger and their own future would be ruined, if they are conqured by the enemy, thus encouraging them to stand up for the survival of the nation as well as themselves. The other is to organize the masses. The huge population will not be able to demonstrate its power until it is organized. Therefore, for Mao mobilization is always linked with organization. In the article "Getting Organized", Mao said: "to mobilize and organize them into a great army of labour, all the available forces without exception."[158] "This is the only road to liberation for the people, the only road from poverty to prosperity and the only road to victory."[159]

The idea of a vast human sea created by the mobilized people has drawn fierce criticism from Mao's adversaries who linked this idea to Mao's principles of concentration of absolutely superior force in war. They denounced it as inhumane, cruel and ruthless because it forced the soldiers to attack the enemy's position in human waves without concern for the loss of lives.

Although the criticism is not completely unfounded regarding the loss of lives in war, it is irrelevant to Mao's idea of the human sea. When Mao talked about the human sea, he meant that under the protection of the mobilized masses, the guerrilla bands would be able to move safely and freely as fish swimming in the water. As long as there is water, it will always be possible for the fish to survive.[160] The enemy, on the other hand, will drown in the vast hostile human sea.

D. The Conflict between the Reds and the Experts

Theoretically, under the Party leadership, the army commanders and the political commissars should have cooperated smoothly and closely. But, as a matter of fact, their relationship is not always as good as expected. The conflict between the two groups at different stages of the revolution has caused serious political problems. Students of Chinese military affairs in the Western world have referred to it as a conflict between the Reds and the experts.[161]

The conflict between these two groups first emerged in the late 1920s when the Red Army was still in its infancy. As mentioned before, the solution of the first conflict was through political control and resumption of the supremacy of Party leadership. The fierce military struggles in the revolutionary wars often forced the military commanders and political commissars to work together closely in order to win the war. But when the war was over and China decided to modernize her armed forces in the early 1950s, the cracks between these two groups of people became prominent again and dominated Chinese political development for more than a decade.

There was a national consensus on the need for military modernization in the 1950s following the end of the Korean War. All agreed that efforts must be made to refine the army's techniques and equipment, and that more time and energy must be devoted to military training in order to elevate the tactical and technical levels of the army.[162] However, under the influence of the Soviet military doctrines, the Chinese military officers began to realize the important role of weapons in modern war and to accord top priority to military rather than political factors in determining the outcome of war. Some Chinese officers apparently accepted this idea and to some extent rejected the revered military thought of Mao Zedong, which stresses political factors above military ones as the key to victory.[163]

This opinion prevailed among the returned soldiers of Korean War units and other young officers. They not only considered the Party committee an obstacle to organizational efficiency but also thought it was incompetent to handle military matters. They started to liquidate and restrict the activities of the Party committees in leadership and political works. Prior to the reorganization of the political control system in July 1960, the number of Party members in the armed forces had gradually declined; about 7,000 companies did not even have Party branch committees, and when they did exist they were inactive.[164]

It is conceivable that the party commissars and even the senior military leaders were offended by this situation and could not wait for long to hit back.

There are many reasons for the political commissars to be offended, but the most important one was the challenge to the supremacy of the Party leadership. When politics takes command all other considerations are subordinate. Under this assumption, the political functionary in the armed force is entitled to meddle in just about everything that goes on within the unit.[165] They cannot tolerate the overenthusiasm of the young officers in striving for modernizations that threaten their status in the army. When they started to hit back, their first targets were Marshal Peng Dehuai, the Minister of National Defence, and Huang Kecheng, the Chief of Staff of the PLA; both were dismissed from their offices in late 1959. Among other charges they were accused of opposing the tightening political control over the army.

In September 1959, Lin Biao replaced Peng and took over the Ministry of National Defence. He carried out a series of reforms to strengthen the political and ideological controls over the armed forces; the Party committees in the companies were reorganized with about 2000 Party members purged from the Party in 1961.[166]

Under Lin Biao's leadership, the drive to strengthen ideological work and the supremacy of the Party leadership reached its peak. His goal was to revolutionize the PLA again and use it to back Mao's struggle against his political rivals. When the Cultural Revolution began in 1966, Lin was able to use the PLA to drive for political power in Mao's name. The PLA were taken out of their barracks and sent to take over the factories, government offices, and the university classrooms and propagate Mao Zedong's thought and Marxism-Lenism. The PLA was described by Western students, in this period at least, as a political army, which implied that it might no longer be competent as a combat unit.

This remark was not entirely groundless. In the wake of the Sino-Soviet border clashes in 1969, the military requirement forced the PLA to reduce their political activities. The Lin Biao Incident in 1971 forced the PLA to return to their traditional military activities. However, the dramatic change occurred only after the Sino-Vietnamese War in 1979. The Chinese Government once again accelerated their military training. Though the importance of political works and ideological education was still being discussed by the leaders, it had not been given a higher priority than military training until hardliners in the Party took over the Party leadership from reformers and suppressed the pro-democracy movement by armed forces in Beijing on June 4, 1989. The dramatic change in the Chinese political mood and the sudden collapse of Communist regimes in the East European countries, above all in Romania, have led nervous Chinese leaders to decide to tighten their control over the PLA. Since then, political indoctrination and political work in the armed forces have once again, at least temporarily, emerged as the top priority.

6. Conclusion

In discussing Mao's military thought, the analysis has consistently emphasized three points: the factors that affected the development of Mao's thought; the process of the development of people's warfare; and the major content of his thought, which includes the basic concept of people's warfare, Mao's epistemology of war, and the development of strategy and tactics.

Several issues have caught my attention through the process of analysis. They are presented below as the conclusion of this Chapter.

A. The Relation between Theory and Reality

Generally speaking, like many theories in social science, military theories are not always testable before engaging the enemy on the battlefield. Rather than culling their ideas from a fantastic imagination, military strategists must conclude their theories from careful observation, investigation, and personal experiences in order to reduce the chance of defeat in war.

As for Mao's military theory, he did not confuse imagination with reality. On the contrary, his basic theory of people's warfare is entirely based on empirical evidence. "The Analysis of Chinese Social Class" and "The Report of Investigation of the Peasant Movement in Hunan", for example, formed part of the theoretical basis for his people's warfare. If one examines Mao's major military writings, one will find that most of them are based on his own experience, except part of his epistemology of war, which was inherited from the political theories of Marxism.

B. The Effect of the Concept of Development on Mao's Theory

Whether it is inherited from the Law of the Unity of Opposites or from the traditional Chinese philosophy of Yin and Yang, Mao fully applied the theory of development to his military theories.

One may or may not agree with his epistemology of war in which he inherited from Marx the theory of the relationship between private property, class struggle, state, and war; but when one refers to his use of force in war and his application of the theory of contradition to change the balance of forces in campaigns and battles, one is inclined to believe that Mao had indeed mastered the application of materialist dialectics to military affairs. His strategy of "pitting one against ten or a hundred strategically by pitting ten against one tactically" helped him to successfully transform his inferiority in strategy to superiority in battle.

Furthermore, by applying the concept of continuing movement and development, he was able to open a new demension for the guerrilla force by constantly improving its organization, equipment, and strategies and tactics in accordance with the development of the situation through different stages. This made people's warfare more powerful than in its original definition.

C. The Effect of Politics Taking Command

Although the armed forces of the Guomindang also have a military political work system, it has never achieved the goals of politics taking command and the Party supremacy in the army, as has the PLA. However, the uniqueness of the PLA political work system is not limited to its political control and the absolute Party authority; it is rather expressed in the political roles performed by the PLA in Chinese society, above all in wartime. The performance of the PLA in propaganda, mass mobilization, and mass organi- zation, was extremely successful and scored an unprecedented record for the armed political work teams in world military history. Nevertheless, the same roles played by the PLA in the socio-political movement, above all when it was involved in the intra-Party power struggles after 1949, became a negative factor, which not only increased the danger of military intervention in politics, but also accelerated the corruption of the PLA in the later years. The aborted coup led by Marshal Lin Biao against Mao in 1971 can be seen as a typical case of the former; the increasing reports of disputes between the PLA units and the local people are the examples of the latter. Since the collapse of the Gang of Four in 1976, the Chinese leaders began to reduce the PLA's political roles and kept them occupied by military training, above all after the Sino-Vietnamese War of 1979 for which the Chinese paid a high price to win an inconclusive victory but exposed their military weakness. However, with the Tiananmen Square incident of June 4, 1989, in which the PLA was ordered to open fire on the pro-democracy movement students, the winds of change are blowing again across the political landscape. Since then, the Party has not only strengthened its political control over the PLA but also required the armed forces to fully commit themselves to the Party lines in the struggle against any political dissent within and without the party. This trend may continue for a while until the political mood changes again.

D. The Armed People--The Militia

The Chinese militia system has had a history almost as long as that of China itself. However, there has never been a single government that has ever created a militia system as large as that of the present Chinese government. From the Red Guards, self-defence corps, and eventually the Everyone-A-Soldier Movement of the 1950s in connection with the communization of the countryside, the mass militia system almost turned the entire country--villages, townships, and cities as well--into a military fortification and a collection of barracks.[167]

The mass militia system still exists but it is not as active as it used to be in the 1960s, except in some sensitive area such as the Sino-Vietnamese border where the militia force is mobilized to maintain local order and guard against sabotage. Generally speaking, when the country has been at peace and has turned her attention to economic development, the militia system has been downgraded or even ignored. However, when the country has been at war or immersed in the process of social mobilization, the militia has been mobilized and kept active. The majority of the Chinese population is still located in the countryside, but there are not enough police to maintain social order. Therefore, the militia has often assumed police functions in the villages and townships even in peacetime.

Mao's major military writings consisted of only about a dozen articles. Most of them were issued primarily to solve strategic problems without trying to include all military subjects. However, in these few writings, it is apparent that Mao had systematically analyzed many important issues and presented a fairly sound system of military thought which is epitomized by the theory of people's warfare. Mao used it to direct the Chinese civil war and win political power. It made potential external enemies think twice about involving themselves in a conventional war on the Chinese mainland.

Footnotes

1. Rice, Edward E., *Mao's Way* (Berkeley, CA:Univ. of California, 1974), p. 17.
2. Schram, Stuart R., *The Political Thought of Mao Tse-tung* (New York: Frederick A. Praeger, 1969), p. 440.
3. The discussion of the use of these principles is found in Ch. 4 to 7 of Sunzi's *The Art of War*.
4. Luo, Guanzhong, *The Romance of the Three Kingdoms* (Taipei: Sanmin Book, 1978), Ch. (Hui) 49, p. 306.
5. Rice, *Mao's Way, op. cit.*, p. 7.
6. Mao Zedong, "On Contradiction", in *Selected Works of Mao Tse-tung* (Beijing: Foreign Language Press, 1967), Vol. I, p. 324. (Hereafter referred to as *Works of Mao.*)
7. Bok, George Tan Eng, "Strategic Doctrine", in *Chinese Defence Policy*, eds. Gerald Segal & William T. Tow (Chicago: Univ. of Illinois, 1984), p. 4. Also see the Introduction of Samuel B. Griffith in Sunzi's *The Art of War*, in which he devoted a whole chapter to the relations of Sunzi and Mao Zedong. He listed many of Mao's words to compare with Sunzi's writings. See Sun Tzu, *The Art of War*, trans. with an introduction by Sammuel B. Griffith (London: Oxford Univ., 1971), Introduction, PP. 45-56, Section 6.
8. Mao, "Role of the Chinese Communist Party", *Works of Mao*, Vol. II, *op. cit.*, p. 209.
9. Sunzi (Sun Tzu), *The Art of War, op. cit.*, pp. 66-69.
10. Mao, "Strategy in China's Revolutionary War", *Works of Mao, op. cit.*, Vol. I, p. 213.
11. Samuel B. Griffith quoted this sentence to indicate the similarity between Mao and Sun. See his introduction, p. 51, in *The Art of War*.
12. Mao, "Strategy in China's Revolutionary War", *op. cit.*, pp. 221-22.
13. Schram, *op. cit.*, p. 169.
14. Mao, "Role of the Chinese Communist Party", *Works of Mao, op. cit.*, Vol. II, pp. 208-09.
15. Idem, "On Contradiction", *Works of Mao*, Vol. I, p. 317.
16. *Ibid.*, p. 316.
17. Idem, "Problems of Strategy in China's Revolutionary War", *Works of Mao*, Vol. I, pp. 179-254.
18. Idem, "Problems of Strategy in Guerrilla War Against Japan", *Works of Mao*, Vol. II, pp. 79-188, and "Problems of War and Strategy", pp. 217-237
19. Griffith, "Mao Tse-tung on Guerrilla Warfare", *The Art of War*, p. 22.
20. Mao, "On Protracted War", *Works of Mao*, Vol. II, p. 153.

21. Sunzi, *op. cit.*, Ch. II, p. 104.
22. *Ibid.*, p. 73.
23. Mao, "Strategy in China's Revolutionary War", *op. cit.*, Vol. I, pp. 190-191.
24. Schram, *op. cit.*, p. 15.
25. Rice, *op. cit.*, pp. 4-5.
26. Mao, "On Protracted War", *op. cit.*, Vol. II, p. 153.
27. *Ibid.*
28. Liu, Zhongping, *Simafa Jinzhu Jinyi:* A Modern Interpretation and Translation of Simafa (Taipei: Shangwu, 1975), p.1. Also see Section 3, Ch. II of this book.
29. Mao, "On Contradiction", *op. cit.*, Vol. I, p. 313.
30. Quoted from *The Works of Lenin*, Vol. 30, by Gao Tiqian in his *Military Materialist Dialectics* (Beijing: The Academy of Chinese Military Science, 1984), p. 3.
31. Marx, Karl & Engels, Frederick, *Manifesto of the Communist Party* (Beijing: Foreign Languages Press, 1972), pp. 30-31.
32. Mao, "Strategy in China's Revolutionary War", *op. cit.*, Vol. I. P. 180.
33. Sunzi, *The Art of War*, Appendix I, Wuzi, Ch. II, Sec. 5:1&2.
34. *Ibid.*
35. Mao, "Strategy in China's Revolutionary War", *op. cit.*, Vol. I, p. 183.
36. *Ibid.*, pp. 182-83.
37. Lenin, "The War Programme of the Proletarian Revolution", *On War and Peace* (Beijing: Foreign languages Press, 1966), p. 60.
38. Idem, "Socialism and War", *On War and Peace*, p. 11.
39. Lenin, "The War Programme of the Proletarian Revolution", *op. cit.*, p. 59.
40. Mao, "Strategy in China's Revolutionary War", *op. cit.*, Vol. I, p. 181.
41. Mao, "Problems of War and Strategy", *op. cit.*, Vol. II, p. 221.
42. *Ibid.*, p. 220.
43. Lenin, "The War Programme of the Proletarian Revolution", *op. cit.*, 59.
44. Mao, "Strategy in China's Revolutionary War", *op. cit.*, Vol. I, p. 183.
45. Lenin, "Socialism and War", *op. cit.*, p. 4.
46. *Ibid.*
47. After Mao arrived in northern Shaanxi in late 1935 from the Long March, he was still under the military siege of the Guomindang army and suffered a series of defeats in 1936. To save his force from total destruction, the Party took advantage of the anti-Japanese mood of the

country and started campaigning for a united front to resist the aggression of Japan; by doing so, he was able to mobilize support from the national bourgeoisie and other socio-political groups to put pressure on the Guomindang government to give up its anti-Communist policy in order to concentrate all forces to fight the Japanese. Meanwhile, the Party was able to persuade General Zhang Xueliang and Yang Hucheng, who were asigned to fight the Communist army, to take Generalissimo Jiang hostage on December 12, 1936, in order to force him to stop the civil war and to fight the Japanese. Jiang was released on December 25 of the same year after an informal agreement was reached between Jiang and the generals. In the process of negotiation, Zhou Enlai represented the CCP and played an important role in securing Jiang's release. After this incident, the civil war stopped and the cooperation between the CCP and the Guomindang resumed within a few months. Against this historical background, it is conceivable that Mao could not have spoken too strong against the bourgeoisie and the existence of the state.

48. Mao, "Strategy in China's Revolutionary War", *op. cit.*, Vol. I, p. 182.

49. Liu, Zhongping, *Simafa*, Ch. I, p. 1.

50. Lenin, V.I. *The State and Revolution* (Beijing: Foreign Languages Press, 1973), p. 19.

51. Sunzi, *op. cit.*, Ch. 1, pp. 27. 70.

52. Mao, "Strategy in China's Revolutionary War", *op. cit.*, Vol. I, p. 184.

53. *Ibid.*, p. 179.

54. *Ibid.*

55. *Ibid.*

56. *Ibid.*, p. 180.

57. *Ibid.*, p. 181.

58. *Ibid.*, p. 189.

59. *Ibid.*, p. 181.

60. Wylie, J. C., (Rear Admiral USN), *Military Strategy: A General Theory of Power Control* (New Jersey: Rutgers Univ., 1966), p.38.

61. *Ibid.*, p. 57.

62. Cai, Xiaoqian, *The Study of Mao Zedong's Military Thought and the People's Warfare* (Taipei: Shanghai Press, 1971), pp. 38-40.

63. Mao, "The Analysis of the Classes of Chinese Society", *Works of Mao,* Vol. I, p. 13.

64. This is paraphrased from Mao's analysis in "The Analysis of the Classes of Chinese Society", *op. cit.*, Vol. I, pp. 13-18.

65. *Ibid.*, p. 19.

66. Mao, "Report on the Investigation of the Peasant Movement in

Hunan", *Works of Mao*, Vol. I, pp. 32-33.

67. *Ibid.*, p. 33.
68. *Ibid.*, p. 40.
69. *Ibid.*, pp. 43-44.
70. *Ibid.*, pp. 23-24.
71. The term "People's War" is first seen in Mao's "On Coalition Government", a political report to the Seventh National Congress of the Communist Party of China on April 24, 1945. See *Works of Mao*, Vol. III, pp. 208-15.
72. Jiang, Jieshi, *The Personal Records of President Jiang* (Taipei: Central Daily News, 1976), Vol. 6, pp. 148-154. Hereafter referred to as *Personal Records of Jiang*.
73. Rice, *op. cit.*, p. 40.
74. Wang Jingwei and the Guomindang Central Executive Committee in Wuhan initiated the purge of the CCP on July 15 but they did not finally make up their mind until July 26, 1927, when Wang personally become the target of attacks of the CCP. The Central Committee of the Guomindang in Wuhan passed a resolution "To Unify the Policy of the Party" on July 26. See *Personal Records of Jiang*, Vol. 6, p. 173.
75. Rice, *op. cit.*, pp. 47-51.
76. Mao, "A Single Spark Can Start a Prairie Fire", *Works of Mao*, Vol. I, p. 118.
77. Idem, "Problems of Strategy in Guerrilla War", *Works of Mao*, Vol. II, p. 97.
78. Chen, Yi, *South of Yangtze River* (Nanjing: the PLA Press, 1985), pp. 118-49.
79. Mao, "Why Is It That Red Political Power Can Exist in China?" *Works of Mao*, Vol. I, pp. 65-67.
80. *Ibid.*, pp. 65, 69-70. Also see Mao's "Pay Attention to Economic Works", Vol. I, pp.129-139, and "Our Economic Policy", Vol. I, pp. 141-45. In *Mao's Way*, Edward E. Rice also made a similar point that the localized agricultural economy is one of two most important circumstances. The other one is the prolonged splits and wars within the white regime, p. 54.
81. Mao, "Struggle in the Chingkang Mountain (Jinggangshan)", *Works of Mao*, Vol. I, p. 80.
82. Idem, "Why Is It That Red Political Power Can Exist in China?" *op. cit.*, Vol. I, p. 66.
83. Idem, "On Correcting Mistaken Ideas in the Party", *Works of Mao*, Vol. I, p. 106.
84. Tien, Chen-ya, *The Mass Militia System and Chinese Modernization* (Toronto: Mosaic Press, 1983), p. 38.
85. *Ibid.*, pp. 40-52.

86. *Ibid.*, pp.79-84.
87. Mao, "A Single Spark Can Start a Praire Fire", *op. cit.*, Vol. I, p. 118.
88. Idem, "On Coalition Government", *op. cit.*, Vol. III, p. 215.
89. *Ibid.*, pp. 215-16.
90. I had discussed this subject in detail in my book, *The Mass Militia System and Chinese Modernization, op. cit.*, pp. 32-52.
91. Mao, "On Coalition Government", *op. cit.*, Vol. III, pp. 209-13.
92. *Ibid.*, p. 214.
93. Mao, "On Protracted War", *op. cit.*, Vol. II, p. 186.
94. *Ibid.*, p. 166.
95. Idem, "On Coalition Government", *op. cit.*, Vol. III, p. 217.
96. Idem, "Strategy in China's Revolutionary War", *op. cit.*, Vol. I, p. 181.
97. *Ibid.*, p. 183.
98. *Ibid.*, p. 190.
99. Ibid., p. 187.
100. *Ibid.*, p. 185.
101. *Ibid.*, p. 183.
102. *Ibid.*
103. *Ibid.*, p. 184.
104. *Ibid.*
105. *Ibid.*
106. Idem, "On Protracted War", *op. cit.*, Vol. II, p. 122.
107. *Ibid.*, p. 123.
108. *Ibid.*
109. *Ibid.*
110. *Ibid.*
111. *Ibid.*, p. 124.
112. Idem, "Problems of Strategy in Guerrilla War", *Works of Mao*, Vol. II, pp. 79-80.
113. Mao, "On Contradiction", *op. cit.*, Vol I, p. 337.
114. Idem, "Strategy in China's Revolutionary War", *op. cit.*, Vol. I, p. 235.
115. *Ibid.*, p. 237.
116. Idem, "Concentrate Superior Force to Destroy Enemy One by One", *op. cit.*, Vol. IV, p.104.
117. *Ibid.*, p. 103.
118. Idem, "Strategy in China's Revolutionary War", *op. cit.*, Vol. I, p. 248.
119. Mao, "Strategy for the Second Year of the War of Liberation", *Works of Mao*, Vol. IV, pp. 141-46.
120. Idem, "The Present Situation and Our Tasks", *Works of Mao*, Vol. IV, pp.161-62.

121. Idem, "On the New Stage", October 1938, quoted from Stuart R. Schram, *The Political Thought of Mao Tse-tung*, p. 289.

122. Lin Piao (Lin Biao), *Long Live The Victory of People's War!* (Beijing: Foreign languages Press,1967), pp. 54-57.

123. Mao, "All Reactionaries Are Paper Tigers", *Works of Mao,* Vol. 5, pp. 517-18.

124. *Ibid.* Also see "Talks with the American Correspondent, Anna Louise Strong", Works of Mao, Vol. 4, pp. 97-101.

125. Lin Piao, *op. cit.*, p. 32.

126. Mao, "Problems of War and Strategy", *Works of Mao,* Vol. II, p. 232.

127. Marx, Karl, Neue Rheinische Zeitung 161 (April 1, 1849) quoted in F.O. Miksche, *Secret Forces: The Technique of Underground Movements* (London, 1950), p. 25.

128. Lenin, V.I., "Partisan Warfare", *Modern Guerrilla Warfare: Fighting Communist Guerrilla Movements, 1941-61.* ed. Franklin Mark Osanka (New York: the Free Press of Glencoe, 1962), p. 74.

129. Mao, "Strategy in China's Revolutionary War", *op. cit.*, Vol. I, p. 213.

130. Idem, "On Correcting Mistaken Ideas in the Party", *Works of Mao,* Vol. I, p. 114.

131. Mao, "Problems of War and Strategy", *op. cit.*, Vol. II, p.227.

132. Idem, "On Protracted War", *op. cit.*, Vol. II, p. 138.

133. *Ibid.*

134. *Ibid.*

135. *Ibid.*

136. In 1948, three years after the war started and when the People's Liberation Army already started their counter-offensive and drove into the Guomindang areas, Mao still publicly predicted that he would expect to overthrow the Guomindang regime completely within five years counting from 1946. However, the war ceased on the mainland around the end of 1949. See Mao, "The Concept of Operations for the Liaohsi-Shenyang Compaign", *Works of Mao,* Vol. IV, p. 261.

137. Mao, "Concentrate Superior Force to Destroy Enemy One by One", *Works of Mao,* Vol. IV, p. 105.

138. In the summer of 1947, Marshall Liu Baicheng broke down the Guomindang's defence position along the south bank of the Yellow River and marched to the Dabie Mountain in the Henan-Anhwei-Hubei border area. After winning several compaigns, he established his base there. The Guomindang was forced to take a strategic defensive on many fronts within a few months. For the story of the march, see *The Memoir of Liu Baicheng,* (Shanghai: Wenyi Press, 1982), pp.40-61.

139. After the Korean War began in June 1950, President Truman declared

the Taiwan Strait a neutral zone and sent the U.S. navy to patrol there in order to prevent any possible military action of the CCP against Taiwan. Consequently, the Guomindang regime is preserved and Taiwan is free from the CCP's control.

140. Engels, F., "Anti-Dubring", in *The Military Essays of Karl Marx and F. Engels* (in Chinese translation) (Beijing: Zhanshi Press, 1981), Vol. I, pp. 38-39.

141. Marx, Karl & Engels, Frederick, *Manifesto of the Communist Party*, p. 56.

142. Lenin, *On War and Peace: Three Articles*, p. 63.

143. Mao, "Problems of War and Strategy", *op. cit.*, Vol. II, p. 223.

144. *Ibid.*, p.224.

145. *Ibid.*

146. Segal, Gerald, *Defending China* (London: Oxford, 1985), p. 66.

147. Mao, "Struggles in the Chingkang Mountains", *op. cit.*, Vol. II, p. 82.

148. *Ibid.*

149. *Ibid.*, p. 81.

150. *Ibid.*

151. Mao, "On Correcting Mistaken Ideas in the Party", *op. cit.*, Vol. I, p. 106.

152. *Ibid.*, pp. 107-08.

153. *Ibid.*

154. *Ibid.*, p. 106.

155. Mao, "On Protracted War", *op. cit.*, Vol. II, p. 186.

156. *Ibid.*

157. *Ibid.*, p. 155.

158. Idem, "Get Organized!" *Works of Mao*, Vol. III, p. 153.

159. *Ibid.*, p. 157.

160. Idem, *General Problems of Guerrilla Warfare in the Sino-Japanese War* (Yanan: Jiefang She, 1938), pp. 287-88.

161. Joffe, Ellis, *Party and Army: Professionalism and Political Control in the Chinese Officer Corps, 1949-1964* (Boston: Harvard East Asian Monographs, 1967), pp. 55 & 145.

162. Hsiao Hua, "The Chinese People's Liberation Army Marching toward Modernization", Report given at People's Political Consultative Conference National Committee Rally Celebrating the 25th Anniversary of the PLA, NCNA (July 31, 1952); in CB, No. 208: 37-39.

163. Hsieh, Alice Langley, *Communist China's Strategy in the Nuclear Era* (Englewood Cliffs, N.J., 1962) Ch. 2; see also pp. 91-92 and 109- 113. Cited from Ellis Joffe, *Party and Army*, p. 42.

164. Kung-tso Tung-hsun (Gong-zao Tong-xiun) No. 23: 1,3. Cited from Ellis Joffe, *Party and Army*, p. 63.

165. Joffe, *Party and Army*, p. 66.

166. *Ibid.*, p. 139.
167 A description of the Everyone-A-Soldier Movement--its historical background, organizations, and functions can be found in Chen-ya Tien's *The Mass Militia and Chinese Modernization* (Toronto: Mosaic, 1983).

CHAPTER 7

Current Trends in Chinese Military Thought

1. Deng Xiaoping's Ideas of Military Reform

Deng Xiaoping is one of the first generation of senior revolutionaries of China still alive. He had long been the General Secretary of the Central Committee of the CCP before the Cultural Revolution which began in 1966. He was disgraced and sent down to the countryside of Jiangxi Province in Central China to be reformed with factory work when the revolutionary turmoil was at its peak.

After Lin Biao's aborted coup d'état of 1971, the drastic deterioration of China's socio-political order and economic situation gave him the opportunity to come back to power again in 1975 with the support of Zhou Enlai, who was sick and close to the end of his life. Though Deng was doomed and dismissed again within a short period of time by Mao and the infamous Gang of Four, he was called back again in 1977 after Mao's death and the collapse of the Gang of Four in a successful coup led by Marshal Ye Jianying and other senior military leaders in 1976.

As the head of the General Staff of the PLA and the senior Vice-Premier of the State Council, Deng did not meet any serious resistance in controlling the armed forces and the political machine of China after he assumed power again. He eventually removed Hua Kuofeng, Mao's hand-picked successor of the Party and the government and others who rose to power during the Cultural Revolution. Although he did not personally assume the supreme leadership of the Party and the nation personally, he nonetheless became the paramount de facto leader of China. He was then able to start his decade-long military and political reforms of China. He changed the face of China, and above all, its armed forces.

A. Weaknesses within the PLA After the Cultural Revolution

As mentioned in Chapter 6, the PLA under Lin Biao's leadership during the Cultural Revolution had dramatically emphasized political and ideological works and was deeply involved in intra-party power struggles. The overindulgence of the PLA in political activities not only increased the danger of military intervention in politics but also strongly affected the military training and, thus, the readiness of the PLA for war.

After he assumed power in 1975, Deng repeatedly pointed out the serious problems within the PLA and pushed hard for reforms. According to Deng's personal point of view, the fundamental weaknesses within the armed forces could be summarized in five Chinese characters. They were *Zhong* (swollen), *San* (undisciplined or unorganized), *Jiao* (arrogant), *She* (extravagant), and *Duo* (lazy).[1]

The swollen size of the PLA, according to Deng, was not limited to the overgrowth of the armed forces in general, but also the over-manned staff organization and leadership in particular. The lack of discipline and disorganization was partly due to the overindulgence of political struggle during the Cultural Revolution and partly due to an excessive officer population, above all, at the higher level of the armed forces.

As for arrogance, though Deng conceded that it had been a long-standing problem in the PLA, he strongly emphasized the recent situation that had developed during the Cultural Revolution, in which the PLA assumed political power in place of the civilian Party leaders under Mao's call for them to support the left faction of the Party in struggle against the leadership of the Party and government. The growth of the PLA's political power resulted in the loss of its traditional mass line. It became isolated from the people, and tensions increased between the PLA and the masses, the military and the government, and even between different units of the PLA itself.[2]

Power leads all too often to corruption and when the PLA came into political power, it too could not finally remain untainted. The last two problems, extravagance and indolence were, as Deng said, actually a manifestation of the corruption of the armed forces. While the former primarily refers to the pursuit of material pleasure and enjoyment, the latter refers to the carelessness and indifference to one's work and duties. They are mutually related factors.

When all of these problems are inherent within an armed force, its fighting power in war is inevitably weaken.[3]

Although Deng pointed out these problems in 1975, his disgrace by Mao and his left faction followers postponed the work of reformation until 1978 when he reassumed power after Mao's death.

B. Deng's Ideas of Military Reform

Deng's military reform includes many things which are closely related to the above-mentioned problems of the PLA. However, in Deng's own words, the goals of his reform programs can be summarized in two words: modernization and regularization. To achieve these goals, he designed a schedule with a series of steps and methods.

(a) The Goals of Deng's Reform

Generally speaking, Deng's idea of military reform paid more attention to modernizing weaponry and regularizing the organization of the PLA without lossing its traditional political characteristics as a Party force. He still emphasized the necessity of using the armed forces to consolidate the regime of the people's democratic dictatorship, that is, the political power of the Communist Party. Among many other things, he emphasized the following ideas as the core of his military modernization and regularization:

First, the PLA must insist on the four basic principles of the Party, strengthen its political ideology, and make itself a model in carrying out party lines, principles and polices. By doing so, it will guarantee its reliability as an armed force of the Party.

Second, it should improve its weaponry and equipment in order to accelerate the modernization of national defence in accordance with the continual development of the national economy.

Third, it has to further improve its relations with the government and the masses, promote its internal unity, strengthen the militia force, and inherit and develop the glorious tradition of the PLA as a people's army.

Finally, it has to reinforce its military and political training in order to raise its quality in both aspects, and it has to devote particular effort to raise its capacity of joint operation with different kinds of armed forces.[4]

In referring to the weight of military and political training, Deng gave more emphasis to the former. He asked military schools, for example, to arrange their curriculum at a three-seven rate. Military subjects should occupy 70 percent of the total time, with the remaining 30 percent alloted to political subjects. On the other hand, when he referred to the curriculum arrangement of the political schools of the PLA, he gave 60 percent of the teaching time to political subjects, but left 40 percent to military ones.[5] Though Deng has moved away from Lin Biao's extreme emphasis on the PLA's political involvement and ideological indoctrination, he continued to count on the political support of the armed forces in domestic politics and, thus, he paid attention to political education in strengthening his control over them. This trend can be recognized after the Tiananmen Incident of 1989.

(b) The Steps of Reform

In discussing his military reforms, Deng often referred to them as the "re-organization of the armed forces". To achieve this goal, his approach included several steps based on his own priorities. According to Deng's perception, the re-organization of the military establishment was his top priority; the improvement of weaponry and equipment follows. Only after these problems have been solved, will strategy be considered.[6]

Reorganization of the Military Establishment: In reorganizing the establishment of the PLA, Deng particularly emphasized the adjustment and re-allocation of its commanding teams in order to reduce the oversized leadership. To solve the problem of overstaffing, Deng not only removed the overstaffed officers and purged the remaining followers of the Gang of Four, but went further to regulate the service of military officers, civil employees of the armed force, the system of retirement, and the system of military ranking. By doing so, he raised the Chinese military force to a higher level of institutionalization, which the Party once planned but failed to achieve in the 1950s when they pursued their first military modernization after the Korean War.[7] These regulations have been adopted one after another since the mid-1980s.

Improvement of Weaponry and Equipment: As mentioned in the third chapter of this book, the first priority in military modernization is the improvement of weaponry and equipment, followed by improvements in military organization and, finally, strategy and tactics.

Though Deng's priority of re-organizing the PLA began with adjusting the military establishment, he did not ignore the importance of weaponry and equipment to the fighting power of an armed force. He clearly understands that in fighting a modern war, the armed force cannot rely on "millet plus rifles" only, nor is it enough for a soldier to fight by knowing only how to shoot, charge with a bayonet, and throw a grenade. To fight a modern war, a soldier not only needs advanced weapons and other modern equipment, but also enough scientific and technological knowledge.[8]

Chinese first began to copy Western weapons as early as the mid-1860s after the Opium War. Under the Communist regime, the Chinese have done even better. Deng's idea of improving weaponry and equipment, however, is not limited to the manufacturing technology of weapons. He has gone further to explore the essential factors which affect the modernization of national defence power and, thus, the result of war. For Deng, a successful modernization of the armed forces must rely on the successful modernization of the national economy in general and of scientific and high-tech development in particular:

The key to complete the Four Modernizations is in the modernization of scientific technology. It is impossible to build up a modern agriculture, a modern industry, and a modern national defence without a modernized scientific technology. It is also impossible to promote the development of national economy quickly unless scientific technology development can meet its needs.[9]

Instead of making the modernization of national defence the first priority, he paid particular attention to the development of the national economy and scientific research.

A rapid development of scientific technology requires that a considerable number of researchers commit themselves consistently to research. Under the Communist regime, the leaders have invested a lot of resources in this project and have been anxious to make some significant headway with their results, but they have been unwilling to allow intellectuals the socio-political freedom to fully contribute their talent and energy. On the contrary, the intellectuals have been treated as a group of pariahs and have often been sacrificed to political movements.

After Deng resumed power in 1975 and 1978, he and some of his staff realized the full extent of the intellectuals' plight and their important role in the success of the Four Modernizations, which consequently led to a conscious improvement of their material well-being and research facilities by the leadership to encourage concentration on research and a greater contribution to the national development. However, he did not entirely depart from Mao's theory of reforming the intellectuals to rid their weaknesses.[10]

Under Deng's open policy in the 1980s, the condition of the intellectuals further improved, both politically and materially. However, the unhealthy condition of the national economy, the corruption of the bureaucracy, and the growing desire for more political democracy and freedom in the intellectual community contributed to the explosive climax on June 4, 1989. The refusal of the current Communist leaders to communicate with the students and intellectuals and meet their requests for more freedom and democracy was the principal factor which set off the fatal chain of events.

The incident may slow down the current drive for the Four Modernizations and, thus, military modernization. However, the most important impact may be revealed in the possible change of Chinese strategies in the 1990s.

Improving Military Training: During the civil war years, the PLA commanders and their soldiers received most of their military training in the battlefield. In peace time, however, the armed forces had to be trained either in school or in the combatant troop units. During the Cultural Revolution, the country was preoccupied with political struggles. Many schools, both military and civilian, were closed and few people paid attention to teaching and learning even if the schools were open.

After his resumption of power, Deng considered the solution of education problems to be primarily a strategic issue, which meant it was given a higher priority and evaluated according to the needs of national development.

As far as military training is concerned, Deng has pushed very hard for both school training and troop training. Without totally excluding their non-military activities, and ignoring their need for political training, he has made significant progress in raising the quality of the PLA officers.

In combatant troop training, Deng has emphasized the learning of modern war and joint operations with various kinds of armed forces through study and field excercises.[11]

The PLA used to train their new recruits with currently enrolled soldiers. Under this mixed training system, the combatant troop was forced to repeat the basic training program and, thus, could not raise its own level of training. Since 1978, however, they have adopted a series of steps to separate themselves from the new recruits. The latter would undergo the higher level training in the combatant units after finishing their basic one. A similar system is also used by the navy and air force.[12]

Compared to combatant troop training, Chinese military schools have done better in institionalizing their training programs. There are more than 100 military schools from the University of National Defence down to the basic military schools. They even developed master and doctoral programs to train the post-graduate students of military science. It is estimated that over 100,000 cadets were enrolled in military schools in 1987.[13] The main programs at these military schools are concentrated on training students to master the knowledge of modern warfare and its commanding skills. Like the combatant troops, the military schools also pay particular attention to joint operations with various kinds of armed forces.[14]

C. Deng's Strategic Considerations in the 1970s

From the early 1960s to the mid-1970s, the Sino-Soviet conflict escalated from ideological disputes to military confrontation along their border areas. After the U.S. withdrawal from Vietnam, the Soviet Union immediately pulled the Vietnamese to their side and opened a second front along the southern Chinese border. This development presented China with a serious psychologic threat.

The Sino-American breakthrough initiated by Mao and Zhou in the early 1970s following the increase of Sino-Soviet conflict has further developed following the U.S. withdrawal from Vietnam. This enabled Deng to develop a united front with the U.S. against the Soviet strategy of containment along the Chinese border.

(a) Winning Time for National Modernization by Postponing Global War

Throughout the 1960s and up to the mid-1970s, under Mao's leadership, the Chinese consistently claimed that a global war was inevitable and that they would, in fact, prefer to see it happen as early as possible. Thus their strategy was to prepare for a full-scale nuclear war. But in the late 1970s, when Deng came to power, the Chinese socio-economic and political situation was at the brink of collapse, and the PLA was not in fighting shape, for a full-scale war. Against this background, Deng and the Chinese government strongly desired a time of peace to commit themselves to domestic reforms.

In 1977, Deng's assessment of the global situation was that the Soviet Union had not completed its organization of global strategy and, thus, was not yet ready for war. The U.S. was committed to a global strategic defence following its withdrawal from Vietnam and, therefore, was not willing to engage in yet another conflict on a global scale. Based on this assessment, Deng believed that China could take the initiative to postpone the possible outbreak of war. [15]

To win time for national modernization, China's global strategy was still based on Mao's notion of unifying the Third World against the hegemonists who, since 1970, have been the Soviet Union rather than the United States. When the Soviet Union tightened its strategy of containment against China in 1979 following the Sino-Vietnamese War, Deng made it clear that Mao's initiative of establishing relations with the U.S. and Japan had become a valuable asset in China's anti-hegemonism. [16]

(b) *Deng's Type of People's War*

While Deng believed that global war could be postponed, he was not willing to leave China unprepared for any unexpected conflict and, above all, regional ones. Considering this situation, Deng thought that "as long as we insist on fighting a people's war with whatever we have, we can still win the war whenever it happens." [17] Nevertheless, Deng's concept of people's war is not identical to that of Mao. Deng has consistently emphasized joint operation trainings among different armed forces and has made it clear that in the future it will not be possible to fight a war with only "millet plus rifles". It will be a war fought with tanks, airplanes, and ships, on the ground, in the air, on the ocean, and underground by cooperative actions of various armed services.

Based on this perception, Deng not only pushed hard to modernize the PLA's weaponry and equipment in order to meet the requirement of modern war, but also paid particular attention to set up a modern rear service system in order to guarantee a reliable supply for the PLA in wartime. He made it clear that the PLA could not supply their weapons and ammunition by relying on war booty in the bettlefield. [18] This is an entirely different vision of war from the real nature of the Chinese civil war, in which Mao's people's war theory was developed. However, Deng still held that even with an improvement of weapons and equipment in the PLA within 10 to 20 years, it would still not be able to completely overcome its inferior position in war against the superpowers. Nonetheless, he continued to maintain that he was prepared to defeat a superior enemy even with inferior equipment. This self-confidence, according to Deng, is based on the belief that it would "be a just war and a people's war".[19]

2. China's Strategic Arrangement in the 1980s

A. Soviet Containment of China and Chinese Reactions

At the end of the 1970s, three developments emerged around the Chinese border that were to strongly affect the Chinese global strategic arrangement for the coming decade. These were the Vietnamese invasion of Kampuchea on December 25, 1978 and the overthrow of the Chinese-supported Pol Pot regime, the Sino-Vietnamese Border War, and the Soviet invasion of Afghanistan on Christmas Day, 1979.

(a) The Invasion of Kampuchea by the Vietnamese and the Sino-Vietnamese War

While Soviet-Vietnamese strategic cooperation had become a clear reality in the mid-1970s, the Chinese maintained a distance and avoided a direct confrontation with their former allies. However, when the Vietnamese began their invasion of Kampuchea, China could no longer stand idly by. Deng Xiaoping made the bold decision to commence his so-called punishment and self-defence campaign against Vietnam in mid-February after returning from the United States and Japan. While the Sino-Vietnamese War accelerated the emergence of the Soviet-Vietnamese Friendship Agreement, China was at the same time further pushed to develop a closer strategic cooperation with the U.S and other Western countries.

(b) Soviet Invasion of Afghanistan

The Soviets' encirclement of China was further reinforced 10 months after the commencement of the Sino-Vietnamese War by the invasion of Afghanistan. The Soviet Union replaced its old Marxist patron with a new one and stationed more than 100,000 troops. Though some political leaders in Europe believed the invasion to be primarily a defensive action, the Chinese, however, saw it from a totally different point of view. They regarded it as part of Moscow's grand design to push into the soft underbelly of Asia, where the oil and strategic routes lie. With Afghanistan and Vietnam under their control, the Soviets, if they decided to push as far south to the Indian Ocean and the oil fields of the Middle East, could easily outflank the West and link the Soviet pressure points in the Pacific and Indian Oceans. This would likely bring the

Strait of Malacca under Moscow's sphere of influence. If events developed to this stage, an upset of the world military balance of power would be inevitable.[20]

Though the Chinese did not publicly state that this development would seriously threaten Chinese security on its southern border and southeastern seashore and, thus, further tighten the Soviet containment of China, it is clear that the Chinese were very upset and nervous. This pushed the Chinese leaders to look for closer cooperation with the United States, Japan, and the Western countries in order to prevent the Soviet Union from expanding to the South and, if possible, to encircle it along its current borders.

B. The Development of Triangular Relations between China, the U.S.A. and the U.S.S.R.

(a) Sino-American Strategic Cooperation

Based on the serious threat to Chinese national security presented by the Soviet invasion of Afghanistan and the Vietnamese expansion in the Indochina Peninsula, the Chinese developed their own global strategy to stop the Soviet Union. Their strategy consisted basically of the following components.

First, China and the Western powers had to support Afghanistan and the Kampuchean people to resist the invaders. Meanwhile, they also had to give material and moral support to Pakistan and Thailand, which were faced with the Soviet and Vietnamese threat.

Second, they had to strengthen their unity and work together to stop the Soviet expansion.

Third, all of these countries also had to support the Arab and Asian countries (including Malaysia, Indonesia, Singapore, Thailand, and the Philippines) to reinforce their self-defence.

Finally, China and the Western powers had to strengthen their own defence in order to maintain a balance of power with the Soviets.[21]

With these strategic perceptions in mind, the Chinese gave top priority to exploring the possible chance of strategic cooperation with the U.S. and other Western powers.

Eight years had passed since Nixon's visit to China in 1972 before formal diplomatic relations were established on January 1, 1979. Deng Xiaoping visited the U.S. in the same month in order to promote their strategic cooperation. It was probably during this visit that Deng gave his permission to the Americans to set up an electronic intelligence-gathering station in China's Xinjiang Uigur Autonomous Region to detect Soviet missile tests, and that he got the silent support of the U.S. for China to begin her war of punishment against Vietnam.[22]

(b) The Emergence of Triangular Relations between China, the U.S. and the U.S.S.R.

It appears that 1979 was the honeymoon period of Sino-American relations. The Chinese leaders may have in fact expected to develop friendly cooperative relations (if not an alliance) with the U.S. For working together to prevent Soviet expansion would assist the Chinese in their four modernizations, above all, the modernization of the armed forces by procuring weapons and high technologies. However, their hopes soon faded not long after Deng's visit to the U.S.

In responding to a question on the issue of Taiwan, in Cleveland in May 1980, Mr. Reagan told his audience that "as a President he will be able to restore official government relations with Taiwan." He went even further to justify his "Two-China" policy by referring to the case of the Two-Germany policy. This statement antagonized the Chinese leaders and, thus, provoked their strong protest.[23]

Though Reagan sent his presidential running mate, George Bush, to Bejing to explain his position and assuage the Chinese, Reagan's pro-Taiwan position did not change, and the newly established strategic cooperative relation was thus marred. After Reagan assumed power, he sent his two successive Secretaries of State, Alexander Haig and George Schultz, to China in 1981 and 1983, respectively, to promote mutual cooperation, but the continued U.S. arm sales to Taiwan only fostered stronger distrust and loss of confidence in them among the Chinese. The result was that quarrels and protests continued for years. The United States tried to placate China by permitting the export of weapons and high technology to China and, at the same time, promised to gradually reduce arm sales to Taiwan. As a measure of the seriousness of the situation, President Reagan made a personal visit to China in 1985 in an attempt to stablize their relations.

The Chinese had begun to improve their relations with the Soviet Union in March of 1982, when President Brezhnev signaled his good faith for compromise in Tashkent.

Sino-Soviet relations did not really improve until the Soviets, to a considerable degree, satisfied China's three preconditions, which were to reduce their armed forces from the Sino-Soviet and Sino-Mongolian borders, to withdraw troops from Afghanistan, and to ask the Vietnamese to withdraw from Kampuchea. Since the mid-1980s, "big triangular" relations among China, the United States and the Soviet Union have gradually taken shape, and the Chinese global strategy has also gradually evolved from one with distinct pro-U.S leanings at the beginning of the decade into one that promotes an independent stand between the superpowers to eventually create a new era of open policy to all countries of the world.[24]

C. Open Policy and Defence Modernization in the 1980s

As the Soviets and Vietnamese became bogged down by guerrilla wars in Afghanistan and Kampuchea, the Soviet strategic offensive in south and southeast Asia was temporarily halted in the early 1980s. Under this circumstance, and with the increasing detente among China, the U.S.A. and the U.S.S.R., the Chinese were able to re-evaluate the global situation and re-design their national strategies. Since then they have given top priority to economic development supported by an open policy in order to strenghten their national defence.

(a) Strenghthening National Defence by Promoting Economic Development

The Chinese leaders realized that a modernized national defence must rely on a fully modernized national economic system supported by advanced technology. Thus the Chinese leaders adopted a two-fold policy to promote their economic development. One way was to expand China's international trade, establish joint business ventures with foreign countries, and even secure international loans in order to solve the shortage of capital and modern technology. The other way was to reduce military expenditures by cutting one-fourth of the PLA's manpower and converting part of the military industry to produce civil goods to solve financial problems.

By the first method, the Chinese have been able to increase their international trade from a few hundred million dollars to more than 100 billion dollars annually in the last decade. Through joint business ventures with foreign companies, they have attracted several billions of hard cash and modern industrial equipment investment in China, which not only promotes Chinese economic development in general but to some extent also helps to transfer advanced technologies to China.[25]

As most Western sinologists know, while the PLA badly needs advanced weapons and equipment to strengthen their fighting power, they can neither afford, nor do they want to buy, them from foreign countries. Instead, they prefer to import foreign modern technologies, above all advanced high technology. The Chinese leaders announced publicly that they hoped to promote their defence modernization by expanding international trade and even desired to undertake joint ventures with other countries in developing and producing modern weapons in China.[26] Though Western countries continue to limit the export of advanced technologies to Communist countries, they have lifted part of the restrictions for China in the past few years. The United States, for example, agreed to help China to improve the radar system of their F-8 fighters and sell their advanced computers. However, after the Tiananmen Square Incident of June 4, 1989, some countries including the U.S. and Japan again tightened their control of technology transfers. It is reported that in the 1980s, the Chinese have imported 27 billion U.S.

dollars of advanced technology and equipment, which created 60 percent of the annual increase in GNP.[27]

(b) Cutting Defence Expenditures and Military Modernization
As mentioned earlier, the Chinese leaders badly needed a time of peace in order to carry out their modernizations. War, even on a regional scale, would divert resources into the armed forces and, thus, change the order of their priorities of modernization. Accordingly, when China felt more relaxed about its relations with the superpowers and a rough military equilibrium emerged around her borders, the Chinese leaders did not hesitate to continue their military reorganization to curb the "swelling" of the PLA and create better conditions for modernization.

Since 1985, the Chinese have reduced the size of the PLA from 4.2 to 3 million people. This has been followed by cuts in military expeditures. The reduction discharged, in fact, only the unnecessary personnel and non-combatant units from the army and thus instead of weakening the army, actually enhanced the real strength of the PLA.

Before the personnel cuts, the Chinese armed forces were about 10 percent more than those of the Soviet Union and two-and-a-half times more than those of the U.S. However, the Chinese military budget was less than one-third of the U.S. and one-fourth of the U.S.S.R.[28] Even so, the government kept cutting defence spending every year. It is said that from 1971 to 1985, it has been reduced from 17.4 percent of the total National Budget to 7.5 percent annually.[29]

To resolve financial difficulty, the PLA is permitted to run businesses to create their own income. Among other things, it has used its defence industry to produce civilian consumer goods sold in domestic and international markets. It is reported that one-third of the defence industry has been committed to this production and three-fifths of the total product is aimed at the civilian market, which includes more than seven hundred kinds of products. Among them, more than 100 kinds have been sold in the international market and they brought in some 300 million dollars U.S. in 1989.[30] In addition, they have also started to sell weapons to Third World countries. In 1988, China was listed as one of the big five weapons suppliers in the international market. If they can improve their management, it would be possible for them to bring in more than 10 billion Yuan (about $2.5 billion U.S.) annually. A report has even predicted that within 20 years the income from weapons and commercial goods trade would be enough to support the national defence expenditure without requiring financial support from the government, if its current trend of development continues.[31]

Due to their continuing reorganization of military establishment and management, though they keep cutting the national defence budget, the Chinese did not slow down their military modernization, above all the modernization of strategic weapons.

(c)   The Organization of Fist Forces and Their Strategic Implication

While the Chinese cut their defence budget and converted part of their military industry to produce consumer goods, they did not cut their defence research fund. Instead, they concentrated their limited defence budget on the development of strategic nuclear weapons and an outer space program. The research fund has been increased consistently since 1978.[32] After the successful testing of a land-based ICBM and its underwater test launched by nuclear submarine in the early 1980s, they have possessed a limited but effective nuclear retaliation power to defend themselves against possible nuclear attacks.

Given their own achievements and the continued progress of limiting and cutting back nuclear weapons between the superpowers, they realized that it is time for China to change her global strategy. The Chinese leaders concluded in 1985 at a plenary meeting of the Military Commission of the CCP that there would be no world war and/or nuclear war for the duration of the 20th century and even early into the next, because the approximate equilibrium of nuclear weapons between the superpowers gave credence to the conviction that a nuclear war would be a war of mutual destruction, and, thus, the superpowers would be unwilling to risk it.

While a full-scale nuclear war may not come to pass, limited war or a low degree of military conflict may occur at any time and that becomes a major problem dominating reginal relations in the near future. To the Chinese leaders, the primary cause of limited war in the future is likely to be regional hegemonism and expansionism. The former refers more specifically to the Vietnamese, the latter to the Soviets. "They are seizing our land and territorial seas. While the border conflict continues, potential threat could be more serious than the current one."[33]

Based on this perception, the Chinese leaders set the tone of their military strategy for the 1980s and even for the early 1990s. Zhao Ziyang, the former General Secretary of the Central Committee of the CCP and First Vice-Chairman of the Military Commission, proposed at a high-level meeting in May, 1988 in Beijing that the Chinese strategy should be primarily aimed at limited war and local military conflict. To meet this challenge, the PLA should build up a "fist force" or quick strike force, while they are re-evaluating the possible war of the future, the long-term national defence strategy, and the direction of military development.[34]

The establishment of a "fist force" has been an important strategic decision since 1988. It is not only carried out in the army but also in the navy and air force. In the army, special battalions or quick action battalions armed with advanced weapons and better equipment have been established. A marine brigade similar to the fist battalion of the army has been also established in the South China Sea Fleet. The Chinese paratroops under the command of the air force also set up a "fist battalion". They are required to carry out attacks on the enemy in any area of the country within one day.[35]

With their emphasis on building a fist force, it would appear that the Chinese have given up their retrograde defence strategy. Instead, they are moving toward a forward and/or positional strategy to deal with border conflict and regional wars. Their fist forces are ready to cross the border and to fight in enemy territory on the ground, in the air and on the sea, if necessary.

The organization of the fist force may also serve as a model for modernizing the PLA. If the PLA is re-organized along the lines of the fist forces, their firepower would be greatly increased, which would inevitably further affect their strategy and tactics.

In addition, if we assume that a regional war takes place and the enemy penetrates into China and occupies part of her land, the Chinese would be forced to fight a guerrilla war again, but it would be totally different from what it used to be.

(d)   The Development of the Chinese Navy and Its Strategy
Though the Chinese have had a relatively large number of naval vessels since the late 1950s, they never used them beyond coastal defence. The strategy of the Chinese navy was dominated by Mao's doctrine of people's war. Under Mao's strategy, in case of war, the Chinese were to eliminate the intruders on the land. This is somewhat similar to those ideas mentioned by Wei Yuan and others in the middle of 19th century, when China was at war against the British Navy (see discussion in Chapter 3). With a strategy of retrogrressive defence in mind, the Chinese leaders opposed the idea of fighting the enemy on the high seas. The navy was asked to protect the Chinese sea coast and fishing boats. Since the beginning of 1970s, when China joined the United Nations and other international organizations, and was influenced by the contention over territorial sea and the 200-nautical-mile economic zone within the continental shelf by the Third World countries, the Chinese began to pay attention to these matters and, thus, commenced to build up their sea power, above all when they began to explore for off-shore oil resources.

After the close of the U.S. - Vietmanese War in 1975, the Soviet navy took over the base in Cam Ran Bay left behind by the U.S. The competition between the U.S. and the Soviet Union to control the South China Sea and Pacific made the Chinese keenly aware of the military threat from the sea and, thus, further reminded them of the need to strengthen their naval force in order to protect their national interest against enemy intrusion from the sea.

Due to strategic perceptions and equipment restrictions, the Chinese naval forces had rarely gone beyond the first island chain around mainland China before 1976. Since then, while they have strengthened their naval force by modernizing their vessels, building new ships, nuclear submarines and missiles, they have also accelerated joint operation training involving differ-ent vessels and armed forces on the open sea.[36]

According to a recent report, the Chinese naval force has been ranked the third largest in the world with 20 destroyers, 40 destroyer escorts, 120 submarines including 5 nuclear ones, and more than a thousand patrol escorts and other vessels. There are about 1,700 to 1,900 vessels in total. Some of them are equipped with new electronic systems and loaded with helicopters and missiles.[37] Since 1983, the Chinese have revealed that they intend to construct five aircraft carriers, each of them with the capacity for handling 25 airplanes. They also plan to deploy 12 nuclear submarines carrying ballistic missiles with nuclear warheads within 10 years.[38]

It is clear that the Chinese leadership is no longer satisfied with its old naval strategy of coastal defence and is actively planning a more ambitious strategy for the years to come.

With their increasing naval training on the open sea, the Chinese leaders addressed their strategic goals of navy building. They wanted to build a naval force which "should be able to control the sea areas connected to Chinese territorial seas, in which we expect to fight, to effectively control the important strait and channels of these areas, and to operate in this area."[39]

While the Chinese are ready to give up their retrogressive defence strategy, it does not necessarily mean that they have now decided to conquer the high seas. When the Chinese talk about naval strategy, they divide naval operations into three levels. The primary level, *Jinan Zuozhan,* means off-shore operation and is to a large degree similar to the term of coastal defence. The highest level is *Yuanhai Zuozhan,* which means operation on the high seas or open oceans. The second level is *Jinhai Zuozhan,* which means the operation area is located between Jinan and Yuanhai. When the Chinese leaders plan to change their naval strategy, their first step is to transfer their off-shore operation strategy to a Jinhai operation strategy, which covers the areas north from Haishenwai (Fuladiwosituoke), down to the south to the Strait of Malacca, and extends to the first chain of islands outside the mainland in the East. It is not limited to the 200-nautical-mile economic zone.[40]

Based on this definition, one finds that the current Chinese naval strategy is primarily aimed at the second level. Their desire is to be able to control the Jinhai area and important channels connected to their territorial seas.

In talking about global strategy, a land-based ICBM system, and other intermediate-range missiles, joined by nuclear submarines with underwater launched nuclear warhead missiles and long-range bombers carrying nuclear bombs, have been seen as the effective strategic triad of a nuclear war. Judged by these criteria, the Chinese strategic weapons system is not yet complete. They do not have long-range bombers that can reach Moscow or penetrate the Soviet air defence lines in the far eastern areas. Though their land-launched missiles and nuclear submarine-launched missiles are able to deter nuclear attacks from the superpowers, they are far from being enough to permit the Chinese to start a nuclear war against any superpower without suffering self-destruction. Therefore, from a global strategic point of view, the Chinese can only temporarily possess limited influence. However, in a regional war within Asia, China can, without a doubt, play an important role. She is strong enough to take a more aggressive strategy in dealing with military conflict and limited wars around her borders. Seen against this background, Chinese leaders are changing their strategy from retrogressive and coastal defence to an active and/or forward defence. This is likely to be the primary thrust of Chinese military strategy until new conditions arise.

3. The Direction of Strategic Development in China in the Near Future
A. The Impact of Revolutionary Changes in the Communist World on Chinese Global Strategy

The years 1989 and 1990 will be remembered as years of dramatic change in Communist countries. It can be said that the Tiananmen Square Incident of June 4, 1989 introduced the first light of change. It was followed by the topling of the European Communist regimes and the chaos in the Baltic states of the U.S.S.R., which eventually led to the dramatic decision of the Communist Party of the U.S.S.R. to renounce its seventy years' monopoly of political power. While the Chinese government cut short the student pro-democratic movement by force and temporarily consolidated its control in China, the economic sanctions imposed by Western countries and the pro-revolutionary policy of the Soviet Union together have intensified the nervousness and sense of isolation within the Chinese leadership. The decision of the old revolutionaries to tighten their authoritarian control over China will inevitably affect their strategies of economic development and national defence.

(a) Economic Slowdown and Its Effect on National Defence

The economic growth of China under the open policy of the last decade has significantly strengthened Chinese defensive power. Many Sinologists have predicted that China would become one of the world's five big powers in the year 2000 based on her contemporary economic development.[41] However, since the June 4th Incident, the Chinese economy has deteriorated significantly as a result of Western sanctions which froze bank loans and banned exports of advanced technologies to China. Though both the American and Japanese governments have refrained from pushing China back into its former isolation, the economic slowdown is inevitable. If the sanctions continue over a long period of time, and if the Chinese government cannot react effectively, the modernization of national defence will be damaged by further economic deterioration.

(b) Increasing Political Activity and Its Effect on the PLA Regularization

In addition to the effect of economic and technological limitations on military modernization, the PLA's regularization program would be more or less interrupted by increasing political activities, as did occur during the Cultural Revolution.

Since June 4th, above all after the Romanian military rebellion which overthrew the Ceausescu regime, the Chinese Communist leaders have repeatedly announced that they want the PLA to obey absolutely the control of the Party by emphasizing political indoctrination.

As mentioned in the first section, in order to achieve military modernization and regularization, the PLA has concentrated on military education and greatly limited their political activity in the past decade. If the Chinese want to create a modernized army, they have to first make it a professional one by regularization. For political reasons, the Party leaders have begun to denounce some public ideas which call for separating the PLA from the Party, nationalizing the armed forces, and neutralizing them from political activities.[42] The leadership may slow down and even sacrifice, temporarily at least, the regularization and modernization process in order to promote the revolutionization of the armed forces.

(c) The Change of Triangular Relations between the U.S.A., the U.S.S.R. and China

Since 1989 when Gorbachev's economic and political reforms first began to encounter serious difficulties and the Communist regimes in Eastern Europe collapsed one after another within a few months, Gorbachev has refrained from using military force to suppress the rebellions in his own country and in the Warsaw Pact countries. On the contrary, he has adopted a conciliatory policy to deal with the rebellious states at home and has taken an appreciative attitude toward the democratic movements in the Warsaw Pact countries. In February 1990, following the renunciation of the constitutional right of monopoly of political power by the Central Committee of the Communist Party, which cleared the way for a multiple party political system, the Soviet Union further reached an agreement on troop reductions in Europe in a joint meeting between the ministers of foreign affairs of the NATO and Warsaw Pact countries in Ottawa, Canada. At their meeting, both sides agreed to further discuss open skies or space and open seas in order to monitor force and weapon movements in the near future. An agreement in principle on a unified Germany was also reached by the ministers at the meeting.[43]

Though the conciliatory policy of the Soviet Union is primarily due to her domestic problems and the need to buy time for reforms, its current moves have substantially changed the 40-year-old cold war between the two super-powers and the East and West blocs.

While the U.S. and most countries in the Western world are praising the Soviet Union for her pro-democratic reforms, the Chinese military suppression of the student movement and their strong stand in reacting to the economic sanctions of the Western world have greatly offended the West. If China still insists on her policies against reform, she is quite likely to incur more condemnation from the U.S. and ruin their strategic cooperation developed in the last decade. However, while the U.S. maintains pressure on China for reform, the American leaders will not let their relations with China deteriorate to such a low point as was reached in the 1950s and 1960s. Thus they would prefer to keep lines of communication with China in both economic and political matters. Sino-U.S. relations may freeze at the current level, but both sides will not let it deteriorate substantially.[44]

Due to its domestic problems, the Soviet Union is likely to do everything possible to maintain a peaceful, if not friendly, relationship with China. Reports show that the old revolutionary leaders in China have been complaining about Gorbachev's policies and denouncing him as a revisionist. Some leaders have suggested raising ideological issues against him; others have even suggested that China must be prepared for military confrontation along its borders as occurred in 1968.[45] If such a report is factual, it would prove a big mistake for the Chinese leaders because the current situation in China and the world at large today is totally different from that of the 1960s. Very few people within and without China will pay any attention to it. Instead of ideological debate, they should concentrate on their economic and political reforms. Assuming, however, that the Chinese leaders do raise these issues, but do not go too far with them, Gorbachev may simply choose to ignore them, for the more the Chinese denounce him, the closer he just might move toward the U.S.

Based on this analysis, Sino-Soviet relations in the coming years may be cool, but there will not be any serious dispute over the border issues or global strategy.

(d) Chinese Response to the Outside Sanctions

After 10 years of opening to the outside world, increasing international trade and economic cooperation with foreign countries have made China an active member of the international community. To a large degree China will need financial and technological assistance to maintain her economic and defensive modernization. Maybe the old revolutionary leaders are willing to sacrifice their national economic development for political reasons as Mao Zedong did in the 1960s. However, the current situation of China is quite different from that of the 1960s. First of all, the majority of the Chinese have lost their confidence in the Party and, therefore, it may not be able to have their support in overcoming the difficulty which the Party may have to face. Secondly, the Chinese financial connection with foreign countries in the past decade has become so deep that, if they abruptly cut off these connections, not only would the Chinese inevitably suffer serious economic recession or even collapse, but they would also experience serious international disputes with many countries.

For these reasons, the Chinese leaders will not close their door again. Rather, they are likely to compromise a little politically in order to attract international financial and technological flows to promote their four modernizations. For this reason, under the slogan of non-intervention, the Chinese leaders are likely to push for a separation of economic and trade affairs from politics.[46]

Recently, they have made some more positive gestures by lifting martial law in Beijing and Lhasa and by releasing several hundred students and intellectuals from detention. Deng Xiaoping has even changed his stance on the Tiananmen incident, saying that the students should not be blamed for the turmoil of last year.[47] While these policies may not do any substantial good for Chinese democracy nor affect the authoritarian rule of the Communist party, they may, however, be able to elicit favourable concessions from the international community. Should this become the case, the Chinese will pursue a policy of openness towards all countries regardless of ideological differences.[48] They will continue their relations with the superpowers with a vigilant eye on their attempts to influence Chinese political development. With the recent dramatic changes in Europe, both the U.S. and the Soviet Union may prefer to have a period of stability in Asia in order to have time to deal with European developments. Accordingly, the Chinese may be able to enjoy a period of stability before any drastic changes occur. They will continue their policy of independence in terms of global politics.

B. Potential Regional Problems and Chinese Strategy

In discussing the Chinese estimate of regional problems in the preceding section, we have seen that Chinese leaders have already shown their concern over border disputes with the Soviet Union and India, and the Sino-Vietnamese dispute over the South China Sea islands, which would be their major strategic considerations in the 1980s and 1990s. Although these problems in different degrees may still dominate Chinese regional strategy, some new factors will have to be added to their strategic planning, such as the rise of Japanese military power, Taiwan, and Korea.

(a) *The South China Sea Islands Dispute*

Due to the drastic changes in Eastern Europe and the U.S.S.R., Soviet leaders will be primarily preoccupied with their internal problems in the coming years or decades. Therefore, they are expected to take a defensive strategy in global politics. They have withdrawn their armed forces from

Afghanistan, reduced their armed forces along the Sino-Soviet border and pressed the Vietnamese to withdraw from Kampuchea. Consequently, not only the Soviet Union itself but its allies in Asia along the Chinese border are expected to refrain from unneccessary confrontations. Though the Kampuchean problem remains unsolved, the big powers have refrained from intervention and reduced weapons supplies, and the fighting factions will be limited to a controllable degree. However, the Sino-Vietnamese dispute over the Xisha Islands (Paracel), and the dispute between China, the Philippines, Viet Nam, and Malaysia over the Nansha (Spratly) Islands, may become hot issues in the near future. Like Dongsha and Zhongsha islands, Nansha and Xisha have been Chinese territories for centuries. China has made it clear that she is determined to protect them from foreign intrusion. As the Chinese increasingly show their forces in that area, regional tensions will inevitably arise except a tentative solution can be worked out satisfactory to all of the related countries.

(b)   Sino-Indian Border Dispute

The Sino-Indian border dispute is a historical problem created in 1914 at the time of the British occupation of India. For their own interests, the British arbitrarily drew the McMahon Line between India and Tibet and annexed a large area of Tibet. The Chinese government refused to sign the agreement.[49] In 1962, the two countries entered a border war over this dispute but did not solve the problem. Though both countries have refrained from another military confrontation since the truce of 1962, there is no indication that either side will give up its claims. Meanwhile, India allied herself with the Soviet Union and Viet Nam for decades in order to compete against China, which stood closer to Pakistan, and, later, the U.S. Partly for this reason, India has for some time been building up her armed forces. It is said that since the beginning of the 1980s, India has doubled her defence budget. In 1986, India was the biggest weapons importer in the world. She spent U.S.$5.2 billion in 1987 to buy weapons in international markets, more than the total amount spent by both Iran and Iraq,which were in war against each other in the Gulf, and twelve times more than what Pakistan spent in the same year. Her 1.36 million strong armed forces is ranked the fourth largest in the world.[50] It is reported that her navy has two aircraft carriers, 18 submarines, and 24 destroyer escorts, which would make it even stronger than that of the Chinese.[51]

Many regional political leaders such as Mr. Li Guangyao, the Prime Minister of Singapore, and the Ministers of National Defence of Malaysia and Australia have worried about the expansion of the Indian armed forces, which may create regional conflict and instability. They expect that India, China, and Japan in the coming decades will compete for regional influence and this will inevitably cause conflict and even war.[52] If so, the Sino-Indian border dispute may become a hot point again. In 1962, the Chinese used force and took a forward defensive strategy in the war. It is not likely that China would take a retrogressive defence strategy in case a border dispute arises again. Such a dispute may not only expand the war into other areas but may also involve a third country such as Pakistan, which has historically engaged in territorial disputes over the Kashmir region.

(c) The Rise of Japan and Possible Alignment in East Asia

The Deterioration of U.S. - Japanese Relations: After the close of the Second World War in 1945, Japan as a defeated country was occupied by the Allied Powers headed by General MacArthur, Commander-in-Chief of the U.S. armed forces in Asia.

Due to the global cold war and regional wars in Asia along the Pacific rim such as China's civil war, the Korean War, the tension in the Taiwan Strait between China and Taiwan, and the Viet Nam War, the United States used Japan as a base to support its military actions in Asia. Under the U.S.-Japanese Security Treaty and the Japanese constitution, Japan was well protected without using her revenue on military expenditures, except maintaining a very small self-defence force. She was therefore able to maintain high economic growth by expanding her exports, including the supply of war materials to the U.S. Consequently, she has become the most affluent economic superpower in the world since the 1970s, while the U.S. is overdrawn by its huge military expenditures and, thus, cannot help but ask Japan to increase her defence expenditures to relieve some U.S. responsibilities. However, the Japanese military build-up incited immediate suspicion and protest among her neighbours in whose minds the bitter memories of Japanese militarism during the Second World War were still fresh.

Japan is not yet a military superpower. It was reported recently that her military force is growing rapidly and is armed with the most advanced weapons. With her tremendous economic power and technological resources, she can become a military superpower within a couple of decades if she decides to follow such a course. This is why political leaders in Asia have expressed their concern over the possible competition and conflict between China, Japan and India in the future.

This potential threat is not only felt by the Asians, but, as a force of the Pacific Rim, the United States has also come to share that concern. While it has been directing its attention to the possible emergence of the so-called "Century of the Pacific", it is particularly concerned about the popular view of the "Japanese Threat", which would require the U.S. to design a proper preventive strategy.[53] To the present American administration, it may not be a bad idea to have a strong China to "contain" Japan in Asia. Explaining his China policy at a news conference on January 24, 1990, Mr. Bush stated that one of his reasons for maintaining close relations with China is to solve Asian problems, which he pointedly referred to as Kampuchea and Japan. He obviously saw China as a key to maintain the balance of power in Asia.[54]

The Japanese, on the other hand, are angered by the American policies. While the U.S. is pressing Japan to reduce her trade surplus and at the same time limiting the transfer of advanced military technologies to Japan, it has revived Japanese feelings of resentment against the U.S. for its role in the Second World War.[55] Therefore, it is not unusual for the Japanese to wish to be rid of U.S. control and pursue an independent foreign policy. It is thus possible that Japan may take diplomatic initiatives in Asia to counter-balance U.S influence. If this is the case, closer Sino-Japanese relations may emerge in the near future.

The Soviet-Japanese Territorial Dispute: Closer Soviet-Japanese relations could be another variable that will affect Chinese relations with Japan. Since the 1980s, Soviet leaders have more than once invited Japan to invest in Siberia. However, the Japanese wish to first resolve their territorial dispute with the Soviets before entering into any economic cooperation. If the Soviets are willing to return to Japan four small but strategically important islands which they occupied after the Second World War, the way would be clear for closer relations.[56] This development, however, would make the Chinese uneasy, because, for their national interests, they would not like to see the Soviet Union succeed in developing her economy in East Siberia, which may sooner or later threaten China's security on her northern border, unless their relations can be improved substantially. However, the Soviet-Japanese joint ventures in Siberia may not be easily worked out because the Soviets are unlikely to accede to Japan's demand for the return of these islands, which are the outposts of the Soviet military bases along the coast of the Sea of Okhotsk. The islands not only make the Okhotsk a Soviet inland sea but they also provide a forward position and springboard of attack in case of war against Japan. With these islands under their control, the Soviets enjoy a great strategic advantage which can put Japanese national defence in jeopardy at any time. Accordingly, as long as the territorial dispute cannot be solved, Soviet-Japanese relations cannot improve significantly.

South Korea's Possible Roles in Regional Confrontation: In Northeast Asia, Korea has long been a hot point in Sino-Japanese confrontations. Japan annexed it after the Sino-Japanese War of 1894. Since the Korean War of 1950, the peninsula has become a major point of international conflict for four decades. The increasing chaos of the Communist camp has reduced the military threat of North Korea. However, potential Sino-Japanese competition in East Asia may once again make South Korea a focus of regional conflict, above all if the U.S. armed forces are withdrawn from the peninsula. Nevertheless, the South Korean government has been actively approaching China in the past few years to establish economic and political relations. If official or semi-official relations can be brought about, it may greatly reduce the military threat from the North Korea and even promote their national unification. The Koreans will, therefore, feel more secure among their competing big power neighbours; it may also be able to serve as a balance of power between China and Japan, if Sino-Japanese competition arises in the future.

Taiwan Problems: Japan may wish to either have Taiwan back under her own control or keep it independent rather than see it integrated into China. Japan does not, however, have any legal right to claim Taiwan. That issue was solved long ago when Japan signed the Sino-Japanese Peace Tready with the Nationalist government in Taiwan, and agreed that Taiwan is a part of China. In 1972, when Japan established diplomatic relations with mainland China, she made the same promise. Thus, there is no dispute between China and Japan over Taiwan's status. Any decision by Japan not to recognize China's claim to Taiwan could lead to a Sino-Japanese confrontation. The outcome will be therefore basically determined by the Japanese attitude.

Though both the U.S. and Japan may in different degrees influence the solution of the Taiwan problem, the policies of the Nationalist regime in Taiwan are the final determinant factor that can affect Chinese policy in this area. The Nationalist government has adopted a flexible and conciliatory policy with China in the last few years. Travel, trade, and semi-official communications between the two regimes have developed rapidly. The new president of Taiwan, Dr. Li Denghui, has even recently taken the first step to suggest possible official negotiations between the two governments.[57] However, the increasing demands of some political forces within and without the island for independence and the growing political instability on the island have alarmed the Chinese government. If current events in Taiwan continue to develop along tumultuous lines, military intervention from China cannot be ruled out. Military intervention would further increase the tension between China and the U.S., and even between China and Japan, which would inevitably affect Chinese global and regional strategies.

The Perspective of Sino-Japanese Cooperation: While U.S.-Japanese and Soviet-Japanese relations are not expected to change substantially, Sino-Japanese relations may become closer in the coming decades. The Chinese and other Asians cannot forget the aggression of the Japanese in the Second World War. However, contemporary China is different from that of the 1930s; she is strong enough to stand on her own feet. Thus, while China may be uneasy about a rearmed Japan, she is no longer intimidated. As long as Japan does not intend to restore her militarism and expansionism in Asia and is willing to cooperate economically with China without trying to interfere in China's domestic politics, China is likely to maintain friendly relations with her. Meanwhile, the Chinese will reciprocate Japan's cooperation by opening their markets to her products and supplying more industrial materials. The fact that the Japanese hesitated to go along with the economic sanctions announced by the U.S. and other Western countries after the Tiananmen Square Incident, and intended to lift the freeze on bank loans to China earlier than other countries can be seen as an indication of their pro-China policy. The Chinese will certainly not jeopardize this opportunity to draw Japan into closer relations with them, and by playing her cards carefully could possibly moderate the balance of power between the U.S and Japan, especially if relations between these two countries continue to deteriorate. Such a possibility has been mentioned by Mr. Nixon, for example, in a recent interview with Time magazine in April 1990.[58]

C. Possible Chinese Strategy in Meeting the New Situation

As the confrontation between the superpowers and their alliances in Europe relax significantly following the drastic changes in the Communist countries, the long-time publicly proclaimed "Century of the Pacific" will only become a reality if the focus of international conflict moves to the Pacific Rim area.

From a global point of view, although Chinese economic and military power has improved enormously in the past decade, it is still not enough to shift the world balance of power. However, when the focus of international confrontation moves to the Pacific Rim, the Chinese roles and strategies in regional conflicts will draw worldwide attention, and, thus, may add their weight to global politics.

If the current global political trend continues, strategic cooperation between China and the U.S. will eventually disappear, but no close co-operation between China and the Soviet Union is expected to emerge while the Soviets are obviously dismantling their Communist empire. A new alignment of the countries in Asia and the Pacific Rim will replace, at least partly, the domination of the superpowers. Based on the current policies of the big powers in East Asia, a balance of power could be maintained between China, Japan, the U.S.A., and the Soviet Union with controllable mutual reactions. No new alliance is expected to emerge in this region in the near future. With their own political and economic problems at home, the Chinese government will be happy to see a peaceful and stable environment in this area in the coming decade which would give it much needed time to consolidate its control and promote the four modernizations.

As far as regional strategy is concerned, above all in South and Southeast Asia, the Chinese are apparently taking a more active forward defensive strategy in dealing with local crises. The potential crises mentioned earlier primarily relate to some historical confrontations over territorial disputes between several regional powers. These problems have continually drawn Chinese attention in the past few decades. The newly strengthened Chinese navy is likely to use the South China Sea as an area to test its power before going out onto the open seas for more aggressive actions. The increasing presence of the Chinese navy in the Xisha and Nansha islands would inevitably raise tensions and even military conflict with the Philippines, Malaysia, and, above all, Vietnam. If the Sino-Indian border dispute breaks out again, the military actions of the two countries may not be strictly limited to the Himalayan area as they were during the 1962 crisis. The Pakistani may take the advantage to raise their territory issue against India, and thus, expand the local conflict to a regional war. It may also expand the military conflict to the Indian Ocean between India and Pakistan, and even China. If so, it would eventually become a major international issue with global impact.

The political crisis of 1989 and its consequences will inevitably have an effect on the power of Chinese national defence. However, while these effects are not likely to be felt on national defence in the short term, they are, however, clearly evident in the extent of damage inflicted on the Chinese economy. The denial of loans from international banks and suspension of business investment from foreign countries have caused significant economic deterioration in China. While the Western countries have also adopted co-ordinated actions in limiting the export of weapons and high technology to China since then, these have not yet had an impact on the power of Chinese national defence. On the contrary, the fighting power of the Chinese armed forces has recently reached a new peak as a result of the impressive achievements of the economy under Deng Xiaoping's reforms and open door policy in the last decade. The full impact of Western actions may only emerge later if current economic sanctions and the ban on advanced technology exports become long and drawn out. According to a recent report, following the establishment of the previously mentioned "Fist Forces" in the army, the PLA has further promoted their professional standards by organizing various kinds of specialized military units such as brigades of artillery, tanks, engineers, anti-airplane guns, and mountain infantry corps, etc.[59] In addition, they also showed their continued achievement in upgrading their naval and air forces by building new patrol escorts, torpedos, and radar systems with high speed and accuracy. Defence experts in Taiwan have recognized the impact of this new equipment in the future if war between China and Taiwan occurs again.[60]

Therefore, in terms of regional defensive strategy, there is no evidence to show that China will go back to its old passive or retrograde defensive strategy based on the principles of people's warfare. On the contrary, the continual improvement of equipment, regularization, reorganization, and joint operation training between different armed forces will push the PLA further away from these old principles unless they can be adapted to the new situation, which is known as people's war under modern conditions.

Footnotes

1.   Deng Xiaoping, "The Works of Military Reorganization", in *The Selected Works of Deng Xiaoping, 1975-1982* (Shanghai, People's Press, 1983), p. 15. (Hereafter referred to as *Works of Deng.*)

2.   *Ibid.*, p. 18.

3.   Idem, "The PLA Has To Be Reorganized", in *Works of Deng, op. cit.*, p. 1.

4.   Idem, "To Build Up A Strong Modernized and Regularized Revolutionary Armed Force", in *Works of Deng, op. cit.*, p. 350.

5.   Idem, "Raising the Military Education and Training to A Strategic Position", in *Works of Deng, op. cit.*, p. 61.

6.   Idem, "The Works of Military Reorganization", in *Works of Deng, op. cit.*, p. 21.

7.   Idem, "To Cut Off the Number of the Armed Force and Strengthen Its Fighting Power", in *Works of Deng, op. cit.*, p. 251.

8.   Idem, "The Current Situation and Our Mission", in *Works of Deng, op. cit.*, p. 228.

9.   Idem, "A Speech on the Open Ceremony of the National Conference of the Scientists", in *Works of Deng, op. cit.*, p. 83.

10.   Idem, "Referring to the Reorganization of National Defence Industry", in *Works of Deng, op. cit.*, pp. 26-7.

11.   Idem, "Raising the Military Education and Training to A Strategic Position", in *Works of Deng, op. cit.*, pp. 57-8.

12.   Shao Huang, "Reform Works of Military Training of the PLA", *Study of the Chinese Communist Monthly* 23:9 (Taipei, Sept. 15, 1980).

13.   *Bejing Review* (August 3, 1987), p. 4.

14.   Deng, "Raising the Military Education and Training to A Strategic Position", *op. cit.*, p. 61.

15.   Idem, "A Speech to the Plenary Meeting of the Military Commission of the CCP", in *Works of Deng, op. cit.*, p. 74.

16.   Idem, "Insisting on the Four Basic Principles", in *Works of Deng, op. cit.*, p. 158.

17.   Idem, "A Speech to the Plenary Meeting of the Military Commission of the CCP", *op. cit.*, p. 74.

18.   *Ibid.*

19.   *Ibid.*, p. 75.

20.   Mark Gayn, "Chinese See Asian Oil as Russia's 'Grand Goal'", *Toronto Star,* 6 August 1980.

21.   *Ibid.* The author had a interview with Mr. Zhang Wenjin, the Vice-Minister of Foreign Affairs of China. Zhang made these points.

22.   The report about the "Joint U.S.-Chinese Station", *New York Times,* June 17, 1981. As to the Sino-Vietnames War, it started 16 days after

Deng returned from the U.S. There was a strong possibility that Deng had consulted the American leaders on this issue when he met with them.

23. "China Remark Haunts Reagan", *Toronto Star,* August 25, 1980.

24. Zhao Qian, "Detente between Sino-Soviet Communists and the Northeast Asia Situation", *The Study of Mainland China* 5:31 (November 1988), p.38.

25. In 1985, the total Chinese two-way trade was Y206.71 billions, which was more than US$ 60.6 billion . See *Britannica, Book of the Year,* 1988, p.574. In 1988, the U.S. investment in China alone was about US$ 3 billion, see the 1989 edition.

26. Zhang Aiping made this announcement, which was carried by *PLA Daily News* on August 20, 1983 and reported in *International Daily News* on August 24, 1983.

27. See "China Imported A Lot of Technology and Equipment", *World Daily News,* February 6, 1990.

28. Jack Anderson, "An Analysis of the Chinese Defence Expenditure", *International Daily News,* May 21, 1983 (Translated by Li Yaping).

29. In L. Brown's *State of the World, 1986* (New York, 1986), p. 207, this figure represents a percentage of the GNP, but the Military Attaché of the PRC in Ottawa suggests that it should be a percentage of the National Budget.

30. *Xingdao Daily News,* February 2, 1990.

31. *Ibid.,* August 16, 1988.

32. Ding Shugan, "The Strategic Nuclear Forces of the PRC Are Changing", *The Study of Mainland China* 2:32 (August 1989), p. 52.

33. *Ibid.*

34. Ying Ru, "The Military of the PRC in 1988", *The Study of Communist China* 23:1 (15 January 1989), pp. 67-8.

35. Chen Minzhi, "The Current Situation of the Quick Strike Forces of the Communist China", *The Study of Communist China* 23:4 (15 April 1989), pp. 111-113.

36. According to Chen Mingzhi, before 1976, there were only three training cruises of Chinese submarines at sea beyond the first islands chain outside Mainland China and one training cruise of surface vessels which could be seen as ocean-going voyages . Since the Chinese have made more cooperative training cruises beyond the second islands chain in the Pacific. See "The Ocean-Going Voyage Training in Joint Fleet of the Chinese Navy", *The Study of Communist China* 23:7 (15 July 1989), pp. 107-8.

37. "The Development of Chinese Navy in the Future", *Zoom Lense* 207 (16 December 1989), pp.28-30.

38. See *Centre Daily News* (Zhong Bao), Novermber 26, 1983.

39.   Chen Mingzhi, "The Ocean-Going Voyage Training in Joint Fleet of the Chinese Navy", *op. cit.*, p. 108.

40.   *Ibid.*

41.   Huang Shuofeng, "Strategy of International Contest of Comprehensive National Strength", *International Strategic Studies* 4 (Beijing Institute for International Strategic Studies, December 1989), p. 34.

42.   "The CCP Strengthening Their Control over the Thought of the PLA", *World Daily News,* February 12, 1990.

43.   The Central Committee of the Communist Party of the U.S.S.R. made the decision on February 5, 1990 after a serious debate and voted with a big majority of approval. The Joint Meeting between the NATO and Warsaw Pact countries was held in Ottawa, Canada from February 13 to 15, 1990. For the major agreement and issues discussed, see the reports in the *Toronto Star,* February 15, 1990.

44.   While President Bush publicly announced economic sanctions against China after the Tiananmen Square Incident, he kept sending his high ranking officials secretly to Beijing in order to prevent relations from deteriorating. When the Congress passed a bill to give the Chinese students and visiting scholars the right to stay in the U.S., Bush vetoed it without hesitation and did his best to stop the Congress from overriding his veto. These moves indicate that the U.S. government does not want to push China back into isolation, and, thus, has brought Japan and many Western countries to follow suit in trade and bank loans.

        As to the Chinese side, the leaders have consistently announced that they are going to keep their open policy of reforms and offer to protect the interests and rights of foreign investors in China.

45.   See *World Daily News,* January 7 and 25, 1990.

46.   After the revolutionary changes in the East European Communist countries, Chinese leaders have repeatedly declared that every country has a right to choose its own political system. The Chinese thus emphasized that the Western world, above all the U.S.A., should not intervene in China's domestic politics.

47.   See *World Daily News,* May 12 and June 7, 1990.

48.   According to recent reports, China has started a joint research program with Israeli scientists in Beijing. It may indicate that China will no longer sacrifice national interest for ideological reasons.

49.   For the story of the McMahon Line, see Neville Maxwell, *India's China War* (Garden City, N.Y.: Doubleday, 1972), pp. 40-42.

50.   See *Xingdao Daily News,* May 9, 1989.

51.   *Ibid.*, October 11, 1989. The Chinese do not have an aircraft carrier; otherwise, the Chinese navy is much larger than the Indian.

52.   *Ibid.* Also see Vice Prime Minister, Wu Zaodong's comment about

the possible regional conflict after the detente of the superpowers in Asia. *World Daily News,* February 5, 1990.

53. Zhao Qian, "Detente between Sino-Soviet Communists and the Northeast Asia Situation", *op. cit.*, p. 38.

54. See "Bush, Japan and China Card", *World Daily News,* February 20, 1990.

55. The FSX bomber issue is an example of limiting advanced technology transfer. It even shows that the U.S. does not want the Japanese to develop their own technology or use the better technology developed by other countries. It may partly be for economic reasons but may also be for military reasons.

　　See Gerald Utting, "Japan's FSX Bomber Struggling to Get Off the Ground", *Toronto Star,* April 23, 1989; also "Japan Seeks Equality in Superpower Relations", *Toronto Star,* April 2, 1989.

56. Based on the Yalta Agreement of 1945 between Stalin and Roosevelt the Soviet Union has occupied Southern Sakhalin and the Kurile Islands north of Hokhaido. The Kurile Islands include four islands: Kunashiri, Etorofu, Shikotan and Habomai. Both the Kurile Islands and the Southern Sakhalin Islands consist of a natural border of Sea of Okhotsk and make it like a lake of the Soviet Union, where the Soviets' biggest military base is located.

57. Dr. Li Denghui's Inaugural Speech on May 29, 1990, *Central Daily News.*

58. *Time,* April 2, 1990, p. 14.

59. See *Xingdao Daily News,* February 27, 1990.

60. See *World Daily News,* February 5, 1990, and *Xingdao Daily News,* February 27, 1990.

EPILOGUE

In analyzing modern Chinese military thought, we have referred to both ancient Chinese military theories and current trends of development in Chinese national strategy. While the former is aimed at the historical continuity of Chinese military theories, the latter is an attempt to give a sense of direction, albeit not in detail, of the development of contemporary Chinese policy of national defence in the post-Mao era. Consequently, the book consists of three major subjects: ancient Chinese military philosophy, modern Chinese military thought and contemporary Chinese national strategies. The discussion here has primarily concentrated on the development of modern military thought. After going through this book, readers are likely to ask whether the ancient Chinese military theories and modern Chinese military thought such as Mao's people's warfare will still be useful in a modern war. It is obviously difficult for the author to answer this question with a simple "yes" or "no", because the answer depends on the perspective of modern war that one may hold, the weapons used in war, and the nature of the theories.

Though the functions of the national armed force are numerous, its most important application is to protect national security by means of war in accordance with national goals. From historical experience, the armed forces of a country are often used by the government to suppress internal violence and rebellion and maintain social order, or are used in war with other countries in pursuit of national goals or national interests. Under modern Marxism and Leninism, Communist countries have repeatedly used their armed forces to support the so-called proletarian revolutionary forces against their ruling class in the civil wars of other countries.

In terms of the scale of war, there are general wars and limited ones. As far as interstate war is concerned, there are those on a global scale and those on a regional scale. With regards to the opponent, the goals of the country and the scale of the war, the means and methods used in handling a conflict may not be the same. While something may be proper to use in a general war of global scale, it may be improper or insufficient in a civil war or a limited and regional conflict. If one thinks about a general war in the future and imagines a type of "star wars" as dramatized in movies, one is likely to conclude that a few kinds of strategic weapons such as the ICBM, long-range bomber or spaceships armed with nuclear bombs and missiles would be able to completely destroy one's enemy. If this is the possible form of future war, all conventional military hardware and armed forces except those using these weapons and delivery instruments would become useless and, thus, be dismantled. However, this may not be a realistic assumption. Although the above-mentioned strategic weapons are indispensable in a modern general war between the superpowers, it is unrealistic to say that conventional armed forces will no longer be needed to finish enemy resistance after the use of nuclear weapons.

As a matter of fact, it has not been a general war, but regional and limited conflicts which have dominated global politics since the Second World War, and which will continue to be a source of political tension in the world in the coming years. Historical experience has shown that most civil wars and even regional wars in the past few decades have been fought primarily in the developing countries which have not yet developed nuclear weapons. Even if a few may now have access to nuclear weapons, they would hesitate to use them on their own land or against their immediate neighbours in war. Therefore, it is highly improbable, if not entirely impossible, that any country would take the nuclear initiative in a civil war and/or local military confrontation.

Furthermore, since the unexpected wave of democratic revolution swept through the eastern European countries in 1989, the Soviet Union has lost much of its confidence and enthusiasm in supporting revolutionary forces as it did before. This dramatic change in attitude has significantly reduced the threat of military confrontation between the superpowers and, thus, the chance of nuclear war. Few of us believe that a general war of nuclear annihilation is unavoidable. On the contrary, more and more people tend to think that nuclear weapons, with their inevitable result of self-destruction, will become less useful and even useless in a future war. This theory may not convince everyone, but it at least indicates that general or regional war with conventional weapons will still play an important role in the future. If this is true, the traditional military theories of China and other countries will not be totally irrelevant in modern wars.

In addition, weapons and technologies can affect the development of strategy and tactics as mentioned in the introduction of this book, but their impact is more significant on tactics than strategies. When firearms replaced spears and arrows as the primary weapons in war, military formation and disposition changed drastically but the general principles of strategy and/or basic military theories did not change very much. For example, some ancient works on the art of war in China discussed formations in great detail as mentioned in Chapter Two, but no modern military strategist bothers to discuss them any longer, nor does any commander try to apply them in battle. Nevertheless, many, if not all, basic military principles developed by the ancient strategists refer to generalizations about war. *Qi* and *Zheng, Xu* and *Shi,* war planning and information collecting, psychological and political warfare, and principles of commanding an army and maintaining its morale in the field, for example, all belong to this category. Modern Chinese military leaders still see them as vital to winning a battle. Their usefulness has never been questioned just because weapons changed. The development of modern technology has strengthened the effectiveness of these principles rather than weakened them.

The same logic can be applied to many modern military theories. The basic theories of people's warfare, for example, require the army to mobilize, organize and rely on the support and cooperation of the people to fight a war. These principles are similar to Sunzi and Wuzi's theory to "mobilize the people to be in complete accord with their ruler, so that they will follow him regardless of their lives, undismayed by any danger" in war, and that "when there is discord within the country, the army cannot be mobilized" for war. No matter what form a modern war may take or how powerful modern weapons can be, these basic theories remain useful and, thus, can be respected. However, many other principles designed for certain circum- stances in the Chinese civil wars and Sino-Japanese War in the 1930s and 1940s may not be applied indiscriminately. For example, Mao required the PLA to supply themselves with weapons looted from the enemy at the front. With weapons and equipment being standardized, it will be unrealistic for them to do so now. This is why Deng Xiaoping referred it as impractical or impossible, as mentioned in the last chapter. In addition, Mao directed his army in the Civil War to occupy the countryside and use it as bases to besiege the cities. When it is applied to a weak revolutionary force against a well- organized modern army, it could be a wise strategy, but it would not apply to regular armed forces equipped with advanced modern weapons and equip- ment. As mentioned in Chapter 6, Mao Zedong himself believed that a particular war has its particular regulations. One must discover these regulations and use them properly. If one unconditionally copies the regula- tions of previous wars, one is likely to suffer defeat. Therefore, though the basic theories of people's warfare can be still useful in accordance with the particular situation of the future, some of Mao's military principles should be changed. In fact, the Chinese military leaders have been discussing those changes for some time, as mentioned in the introduction of this book. "A people's war under modern conditions" is an accepted conclusion among the Chinese leaders. It would give them breathing space to adapt to the new conditions they may face in the future.

Under Deng Xiaoping's leadership, Chinese defence modernization has had impressive achievements and has made Chinese forward defensive strategy more realistic than before. However, the impact of the 1989 Incident has drastically changed Chinese political and economic development. The current Chinese leaders are tightening their control over the armed forces and the direction of economic-political development and are trying to steer Chinese society back to the orthodox doctrines of Marxism. Though it is difficult for one to know how far they will go, and how long this trend will persist, one thing is certain that political instability will inevitably have a significant impact on the economy in general and defence modernization in particular in the coming years. A steady decline of the Chinese economy would weaken their national defence power and, thus, affect the balance of power in the regional politics of Asia.

It has long been a popular myth that the 19th century was a British century, the 20th an American century and the 21st a Chinese century. With the possibility of the century of the Pacific Rim in mind, one is likely to think that the Chinese reforms of the last decade and the economic development of the East Asian countries have been pushing the popular notion closer to reality. However, since the Tiananmen Incident of 1989 and the democratic revolution in the East European countries thereafter, such an anticipation is becoming increasingly less realistic. For instead of continuing military confrontation, NATO and the Warsaw Pact countries have begun to work together in political and economic cooperation. If this approach succeeds (and it looks likely), it would inevitably attract the powerful financial groups to take their business ventures to Europe, thus excluding the Asian countries, above all China, which badly needs foreign capital.

If the current economic sanctions and ban on technology exports imposed by western countries continue into the long term, and if the Chinese government fails to break out of its self-created economic and political stalemate as soon as possible, the Chinese will forfeit any claim to distinction they may have in the 21st century. With their explosive population growth, increasingly deteriorating ecology and limited resources, not only would the forecasted Chinese century recede as unfulfilled fantasy, but it would even become questionable as to whether China could maintain her current standard of development.

If the Chinese wish to play a positive role in global and regional politics in the coming century, and to feed their 1.2 billion population properly, they must build up a strong national power based on a modern economic system and technology. However, judging from historical experience, this goal can only be achieved by means of peaceful reformation in a stable and harmonious society and not by violent revolution. A stable and harmonious country can be achieved by various means but not by endless class struggle which results, not in progress and construction, but only more destruction and sorrow to the society.

Bibliography

1. **Publication in Chinese:**

The Essays of Modern Chinese History. Beijing: Zhonghua, 1979.

Association of Chinese Cultural Construction, ed. *China, Ten Years Prior to the Resistance War.* Hong Kong: Lungmei, 1965.

Association of the CCP History of Jiangsu, ed. *A New Treatise of the History of the Sino-Japanese War.* Nanjing: Nanjing College of Engineering, 1986.

Bai, Guangya. *The History of Political Warfares of the Nationalist Army.* Taipei: College of Political Cadres, 1970.

Cai, Songpo (E). *The Posthumous Works of Mr. Cai Songpo.* Taipei: Winxing Press, 1962.

Cai, Xiaoqian. *The Study of Mao Zedong's Military Thought and the People's Warfare.* Taipei: Shanghai Press, 1971.

Cao, Boyi. *The Eastablishment and Collapse of the Jiangxi Soviet Regime.* Taipei: Institute of East Asia Study of National Chengzhi Univ., 1969.

_____. *The Political Experience of the CCP in Yanan Period.* Taipei: Institute of East Asia Study of National Chengzhi Univ., 1973.

Chen, Wenshang & Lei, Jiaji. *The Study of Strategical Theory.* Taipei: Lianming, 1981.

Chen, Xulu; Gu, Tinglong; & Wang, Xi. *The Sino-Japanese War of 1894 (Year of Jiawu).* Shanghai: People's Press, 1982.

Cheng, Xi. *Ancient Chinese Tactics and Arts of War*. Hong Kong: Xin Shidai.

Chinese Revolution Museum, ed. *Su Yu - - the Prominent General*. Baijing: Xinhua, 1986.

Collins, John M. *The Grand Strategy*. (in Chinese) Translated by Niu Xianzhong. Taipei: Liming, 1975.

Deng, Yibing. "The Xunfeng Dui of the Last Years of Qing Dynasty and the 1911 Revolution. *In The Front of Social Science* (Shehui Kexue Zhanxian),No. 4, 1983.

Engels, F. *The Military Essays of Karl Marx and F. Engels*. 5 Vols. (trans. in Chinese) Beijing: Foreign Languages Press, 1981.

Feng, Guifen. "A Discussion on Learning the Teachnology of Making Foreign Weapons." In *The Reference Materials of Modern Chinese History of Thought*, edited by Shih Jun. Beijing: Sanlian, 1957.

Feng, Yulan. *The Essays of Modern Chinese History of Thought*. Sanghai: People's Press, 1958.

_____, *Chinese History of Philosophy*. Beijing: Shangwu.

Fu, Zhong. "Mao Zedong's Military Thought Is Always the Precious Treasure of the Chinese People," *Hongqi*, No. 15, Aug. 1, 1981.

Gao, Tiqian. *Military Materialist Dialectics*. Beijing: Party School Press of the CCP, 1985.

_____ & Deng, Guangrong. *A Preliminary Study of the Military Philosophy of Mao Zedong*. Chengdu: the Social Science Research Council of Sichuan Province, 1986.

Gu, Jiguang. *An Annotation of the Fu Bing System*. Shanghai:People's Press, 1962.

Guo, Huaruo, ed. & trans. *An Annotation of Sunzi's Art of War*. Shanghai: Guji Press, 1984.

Guo, Qingshu, ed. *A Short History of the Chinese People's Liberation Army*. Shenyang: Liaoming Univ., 1985.

Hang, Thaddaus. *A Study of the Chinese Nation*. Taipei: Shangwu, 1966.

He, Liangchen. *A Note of Formation (Zhenji)*. In *The Collections of Chinese Books on the Art of War*, edited by Li Yuri. Taipei, 1957.

He, Yingqin. *The Eight Year History of the Resistance War*. Taipei: Liming, 1982.

Hu, Sheng. *From Opium War to May 4th Movement. Beijing*: Rimin Press, 1980.

Huang, Keqiang. *The Works of Huang Keqiang*. Taipei: the Commission of Party History of Guomindang, 1967.

Huilu Jiumin. *Bingpi Baijing Fang. In The Collections of Chinese Books on the Art of War*. Edited by Li Yuri, Taipei, 1957.

Hunan People's Press. *One Hundred Topics of Modern Chinese History*. 2 Vols. Changsa, Hunan: Hunan People's Press, 1983.

Institute of Modern History, Science Research Council of China. *The Selected Materials of History of Thought in the Opium War Period.* Beijing: Zhonghua, 1963.

Institute of Qing History, People's Univ. of China. *Essays of Modern Chinese History.* Beijing: Zhonghua, 1979.

Jiang, Jieshi. *The Collections of Military Speeches of President Jiang,* 4 Vols. Taipei: the Editorial Committee of the Zhongzing Speeches Collection of President Jiang, 1971.

_____. *The Collections of President Jiang's Speeches and Essays.* 2 Vols. Taipei: Zhongyang Winwu Gongyingshei, 1977.

_____. *The Digest of the Instruction of the Late Leader on Political Warfare.* Taipei: General Dept. of Political Warfare of the Ministry of National Defense, 1975.

_____. *The Personal Records of President Jiang,* 12 Vols. Taipei: Central Daily News, 1976.

_____. *The Quotations from the Late President Jiang,* ed. Qin Xiaoyi. Taipei: Zhongyang Winwu Gongyingshei.

_____. *The Works of President Jiang,* 2 Vols. Taipei: Institute of National Defense Study, 1963.

Jiang, Tingfu, ed. *Selected Materials of Diplomatic History of Modern China.* Taipei: Shangwu, 1958.

Jiang, Weiguo. *Selected Military Essays.* 3 Vols. Taipei: The Military Univ., 1973.

_____. *The Sino-Japanese War (Kangri Yuwu) -- the 3rd Part of National Revolution War History.* Taipei: Liming, 1978.

_____. *The Special Essays of T.V. Broadcast Program on President Jiang's Military Thought.* Taipei: Ministry of Education, 1979.

Ke, Gang; Zeng, Ke & Xie, Hongxing. *Liu Bocheng's Fighting Among Rivals for the Throne.* Beijing: PLA Press, 1983.

Lei, Bailun. *Chinese Culture and the Chinese Soldier.* Taipei: Wanniang-ing, 1971.

Leng, Jiepu. *The Campaign of Huaihai.* Fuzhou: People's Press, 1983.

Lenin, F.L. *The Military Essays of F.L. Lenin.* (in Chinese) B e i j i n g : Zhanshi Press, 1981.

Li, Dingfong. *Zeng Koufan and His Staffs.* Hong Kong: Yuandong, 1978.

Li, Hongzhang. *The Works of Li Winzhong Gong.* 6 Vols. Taipei: Winhai.

Li, Jing. *The Collection of Weigong's Art of War.* In *The Collections of Chinese Books on the Art of War.* Taipei, 1959.

Li, Minhua. *The Land Struggle of the CCP.* Taipei: Institute of Int'l Relation, 1965.

Li, Shoukong. *Biography of Li Hongzhang.* Taipei: Xuesheng, 1978.

Li, Tianmin. *A Critical Biography of Lin Biao.* Hong Kong: Mingpao, 1978.

Li, Yuri. *A General Comment on Sunzi's Art of War.* Hong Kong: Zingfung Wenhua.

_____, ed. *The Collections of Chinese Books on the Art of War.* 5 Vols. Taipei, 1957.

Li, Zhen. *The History of Chinese Military Education.* Taipei: Zhongyang Winwu Gongyingshei, 1983.

Lin, Zexu. *Political Writing of Lin Winzhong Gong.*

Liu, Bocheng. *The Memoirs of Liu Bocheng.* Shanghai: Winyi Press, 1982.

Liu, Dawu. "The Chronicle of Cai Songpo." In *The Posthumous Works of Mr. Cai Songpo.* Taipei: Winxiang Press, 1962.

Liu, Yungyo. "Quotation from Yuefi's Military Work." In *The Collection of Chinese Books on the Art of War,* edited by Li Yuri, Taipei, 1957.

Liu, Zhongping. *Simafa Jinzhu Jinyi: A Modern Interpretation and Translation of Simafa.* Taipei: Shangwu, 1975.

_____. *Weiliaozi Jinzhu Jinyi: A Modern Interpretation and Translation of Weiliaozi.* Taipei: Shangwu.

Lu, Dajie. *An Introduction to Books on Art of War of All Ages (of China).* Hong Kong: Zhongson, 1969.

Lu, Fungge. *A General History of the West Expedition of Zuo Winxiang Gong.* Taipei: Winhai, 1972.

Luo, Guanzhong. *The Romance of the Three Kingdoms.* Taipei: Sanmin Book, 1978.

Mao, Yingbai. *An Introduction to the Arts of War of Sunzi and Sunbin.* Hong Kong: Yinghua, 1979.

Mao Zedong. *The Selected Works of Mao Zedong.* Beijing: People's Press, 1965.

Mao, Zhuqing, ed. *The Works of Cai E. Changsa,* Hunan: Hunan People's Press, 1983.

Military Science Council of the PLA. *A New Annotation of Sunzi's Art of War.* Beijing: Zhonghua, 1981.

Mu, Anshih. *The Opium War.* Shanghai: People's Press, 1982.

Nanjing Univ. ed. *A Memorial Essays of the One Hundred Thirty Anniversary of the Founding of Taiping Heavenly Kingdom in Nanjing.* Nanjing: Nanjing Univ., 1983.

National Council of Military Science of China. *Modern Chinese History of War.* Beijing: Military Science Press, 1985.

Peng, Daxiong. *Wuzi and Weiliaozi on the Art of War.* Taipei: Dahua.

Peng Dehuai. *An Account on His Own Words.* Beijing: People's Press, 1981.

PLA Military Science Council. *Essays of Military Materialist Dialectics.* Beijing: PLA Military Science Council, 1984.

_____. *The Study of Military Materialist Dialectics.* Beijing: PLA Military Science Council, 1985.

PLA Press. *The Great Military Strategy of Modern Sunzi and Wuzi (Hulue Longtao Xin Sunwu).* Beijing: PLA Press, 1983.

_____. *Under the Commanding of Marshal Xu Xiangqin.* Beijing: PLA Press, 1984.

_____. *Chinese Military History - - with Tables of Wars in History*. Beijing: PLA Press, 1985.

Qin, Xiuhao. *The Military Service System of China and Foreign Countries*. Taipei: the Guomindang Central Committee, 1983.

Qiu, Shaohua & Niu, Hongen. *The Various Schools in the Pre-Qin Times*. Beijing: Military Science Press, 1985.

Second History Archives Centre of China, ed. *The Civil War Between the Hepei and Anhui Warlords*. Jiengsu: People's Press, 1980.

Shen, Yunlung, ed. *Collections of Modern Chinese Historical Documentations*. Taipei: Wenhai.

_____, ed. *The Essays of Jiang Baili* (Fang-zhen). Selected and pub. by Institution of National Denfense, 1972.

Shi, Yan & Wu, Kebin. *Chen Yi Crossed the Yangtze River to theNorth*. Nanjing: Zhanshi Press, 1983.

Shi, Zhi. *The Evolution of the Military System and Staff Organization*. Taipei: Guomindang Central Committee, 1981.

Shih, Jun, ed. *Reference Materials of Modern Chinese History of Thought*. Beijing: Sanlian, 1957.

Sihu Yishi. Toubi Futan. *In The Collections of Chinese Books on the Art of War*. Ed. Li Yuri. Taipei, 1957.

Social Science Front. *The Collections of Studies of Modern Chinese History*. Jilin: People's Press, 1981.

Song, Shilun. "Mao Zedong's Military Thought Is the Guidebook for t h e PLA to Victory," *Hongqi*, No. 16, 1981.

Song, Zhi. *Chen Yi in the South of Yangtze River*. Beijing: Jiefang Press, 1985.

Stalin, Joseph. *The Military Essays of Stalin*. (in Chinese) Beijing: Zhanshi Press, 1980.

Sun, Shuping. *The Manuscript of History Chinese Philosophy*. Shanghai: People's Press,1981.

Sun Tzu (Sunzi). *The Art of War*.

Sun, Yatsen. *The Works of Dr. Sun Yatsen* (Guofu Quansu). Taipei: Institution of National Defense, 1963.

Tao, Diya. *The Strategies of Dr. Sun Yatsen and Jiang Jieshi.*. Taipei: Liming, 1985.

Tao, Hanzhang. *An introduction to Sunzi's Art of War*. Beijing: PLA Press, 1985.

Tao, Juyin. *The Biography of Jiang Baili*. Baijing: Zonghua, 1985.

_____. "The History of the Beiyang Warlord Governing Period." *Life, Study and New Knowledge* (Shanghai), Vol. 1, 1957.

Tao, Luzi. *A Note of the Use of Formation (Yunzhen Zhalu)*. In *The Collections of Chinese Books on the Art of War*, edited by Li Yuri. Taipei, 1957.

Tian, Buyi. A History of the Beiyang Warlords. Taipei: Chunqiu, 1967.

Tian, Ping. "A Discussion on the Historical Functions of the Yangwu Movement." In The Essays of Modern Chinese History. Beijing: Zhonghua, 1979.

Wang, Ermin. The Collections of Studies of Military History of Qing Dynasty. Hong Kong: Luanyu Press, 1979.

_____. A Record of the Hueijun, Hong Kong:

Wang, Heming. Bingfa Baizhanjing. In The Collections of Chinese Books on the Art of War, edited by Li Yuri. Taipei, 1957.

Wang, Qingcheng. The History and Thought of the Taiping Heavenly Kingdom. Beijing: Zhonghua, 1985.

Wang, Ranzhi. General Jiang Baili and His Military Thought. Taipei: Shuaizheng Press, 1975.

Wang, Tongling. Chinese History. 2 Vols. Taipei: Qiming, 1960.

Wang, Xianchen & Xu, Baolin. A Miscellaneous Discussion of Ancient Chinese Art of War. Beijing: Zhanshi Press, 1983.

Wei, Rulin. Huangshigong Sanlie Jinzhu Jinyi. Taipei: Shangwu, 1975.

Wei, Yuan. "The Overall Planning of the Coast Defense." In The Reference Materials of Modern Chinese History of Thought. Ed. Shih Jun. Beijing: Sanlian, 1957.

Win, Gongzhi. The Chinese Military History of the Last Thirty Years. Taipei: Winhai, 1971.

Winwu Press, ed. The Books of the Political Strategists in the Warring States Period (Zhanguo) - - Unearthed from Mawangdui Han Tomb. Beijing: Winwu Press, 1976.

Wu, Rusong. An Elementary Introduction of Sunzi's Arts of War. Beijing: PLA Press, 1983.

Wuzi (Wu Tzu). The Arts of War, ed. Pang Daxiong. Taipei: Dahua Press.

Xiang, Dakun. The People's Commune of the CCP. Taipei: the Institute of Mainland China Studies, 1966.

Xu, Dong. Huqianjing. In The Collections of Chinese Books on the Art of War, edited by. Li Yuri. Taipei, 1957.

Xu, Peigen. Taigong Liutao Jinzhu Jinyi: A Modern Interpretation and Translation on the Six War Doctrines of Taigong. Taipei: Shangwu, 1976.

_____. History of Chinese National Defense Thought. Taipei: Zhungyang Wenwu, 1983.

Xu, Shiyou. My Ten Years in the Red Army. Beijing: PLA Press, 1983.

Xu, Xiangqian. A Historical Retrospect. Beijing: PLA Press, 1984.

Xue, Guangqian. The life of Jiang Baili's Old Age and His Military Thought. Taipei: Zhuanji Winzue Press, 1969.

_____ & Jiang, Fucong, eds. The Works of Jiang Baili. Taipei.

Yang, Dezhi. Fight on the Horseback (Hongge Mashang). Beijing: PLA Winyi Press, 1984.

Yang, Guoyu; Chen, Feiqin; Li, Anmin & Wang, Wei. *The Military C a - reer of Liu Bocheng*. Beijing: The Chinese Youth Press, 1982.

Yang, Guoyu & Chen, Peiqin, eds. *The Record of Liu Bocheng's Manoeuvring Troops*. Beijing: Zhanshi Press, 1983.

Yang, Shangkun. "Building A Strong Revolutionized and Modernized Army," *Hongqi*, No. 15, 1982.

Yi, Guogan, ed. *The Official Documents of Vice-president Li: A Collection of Documents of Modern Chinese History*. Taipei: Winxing, 1915.

Zeng, Guangxing & Wang, Quanying. *The Northern Expedition War in Henan Province*. Henan: people's Press, 1985.

Zeng Guofan. *The Works of Zeng Wenzheng Gong*. Taiwan: Zonghe Press, 1982.

_____. *Zeng Wenzheng Gong 's Letters to His Family*. Taipei: Dafang.

Zeng, Guoyuan. *The Philosophy of War Before Qin Dynasty*. Taipei:Shangwu, 1972.

Zhang, Guangya, ed. *The History of Political Warfare in the N a t i o n a l Army*. Taipei: Zhenggong Ganbo Xuexiao,1970.

Zhang,Jiayun. *Zuo Zongtang. A Collection of the Strategists*, Vol. 4. Taipei: Lianming, 1981.

Zhang, Jungu. *The Biography of Li Yuanhong*. Taipei: Zhong Wai Press,1971.

Zhang, Yanshen, ed. & tran. *Yangwu Movement: The Selected Materials of Modern Chinese History*.

Zhang, Yutien, et al. *Modern Chinese Military History*. Shengyang, Liaoning: People's Press, 1983.

Zhao, Zenghui. *The System of Zeng Kuofan's Words and Deeds*. Taipei: Lanhi, 1975.

Zhu, De. *The Selected Works of Zhu De*. Shanghai: People's Press, 1983

Zhu, Jiaxiang. *The Theory and Practice of Dr. Sun Yatsen's Mass Warfare*. Taipei: Liming, 1978.

Zhuge, Liang. *Xinshu*. In *The Collections of Chinese Books on the Art of War*, editedby Li Yuri. Taipei, 1957.

Zuo Zongtang. *The Works of Winxiang Gong*. In *The Collections of Modern Chinese Historical Documentations*, edited by Shen Yunlung. Taipei: Winhai, 1979.

中文書目

（依上列英譯中文書目之號碼順序排列。）

1. 中國文化建設協會編：<u>抗戰前十年之中國</u>，香港：龍門，
  一九六五。

2. 江蘇省中共黨史學會：<u>抗日戰爭史新論</u>，南京工學院出版社
  一九八六。

3. 白光重：<u>國軍政戰史</u>，政工幹校（台灣），一九七〇。

4. 蔡松坡（鍔）：<u>蔡松坡遺著</u>，台北：文星，一九六二。

5. 蔡孝乾：<u>毛澤東軍事思想和人民戰爭之研究</u>，台北：上海
  出版社，一九七一。

6. 曹伯一：<u>中共延安時期之政治經驗</u>，國立政治大學東亞研
  究所，一九七三。

7. 曹伯一：<u>江西蘇維埃之建立及崩潰</u>，台灣：國立政治大學東
  亞研究所，一九六九。

8. 陳明知：「中共組訓快速打擊部隊之近況」，<u>中共研究</u>，卷
  廿三，四期，台北，一九八九年四月十五日。

9. 陳明知：「中共海軍的聯合編隊遠航訓練」，<u>中共研究</u>，卷
  廿三，七期，台北，一九八九年七月十五日。

10. 陳文尚：<u>戰略理論研究——戰略叢書</u>（1），台北：聯鳴，
  一九八一。

11. 陳旭麓等：<u>甲午中日戰爭</u>，上海人民出版社，一九八二。

12. 程義：<u>中國古代戰術與兵法</u>，香港：新時代出版社。

13. 鈕先鍾譯：<u>大戰略</u>（John M. Collins, The Grand Strategy）
  台北：黎明，一九七五。

14. 鄧小平：<u>鄧小平文選</u>（一九七五一八二），上海人民出版社，
  一九八三。

15. 鄧亦失：「清末的巡防隊與辛亥革命」，<u>社會科學戰線</u>
  四期，一九八三。

16. 丁樹範：「演變中的中共戰略核子武器」，<u>中國大陸研究</u>
  卷廿三，二期，一九八八年十一月。

17. 恩格斯：<u>馬克斯和恩格斯軍事論文集</u>，五冊，北京：
  外語學院，一九八一。

18. 馮桂芬：「制洋器議」，石峻編：<u>中國近代思想史參考
  資料</u>，上冊，北京：三聯書店，一九五七。

19. 馮友蘭：中國近代思想史論文集，上海人民出版社，一九五八。

20. 馮友蘭：中國哲學史，北京：商務。

21. 傅鈡：「毛澤東軍事科學永遠是中國人民之瑰寶 —慶祝中國共產黨成立六十週年和中國人民解放軍建軍五十四週年，紅旗，十五期，一九八一年八月一日。

22. 高体乾：軍事唯物辯証法，北京中共中央黨校，一九八五。

23. 高体乾：毛澤東軍事哲學初探，四川社会科學院，一九八六。

24. 谷霽光：府兵制度考釋，上海人民出版社，一九六二。

25. 郭化若：孫子譯註，北京古籍出版社，一九八四。

26. 郭清樹：中國人民解放軍歷史簡編，瀋陽遼寧大學，一九八五。

27. 項退結：中國民族研究，台北商務，一九六六。

28. 何良臣，「陣紀」，李浴日編 中國兵法大系，台北古界兵學社，一九五七。

29. 何應欽：日軍侵華八年抗战史，台北：黎明，一九八二。

30. 胡繩：從鴉片战爭到五四運動，北京人民出版社，一九八〇。

31. 黄克強：黃克強全集，台北：中國國民黨中央委員會，一九六七。

32. 惠麓酒民：「荡游百金方」，李浴日編：中國兵法大系，台北古界兵學社，一九五七。

33. 湖南人民出版社：中國近代史与題，一九八二。

34. 中國科学院近代史研究所：鴉片战爭时期思想史資料選輯，北京，中華書局，一九六三。

35. 中國人民大学清史研究所：中國近代史論文集，北京中華書局，一九七九。

36. 簡鉄：「論当前中共对毛澤東『十大軍事原則』之檢驗」，匪情月報，卷廿四，六期，一九八一。

37. 簡鉄：「中共的國防現代化問題」，匪情月报，卷廿五，一期，一九八二。

38. 蔣介石：蔣總統軍事建設講詞，四冊，蔣總統中奧講詞總集編輯委員會，一九七一。

39. 蔣介石：蔣總統言論集，台北中央文物供應社，一九七七。

40. 蔣介石：領袖政治作战遺訓專錄，國防部總政治作战部，一九七五。

41. 蔣介石：蔣總統祕錄，十二冊，台北中央日報，一九七六。

42. 秦孝儀編：蔣總統語錄，台北：中央文物供應社。

43. 蔣介石：蔣總統集，二冊，台北國防研究院，一九六二。

44. 蔣廷黻：中國近代外交史資料輯要，二冊，台北商務，一九五八。

45. 蔣緯國，軍事論叢，三冊，台北三軍大學，一九七三。

46. 蔣緯國：國民革命戰史第三部—抗日禦侮，台北：黎明，一九七八。

47. 蔣緯國：總統蔣公軍事思想廣播講座專輯，教育部，一九七九。

48. 金千里：「中共軍事犯台之軍事佈署」，九十年代，第五期，香港，一九九〇。

49. 柯崗等：劉伯承逐鹿中原，北京解放軍，一九八三。

50. 雷伯倫：中國文化和中國的兵，台北萬年青出版社，一九七一。

51. 冷杰甫：淮海戰役，福州人民出版社，一九八三。

52. 列寧：列寧軍事文集，北京戰士出版社，一九八一。

53. 李定方：曾國藩和他的幕僚（府），香港：遠東，一九七八。

54. 李鴻章：李文忠公全集，台北：文海，一九八〇。

55. 李靖：「衛公兵法集」，李浴日編：中國兵法大系，台北：去界兵學社，一九五七。

56. 李際均：「毛澤東軍事思想的特點和歷史地位」，紅旗，十四期，一九八二。

57. 黎明華：中共的土地鬥爭，台北：國際關係研究所，一九六五。

58. 李守公：李鴻章傳，台北：學生出版社，一九七八。

59. 李天民：林彪評傳，香港：明報月刊出版社，一九七八。

60. 李浴日：孫子兵法總檢討，香港：新風文化出版社。

61. 李浴日：中國兵法大系，五冊，台北：去界兵學社，一九五七。

62. 李震：中國軍事教育史，台北：中央文物供應社，一九八三。

63. 林彪：林副主席軍事論文集，昆明軍區司令部，一九七〇。

64. 林則徐：林文忠公全集，台北：德志，一九六三。

65. 凌宇：「中國海軍的未來發展」，廣角鏡，二〇七期，香港，一九八九年十二月十六日。

66. 劉伯承：劉伯承回憶錄，上海：文藝出版社，一九八二。

67. 劉仲平：司馬法今註今譯，台北：商務，一九七五。

68. 劉仲平：尉繚子今註今譯，台北：商務，一九七五。

69. 陸達節：中國歷代兵書概論，香港：中山，一九六九。

70. 盧鳳閣：左宗棠西征史略，台北：文海，一九七二。

71. 羅貫中：三國誌演義，台北：三民書局，一九七八。

72. 毛膺白：孫子兵法與孫臏兵法簡介，香港：英華，一九七九。

73. 毛澤東：毛澤東選集，北京人民出版社，一九六六。

74. 毛澤東：毛澤東選集，第五卷，北京人民出版社，一九七七。

75. 毛注青：蔡鍔集，長沙：湖南人民出版社，一九八三。

76. 牟安右：鴉片戰爭，上海人民出版社，一九八二。

77. 中國革命博物館：名將粟裕，北京：新華，一九八六。

78. 南京大學學報編輯部：太平天國建都天京一百三十週年紀念文集，南京大學，一九八三。

79. 軍事科學院戰學理論研究部：孫子兵法新註，北京：中華，一九八一。

80. 軍事科學院軍事辯証法研究室：軍事辯証法論文集，北京：軍事科學出版社，一九八四。

81. 軍事科學院中國近代戰爭史編寫組：中國近代戰爭史，三冊，北京軍事科學出版社，一九八四至一九八五。

82. 軍事科學院軍事辯証法研究編寫組：軍事辯証法研究，北京軍事科學出版社，一九八五。

83. 國家安全會議戰地政務委員會：戰地政務專題研究彙編，台北：國家安全會議戰地政務委員會，一九六八。

84. 彭達雄：吳子.尉繚子兵法，台北：大華。

85. 彭德懷自述編輯組：彭德懷自述，北京人民出版社，一九八一。

86. 解放軍出版社：虎略龍韜斬孫吳——學習「朱德選集」体会文章專輯，北京：解放軍出版社，一九八三。

87. 解放軍出版社：在徐帥指揮下，北京解放軍出版社，一九八四。

88. 解放軍出版社：中國軍事史——附歷代戰爭年表，二冊，北京解放軍出版社，一九八五。

89. 秦修好：中外兵役制度，台北中央文物供應社，一九八三。

90. 邱少華：先秦諸子軍事論譯注，二冊，北京：軍事科學出版社，一九八五。

91. 中國第二歷史檔案館：直皖戰爭——中華民國史檔案資料叢刊，江苏，人民出版社，一九八〇。

92. 邵國華：「社會主義建設的可靠保障」，紅旗，廿一期，一九八二。

93. 紹晃：「中國軍隊的訓練改革工作」，中共研究月刊，二三卷第九期，一九八九年九月十五日。

94. 沈雲龍：中國近代史料叢刊續編，台北：文海，一九七九。

95. 沈雲龍：蔣百里論文集，台北國防研究院，一九七二。

96. 沈雲龍：袁世凱史料彙刊，台北：文海，一九六六。

97. 石峻：中國近代思想史參考資料，北京：三聯，一九五七。

98. 石言：陳毅北渡，南京：戰士出版社，一九八三。

99. 施治：中外軍制和指揮參謀體系的演進，台北中央文物供應社，一九八一。

100. 社會科學戰線編輯部：中國近代史研究論叢，吉林：人民出版社，一九八一。

101. 宋時輪：「毛澤東軍事思想是我軍勝利的指南」，紅旗，十六期，一九八一。

102. 松楨：江南陳毅，北京解放軍出版社，一九八五。

103. 史大林：史大林軍事文集，北京戰士出版社，一九八〇。

104. 孫述圻：中國哲學史稿，上海人民出版社，一九八一。

105. 孫中山：國父全書，台北國防研究院，一九六三。

106. 陶滌亞：國父與領袖的戰略思想，台北：黎明，一九八五。

107. 陶漢章：孫子兵法概論，北京解放軍出版社，一九八五。

108. 陶菊隱：蔣百里傳，北京中華書局，一九八五。

109. 陶菊隱：北洋軍閥統治史話，北京生活、讀書和新知三聯出版社，一九五七。

110. 鮑盧子：「用陣雜錄」，李浴日編：中國兵法大系，台北：世界兵學社，一九五七。

111. 田布衣：北洋軍閥史話，台北：春秋，一九六七。

112. 田平：「關于洋務運動歷史作用之討論」，中國近代史論文集，北京：中華，一九七九。

113. 王爾敏：清朝軍事史論集，香港：聯經，一九七九。

114. 王爾敏：淮軍誌，台北：中國學術著作獎座委員會，一九六七。

115. 王鳴鶴：「兵法百戰經」，李浴日編：中國兵法大系，台北：世界兵學社，一九五七。

116. 王慶成：太平天國的歷史和思想，北京：中華，一九八五。

117. 王冉之：蔣百里將軍與其軍事思想，台北：率真，一九七五。

118. 王桐齡：中國全史，二冊，台北：啟明，一九六〇。

119. 王顯臣：中國古代兵書雜談，北京：戰士出版社，一九八三。

120. 魏汝霖：黃石公三略今註今譯，台北：商務，一九七五。

121. 魏源：「籌海篇」，石峻編：中國近代思想史參考資料，北京：三聯，一九五七。

122. 文公直：最近三十年中國軍事史，台北：文星，一九七一。

123. 馬王堆漢墓帛書：戰國縱橫家書，北京文物出版社，一九七六。

124. 吳如嵩：孫子兵法淺說，北京解放軍出版社，一九八三。

125. 向大鯤：共匪人民公社問題，中國大陸問題研究所，一九六六。

126. 肖克：「學習列伯承同志」，紅旗，十六期，一九八二。

127. 西湖逸士：「投筆膚談」，李浴日編：中國兵法大系，台北法界兵學社，一九五七。

128. 許洞：「虎鈐經」，李浴日編：中國兵學大系，台北世界兵學社，一九五七。

129. 徐培根：太公六韜今註今譯，台北：商務，一九七六。

130. 徐培根：中國國防思想史，台北：中央文物供應社，一九八三。

131. 許世友：我在紅三軍十年，北京：解放軍出版社，一九八三。

132. 徐向前：歷史的回顧，北京：解放軍出版社，一九八四。

133. 薛光前：蔣百里的晚年及其軍事思想，台北：傳記文學出版社，一九六九。

134. 薛光前、蔣復聰編：蔣百里先生全集，台北：傳記文學，一九七一。

135. 楊得志：橫戈馬上，解放軍文藝出版社，一九八四。

136. 楊國宇等：劉伯承軍事生涯，北京：中國青年出版社，一九八二。

137. 楊國宇等：劉伯承用兵錄，北京：戰士出版社，一九八三。

138. 楊尚昆：「建設強大的革命化現代化的軍隊－紀念中國人民解放軍五十週年」，紅旗，十五期，一九八二年八月一日。

139. 尹國幹：「黎副總統政書」，見中國近代史檔案選輯，台北：文星，一九七五。

140. 影儒：「中共一九八八年之軍事」，中共研究，卷廿三，一期，一九八九年元月十五日。

141. 袁世凱：「訓練操法詳晰圖解」及「新建陸軍兵略錄存」，沈雲龍編：袁世凱史料彙刊，台北：文海，一九六六。

142. 曾廣奐：北伐戰爭在河南，河南：人民出版社，一九八五。

143. 曾國藩：曾文正公全集，台南：綜合，一九八二。

144. 曾國藩：曾文正公家書，台北：大方文化事業。

145. 曾國垣：先秦戰爭哲學，台北：商務，一九七二。

146. 張家昀：左宗棠 ─ 战略家叢書 (4)，台北：聯鳴，一九八一。

147. 章君穀：黎元洪傳，台北：中偉．一九七一。

148. 張雁深摘譯：「田鳧號航行記」(Shaule, the Lapwing)
中國近代史料叢書 ─ 洋務運動 (八)，上海人民出版社，
一九七三。

149. 張玉田等：中國近代軍事史，遼寧人民出版社，一九八三。

150. 趙倩：「中蘇、共和解與東北亞情勢」，中國大陸研究，卅一期，
一九八八年十一月。

151. 趙增輝：曾國藩言行体系，台北：蘭溪出版社，一九七五。

152. 朱德：朱德選集，上海人民出版社，一九八三。

153. 祝嘉祥：國文群眾战之理論與实踐，台北：黎明，一九七八。

154. 諸葛亮：「心書」，李浴日編：中國兵學大系，台北：世界兵學社，
一九五七。

155. 左宗棠：左文襄公全集，台北：文海，一九七九。

2. Publication in English:

Barnet, Richard J. *Roots of War*. New York: Atheneum, 1972.

Bianco, Lucien. *Origins of the Chinese Revolution, 1915-1949*. Trans. from French by Murrid Bell, Stanford, CA: Stanford Univ., 1971.

Bidwell, Shelford. *Modern Warfare: A Study of Men, Weapons and Theories*. London: Allen Lare, 1973.

Bill, Jame A. & Gardgrave, Robert L. (Jr.) *Comparative Politics: The Quest for Theory*. Columbus, Ohio: Charles E. Merrill, 1973.

Bok, George Tan Eng. "Strategic Doctrine." In *Chinese Defence Policy*, eds. Gerald Segal & William T. Tow. Chicago: Univ. of Illinois, 1984.

Bourdet, Jacques. *The Ancient Art of War*. London: Barrie & Rockliff, 1966.

Brodle, Bernard. *Escalation and the Nuclear Option*. Princeton, N.J.: Princeton Univ., 1966.

Buzzard, Anthony, W. *Massive Retaliation and Graduated Deterence*. Princeton, N.J., 1956.

Cheng, Shih. *A Glance at China's Economy*. Beijing: Foreign Language Press, 1974.

Cherepanov, A.I. *As Military Adviser in China*. Moscow: Progress Pub., 1982.

Chesneaux, Jean et al. *China: From Opium Wars to the 1911 Revolution*. New York: Pantheon, 1976.

Clausewitz, Karl Von. *On War*. New York: Barnes & Noble, 1966.

Dixon, Cecil A. *Communist Guerrilla Warfare*. New York: Praeger, 1954.

Feuerwerker, Albert. *China's Early Industrialization*. New York: Atheneum, 1970.

Foreign Language press. *China: A Geographical Sketch*. Beijing: Foreign Language Press, 1974.

_____. *The Reform Movement of 1898*. Beijing: Foreign Language Press, 1976.

_____. *The Taiping Revolution*. Beijing: Foreign Language Press, 1976.

Fuller, J.F.C. *War and Western Civilization, 1832-1932*. London: Duckworth, 1932.

Gao, Tiqian. "An Outline of Military Materialist Dialectics." In *The International Strategic Studies*, No. 4, 1987, & No. 2, 1988.

Garthoff, Raymond L. *Soviet Military Doctrine*. Glencoe, Ill.: Free Press, 1953.

Gromyko, Anatoly & Hellman, Martin, eds. *Breakthrough: Emerging New Thinking* - - -Soviet and Western Scholars Issue a Challenge to Build a World Beyond War. New York: Walker, 1988.

Halperin, Morton H. *Contemporary Military Strategy*. Boston: Little, Brown, 1967.

Harrison, James P. *The Communists and Chinese Peasant Rebellians* - -A Study in the Rewriting of Chinese History. New York: Atheneum, 1971.

_____. *The Long March to Power*: A History of the Chinese Communist Party, 1921-72. New York: Praeger, 1972.

Hsieh, Alice Langley. *Communist China's Strategy in the Nuclear Era*. Englewoodcliff, N.J., 1962.

Huntington, Samuel P. *Political Order in Changing Societies*. New Harven: Yale Univ., 1970.

Jiang, Jieshi (Chiang Kai-shek). *Soviet Russia in China: A Summing-up at Seventy*. N.Y.: Farrar, Straus, and Cadahy, 1957.

Joffe, Ellis. *Party and Army: Professionalism and Political Control in the Chinese Officer Corps, 1949-1964*. Boston: Harvard East Asian Monographs, 1967.

Kaplan, Morton A., ed. *Great Issues of International Politics: The International System and National Policy*. Chicago: Aldine, 1970.

Kau, Yingmao. *The People's Liberation Army and China's Nation-Building*. New York: International Arts and Science Press, 1973.

Kautsky, John H. *The Political Consequences of Modernization*. NewYork: John Wiley, 1972.

Kennedy, Paul. *The Rise and Fall of the Great Powers*: Economic Change and military Conflict, from 1500-2000. London, England: Unwin Hyman, 1988.

Legge, Jame, trans. *The Four Books*. Taipei: Culture, 1981.

Lenin, V.I. "The Armed Forces and the Revolution." *In Collected Works of Lenin*, Vol. 10. London: Lawence & Wishart, 1962.
_____. On War and Peace. Beijing: Foreign languages Press, 1966.

Lenin, V.L. "Partisan Warfare." In *Modern Guerrilla Warfare: Fighting Communist Guerrilla Movements, 1941-61*, edited by Franklin Mark Osanka.
_____. *The Selected Works of Lenin*. 3 Vols. Moscow: Progress, 1970.

Leonhard, Wolfgang. *Three Faces of Marxism*: the Political Concepts of Soviet Ideology, Maoism, and Humanist Marxism. New York: Holt, Rinehart & Winston, 1970.

Li, Dun J. *The Ageless Chinese*. N.Y.: Charles Scribner's Sons, 1971.

Mao, Tse-tung (Zedong). *Selected Works of Mao Tse-tung*. 5 Vols. Peking: Foreign languages Press, 1967.

Mark, Karl & Engels, Frederick. *Manifesto of Communist Party*. Beijing: Foreign languages Press, 1972.

Merkl, P.H. *Modern Comparative Politics*. New York: Hold, Rinemart & Winston, 1970.

Maxwell, Neville. *India's China War*. New York: A. Doubleday Anchor, 1972.

Rice, Edward E. *Mao's Way*. Berkeley: Univ. of California, 1974.

Saywell, William G. & Johnston, Iain. "Chinese Defence Doctrine and Foreign policy:Option for the Future." Working Paper #11. Univ. of Toronto - York Univ., Joint Centre on Modern East Asia. Univ. of Toronto.

Schram, Stuart R. *The Political Thought of Mao Tse-tung.* New York: Frederick A. Fraeger, 1969.

Schurmann, Franz. *Ideology and Organization in Communist China.* Berkeley & Los Angeles: Univ. of California, 1968.

Schwartz, Benjamin I. *Chinese Communism & the Rise of Mao.* New York: Harper Torchbooks, 1951.

Seagrave, Sterling. *The Soong Dynasty.* N.Y.: Harper & Row, 1985.

Segal, Gerald. Defending China. London: Oxford, 1985.

_____ & Tow, William T., eds. *Chinese Defence Policy.* Chicago: Univ. of Illionis, 1984.

Sokolovsky, V.D. *Military Strategy.* London: Pall Mall, 1963.

_____. *Soviet Military Strategy.* N.Y.: Crane, Russak, 1975.

Sun, Tzu. *The Art of War.* Translated with an introduction bySamuel B. Griffith. London: Oxford Univ., 1971.

Sun, Yatsen. *San Min Zhu I* (The Three Principles of the People). With Two Supplementary Chapters by Jiang Jieshi. Taipei: China Publishing.

Tien, Chen-ya. The Mass Militia and Chinese Modernization. Toronto: Masiac, 1983.

Titzgerald, C.P. The Birth of Communist China. N.Y.: Pelican, 1964.

Ward, Robert E. "Political Modernization and Political Culture in Japan." In *Political Modernization,* ed. Claude E. Welch. Belmont, CA: Wadsworth, 1967.

Welch, Claude E. *Political Modernization: A Reader in Comparative Political Change.* Belmont, CA: Wadsworth, 1967.

Wylie, Joseph C. *Military Strategy: A General Theory of Power Control.* N.J.: Rutgers Univ., 1966.

GLOSSARY OF CHINESE TERMS & NAMES

Anfu	安福	Chen Duxiu	陳独秀
Anhui	安徽	Chen Jiongming	陳炯明
Anjun	安軍	Chen Qimei	陳其美
Anqing	安庆	Chengcheng School	成城学校
Anxi	安西	Chengdu	成都
Ba Zhen	八陣	Chongqing	重庆
Bagua	八卦	Chouhai Pian	筹海篇
Bai Guangya	白光亚	Chu	楚
Bao Fa	保法	Chuanbi Treaty	穿鼻條約
Baoding	保定	Chuanjian Paoli	船堅炮利
Baojia System	保甲制	Chujun	楚軍
Bei	備	Chunqiu	春秋
Beijing	北京	Chuyu	楚豫 (兵艦)
Beiyangjun	北洋軍	Ci-xi	慈禧
Biao	標	Cun	村
Bing Fa	兵法	Dabieshan	大别山
Bing Jing	兵经	Daguko	大沽口
Bing Li	兵力	Dai Bing	呆兵
Bingbu Shilang	兵部侍郎	Dali	大里
Bingfa Baizhanjing	兵法百战经	Dangjun	党軍
Bingguan Xuetang	兵官学堂	Dangyi	党義
Bingmu	兵謀	Dao	道
Bingnong Heyi	兵農合一	Daoism (Taoism)	道家思想
Bingpi Baijin Fang	浒湃百金方	Daojia (Taoist)	道家
Boning	包寧	Daxue	大学
Bushido	武士道	Deng Xiaoping	鄧小平
Cai E	蔡鍔	Deng Yibing	鄧亦兵
(Cai Songpo)	（字松坡）	Dinghai City	定海城
Cen Chunxuan	岑春煊	Dizai	地載
Changbei Jun	常備軍	Donghuali	東華里
Changsha	長沙	Dongsha	東沙 (群岛)
Changshan	常山	Dongyang	東洋

309

Duan Qirui	段祺瑞	Gu Qinglian	顧清廉
Duban	督辦	Gu Zhenggang	谷正剛
Dudu	都督	Guan Zhong	管仲
Dujun	督軍	Guangdong	廣東
E Jun	鄂軍	Guangxi	廣西
Fa	法	Guangxu	光緒
Fan Zengxiang	樊增祥	Guangzhou (Canton)	廣州
Fei E Zhen	飛鶚陣	Guanmi	觀彌
Feidu Caijun	廢督裁軍	Guanyinshan	觀音山
Feigong	非攻	Gui jun	桂軍
Feng Guifen	馮桂芬	Guizhou	貴州
Feng Guozhang	馮國璋	Guo Ben	國本
Feng Youlan	馮友蘭	Guo Li	國力
Fenghou	風后 (人名)	Guomin Canzheng Yuan	國民參政院
Fenghwa	奉化 (縣)		
Fenglu School	鳳麓學堂	Guomindang	國民黨
Fengyang	風揚	Haishenwai	海參威
Fenjun	分軍	Haiyan	海岩 (縣)
Fenzhou	汾州	Hami	哈密
Fujian	福建	Han Fei	韓非
Fuxi	伏羲	Hangzhou	杭州
Fuzhou	福州	Hankou	漢口
Gan-Shan	甘陝	He Shen	和珅
Ganchuan	甘泉	He Yucheng	何玉誠
Ganpu (Kanpu)	甘浦	He Liangchen	何良臣
Gansu	甘肅	Hebei	河北
Gelaohui	哥老會	Henan	河南
Geming Shixing Jia	革命實行家	Hetu	河圖
		Houbei Jun	後備軍
Gongqiang Yiqiang	攻強益強	Hu Baili	胡柏立
Gongzao Tongxun (Kung-tso Tung-hsun)	工作通訊	Hu-Guang	湖廣
		Hu Linyi	胡林翼

310

Hu Sheng	胡繩	Jiangxi	江西
Hua Guofeng	華國鋒	Jianjin School	箭金學堂
Huaijun	淮軍	Jianyuan	間遠
Huan Jin Su Zhan	緩進速戰	Jiaofi Shaoben	剿匪手本
Huang Biao	黃彪	Jileu	紀律
Huang Kecheng	黃克誠	Jin	晉
Huang Keqiang	黃克強	Jinan	济南
Huang Shaogu	黃少谷	Jinan Zuozhan	近岸作战
Huang Shigong	黃石公	Jinggangshan	井崗山
Huang Xing	黃興	Jinggong	景公
Huangdi	黃帝	Jingzhi Bing	经制兵
Huangong	桓公(齊)	Jinhai Zuozhan	近海作战
Huangpi	黃陂	Jinling	金陵
Huangpu	黃埔	Jinshi	進士
Huaxinghui	華興會	Jiujiang	九江
Hubei	湖北	Jixia	嵇瑕
Huguo Zhanzeng	護國战爭	Jun Guomin Pian	軍國民篇
Huilu Jiumin	惠籠海民	Jun Ling	軍令
Hunan	湖南	Jun Xue	軍學
Huo Bing	活兵	Jun Zheng	軍政
Huqianjing	虎鈐經	Junguan	軍管
Huyi	虎翼	Junji Chu	軍機处
Jiang Baili	蔣百里	Junwu Chu	軍務处
Jiang Jieshi	蔣介石	Juren	舉人
(Chiang Kai-shik)		Kangxi	康熙
Jiang Jingguo	蔣经国	Kebuduo	科布多
Jiang Shang	姜尚	Lanzhou	蘭州
Jiang Weiguo	蔣緯國	Laowu Jiehe	劳武结合
Jiangbing Xuetang	將并學堂	Laozi	老子
Jiangnan	江南	Lei Bailun	雷伯倫
Jiangsu	江蘇	Leo Zhongkai	廖仲愷

Li Dazhao	李大釗	Longyou	隴右
Li Denghui	李登輝	Longzhong, Dialogue of	隆中對
Li Hongzhang	李鴻章	Lu Dajie	陸達節
Li Jing	李靖	Lu Fengge	盧鳳閣
Li Li	李悝	Lu Rongting	陸榮廷
Li Quan	李荃	Luhua	蘆花
Li Weigong	李衛公	Luhua Qijun Zhen	蘆花奇軍陣
Li Yuanhong	黎元洪	Luo Guanzhong	羅貫中
Li Yuri	李洛日	Luoshu	洛書
Li Zhen	李農	Luoyang	洛陽
Lian	連	Mao Yingbai	毛膺白
Lianbing Chu	練兵処	Mao Zedong	毛澤東
Liang-Jiang	兩江	(Mao Tse-tung)	
Liang Qichao	梁啟超	Mao Zhuqing	毛注青
Lianghui	梁惠(王)	Mawei	馬尾
Liangzhou	涼州	Mazu	馬祖
Lianhe Zhanxian	聯合战線	Mianhu	棉湖
Lianzuo Fa	連坐法	Min-Zhe	閩浙
Lin Biao (Lin Piao)	林彪	Ming Dynasty	明朝
Lin Fuxiang	林福祥	Mintun	民屯
Lin Zexu	林則徐	Minzheng Zhang	民政長
Liqin	離親	Mo Di	墨翟
Liu Baicheng	劉伯承	Mo Rongxin	莫榮新
Liu Bei	劉備	Moist	墨家
Liu Dawu	劉達武	Mu	畝
Liu Wendao	劉文島	Mu Anshi	牟安世
Liu Yangyang	劉泱泱	Mulan	木蘭
Liu Zhenhuan	劉宸襄	Nanjing	南京
Liutao	六韜	Nansha	南沙(群島)
Lixing Zhexue	力行哲學	Nanyangjun	南洋軍
Lixue	理學	Nian	捻
Longfi	龍飛	Nioxiang	鳥翔

312

Niulangang	牛欄崗	Sanzhong Yizhong	散眾益眾
Pai	排	Shan-Gan	陝甘
Pan Rong	潘榮	Shandong	山東
Pei Xu	裴續	Shang Dynasty	商朝
Peng	棚	Shang Yang	商鞅
Peng Daxiong	彭達雄	Shanghai	上海
Peng Dehuai	彭德懷	Shanxi	山西
Qi Shan	琦善	Shaanxi	陝西
Qi Zheng	奇正	Shaoquan	少泉(李鴻章字)
Qianlong	乾隆	Shaoshan	紹山
Qibing	奇兵	Shaoyang	邵陽
Qin Dynasty	秦朝	Shen Baozhen	沈葆楨
Qin State	秦國	Shen Buhai	申不害
Qing Dynasty	清朝	Shen Dao	慎到
Qinghai	青海	Shen Dingyi	沈定一
Qinghe Zhen	清河鎮	Shen yunlong	沈雲龍
Qinzhou	欽州	Shengjing	盛京
Qu	區	Shengjun	聖君
Quan	全	Shexue	社學
Quanrong	犬戎	Shepan	蛇蟠
Quantixing Zhanzheng	全体性战争	Shi	士
		Shiji	姶計
Rehe	熱河	Shijian	實踐
Ren	仁	Shijing	詩経
Ren Zequan	任澤全	Shu	蜀(國)
Rong Lu	荣祿	Shuishi Xuetang	水師學堂
San Cai	三才	Shujing	書経
San Min Zhu Yi	三民主義	Shun	舜
Sanhehui	三合會	Si Ku Quan Shu	四庫全書
Sanlue	三略	Sichuan	四川
Sanyuanli	三元里	Simafa	司馬法

313

Simo	思苗	Tongzhi	同治
Song	宋	Toubi Futan	投筆膚談
Song Jiaoren	宋敎仁	Tu (Du)	都
Song Shilun	宋時輪	Tuan	團
Song Yuren	宋育仁	Wan	皖
Sucheng Xuetang	速成學堂	Wang Dengyun	王登雲
Sun Chuanfang	孫傳芳	Wang Jingwei	汪精衛
Sun Bin	孫臏	Wang Minghe	王鳴鶴
Sun Wen Xue Shuo	孫文學說	Wang Ranzhi	王冉之
Sunzi (Sun Tzu)	孫子	Wang Tongling	王桐齡
Sushu	素書	Wang Yangming	王陽明
Suzhou	蘇州	Wang Zhongyi	王仲義
Suzhou	肅州	Wei	魏(國)
Taibaiyinjing	太白陰經	Wei Rulin	魏汝霖
Taigong	太公	Wei Shu	僞書
Taiping	太平	Wei Tao	僞託
Taiqiang	抬槍	Wei Yuan	魏源
Taizong	太宗	Weiliaozi	尉繚子
Tang	唐	Wenfa	文伐
Tang Jiyao	唐繼堯	Woqi	握奇
Tang Shengzhi	唐生智	Woqijing	握奇経
Tao Juyin	陶菊隱	Wu (State)	吳(國)
Taolue	韜略	Wu (King)	武王
Tianfu	天覆	Wu Peifu	吳佩孚
Tianjin	天津	Wu Qi	吳起
Tianshan	天山	Wuchang	武昌
Tianshui	天水	Wuda Zhanfa	五大战法
Tidu	提督	Wuhan	武漢
Tiyong	体用	Wuhou	武侯
Tongmonhui	同盟會	Wuhou Bazhen	武侯八陣
Tongyi Zhanxian	统一战线	Bingfa Jiyao	兵法輯要

314

Wuhua	五花	Xinjian Lujun	新建陸軍
Wulivasutai	烏里雅蘇台	Binglue Lucun	兵略錄存
Wutai Mountain	五台山	Xinjiang	新疆
Wuwei Jun	武衛軍	Xinjun	新軍
Wuxing	五行	Xinshu	心書
Wuyuan	烏垣	Xisha	西沙(群島)
Wuyunzhen	烏雲陣	Xiu Dao	修道
Wuzi (Wu Tzu)	吳子	Xiucai	秀才
Xian	西安	Xu Chongzhi	許崇智
Xian Qin	先秦	Xu Dong	許洞
Xianfeng	咸豐	Xu Peigen	徐培根
Xiang	鄉	Xu Shi	虛實
Xiangjiang Pinglun	湘江評論	Xuannu	玄女
Xiangju	襄咀	Xuantong	宣統
Xiangjun	湘軍	Xubei Jun	續備軍
Xiangshan	香山	Xue Guangqian	薛光前
Xiangtan	湘潭	Xue Huan	薛桓
Xiangxiang	湘鄉	Xunfang Dui	巡防隊
Xiao Zhizhi	蕭敬治	Xunfang Jun	巡防軍
Xiaojun	校軍	Xunfu	巡撫
Xiaozhan	小站	Xunlian Caofa	訓練操法
Xie	協	Xiangxi Tushuo	詳晰圖說
Xihu Yishi	西湖逸士	Xuzhou	徐州
Xikou	溪口	Yanan	延安
Xin	心	Yang Changji	楊昌濟
Xin Fa	心法	Yang Dezhi	楊得志
Xin Qing Nian	新青年	Yang Hucheng	楊虎城
Xing	形	Yangwu Movement	洋務運動
Xinghanhui	興漢會	Yangwu Warship	楊武号軍艦
Xingzhonghui	興中會	Yao	堯

Zhi Liang Zhi	致良知
Zhili	直隸
Zhiqi	治氣
Zhixin	治心
Zhonghua Diguo	中華帝國
Zhonghua Gemingdang	中華革命党
Zhongguo Guomindang Lujun Junguan Xuexiao	中國國民党陸軍軍官學校
Zhongsha	中沙（群島）
Zhongxing	中興
Zhou	周
Zhou Enlai	周恩來
Zhoushan	舟山
Zhu and Ke	主和客
Zhu River	珠江
Zhu Xi	朱熹
Zhu Zongzhen	朱宗震
Zhuge Liang	諸葛亮
Zhuyi	主義
Ziqiang	自强
Ziqiangjun	自强軍
Zongli	總理
Zongli Yamen	總理衙門
Zongti Zhan	總体战
Zuo Zhuan	左傳
Zuo Zongtang	左宗棠

INDEX

319